Elizabeth & Leicester

Sarah Gristwood

D0104569

PENGUIN BOOKS

PENGUIN BOOKS

Published by the Penguin Group

Penguin Group (USA) Inc., 375 Hudson Street, New York, New York 10014, U.S.A.
Penguin Group (Canada), 90 Eglinton Avenue East, Suite 700, Toronto,
Ontario, Canada M4P 2Y3 (a division of Pearson Penguin Canada Inc.)
Penguin Books Ltd, 80 Strand, London WC2R 0RL, England
Penguin Ireland, 25 St Stephen's Green, Dublin 2, Ireland
(a division of Penguin Books Ltd)
Penguin Group (Australia), 250 Camberwell Road, Camberwell,
Victoria 3124, Australia (a division of Pearson Australia Group Pty Ltd)
Penguin Books India Pvt Ltd, 11 Community Centre,
Panchsheel Park, New Delhi – 110 017, India
Penguin Group (NZ), 67 Apollo Drive, Rosedale, North Shore 0632,
New Zealand (a division of Pearson New Zealand Ltd)
Penguin Books (South Africa) (Pty) Ltd, 24 Sturdee Avenue,
Rosebank, Johannesburg 2196, South Africa

Penguin Books Ltd, Registered Offices:
80 Strand, London WC2R 0RL, England

First published in Great Britain by Bantam Press, a division of Transworld Publishers 2007
First published in the United States of America by Viking Penguin,
a member of Penguin Group (USA) Inc. 2007
Published in Penguin Books 2008

1   3   5   7   9   10   8   6   4   2

Illustration credits appear on pages 389–91.

ISBN 978-0-670-01828-4 (hc.)
ISBN 978-0-14-311449-9 (pbk.)
CIP data available

Printed in the United States of America
Set in Sabon

Praise for *Elizabeth and Leicester*

"Quite simply one of the most enthralling history books I've ever read. Packed with riveting detail, it is full of engaging and perceptive insights into the truth about the Virgin Queen and the man who meant more to her than any other. You must read this!"
—Alison Weir, author of *The Life of Elizabeth I*

"Elizabeth Tudor and Robert Dudley first crossed paths as children, in the court circles of her father, King Henry VIII. . . . Many accounts emphasize the early, passionate phase of the relationship; Gristwood chronicles an enduring bond at turns romantic, affectionate, quarrelsome, and distant, and she skillfully explores the intersection of personal relations and politics. . . . The book is especially engaging in suggesting what drew the two together, what made them friends and working partners. . . . Whether they had sex or not, Gristwood convinces us, theirs was a great love story."
—*The Boston Globe*

"Sarah Gristwood manages to contribute something new to the colorful noise of 'the Elizabeth industry' . . . [and] distills the mighty queen and her thwarted lover down to two very real, very complicated human beings. . . . [The] success with this book is even more impressive considering the heightened expectations readers have about private details and public lives. . . . For anyone with an appetite for history, Gristwood pulls off a neat feat. She offers a lively and real picture of this pair that draws heavily on the absence of fact."
—*Chicago Sun-Times*

"Vivacious and absorbing. Gristwood is a mistress of the trivial details that enthrall. Full of intriguing suggestions, stimulating analogies and shrewd connections."
—*The Sunday Times* (London)

"Gristwood disentangles the many myths and stories that have, since the start of Elizabeth's reign, been spun around the lifelong love and loyalty between the queen and her 'Sweet Robin.' This is rich terrain, taking us into the heart of our feelings about femininity, power, and nationhood. Makes one feel that Freud's question 'What do women want?' might have been inspired by the enigmatic behavior of Elizabeth herself."
—*Telegraph* (London)

"As well as producing an enthralling account of one particular relationship, Gristwood crams her book with fascinating details of life at court."
—*The Mail on Sunday* (London)

"The tangled and enigmatic relationship of Leicester and Elizabeth has always fascinated posterity. . . . One of the most gratifying aspects of Gristwood's exhaustive and perceptive new look at Leicester and the queen is that it traces the whole arc of the relationship as it both cooled and deepened with the dramatic changes in the political landscape through the long decades of Elizabeth's reign."
—*The Philadelphia Inquirer*

ABOUT THE AUTHOR

After leaving Oxford, Sarah Gristwood worked as a journalist specializing in the arts and women's issues. She was a regular contributor to the *Times*, *Guardian*, *Independent*, and *Evening Standard*.

When I was fair and young, and favour graced me,
Of many was I sought their mistress for to be.
But I did scorn them all, and answered them therefore,
'Go, go, go seek some otherwhere,
Importune me no more.'

How many weeping eyes I made to pine with woe;
How many sighing hearts I have no skill to show.
Yet I the prouder grew, and answered them therefore,
'Go, go, go seek some otherwhere,
Importune me no more.'

Then spake fair Venus' son, that proud victorious boy,
And said: Fine dame, since that you be so coy,
I will pluck your plumes that you shall say no more
'Go, go, go seek some otherwhere,
Importune me no more.'

When he had spake these words, such change grew in my
  breast
That neither night nor day since that, I could take any rest.
Then lo, I did repent that I had said before,
'Go, go, go seek some otherwhere,
Importune me no more.'

Finis

Elizabetha Regina
*c.*1580s

O! mistress, why
Outcast am I
All utterly
From your pleasaunce?
Since ye and I
Or this, truly,
Familiarly
Have had pastaunce.

And, lovingly,
Ye would apply
Thy company
To my comfort:
But now truly,
Unlovingly,
Ye would deny
Me to resort.

But since that ye
So strange will be
As towards me
And will not meddle,
I trust, percase,
To find some grace
To have free chase
And speed as well.

Anon.
earlier sixteenth century

Contents

Preface		1
1	'Some secret constellation': 1533–1536	7
2	'Her eighth year': 1536–1547	25
3	'The occasion of his utter undoing': 1547–1553	38
4	'This night I think to die': 1553–1559	56
5	'The King that is to be': spring 1559–summer 1560	76
6	'So sudden a chance': autumn 1560	99
7	'Maiden honour and integrity': 1560–1561	125
8	'Not yet towards a marriage': 1561–1565	147
9	'Majesty and love do not sit well together': 1565–1567	164
10	'The daughter of debate': 1568–1569	180
11	'The great Lord': the 1570s	192
12	'Our estate requireth a match': 1570–1572	207
13	'I have long both loved and liked you': 1573–1575	225
14	'Dishonorable brutes': 1576–1579	249
15	'The greatest prince in Christendom': 1578–1582	265
16	'In times of distress': 1582–1584	288
17	'Her Majesty will make trial of me': 1585–1588	305
18	'A thing whereof we can admit no comfort': 1588	325
19	'To end this life for her service'	339

Appendix I: The second Robert Dudley   343
Appendix II: The Arthur Dudley mystery   351
Afterword: some fictional treatments   364
Notes on sources   371
Acknowledgements   388
Picture acknowledgements   389
Index   393

Preface

IT IS ALMOST HALF A CENTURY SINCE THERE HAS APPEARED A NON-fiction book specifically on Elizabeth Tudor and Robert Dudley. It seems almost incredible to write it. There has, of course, been every other kind of version of the story. Two major new television series on England's most frequently filmed monarch; Philippa Gregory's best-selling novel about the relationship itself; a great theatrical revival of Schiller's play *Mary Stuart*, with Robert caught between a queen of hearts and a queen of heads . . . and before that, the feature film entitled simply *Elizabeth*, its themes echoed in the sequel, *The Golden Age*. And this is to ignore all new biographies of Elizabeth, popular or academic, and all the new work on Robert Dudley; to ignore, too, those old enough to have seen Glenda Jackson in *Elizabeth R*, or to have read the myriad novels by Margaret Irwin or Jean Plaidy.

This is clearly an appetite that grows by what it feeds on – luckily for me. There is, it might seem, a risk in offering a factual version of the Elizabeth and Leicester story: a risk that, with all the necessary cavils, all the quibbles about the fluidity of the source material (rumours of doubtful attribution; ambassadors' letters we've read only in translation), it may always be less palatable than quick, colourful fantasy. But in fact, the more attractive and convincing the recent fictions have been, the more one's curiosity is sparked for the real story. We want to weigh the evidence for ourselves – like successive generations of historians; like Robert and Elizabeth's contemporaries.

The last book specifically on this subject was published in 1961 by Elizabeth Jenkins, whose earlier biography of the Queen had pictured her repeatedly rescued from herself by 'protective masculine authority'. More recently, feminist study of Queen Elizabeth has tended, inevitably, to downplay the role of the men in her life, while fresh work on the long-maligned Robert has concentrated on his own background, beliefs, financial affairs – on viewing him as an independent entity. I set out, in beginning this book, to examine the relationship in its long entirety (rather than just the first few years of it, as has more often been done); to try to discover what it meant not only personally, but politically. What was its impact on Elizabeth's reign and on her kingdom? What might one learn by using the relationship (and the perceptions of Robert Dudley himself, a man who knew his queen better than any) as a prism through which to re-examine one of the best-known, and still most fascinating, pieces of English history?

If the Elizabeth industry in general will never go into recession, then the love of Elizabeth and Leicester has a particular fascination – and the question, of course, is why? The answer is not just simple prurience, our greedy curiosity about the private lives of royalty. Perhaps it is that the unusual balance of power in this relationship gives it a peculiar modernity. And perhaps, too, we feel the need, today, to explore those relationships that were of memorable, enduring, support and passion – and yet did not follow the course of the traditional romantic story.

For in many ways this is unpromising material. Elizabeth's relationship with Robert Dudley, Earl of Leicester, was perhaps the most important in her life. The savage possessiveness with which she wrote of him – 'a creature of our own', as she described him, with all the imperiousness of the royal 'we' – in no way diminished his importance in her eyes. For a woman so short of surviving blood relations, he was the nearest thing she had to family. By the time Robert died in 1588 (at which point Elizabeth shut herself up in grief, until her ministers broke down the door of her room), he had been her councillor, her unofficial consort and commander of her army. He had loved her, advised her, understood her, sat by her bed in sickness and represented her on state occasions; she had raised him, the son and grandson of convicted traitors, to be the greatest man in the land.

But she had also humiliated him, held him dangling on a string, made him dance attendance on her other suitors and tried to have him clapped in prison when finally he broke loose; and he had made commitments to two other women, even after the shocking death of his first wife Amy Robsart. This is no easy Romeo and Juliet love story. It is, what is more, a relationship in which we have to come to terms with several lasting uncertainties.

One of them, of course, concerns the couple's sexual relationship. The King of France in Elizabeth's own lifetime would jest that one of the three great questions of Europe was 'whether Queen Elizabeth was a maid or no'. The fascination has not gone away. Indeed, in the course of writing this book, I found, somewhat to my consternation, that this was the one question every single person asked on hearing that I was to write on Elizabeth and Robert Dudley. (I had – before I stopped counting – been asked it by several journalist friends, a Cambridge paleontologist, a retired diplomat, an eleven-year-old, a brigadier and the man who came to mend the dishwasher. Several of them prefaced the question with: 'I'm not really interested in history, *but* . . .') When Helen Mirren's television portrayal came out in the autumn of 2005, every single one of the hugely popular listings magazines devoted some of their valuable space to a feature. Then, when the BBC's series came out four months later, they did it all over again. Every article asked the same question – did they or didn't they?

The massive interest in this point is not just simple prurience – at least, I don't think so. (Anyone who just wants to read about the sex lives of royalty can do it without trawling through four hundred years of history.) In part, perhaps, there is a genuine interest in just how Elizabeth's private life meshed with her public career: she is, after all, a rare early female role model. But far more importantly, it's because Elizabeth's iconic maiden status is one of the things we all think we know about our past. The Virgin

Queen has always been at once as magical a myth as Arthur's Camelot and – we hope – as solid and splendid a fact as Nelson's Trafalgar victory. But now we need to know if we've been sold a pup. We want (in an age of spin and of its converse: the debunking of many of the old popular stories) to know if this legend too will crumble, or if it is trustworthy.

And yet it is a question to which there can never be a wholly authoritative answer. All one can do is to present the evidence – the stories and the statements that have been fuelling speculation since Elizabeth's own day. At the end of them, I felt had an answer. Others may think differently. In an afterword and an appendix, I briefly discuss the different historical views of Elizabeth and Leicester, some of the most popular of the recent fictional treatments, and the old canard that Robert and Elizabeth secretly had a son called Arthur Dudley. It's fascinating to see how the sexual scandals are always the ones that persist. (And, since I've tried to keep intrusive modern references out of the text itself, let me just remember here all those stories that circulated around the death of Diana, and her supposed secret pregnancy.) By the same token, we will never know for sure whether Robert Dudley killed his wife Amy to enable him to marry Elizabeth – or whether Elizabeth had Amy killed in the most scandalous fashion possible so as *not* to have to marry Robert Dudley. But we seem happy to live with, even to relish, the uncertainty. I say 'we' because it would be naïve to think that anyone comes to this story fresh. It is one with which we all have some sort of a history.

That, indeed, is one of the problems for a researcher. It would be all too easy to turn to sources only to confirm what we have been told is there. We gaze at an established icon of Elizabeth, and mouth the familiar sayings. But if, instead, you turn an enquiring eye onto your subjects' own words, you can find yourself struck with surprise – and with gratitude for being granted material so extraordinary.

The picture of Elizabeth painted in recent decades has shown a woman of sexual impulses, indeed, but one in whom those impulses were subdued to political necessity. Her priorities seemed part of her modernity. Our picture of Robert Dudley has been less successfully updated; and here is an area where we have something to gain from taking a broader historical view. The romantic hero of fictional tales – tall, dark and handsome, arriving on his white horse – has never meshed easily with the venal and impotent hanger-on of the older histories. But then, the position of a favourite (and in particular a male favourite) has never been easy; has represented, indeed, an unease that echoes down the centuries.

Of course, restoring Robert to his due dignity as a politician and a patriot has prepared the way for our being able to take his relationship with Elizabeth seriously. While he was regarded as something of an embarrassment, capable of no motive beyond unenlightened self-interest, his alliance with the Queen represented a problem, a bone in the throat, to even her most ardent admirers. Remove that obstacle, and we may understand Robert as an independent political and social intelligence, while still accepting that much of his function was so personal – so bound into his emotional link with Elizabeth – as to be close to what we think of as feminine.

Perhaps what interests us so much today is this very blurring of conventional gender identities – and the feeling that sex, present or absent, is not necessarily the be-all and end-all of a relationship. Perhaps today we are inclined to look beyond the hearts and flowers love story; to feel that sex often comes easy, and that the holy grail is a relationship with longevity.

As I began to work on this book, I became fascinated by two things in particular. The first was the question of evidence: what we know, as opposed to what we guess. The notes on sources that follow at the end of this book are purposely limited. Almost all available quotations that have any direct bearing on Elizabeth I have been batted around like ping-pong balls for centuries. Such notes as there are aim to offer the general reader some insight into the patchwork of different accounts of her reign – fragmentary, prejudiced, often contradictory as they are. These are the materials from which the traditional story has been drawn; but, when questioned more closely, when set side by side with one another, they sometimes serve instead to undercut it.

The second thing that struck me was that very question of the longevity of this relationship. After the first phase of their love, Elizabeth Tudor and Robert Dudley settled down into a platonic alliance that yet had the frisson of passion about it, a political partnership with the personal pique still fresh. But it still surprises me to reflect on quite how brief a patch of time was occupied by what everyone *thinks* of as that relationship: a bare eighteen months from the moment the evidence first places Robert and Elizabeth together as adults to the scandal that followed the death of Robert's wife Amy. This out of an association that in fact lasted the first three decades – decades! – of Elizabeth's reign . . . Even icebergs only boast a submerged nine-tenths. Here, we seem to have lost nineteen-twentieths of the story. It is hard to think of a better reason for a new biography.

1

'Some secret constellation'
1533–1536

THE TALE OF ELIZABETH'S ACCESSION IS A FAMOUS ONE. IT MAKES A favourite 'scene from history'. We see the princess walking in the park at Hatfield when the councillors came to tell her that her sister Mary was dead and she was Queen of England; caught by surprise, overtaken by her destiny under a great oak tree . . . We all know the words she is supposed to have uttered, after catching her first startled breath: 'This is God's doing, and it is glorious in our eyes.' The words come, so appropriately, from the Psalms.

But in fact Elizabeth was far from surprised by the news that came to her that autumn day. When the cold light dawned on 17 November 1558, a loyal supporter of her own was waiting at the court in London, to make sure she got word early; and William Cecil, Elizabeth's future secretary, was waiting at Hatfield, ready to send out the letters that would get a new government under way. As for Elizabeth herself, she had been waiting all her life: more than twenty years since her mother was beheaded, during her own infancy; eleven years since her father's death plunged the country into uncertainty; five since another death, that of her brother Edward, brought England back under the Pope's sway, and Elizabeth herself closer to death than any twenty-year-old ought to be.

How many years had it been since she had realized Mary was

unlikely to have a child, and that her own accession, could she but survive, was a real possibility? Three, maybe – since Mary's first phantom pregnancy? A year – since Mary's husband, Philip of Spain, sailed away from a barren wife and a hostile country? It was hardly more than a month since Mary's ill-health had taken a turn that could end only one way; three weeks since Mary had added a codicil to her will, accepting that if God continued to give her 'no fruit nor heir of my body', then England would go to the one 'the laws of this realm' decreed (she still could not bear to name her heretic sister, Elizabeth, directly); ten days since one of Mary's most trusted ladies brought her jewels north to Hatfield, in token of everything else Elizabeth would inherit shortly. Mary begged only that Elizabeth would pay her debts and preserve the Catholic faith. To the Catholics and to the Protestants alike, Elizabeth seemed to promise everything, readily. It was a week since King Philip's ambassador had brought word to both sisters that Spain, with all its vested interests in England, would not oppose Elizabeth's accession; six days since the last Protestants of 'Bloody' Mary's reign had been burned, at Canterbury. In the final days of her life Mary had lapsed into a semi-coma, murmuring about the absence of her husband, and of England's loss of its French stronghold, Calais. She was given the last rites at midnight on 16 November and died before dawn the next day.

So on 17 November Elizabeth was already well prepared; surrounded by those who would be central to her reign. And soon among them – arriving, story says, on the hero's traditional white horse – was Lord Robert Dudley.

For the known, the certain, story of Elizabeth Tudor and Robert Dudley begins with her accession day. It is only from this time onwards that we can see surviving evidence of contact: letters sent and docketed; bills; records of ceremonies. We know, from later statements they both made, and from the easy assumptions of agents and ambassadors in the first days of the new queen's reign, that theirs was no brand new acquaintance-ship. But precise information is scarce.

On the other hand, perhaps we hardly need the time and the place where the two first met among the palaces and courts of

Henry VIII's day. The history of the Dudleys and the Tudors had been so closely linked that they have been compared to the ivy and the oak tree around which it wraps. (And it is only in recent years that it has been conceded that the Dudleys were not necessarily the parasites – indeed, that the Dudleys had a better record of fidelity in giving service than the Tudors did of gratitude in receiving it; that the Dudleys' motto, 'Droit et loyal', was one they could claim in all honesty.)

Even their contemporaries felt that the relationship of Elizabeth and Robert transcended the details of practicality. There had to be some explanation for their lifelong fidelity, and those contemporaries put it down to 'synaptia', a hidden conspiracy of the stars, whose power to rule human lives no-one doubted: 'a sympathy of spirits between them, occasioned perhaps by some secret constellation', in the words of the historian William Camden, writing at the beginning of the seventeenth century. Theirs was a relationship already rooted in history and mythology. And that moment when Elizabeth heard she had come to the throne encapsulated much about their story. If our well-loved picture of Elizabeth's accession is something of a fantasy – if the reality is on the whole more interesting – you might say the same about our traditional picture of her relationship with Robert Dudley.

The site of the oak under which Elizabeth is said to have heard of her accession is marked in Hatfield House today. But a neighbouring estate – then belonging to Sir John Brockett, and still in the family – has, like Hatfield, its own marked oak, where they claim Elizabeth heard the news. The pretty picture of a girl surprised by destiny, complete with biblical quotation, was written down seven decades after the event by Sir Robert Naunton, and even then, the author doesn't mention any tree. The first known records of the Hatfield oak are of its being displayed to later royal visitors – as late as the nineteenth century.* Was the romantic

---

* When the tree died in the 1970s, another sapling was planted by another Queen Elizabeth, while the dead trunk was temporarily resurrected in the Hatfield gift shop, sheltering a waxwork effigy of the princess.

story an antiquarian's invention, or accurate folk memory? Or was it constructed in Elizabeth's own day? Two avenues of trees converge on the very spot where the royal oak stands. They were planted almost within living memory of that day, in the great Hatfield rebuilding of the early seventeenth century. One might speculate that Elizabeth and those around her are unlikely to have ignored so promising a piece of symbolism as England's stout-hearted queen, declared under England's stout-hearted tree. Coincidentally, of course, the oak (since *robur* is the stout oaken wood in Latin) was the self-appointed symbol of Robert Dudley, the man who understood Elizabeth's image – and Elizabeth herself – better than any.

These two met each other now not just as courtier and queen, but as a man and a woman who would draw each other enormously. She was tawny-haired and slender, with the long fingers of which she was so proud and 'a spirit full of incantation', as one ambassador memorably had said. (Or see her in Sir John Hayward's words: 'her forehead large and fair . . . her eyes lively and sweet, but short-sighted, her nose somewhat rising in the middlest; the whole compass somewhat long, but yet of admirable beauty . . . a most delightful composition of majesty and modesty'.) Robert, too, was notably good-looking: tall, for the sixteenth century, at almost six feet, 'and singularly well-featured', Naunton later wrote, with the dark eyes that gave him the nickname of 'the Gypsy'.* But that easily understood attraction is only part of the story.

At that time of her accession, Elizabeth would have needed her spiritual kin about her; her 'old flock of Hatfield'. This was a moment of extraordinary triumph – the realization of everything she had worked for, as well as waited for, so long. After the careful watchings of Mary's reign – the keys turned in the lock by a gaoler's hand, the covert dealings, the constant fear of being caught up in some foolish fellow traveller's rebellious fantasy – it must have seemed like day after night. But it was also a moment

---

* 'Graceful in behaviour', said another writer, Clapham, and 'much addicted to sensual pleasures'; others again wrote of his 'stately carriage' and 'grave look'.

of extraordinary tension, a moment at which huge demands were made of her, when she would need to call upon all the resources available to her. She was, after all, a female ruler – at the time, a contradiction in terms – of an impotent kingdom, many of whose inhabitants viewed her religion with scant sympathy. She would have wanted her friends beside her, and not just the fair-weather friends but those of proven loyalty: those who (like Robert Dudley) had known her as a child; those who perhaps (like Robert) had sold lands, in her time of need, to raise money for her.

Now that Elizabeth was queen, she could expect to be surrounded by a mob of good-time glad-handers, eager to assure her that they had always supported her . . . really. But the people she needed (she, with her long history of nervous strain, of illness following on a period of exhilarating effort) were the ones who had always known where their loyalties lay – and who had seen the bad side of life under her Catholic sister Mary.

When Robert kissed Elizabeth's hand at Hatfield – when she made him instantly her Master of Horse, a position his father and brother had held before him – we have no sound reason to believe he already had a place in her heart. That, perhaps, still lay ahead. We cannot know with certainty. But, looking back through the shared years of their common childhood, at a hundred tiny ties, it is hardly surprising that he certainly did have a place waiting in her hierarchy.

Camden said that, though young to rule at twenty-five, Elizabeth was 'rarely qualified by resolution and adversity'. So was Robert Dudley. Like the phoenix that was her emblem, she had risen from what (given the fate meted out to heretics) could almost literally have been her ashes. She had survived by shrewdness, by her sharply honed wits and by a self-control so savage it must have hurt a young soul – and yet, it was of Dudley that Robert Naunton wrote he could 'put his passions in his pocket' to keep them safely hidden away. Robert Dudley too had had to make some harsh decisions to survive, had had to curb his young man's impetuosity. Camden wrote of him, with dubious approval, that he was 'very skillful in temporising, and fitting himself to the times'; but Elizabeth, who had no use for hotheads, valued this determined resilience.

A prayer Elizabeth published in the first years of her reign cast an eye back over her youthful history.

> Thou hast willed me not to be some wretched girl from the meanest rank of the common people, who would pass her life miserably in poverty and squalor, but to a kingdom Thou has destined me, born of royal parents and nurtured and educated at court. When I was surrounded and thrown about by various snares of enemies, Thou has preserved me with Thy constant protection from prison and the most extreme danger; and though I was freed only at the very last moment, Thou has entrusted me on earth with royal sovereignty and majesty.

Robert Dudley too had been educated at the court; though born of the nobility, he too had been imprisoned and in danger. The scaffold that had claimed her mother had taken his father and brother. There is no evidence for the pretty timeworn tale of a stolen romance between the two when they were both imprisoned in the Tower. But though they may never have loved or lusted there, the place represented a bond between them – a shared experience of fear and loss unusual in even the Tudor century.

Legend says they were born on the same day. In fact Elizabeth was born on 7 September 1533, Robert Dudley on 24 June (as he mentioned many years later, in a letter to William Cecil), either of that year or of the year before; no-one was recording his life precisely. Not that he was a nobody. Many years later, Philip Sidney – Robert's nephew, remembered as the epitome of a young aristocrat – wrote, in rebutting an attack on his uncle, that 'my chiefest honour is to be a Dudley, and truly I am glad to have cause to set forth the nobility of that blood whereof I am descended'.

The Dudleys – like Elizabeth's maternal relations, the Boleyns – live in legend as arch-arrivistes, with all the implied sneers about those who rose too rapidly. They were undoubtedly – like the Boleyns – arch-servants of the state. But, just as Anne Boleyn (with the Duke of Norfolk for her uncle) was not entirely the outsider of legend, so there were some of the famous old names in Robert Dudley's family tree. Even Richard Neville, Richard 'the Kingmaker' – Earl of Warwick, the title Robert's brother would bear – was related to the Dudleys, a connection that cast an interesting sidelight on the position the family might occupy in relation to the monarchy. (Previous earls of Leicester, Robert's own future title, had included Simon de Montfort, who in the thirteenth century led an aristocratic revolt against the incompetent government of Henry III, and Henry 'Bolingbroke', who deposed the equally inefficient Richard II.) Over the years it had often been descent in the female line that had given the Dudleys their claims to the aristocracy, the Lisle title and the Warwick earldom; and it was the female line that linked them, so they would boast, even to the Saxon nobility.

Robert's great-grandfather was a younger son of the great Midlands landholder Baron Dudley. His grandfather Edmund Dudley trained as a lawyer, and was already known as a coming man when Henry VII achieved the throne. Twenty years later he was Speaker of the House of Commons, and a member of the royal council; prominent and wealthy. The tactics which made him rich (with his neighbour and partner, Sir Richard Empson) still more greatly enriched the monarchy. Dudley and Empson increased the royal revenue by squeezing the nobility: hunting out carefully hidden assets, exploiting old laws to claim fines for their king. If they also accepted bribes for themselves, it was hardly more than common practice.

Men did not love Henry VII for what they saw as his mercenary attitudes, but you did not complain of an anointed king with impunity. Safer by far to blame Empson and Dudley: 'his horse-leeches and shearers', that partial historian Francis Bacon called them a century later, 'bold men and careless of fame, and that took toll of their master's grist'. When Henry VIII succeeded to the throne in 1509, one of his first acts was to order the arrest of his father's hated agents. It was a singularly ruthless bid for popularity. That it was nothing more is shown in the details of the two men's trial and treatment: the absurdity of the charge that they had tried to take over the country, and the fact that their bodies were never subject to the torments and disgraces that would have been inflicted upon genuine traitors. None the less Dudley, like Empson, was beheaded – nominally for treason – in August 1510.

John Dudley, Robert's father, was a child of seven when his father Edmund went to the block. His mother rapidly remarried, taking as her new husband one Arthur Plantagenet, illegitimate son of Edward IV, and the boy was sent as ward to another gentleman, the Kentish landowner and family friend Sir Edward Guildford, who, having no sons of his own, effectively adopted John, and betrothed him to his own daughter Jane. The marriage was to be a long and unusually happy one: witness the many references, in Jane's eventual will, to her 'lord, my dear husband'; witness the loving messages that found their way into her husband's official despatches.

John found early prominence as a fighting man: first as a youthful veteran of the French wars of the 1520s and then as star jouster of many a court tournament. But if the King valued him in tilt yard and hunting field, the King's ministers found John equally apt and enterprising in political tasks. First employed by Cardinal Wolsey, he was then – after Wolsey fell from power, having failed to secure the King his annulment – employed by Thomas Cromwell, who rose to prominence alongside Anne Boleyn. He was, in fact, an intelligent and dutiful tool for any government of the day. By the time of Robert's birth, he had begun to purchase the old territories of Baron Dudley, and had succeeded his surrogate father as Master of the Tower Armouries. A year later Sir Edward Guildford died, and John (through his wife) inherited Sir Edward's seat in the House of Commons and his lands around Tenterden in Kent. (Robert may have been born at Halden Place near Rolvenden – or 'Rounden' – rather than in London. A font in the village still bears the arms of the Guildford family. Indeed, the Dudley children probably did much of their growing up in the country, since besides the inherited estates in Kent and Sussex, John Dudley went on buying lands in the West Midlands, close to the Welsh border, and transformed the ancient family seat of Dudley Castle.

The Dudleys were an intensely clannish family. All his life, Robert would stick close to those siblings who survived into adulthood, bonded to them in a strong defensive alliance based not only on loyalty, but on a communality of ideas and ideals. Perhaps this explains the two different faces John Dudley seemed to show: one often inimical to the outside world, the other warm and indulgent to his own brood. Two more boys were born after Robert, and another four girls; and of the thirteen children born to the prolific Jane Dudley, nine survived infancy, at a time when half of all babies died before they were five years old. Robert's earliest youth seems to have been uneventful; there is no reason (with all those acres, and all those siblings to play with in them) to doubt it was also happy. But the hard facts about it are not many.

Elizabeth's babyhood, on the other hand, gets the careful chronicle due to royalty – and to a royal baby awaited with especial eagerness. This was, after all, the early 1530s, a time when the English Reformation was just barely under way: almost a decade since Henry VIII's interest had first been piqued by Anne Boleyn; six long years since he had started trying to divorce his first wife, Katherine of Aragon; four years since the overthrow of Anne's enemy, Cardinal Wolsey. But no papal court had yet granted the King a decree nisi. Now past forty, he was beginning to change from the Adonis of his early reign into the bloated and temperamental autocrat of story. But it would not be until the middle of the decade that Henry (conservative by temperament and no Lutheran) finally broke off relations with the Pope, declared himself Supreme Head of the English church and launched a general visitation of the monasteries. It would be more than a decade after that before, under a new young king, the old church rites were swept away.

With hindsight, we tend to see the Reformation in England as the logical, the inevitable, fruit of the European movement. Look backwards to how, in Martin Luther's Germany, the call for reformation of corrupt church practices grew to become a revolution in doctrine and belief. Look onwards to the rise of

English puritanism, and how Protestantism came to be strongly associated with the national identity. But at the time of Elizabeth's birth, the English Reformation was so new as hardly to be firmly established as an ideal. Contemporaries, when they looked at the King and his new queen, must have seen first and foremost the consequences of a wild, unsanctioned passion; everything done for Anne, and for Anne's expected baby.

At the time Elizabeth was born, her parents' marriage was very recent – a secret ceremony in January, when Anne was already pregnant, with the coronation festivities postponed until the very end of May. Even so, Europe had had ample time to be scandalized by the love story: not by the King's taking a mistress (the thing was commonplace; Henry's mistresses had already included Anne's sister Mary) but by the way in which, over the course of the six-year wooing, he had come to confuse the roles of consort and concubine. The Habsburg ambassador Chapuys, commenting before the relationship was official, had described how Anne was made 'to sit by the King's side, occupying the very place allotted to a crowned Queen ... After dinner there was dancing and carousing, so that it seemed as if nothing were wanting but the priest to give away the nuptial ring and pronounce the blessing.' Thirty years on, another Spanish ambassador would be saying much the same about Robert Dudley.*

Anne had performed well as mistress, both in the sense of unwedded lover and in the old courtly sense of unattainable adored. Now she had to perform as a married woman. Even the pageantry of her longed-for coronation had told the new queen her duty. 'Queen Anne, when thou shalt bear a new son of the King's blood; there shall be a golden world unto thy people!' The play was over. It was time to pay.

The hour of Elizabeth's birth is matter of public record – three o'clock of a Sunday afternoon, at Greenwich, the Thames-side

---

* Spain and the Holy Roman Empire were both at this time ruled by Charles V. It was only in the last years of Mary's reign that, after Charles V's abdication, the two great Habsburg territories came to be governed separately – Spain by Charles's son Philip, the Empire by Charles's brother's kin – and their ambassadors have to be distinguished.

birthplace of her father Henry VIII. There was, of course, over-whelmingly special reason to note this particular accouchement. Everyone had hoped – and almost every physician and astrologer had predicted – that it would bring forth the longed-for male heir. For this (or so it must have seemed), Henry had cast off his first wife Katherine and bastardized his daughter Mary; offended Queen Katherine's nephew Charles V, and cut himself and his country off from the mainstream of Europe; and, at the risk of his eternal damnation, defied the Pope, whom he and all his subjects had been raised to believe God's representative on earth. For this: that Queen Anne's son should be born legitimately.

Everyone put a good face on the arrival, instead, of a daughter, expressing their pleasure and relief that Anne had at least come through her ordeal safely, and had, moreover, produced a healthy child at her first attempt. Surely a boy would follow shortly. The splendid tournament planned for the arrival of a prince was cancelled, but the pre-written letters of announcement were sent out with 'prince' altered to 'princes[s]', the *Te Deum* was sung, and Elizabeth's first progress, the brief journey back from her christening, was accompanied by five hundred men carrying lighted torches.

Underneath this public show of rejoicing, however, there was a darker story. There are no records of what her parents actually felt when the child's sex was announced. But then, there hardly need to be. The disappointment can only have been overwhelm-ing – a new and intolerable strain on a relationship that was already carrying a crushing burden of guilt and responsibility. Anne has to have known, from the moment the midwife held up the long baby, that she had failed to deliver on her implicit promise – and to have known, too (since she was very far from a stupid or an imperceptive woman), that it was in Henry's nature to try to rid himself of any guilt for the trauma that surrounded this marriage, and to throw the blame her way. To Henry the sex of this child was not just a misfortune, it was a gesture from God; a potential warning that perhaps, after all, His will had not been interpreted clearly. From the moment of her actual delivery, you could say, Elizabeth's potential importance declined rapidly.

Henry, in accordance with contemporary thinking, had long believed that God was showing His displeasure in allowing him no living male issue – he had, indeed, promised the Pope he would go on crusade, if he were only granted a male heir. (What a contrast with the Dudleys' fecundity.) Possibly, Anne herself had encouraged the idea that Henry's marriage to Katherine was demonstrably wrong, since it could produce only Mary. Had she borne a son, she would have had a position in the country and the hierarchy secure enough no longer to need the constant endorsement of Henry's passion. As long as she was mother only to a daughter, there was no reason why her many enemies should abate their attack.

For the first three months of her life Elizabeth remained at Greenwich, with her mother – not that Anne was expected to take a primary role in her care. In the special nursery suite, a wet nurse fed the child under the supervision of the Lady Mistress of the Nursery, Lady Bryan, who had similarly had charge of Princess Mary, and would perform the same function for Edward. The seventeen-year-old Mary – now disinherited by the annulment of her parents' marriage – was required to yield the jewels and the title of princess to her half-sister, and to acknowledge her own bastardy. Her refusal on the latter two points confirmed her on a collision course with Anne.

At three months, Elizabeth and her dozen or so attendants were sent away from court to reside in the fresher air of Hertfordshire. This meant the formation of a separate household for England's new heiress, including a host of mostly male servants to run everything from the stables to the buttery. To the hostile eyes of the Habsburg ambassador, it seemed to be Anne herself who decreed that Mary should form part of Elizabeth's entourage and dance attendance on the infant who had supplanted her. Mary was compelled to move to Hatfield where, in everything from diet to seating, she would be treated as a person of secondary importance. She fought a formidable rearguard action – even down to eating a large breakfast in her room, in order to avoid having to go into hall and accept a lower place at dinner. Anne lashed back with savagery. If Mary called herself princess, her ears should be boxed 'as the cursed bastard that she was', Anne declared – or so Chapuys reported – and she should be starved into hall. No-one (least of all Anne) seems to have considered what it might mean for a baby and toddler to grow up in the enforced presence of someone with reason to resent her so bitterly. That was not the thinking of the sixteenth century.

When Katherine died, in the early days of 1536, Mary was not allowed to go to her mother's deathbed. The two-year-old Elizabeth was at court with her parents for the Christmas festivities – more festive than ever, after the news of Katherine's demise, which (said Chapuys) sent Henry into a celebratory suit of yellow velvet, and Anne's ladies into a frenzy of joy. Elizabeth was paraded around the courtiers in her father's arms. Everything – not just Henry's suit – seemed sunny. But again, underneath the dance music there was a darker melody. Chapuys heard that the King had already whispered to one confidant that he had been seduced by witchcraft into the marriage with Anne, and therefore considered it null: as witness the fact he still had no male heir. Anne herself seems already to have had an early sense of foreboding, even sending a half-conciliatory message to Mary – hoping to recruit future sympathy for her own daughter, maybe? She was pregnant again, but lost the male foetus; perhaps because news was brought to her that Henry had fallen, and could easily have been fatally injured, in a jousting tournament. ('She has mis-carried of her saviour,' her uncle said.) In the same breath as he reported it, Chapuys mentioned that the King was making much of one Mistress Seymour. Anne must have been aware that if she fell, Elizabeth would be left very vulnerable.

One of the great imponderables about Elizabeth's early life is her relationship with her mother. Were those first three months together at Greenwich enough to forge a bond? Or did Elizabeth effectively find mother figures, adequate or otherwise, in the parade of women who raised her – to some of whom she would remain close until their dying days? Later, she would write that 'we are more indebted to them that bringeth us up well than to our parents'. Even had Anne lived, she would not necessarily have shared an establishment with her daughter. She visited the nursery, alone and with Henry; wrote to and heard from Lady Bryan. She sent many gifts up the north road, from a fringed crimson canopy for the cradle to a gadget for straightening the fingers of which Elizabeth would later be so proud. We may if we choose deduce a doting mother from the lavish items of clothing she bestowed on the infant, but evidence as to direct involvement is limited. Having given birth to a royal child, her emotion or lack of it was not an issue. In either case, she was required now merely to step back and leave matters to King and council. From now on even the decision to have Elizabeth weaned at twenty-five months would be ratified 'by his grace, with the assent of the queen's grace'. It is true that Elizabeth's half-sister Mary had been un- usually close to her mother Katherine (who, when the child Mary was ill, had her in her bed to nurse her). But even Katherine had bent the rules of royal matrimony only with difficulty. And Katherine did not have Anne's other fish to fry: was not, at that time, surrounded by enemies; did not have a religious reform to promote and a political party to rally.

Elizabeth may have stayed with or near her parents that spring. If so, it is not clear why. Perhaps now Anne felt the need to spend time with her daughter; perhaps the King was too distracted to order her return to Hertfordshire. Perhaps Katherine's death (which, as Anne well knew, paved the way for her own replace- ment by a third wife, less controversial and more fecund) made them feel the child was indeed better away from Mary. Two decades later, the Scottish reformer Alexander Alane (also known as 'Alesius'), then living in England, told Elizabeth that he remem- bered a scene: 'your most religious mother carrying you, still a little baby, in her arms and entreating the most serene King, your father, from the open window . . . the faces and gestures of the speakers plainly showed that the King was angry'. But that may have been fantasy rather than memory; and Elizabeth may have been in Hertfordshire, well away from the court.

A surviving clothing bill to Queen Anne, presented by the mercer William Lok in that spring of 1536, shows that in the three months from January to April alone, the two-year-old

Elizabeth was supplied with a gown of orange velvet; kirtles of russet velvet, yellow satin, white damask and green satin; embroidered purple satin sleeves, ribbons, a damask bedspread, and carefully fitted caps, one made of purple satin, another in a net of gold. But the lavish spending stopped abruptly. At the beginning of May, Anne was arrested.

She was charged with committing adultery with a handful of men, including her musician Mark Smeaton (the only one to have confessed, almost certainly under the fear or fact of torture) and her own brother George. From the start she seems to have had few illusions about her fate. A few days before her arrest, Anne had had a conversation with her chaplain Matthew Parker (later Elizabeth's first Archbishop of Canterbury) about Elizabeth's future upbringing. As he recounted it later, with the dubious benefits of hindsight, he was convinced that Anne was in some way entrusting Elizabeth to his care.

Just as it has always been one of the great 'what ifs' of history whether, if Henry had never met Anne, England would still be a Catholic country, so it has always been a puzzle just why Anne had to die. We realized a while ago that Anne was not the villainess of earlier legend, just as we know how unsubstantiated were the charges of adultery that prefaced her death. But it has proved curiously hard to replace that biblically colourful image of a scheming Jezebel with another that convinces entirely. Was this a woman who combined a genuine religious fervour with personal ambition? It is possible Anne had become a political liability – that diplomatic pressures in Europe, and her own very sincere espousal of a kind of moderate religious reform, came to threaten her former ally Cromwell over the great land grab that was the dissolution of the monasteries.* Anne's vulnerability (just like Robert Dudley's, later) was that she had set herself up as a natural scapegoat – too aggressive, too rapid a riser, ever to command much sympathy.

* This is the theory convincingly expounded by her biographer Eric Ives. An alternative has, however, recently been put forward by Retha Warnicke, who suggests that Anne's miscarriage of a possibly deformed foetus convinced Henry of her corruption and adultery.

We do not know how or when Elizabeth heard of her mother's death. She was probably told by her own household, and kindly – but did the news come all at once, or in gradual stages? Did she hear first that her mother was dead, and only later the manner of it? Did anyone, in her childhood, throw in her face her mother's supposed failings? It is hard to doubt that the gossip of servants, and the bitterness of her sister Mary, told her enough to mark her indelibly. The more so if the two half-sisters were together when Lady Kingston (wife to the Lieutenant of the Tower) came hotfoot from London, where she had accompanied Anne to the scaffold, with news that was the best of all to one girl, the worst of all for the other.

Did Elizabeth herself, as she grew, believe Anne innocent? Presumably. As queen, she would favour her mother's kindred; would adopt her mother's motto 'Semper eadem', 'Always the same', and her badge of a falcon. She cherished a jewel that showed her portrait and her mother's side by side. Unlike her sister Mary, she made no attempt to revive and clear her mother's memory when she came to the throne (any more than did Robert Dudley to clear his family). But one might argue that she paid her debt to her own past in many tiny ways. They permeate the relationship she and Robert shared.

If Elizabeth's mother was innocent, then her father was the more guilty ... Did Elizabeth learn here the downside of a marriage based on mere personal attraction? It is anachronistic to suggest that Elizabeth felt precisely the same guilt and trauma we today impute to the child of quarrelling parents. But she must have had her own horrors to contend with; must have been aware that her mother was widely credited with the heinous crimes of treason and adultery – aware, too, that her mother's fate might have been very different, had she herself been a boy. Later in life her refusal to look facts squarely in the face amounted almost to a flair, a distinct element in her governing style. It is tempting to speculate that she was forced to learn the skill early.

As a parent, Henry had one thing going for him (besides being there, alive) – his royalty. It was his name (not her mother's, unless you count her pride in her 'most English' descent) that the adult Elizabeth would invoke so frequently. Did Elizabeth perceive a class element in her parents' relationship, which would be replicated in her own with Robert Dudley? Years before her birth – before her mother yielded – Henry had written to Anne a letter in which (though he spoke of himself as her 'very loyal servant', in the language of courtly fantasy) the King urged the commoner to 'do the duty of a true, loyal, mistress and friend, and give yourself body and heart to me'. There was something consuming in his passion. It sounds as if he wanted to gobble Anne up whole, which is effectively what Elizabeth would do with her favourites. Elizabeth surely found the relationship a thankless one, in that she was to give her head and heart to a man who – when he had a living daughter, but no legitimate son – would describe himself as 'childless'. And for the first half of the period – hardly more than a decade in all – that passed between Anne's death and that of Henry himself, Elizabeth's father was effectively an absentee from her life.

As the 1530s gave way to the 1540s – while Jane Seymour gave birth to a son and died; while Henry made his brief fourth marital experiment with Anne of Cleves; and even while he took as his fifth wife the pretty, teenaged Katherine Howard – the royal sisters were chiefly living in Hertfordshire; and all the better for being away from the court, no doubt. Even Mary, at this stage of Elizabeth's early life, managed to separate her hatred of the mother from her feelings towards the child. Now that Anne, like Katherine, was dead, she managed to see both herself and her half-sister as victims.

Mary had quickly learned that Anne's death had not ended her problems, and had fought long and hard before, in that summer of 1536, she signed the 'confession' of her own bastardy. Two days before Anne's execution, the Archbishop of Canterbury had annulled her marriage, so that Elizabeth too was *ipso facto* a bastard. The Act of Succession passed that summer decreed that the throne should go only to Henry's children by Jane or by some subsequent wife, Elizabeth, like Mary, being 'illegitimate . . . and utterly foreclosed, excluded and banned to claim, challenge or demand any inheritance as lawful heir'.

None the less, if they were bastards they were still royal bastards, and would (while they pleased their father) be treated royally. While Mary stood as godmother at the new Prince Edward's christening, Elizabeth (herself still so small she had to be carried) held up the chrisom.

Soon after Anne Boleyn was executed, Lady Bryan was complaining to Cromwell that

> my Lady Elizabeth is put from that degree she was afore, and what degree she is of now I know not but by hearsay. Therefore I know not how to order her, nor myself, nor none of hers that I have the rule of – that is, her women and grooms, beseeching you . . . that she may have some raiment. For she hath neither gown, nor kirtle, nor petticoat, nor no manner of linen, nor smocks, nor kerchiefs, nor rails, nor body-stitchets [nightgowns or corsets], nor handkerchiefs, nor sleeves, nor mufflers, nor biggens [nightcaps].

The white damask and the russet velvet had clearly been outgrown and would not necessarily be fast replaced. They were, in a sense, representative of the devoted care which Elizabeth would never again be able to take for granted, as her right, from those in authority.

In this portrait of Elizabeth, painted when she was about thirteen, the richness of the damask and the pearls that deck her dress is undercut by the studious message of the books close at hand.

Portraits of Anne Boleyn (above), Elizabeth's mother, demurely coiffed in the French fashion, none the less suggest something of her fascination.

The Family of Henry VIII (above) is an allegory (of the Tudor succession, showing Henry flanked by his s(on) Edward and Jane Seymour, the only one of the King('s) six wives to produce a male heir. Mary Tudor, as the elder daughter, stands to the King's right, and Elizabeth to his left.

...st of Hatfield House *(below left)*
...been rebuilt, but the great hall
...re Elizabeth held her first council
...ting survives. It is used for
...quets today.

*Thomas Seymour, the first
man with whom scandal
linked Elizabeth.*

LONDINVM
GLIAE R

Clarkenwell

Smyt
Field

Cecell

Suffolke P. Purrine P. D.? Somer set Place

Yuere house

The Corte

Mildesse

The Temple Rd Ferie

Rd Ferie

Sterey bridge

Lamberth Marsh

Lambeth Coumon

Y Cupids Bridge.

The Stewas
ter house

Lamberth

Hæc eſt Regia illa totius Angliæ ciuitas LONDINVM, ad flu-
uium Thameſim ſita: Cæſari, vt plures exis ſimat, Trinobantum
nuncupata, multarum gentium commertio nobilitata, exciſa domib. ornata te-
plis, exelſa arcibus, claris ingenijs, viris omnium artium doctrinarumq; gene-
re præſtantibus, percelebris. Demq, omnium rerum copia, atque opum excelletia
mirabilis. ſuccrebr in eam totius orbis opes ipſe Thamaſis, onerarijs nauibus per
ſexaginta millia paſſuum, ad vrbem præalto alueo naugabilis

A map of London in 1572 clearly shows the Tower, where Elizabeth and Robert (top left) were both held prisoner. The carvings the Dudley brothers made there (top right) can still be seen today. In a contemporary illustration of Elizabeth's coronation (bottom right), Robert rides behind her, in his capacity as Master of Horse.

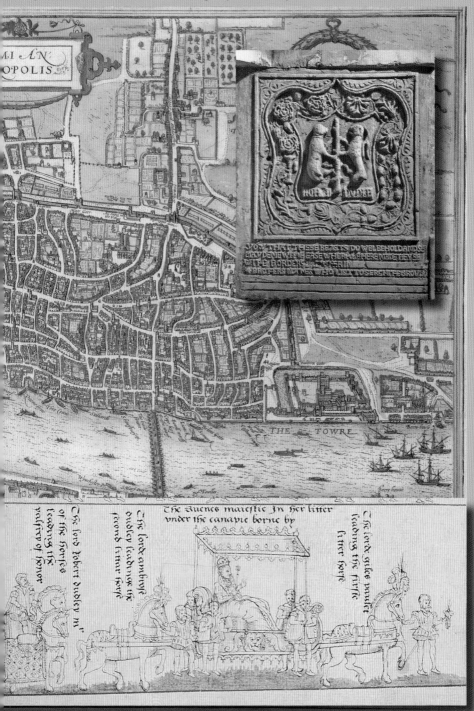

The sketches for matching portraits of Elizabeth and Robert (now lost) were made by Zuccaro in 1575. Robert has chosen to have himself portrayed with the armoured trappings of chivalry.

This picture at Penshurst Place has long been described as showing Elizabeth and Leicester dancing the Volta. In fact it is less likely to be an actual depiction of the pair than a piece of political propaganda.

Elizabeth, on one of her legendary progresses, approaches her magical palace of Nonsuch (long since destroyed).

For as long as Mary, Queen of Scots (top left) remained the Catholic pretender to the throne of the Protestant Elizabeth (top right), the two were locked in a dance of death that ended only with Mary's execution at Fotheringhay (above).

2

'Her eighth year'
1536–1547

IN FACT, ELIZABETH'S DAILY LIFE DID NOT CHANGE INSTANTLY WHEN her mother died. It is both tempting and easy to paint too gloomy a picture. (In the same letter as she bemoans Elizabeth's lack of clothing, the lady governess discusses how frequently Elizabeth should dine under her canopy of state.) When, later that year, the north rose in revolt against the dissolution of the monasteries, Mary and Elizabeth were both brought to court for safety; and though Elizabeth was placed less prominently than Mary, a French agent reported that the King was 'very affectionate' to her. The royal daughters moved between Hatfield and Hunsdon, Ashridge and Hertford Castle, when one great set of rooms needed to be cleansed and 'sweetened' as fresh herbs were strewn on the floor and the old unhygienic layer carted away. Each house was an encampment as large as a village, with its kennels and stables, its brewery and bakery. Most of those Hertfordshire houses where the princesses spent their time are long gone today, but a glowing red wing of old Hatfield still stands, facing the ancient church dedicated to St Etheldreda – another queen who took a hand in the destiny of her realm.*

---

* The chapel of Ely Place is also dedicated to St Etheldreda. It seems an odd coincidence that both Robert and Elizabeth should have grown up with churches dedicated to a saint and queen celebrated for her virginity.

Elizabeth was not reared specifically for the throne. She had no actual training in statecraft, of the sort that was crammed into Edward (and had, at one time, been given to Mary, who before she was ten had been declared Princess of Wales, while governorship of the principality was formally – if briefly – turned over to herself and her advisers). All the same, Elizabeth too was given a royal training in the most important sense: that she was educated like a boy, instead of being fobbed off with the informal and domestic training traditional for a girl.

Katherine of Aragon had received her education at the hands of her formidable mother, Isabella of Castile, and it had been formal and rigorous. Anne Boleyn had had her – also impressive – training, with a different gloss, at what was effectively the finishing school of the great European households. She was still a child when she was entrusted to the care of Margaret, the Regent of the Netherlands, and reared with the three Habsburg girls who would become the queens of France (and Portugal), of Denmark and of Hungary. In a centre of humanist studies, famed for its painting and music, Anne was trained in not only the literary but the worldly arts of the courtier. Elizabeth, of course, would end up skilled in both spheres; but the actual training she got was more akin to the model Katherine had instituted for her daughter: the model of royalty.

In 1536 Elizabeth's household had been augmented by a Devonshire gentlewoman, Kat (Katherine) Champernowne, whose subsequent marriage to a cousin of Anne Boleyn's gave her her better-known name of Kat Ashley (or Astley). It was she who first, Elizabeth later said, took 'great labour and pain in bringing me up in learning and honesty'; and though Kat's later career has left lasting doubts as to her sense and scruples, her learning seems to have been well up to the task of instructing Elizabeth's first steps. The young princess started to acquire fluent French (though a Frenchman later mocked her clumsy accent), Italian, Spanish and even Flemish; history and geography, astronomy and mathematics, as well as dancing and riding, music and embroidery. As she would write later, in her teens: 'the face, I grant, I might well blush to offer, but the mind I shall never be ashamed to present'.

In later years, Elizabeth's formidable list of skills and accomplishments made up part of her equipment as a ruler. But at the time it must have been a little unclear for just what destiny, in fact, she was being educated. The grand marriage that was conventional for royal daughters already looked unlikely for her (or for Mary). When she was a baby she had been displayed 'quite naked' to French ambassadors, with a view to betrothing her to the French king's younger son – but that was before she was declared bastard. When illegitimate Elizabeth, daughter of the Protestant adulteress, was offered for a Habsburg nephew, Charles V received the offer coldly. Even Henry's own council noted that the girls were unlikely to be marriageable abroad unless they were made 'of some estimation' at home. The mature Elizabeth would be famous for her appetite for flattery – her urge to keep herself desirable, but ultimately unattainable. Perhaps that later attitude was coloured by this experience of knowing herself a drug on the market, before she was restored to the succession and to marriageability.

Robert's education, meanwhile, was not being neglected. Through the boy's early years, his father's fortunes rose steadily. At the time Anne Boleyn died, John Dudley was already a friend and sometimes business partner of Edward Seymour, the brother of Henry's third queen, Jane. John and his wife held office under Anne of Cleves as Master of Horse and lady-in-waiting. (They would also be close to Katherine Parr. You could say that they did well out of Henry's marital history.) Their sons were educated at home, not – as was so common among the English nobility – sent away to another noble house or, as would soon become possible, to a school. Perhaps it was no coincidence that, as Edmund Dudley had once written, the English nobility were 'the worst brought up for the most part of any realm in Christendom'. John Dudley would not make that mistake; though possessed himself of only moderate linguistic and literary training, he had all the respect for book-based education to be expected from one who enthusiastically followed his royal master into the new religion and the new learning. Robert's mother Jane Dudley had herself been well educated on elevated lines; her uncle was one of

Katherine of Aragon's closest supporters, so that Jane's youthful times at court had brought her into contact not only with Princess Mary, but also with the future Katherine Parr, whose mother was one of Katherine of Aragon's most respected ladies-in-waiting.

The programme laid down some years later for the twelve-year-old Earl of Oxford gives some idea of that the Dudley boys might have followed. (There was little idea of segregating children, or their studies, according to age.) Dancing, French, Latin, writing and drawing from early in the morning (for even lie-abed Londoners rose at six) until the ten-thirty break for prayers and dinner; then from one o'clock more of the same, with a little cosmography. This – a mixture of geography and astrology, with oddments from natural science and anthropology – was likely, to judge by the eagerness of his future patronage of explorers and merchant adventurers, to have been one of Robert's favourite subjects.

John Dudley's personal interests led him towards the more practical subjects of study. Astronomy could be used for navigation, and mathematics had, after all, an application in ballistics; like history, it was considered useful to a nobleman for the conduct of a war. Dudley's professional interests were naval as well as military, and the presence of seafarers and explorers like Cabot around his house must have meant that his sons were vividly aware of the romantic possibilities offered by the new frontiers of the sixteenth century. At some point in his early career, Robert came under the extraordinary influence of 'Dr' John Dee, the scientist and astrologer who had himself been a pupil at Cambridge of John Cheke, and who would later be called in to give lessons in cosmography to the explorers Elizabeth and Robert both patronized.* Such company cannot but have helped fire an imagination to which the age gave ample fuel. The adventurers of the late Tudor era brought back stories of 'extreme and horrible cold', of perpetual days 'upon a huge and mighty

* Dee is often described as having been Robert's tutor, but this can only have been as an adult's companion in study rather than a schoolmaster since Dee, born in 1527, was working abroad until Robert was almost twenty.

sea', where might be found the unicorn's horn (probably from a narwhal) that Frobisher would present to the crowned Elizabeth; of the giant 'oliphant' and its strange snout; of lands dripping with sweet gums.

Besides lecturing the explorers, Dee, in the years Robert and his siblings remained close to him, would speak to spirits through his mediums – or so he said, and why should any doubt it? If the tales of the travellers could be true, then why should those other realms of the imagination not also open themselves to man's curiosity? Why should the grown-up Robert not subscribe with the same hopes to an experiment to turn iron into copper and to the Muscovy Company? Elizabeth and Robert both shared the age's belief in the supernatural: how could Elizabeth not, when her mother had been suspected of witchcraft? (And what besides magic, after all, was the coronation ceremony that transformed a fallible, fleshly, 'natural' woman into the earthly embodiment of the body politic, a being so endowed with grace that even her touch could cure certain maladies?) If Robert was to become Elizabeth's 'Eyes', as she called him, then perhaps one thing he helped to show her was this amazing new world of earth and sky.

Noble children read the classical authors like Cicero and Virgil, Horace and Livy, to pick up precepts, pithy pieces of wisdom and an elegant turn of phrase; they might be taught logic and rhetoric to the same end. Robert's linguistic and literary gifts would never compare with Elizabeth's. In later life the great educationalist Roger Ascham, famous for his part in Elizabeth's training, would chide him: 'I think you did yourself injury in changing Tully's wisdom for Euclid's pricks and lines.' But other Renaissance scholars valued more highly the newly fashionable geometry of Euclid, as well as the observations of Pliny and Ptolemy. And Robert seems, later in life, to have acquired a working knowledge of the languages he needed. Music was essential; even barber shops kept a lute so that customers might amuse themselves while waiting in the queue. Robert's later inventory included lutes, flutes and virginals, a particularly fine collection of paintings, and chessmen of crystal set with precious stones. The old requirements that a gentleman should be a fighter and a sportsman were changing (like the old medieval curriculum of learning); Castiglione's *The Courtier* had been published in Italy in 1528, and although it was not published in England for more than thirty years after that, the Italian's ideal of a connoisseur and conversationalist, a dancer and a diplomat, was current far earlier.

Even the idea of a young gentleman's education given by so dedicated a scholar as Roger Ascham included 'courtly exercises' as well as book learning: 'to ride comely, to run fair at the tilt or ring, to play at all weapons, to shoot fair in bow and surely in gun, to vault lustily, to run, to leap, to wrestle, to swim, to dance comely, to sing and play at instruments cunningly, to hawk, to hunt, to play at tennis . . .'; and Thomas Elyot's *Book Named the Governor* (first published in 1531 and often reprinted) describes the training that would build a young nobleman's 'hardness, strength and agility and to help therewith himself in peril, which may happen in wars or other necessity'. The hunting in which Robert and Elizabeth both delighted was seen as a training for war. Robert would early have been taught to fight with a variety of weapons: not only the staff and the pike, and the broadsword, but also the rapier. Archery was a required skill for boys and men of all ranks; with invasion from abroad a recurrent possibility, it was obligatory to keep bows for children over seven. At the time of Robert Dudley's death (a time when archery, while still compulsory, was becoming perhaps a little old-fashioned), the inventory of his possessions would include 280 bows, with their arrows.

As the years wore on and the children grew, John Dudley took a lease on Ely Place, Holborn, as a town base in which to house his brood. The rambling fourteenth-century mansion, once the London residence of the Bishop of Ely, was a huge sprawling complex of courtyards and cloisters, state rooms and gardens. Robert thus had an early training in the ways not only of the court, but of London. Those who lived there knew the problems of the overcrowded city, where pestilence was a perennial threat. But the criers offering fresh periwinkles and ripe cowcumbers, the footpads and great fairs, the busy sparkling river and stinking alleys must have been colourful and romantic enough to attract a rich man's son, escorted by servants through the cramped, lively streets on an occasional holiday. For in the sixteenth century Ely Place itself would almost have been in the country, or at least the healthy suburbs where plague was less of a danger. Contemporary maps show the rectangular flower and fruit beds of the huge enclosed space behind the palace, large as a market garden. Shakespeare wrote of the strawberry beds of Ely Place; and when Queen Elizabeth forced a later bishop of Ely to lease the house to another favourite, he stipulated that he should be able to pick a bushel of roses – some versions said an extraordinary twenty bushels – from the garden each year.*

This was a time when London meant the City of London; when royalty could ride in the green spaces between the city walls and the royal complex of Westminster and Whitehall, and hounds kill their quarry in St Giles; when laundrywomen laid their sheets to dry on Moorfields; and when Covent Garden was literally the property of a monastery – one of the many whose inhabitants were turned out of doors in the first years of Robert's childhood, in the successive depredations of the dissolution of the monasteries. In 1536 London saw its smaller monasteries, like Kilburn Priory, fall; in 1539, the larger, like Southwark and St Bartholomew's, went the same way; and in 1540, finally, there followed the suppression of Westminster Abbey. No-one was better placed to profit from this dispossession than the King's henchman John Dudley. But the head of the Holy Maid of Kent (executed for daring to prophesy disaster if the King married Anne Boleyn) on London Bridge, and the limb of the executed prior of Charterhouse nailed up over his monastery doors, must have spelt a kind of warning to any family for whom Edmund Dudley's death was a recent memory. Violent death by process of law haunted both Tudors and Dudleys.

In later life Robert and Elizabeth each made one recorded statement – just one – concerning their relationship before her accession day.

---

* That favourite was Christopher Hatton, who gave his name to Hatton Garden, which stands on the site today. All that remains of the old palace is the crypt below St Etheldreda's chapel – 'reclaimed for the old religion', as the plaque outside puts it, in the 1870s.

Robert's, made to the French ambassador in 1566, was that he had known Elizabeth 'from her eighth year' (known her 'better than any man on earth'; and that, since that time, she had invariably declared she would never marry). The passing of that eighth year brings us to the autumn of 1541 – a point at which several things were about to happen.

In 1542 Robert's father was elevated to the peerage, increasing the possibility that his sons might be placed in the young Prince Edward's household; and Elizabeth, for the first time since baby-hood, spent time with her father Henry. Over the next few years, both Robert and Elizabeth would be in and out of court circles. The children of prominent courtiers were often roped in as class-room companions for juvenile royalty, and the scholars who enjoyed John Dudley's patronage included the tutor to the royal children, John Cheke. It is dangerous to paint, as some writers have done, too sure a picture of a childhood friendship between Robert and Elizabeth. But their circles overlapped to such an extent that some degree of contact is a virtual certainty – and would have been even without the friendship between Katherine Parr, the King's last wife, and Jane Dudley.

Because something else had happened in 1542. That February, Elizabeth's kinswoman – giddy, sexy Katherine Howard – died on the block, with unexpected bravery. Where her cousin Anne had cracked jokes about her 'little neck', Katherine asked to have a rehearsal of the execution ceremony: this, at least, she wanted to do properly. But Elizabeth was not close enough to Kat to suffer in her fall (unlike her aunt, George Boleyn's widow, Lady Rochford). When, in the summer of 1543, the King married Katherine Parr, Jane Dudley was one of the few present at the ceremony. The first surviving letter to contain some hint of the news was written by John Dudley, reporting that Katherine was 'here at court' in Greenwich with Mary and Elizabeth.

After the wedding, while Mary stayed at court, Elizabeth was returned to the schoolroom – to the company of Edward, and those around him. But the new couple's progress brought them round to Ashridge, and to the inhabitants of the royal school-room. English ambassadors abroad, used to passing off the latest scandal, found themselves asked, as a novelty, whether it was true that the English royal family lived now as one household? For Elizabeth, it was perhaps the nearest thing she would ever know to ordinary family life. At the beginning of 1544 Henry – now aged fifty-two, and with no sign of the longed-for second son – laid down another Act of Succession. If he had no further child, if Edward died without heir, then the throne passed to Mary; if she too died childless, to Elizabeth. That is a lot of 'ifs' – and nothing was done about removing the stigma of bastardy. But all three of Henry's children were there at a formal dinner in May 1544 to mark the betrothal of the King's niece Margaret Douglas to the Scottish Earl of Lennox.

In July came a kind of break-up of the family group. As the King himself set off to the wars in France, Prince Edward was to move into Hampton Court, where there had been constructed a 'Prince's side', a shadow establishment above a sunny small court, next to the Chapel Royal, with the prince's chamber between that of the master of his horse and his bowling alley; rooms that, to protect the prince's most precious person from infection, were washed down three times a day.

It was those French wars of the 1540s that gave John Dudley his real opportunity. Appointed a general (like Edward Seymour, now Earl of Hertford), he had been raised to the peerage as Viscount Lisle in 1542 and, within another year, to the posts of Lord Warden of the Cinque Ports and Keeper of the Scottish Marches; to the head of the Admiralty and the Order of the Garter; and even to the privy council. In 1544 he was at the head of the army that quelled Scotland with professional ferocity, and then (heading rapidly southwards again) in command of the fleet that carried an English army to France. The recapture of Boulogne was in part his triumph – a coup of limited practical use, but a huge propaganda victory. Boulogne made Dudley a public hero, but at great personal cost: his eldest son, Robert's elder brother, died in the affray.

So, when it was deemed time for the six-year-old Edward no longer to be brought up 'among the women', as he himself later put it, but given male tutors, the young nobles and 'henchmen' around him were always likely to have included some at least of the young Dudleys. The State Papers mention the appointment of the prince's tutors 'for the better instruction of the Prince and the diligent teaching of such children as be appointed to attend on him'. The fact that Robert was a few years older than Edward would have been no impediment: royalty was expected to show an unusual precocity.

Robert's political education would have continued in the prince's entourage. Every child in the royal service knew that they carried with them, like a heavy load of schoolbooks, the interests of their family. Robert, of course, was used to seeing his father conducting the business of governance at home, where he presided over sessions of the High Court of Admiralty and meetings of the Navy Board he himself had founded. But he was learning another kind of politics, too (at a different level from Elizabeth): learning how a huge household meshed together; how this microcosm of a world, with its wildly differing social strata, functioned and was managed.

The young lords around the prince had their own tutors, preachers, masters. But they must surely also have rubbed up against the different rank of rowdy 'boys' who feature so regularly in the kitchen ordinances. It is still possible to walk round Hampton Court today and get some sense of the bustle of those huge kitchens, as organized as any factory: kitchens where the game hung in larders on the shady side of the passage, and the pastry chefs and confectioners needed the drier side of this small street to prepare their 'subtleties' and their huge pork pies; where rabbits came fresh-killed from pens in the grounds, and carp from the palace fishponds were cooked with prunes to supplement the crab and the bream, the plaice or even porpoise, that arrived packed in seaweed every day.

During his absence abroad, the King left Queen Katherine to govern in his stead, and to keep her state amid the colour of the great hall: its friezes and tapestries and painted roof; its green and white tiles on the floor (and its carvings from which not quite all the letters HA – Henry and Anne – had been excised successfully). Elizabeth was with her stepmother's court, watching the skill with which she presided. Until she was eleven or so, Elizabeth's education had been slightly erratic, requiring lessons from Edward's teachers, Dr Richard Cox and Sir John Cheke, to supplement the efforts of Kat Ashley. In 1544, however, she was given her own tutor, William Grindal, who was not only a fine Latinist and a notable Grecian but also a pupil of the great Ascham. Ascham himself, a friend of Kat Ashley and her husband, taught the royal brother and sister the difficult italic hand, sent books of prayers, mended Elizabeth's 'silver pen', wrote frequently and, on visits, joined them in archery. Elizabeth owed a lot to his famously progressive ideas, rare at a time when common belief held that to spare the rod was to spoil the child. Ascham, by contrast, urged Kat Ashley to 'favour somewhat' Elizabeth's agile young intelligence: 'the younger, the more tender, the quicker, the easier to break'. Just as influential, however, must have been the position of Ascham, Ashley and all their circle in the vanguard of the reformed faith, along with Katherine Parr's own advanced views.

Robert, too, would have been learning strict Protestant tenets – indeed, he would later boast that he had been reared in them 'from my cradle'. If Robert spent time with his father, he was in the company of one of the two men the Spanish ambassador called 'these stirrers of heresy' (the other being Jane Seymour's brother, the Earl of Hertford) – adding that both men's wives were using their religious influence on Queen Katherine. If Robert were attendant on the young Edward, then he was living at the court of a prince who (precociously and, it has to be said, not terribly likeably) insisted on being given a copy of every sermon he heard, and quizzing his adolescent companions on the content of it. The latter part of Robert's career would amount to a crusade for what would come to be called puritanism; a cause pursued with such commitment, so often privately expressed, that it could only be sincere, little though it might seem to fit with the image of the popinjay. His tenets, indeed, would in the end be considerably more radical than Elizabeth's.

In 1544 (in a startlingly elaborate showpiece letter) Elizabeth wrote to Queen Katherine that 'Inimical Fortune, envious of all good, she who revolves things human, has deprived me for a whole year of your most illustrious presence'. But by 1546 Elizabeth was of an age to be brought to court and live under her stepmother's eye as lady-in-waiting: after Mary, the first of the ladies 'accustomed to be lodged within the King's Majesty's house'. When she arrived, she might have been greeted by a painting (now in Hampton Court, where it had been hung by the middle of Elizabeth's reign) that embodied in one huge canvas her place in the royal family.

The shape of the anonymous painting, *The Family of Henry VIII*, is so oddly elongated as to invite speculation that it may have been designed for deletion as necessary – cut down, perhaps, to the point of leaving only the trinity at its core. In the centre sits Henry himself enthroned, with the young Edward at his right hand, and at his left the long-dead Jane Seymour, as mother of the all-important boy. (No sign of Queen Katherine, although she had married Henry in 1543; and it is unlikely the painting was made that early.) These three are framed in a network of gilded pillars. Outside the magic circle – framed by another set of rather less conspicuous pillars – stand the two royal daughters, separately: Mary, as elder, to Henry's right, and Elizabeth to his left.

In December 1546 the message of the portrait was ratified by the King's will, which confirmed Elizabeth's place in the succession, after any heirs of her brother or Mary. Each daughter was left £3,000 a year until she married, with a further £10,000 to be made as a single payment on that marriage – but only if it were made with the approval of the privy council. Should Elizabeth marry without such approval, she would be out of the succession itself, 'as though the said Lady Elizabeth were then dead'.

But it was Henry himself who was dying. One recent theory suggests that he was suffering from Cushing's Syndrome, a rare hormonal disorder, which would account for the bloated face that stared grimly out of later portraits, and for the massive bulk of the body. It can cause irritability, depression, aggression, psychosis – and, in men, impotence – as well as the fatty deposits on face and trunk so conspicuous in the pictures. But it remains possible that the fairly unspecific set of symptoms Henry exhibited could have been caused by general self-indulgence and debility; or by the lingering effects of that jousting injury, which produced recurrent agonizing abscesses on his legs, while forbidding him to exercise in any way.

When, on 28 January 1547, King Henry died, his brother-in-law Edward Seymour, the Earl of Hertford, rode out to Hertfordshire to collect the new child king – telling him only, however, that he had to return to London to be invested as Prince of Wales, and waiting till they halted to spend the night with Elizabeth at Enfield before breaking the news to both children together. Their shared grief, however, was the last moment at which brother and sister would meet together on anything like equal terms. From now on, the one was King and the other subject. While her brother moved straight into the dramas of Henry's funeral and his own coronation (a rushed progression of less than three weeks), Elizabeth was not present at either ceremony.

It is far more likely that Robert was there as the new Edward VI heard Archbishop Cranmer assure the congregation that he himself was now accountable only to God; and that to God was he answerable for the reformations of his church. Robert's father, after all, would wish to display his new dignities as Earl of Warwick, the title bestowed upon him a few days before the ceremony. Edward Seymour, already Earl of Hertford, became also Duke of Somerset and, more to the point, took for himself the title of Lord Protector during Edward's minority.

Yet over the next few years, Elizabeth's were to be the more dramatic adventures. Soon after her brother's coronation came the sequence of events that would mark the end of her childhood – and, it has always been assumed, colour for ever her relationships with men.

3

'The occasion of his utter undoing'
1547–1553

IT HAD BEEN OBVIOUS BEFORE HENRY DIED THAT EDWARD SEYMOUR and John Dudley would play leading parts in the rule of the country. John Dudley's closeness to the King had endured through the last months of the monarch's life – increased, even, with the bond of a shared religious policy added to the masculine good fellowship they had previously enjoyed. In the tug of war between conservatives and radicals, each pulling at Henry's religious settlement, the King (whatever his personal convictions) finally came down on the reformers' side. This, in the end, was the legacy he wanted to leave his son. (One of his last acts was to order the arrest of the Duke of Norfolk and the execution of his heir: politically and religiously conservative, they were the kind of over-mighty subjects who might threaten the succession of a vulnerable boy.) And if the future were to be a reformed one, there were only a few people who could administer it. As Charles V's ambassador put it, in the first weeks of 1547, 'it is probable that these two men, Seymour and Dudley, will have the management of affairs, because, apart from the King's affection for them, and other reasons, there are no other nobles of a fit age and ability for the task'.

But for the moment, by the sacred ties of blood, the pre-eminent individual was Seymour: a slightly shadowy figure, whose strong religious beliefs and altruistic rhetoric masked both his ambitions and his weaknesses. All the same, the Dudley sons – now often at court, in attendance on their father, if not directly on the young King – were close to the heart of the political intrigues that were bound to mark a royal minority. This grounding in every level of court life would later prove to have been invaluable training for Robert Dudley, enabling him rapidly to rise to the top when Elizabeth's accession brought him his opportunity. He saw at first hand – still, at this point, from the sidelines, but from the favoured position of one whose own family were riding high – the spites, the slights and the endless spying; the webs woven between the men who mattered; the frantic clamour for place and favour; and the drama of disappointment played out every day. Robert's nephew Philip Sidney would write of the need 'that obeys no law and forgets blushing'; his protégé Gabriel Harvey of how the courtier should 'Learn of the dog how skillfully to treat a Lord or King. Endure anything in the way of wrongs, and fawn none the less.' Though this was a different kind of court from the one that eventually clustered around the dominant figure of Elizabeth, there were particular lessons to be learnt from these years of a royal minority: lessons about the use of counsel and the machinery of state (now more in evidence than it had been under the powerful Henry); lessons about the extent, and the limitations, of monarchy. Elizabeth, meanwhile, was learning lessons of her own; and they – unlike Robert's, at this stage – would be traumatic to a degree.

After her father's death, Elizabeth was sent to join her stepmother Katherine Parr, who had now set up her own establishment at Chelsea. Probably the arrangement pleased her well enough. But Katherine's life of legendary prudence and piety was about to take a more skittish turn. Before Henry's eye lighted upon her, she had dreamt of marriage with Thomas Seymour, the younger, less responsible and infinitely more charismatic brother of the Lord Protector. The two resumed their old amour, and were married secretly in April. This – since Elizabeth continued to share a house with her stepmother and her stepmother's new husband – brought her effectively into Seymour's guardianship.

Seymour may have loved Katherine both before and after her life with Henry, but marriage appeared to him first as a political opportunity. Rumour claimed that his immediate thought, on the death of the old King, had been to marry either of the two princesses, Elizabeth herself or Mary. It was of course a grandiose and ludicrous fantasy – but he renewed his attentions to Katherine only after it was made clear to him that the council would never sanction this other, yet more inviting, possibility.

Now it seemed as if he might be able to have his cake and eat it too, in some confused way. It is unclear whether the advances he made to Elizabeth were consciously sexual or merely inappropriate – or whether sex was just, in dealing with any woman, his normal *modus operandi*. He may have seen a nubile teenager when he looked at Elizabeth. A portrait she had painted in her early teenage years is a study of seriousness, her hair demurely smoothed, her lips set, her dark eyes veiled and her fingers clasping a book – but perhaps a Thomas Seymour might find a hint of invitation in that very composure. More certainly, when he looked at Elizabeth he saw a chance of advancement. In this, of course, he would be the first man of many.

In these first months of his nephew's reign, Thomas Seymour was a disappointed man. He had been given the Lord Admiralship (John Dudley having progressed to Lord Great Chamberlain), and lands, and a barony. But he felt he should have had an equal hand with his brother in the governance of the King and the running of the country. As one contemporary, Sir Nicholas Throckmorton, put it neatly and damningly, he was 'fierce in courage, courtly in fashion, in personage stately, in voice magnificent but somewhat empty of matter'. Of much wit and little judgement, as Elizabeth is famously supposed to have summed him up ... but the quote is probably apocryphal, and the assessment is not a teenager's. On the plus side, Seymour was tall, and bold, and handsome. Very much, in other words, like the future Robert Dudley.

What happened next is familiar to any amateur of Tudor history, though our knowledge comes from a very limited number of sources: the testimonies of Elizabeth's attendants, Kat Ashley and Thomas Parry, extracted under pressure and the less reliable for it. How the Lord Admiral would come bursting into her bed-chamber early in the morning, pulling back the bedcurtains to 'make as though he would come at her' while she scooted away – all this in the name of play; how, if he caught her getting dressed, he would 'strike her on the back or buttocks familiarly'. Next, he appeared 'bare legged', in his nightgown; tried to snatch kisses from Elizabeth even as she lay in bed.

Kat Ashley told him he went too far, for 'These things are com-plained of, and my lady is evil spoken of.' He answered hotly that he meant no evil, that he would not leave off. That Elizabeth was like a daughter to him . . . And Elizabeth? She tried (so her servants asserted) to hide, to avoid him, to get away. Small wonder, for these approaches can only have been disconcerting (to put it at its lowest) to a girl of thirteen or fourteen – out of childhood but not yet into maturity. But her feelings were clearly mixed – it would soon be reported that she blushed when his name was mentioned, showing 'a glad countenance', that she loved to hear him praised. Modern ideas about exploitation, about power and sexuality, should not obscure the fact that women as young as Elizabeth (or Juliet!) were married in the sixteenth century, and that Seymour was a famously attractive man.

Katherine seems to have been as uncertain as anybody over what her husband intended, or how best to respond. That, at least, is the best explanation for the fact that (as Kat Ashley told it) she sometimes joined in Seymour's mock assaults on their step-daughter, helping him tickle Elizabeth in bed, and once holding her when, in the garden, he cut her dress into pieces. You could, perhaps, take her participation as proof that Seymour's behaviour was innocent . . . or proof that Katherine was trying to demon-strate it was innocent. Trying to convince herself, maybe.

But by the spring of 1548 the matter had gone beyond a game. If Kat Ashley's tearful testimony is to be believed, there came a time when the Queen Dowager, 'suspecting the often access of the Admiral to my Lady Elizabeth's Grace . . . came suddenly upon them, where they were all alone, he having her in his arms.

Wherefore the Queen fell out, both with the Admiral and with Her Grace also.' As well she might have; the more so since Katherine by this time was five months pregnant with Seymour's child, and in a state of some vulnerability. After a difficult interview between the woman and the girl – in which the younger 'answered little', suggesting she did feel herself guilty – Elizabeth was sent away, to the household of Sir Anthony Denny. It was hardly a punitive measure, since Lady Denny was Kat Ashley's sister, and the household a prominent and congenial one. The affection between Elizabeth and Katherine had been strained but not broken, if we heed the exchange of loving letters, in which Elizabeth thanked the Queen for the 'manifold kindnesses' she continued to show: 'thank God for providing such friends for me'. But, as so often in her life, sexuality had threatened to spoil a relationship important to her. Thanks to Seymour's ambition and/or lack of control, the tentative experimentations of an adolescent girl had been distorted into something very risky.

On 30 August, at her husband's castle of Sudeley, Katherine gave birth to a daughter. Both mother and baby seemed to be doing well, but within a few days Katherine developed puerperal fever. She died on Elizabeth's fifteenth birthday. Seymour was at Sudeley, as was Elizabeth's young kinswoman Lady Jane Grey, but Elizabeth herself remained at Cheshunt with the Dennys – possibly because of her health. Elizabeth had been ill about midsummer, remained unwell and edgy through into July, and was sick in bed when Kat Ashley told her Katherine was dead. (Her new tutor, Roger Ascham – who had succeeded to the post earlier in the year when Grindal had unexpectedly died – had hoped to return to Cambridge for the summer, but could not get Elizabeth's permission to go, 'for she favours me wonderfully'; a prime example of the way she would cling to her favourites.) Her illness may well have been emotional in origin; the first but not the last of the nerve storms that would continue to plague her throughout her life. The symptoms – migraine, panic attacks, menstrual problems – certainly fit that diagnosis, but some contemporaries suspected otherwise. It was suggested that Elizabeth had miscarried Seymour's baby. Later there would be other tales of a country midwife summoned to attend on a very young and obviously noble lady; of a child born only to be killed at birth. For none of this is there any evidence – and improbable tales of secret pregnancies would continue to haunt Elizabeth's career.

With Katherine's death came the possibility, again, of Elizabeth's marrying Seymour. Seymour, at least, obviously thought so. When he refused to disband his wife's household of ladies, there was debate as to whether they were to attend on his second royal wife, or merely on the ever-present Lady Jane Grey. His thoughts of Elizabeth must be seen in the context of his ever more frantic political forays; for Thomas Seymour, by now, was even travelling to the West Country to assure himself that the fleet would be on his side in the event of his launching a coup against his brother. So noticeable had his intentions become by late autumn, when Parliament reassembled, that the Lord Privy Seal, Lord Russell, took the occasion to warn Seymour that if he – or any other Englishman – attempted to set himself so far above his peers as to marry either of the princesses, he would 'procure unto himself the occasion of his utter undoing'. (So much for the theory put forward by Seymour – and those who came after him – that 'It is convenient for princesses to marry, and better it were that they are married within the realm than in any foreign place.')

Thomas Seymour was in fact (possibly encouraged by John Dudley, who hoped to divide the brothers) using presents and pocket money to win the affection of the young King, who was kept by the Lord Protector under a somewhat oppressive regime, and planning in the end to take possession of the King's person, by force if necessary. In the middle of January 1549 he burst into Edward's bedroom with a party of armed men and, when the barking of Edward's pet spaniel aroused the guards, shot the dog dead. The council had almost no choice but to arrest him, and to call in for questioning his associates, who by now included Kat Ashley and Elizabeth's cofferer Thomas Parry. Seymour had bribed or flattered these key members of Elizabeth's household into support of his plans; nor did it seem that Elizabeth heard of his ambitions unwillingly. But the key question was, with precisely what provisos had Elizabeth even tacitly conceded she and Seymour might possibly marry? With Elizabeth's favourite servants on their way to the Tower, her household was taken over by Sir Robert Tyrwhit, with instructions from the council to obtain evidence of Seymour's treasonable activity. He had, he said confidently, good hopes 'to make her cough out the whole'.

But in Elizabeth Tyrwhit had met his match. Parry and Kat Ashley talked quickly, terrified, and Elizabeth, once her first tears were over, was brought to confirm the basics of what they had to say. They 'all sing one song', Tyrwhit reported disgustedly. Yes, Seymour had quizzed Parry about exactly what lands and possessions Elizabeth had. Yes, she had been in contact with the Admiral, but only about matters of business, open for anyone to see. Yes, there had been rumours, but was that her fault? Hardly. Even if it were true that Kat and Parry had discussed the possible marriage between themselves, the point – the only real point – was that (as Elizabeth declared) Kat Ashley 'would never have me marry, neither in England nor out of England, without the consent of the King's Majesty, Your Grace's [Somerset's] and the Council's'. Elizabeth's servants – frailer (and more vulnerable to threat) than she was – were none the less loyal to her, by their lights, and she (as Tyrwhit wonderingly noted) remained wholly committed to them. Indeed, the whole long night she wept when she heard Kat Ashley was to be taken away from her, the way she clung to familiar faces over the next months, foreshadowed the way she would hold fast to Robert Dudley, clamping him in fetters at the same time as she gave him his opportunity.

In February she had to hear the distasteful news that Kat had been pressurized into blabbing details of those early-morning romps. Elizabeth was never one to take humiliation lightly. She wrote indignantly to Somerset. She had to accept the further indignity of hearing that Lady Tyrwhit would replace the disgraced Kat Ashley. But effectively, she had got away with it; had kept her head, literally. It was only Seymour who, faced with thirty-three counts of treason, was sentenced to the death penalty. His brother refrained from any effort to save him – urged to this harshness by John Dudley. Elizabeth, as Tyrwhit reported, 'beginneth now a little to droop'. But when, on

20 March, Seymour's head was cut off, she was safe in the country. David Starkey has discussed this formative episode in Elizabeth's history, noting that 'Almost all the men that she subsequently loved, or pretended to love, resembled Seymour. And all the affairs ended in the same way, in frustration and, in the case of the last [Robert's stepson, Essex], again in death.' To a psychologist – he says – Elizabeth might seem the victim of abuse, who herself would become a kind of abuser. To the eyes of a religious age, on the other hand, she would simply have learnt a great truth: that sex is sin and sin is danger. Both explanations, as he says, are far too simple. But there can be no doubt that her relationship with Thomas Seymour both affected and foreshadowed that with Robert Dudley – and perhaps not least in this: that marriage with royalty had been too dangerous an advancement for Seymour's rivals to stomach; a rehearsal for the way Robert Dudley's contemporaries would regard the possibility of Elizabeth's marrying him. (Anne Boleyn, too, of course, had died for daring to mate too high.) Nor can the similarities have failed to strike Elizabeth herself: is it conceivable that, in the curbs she would eventually place upon Robert, she was trying to protect him in some way? Aspiring to marry her, after all, had brought Thomas Seymour to the block, as well as bringing Elizabeth herself into the spotlight of a dangerous and damaging inquiry. Paradoxically, the episode can only have reinforced the link in her mind between sex and danger: teaching not only that sex brought danger, but that the dangerous was somehow sexy. It is possible that Robert would not have held her interest so long had she not known he was both forbidden fruit, and a man from an ambitious family.

As the dust of the Seymour affair settled, Elizabeth retreated for the moment into her own household and what seemed a life of almost monastic study. Kat Ashley's husband John later recalled the companionship of the household that centred on Elizabeth and her tutor, Ascham: the 'free talk' and 'trim conferences', the 'friendly fellowship' and 'pleasant studies' of Aristotle and Cicero. The picture was an idyllic one, somewhere between a reading group and an office awayday. Spoiling the image slightly are Elizabeth's continued bouts of illness, which do indeed sound as if they may have been nervous in origin. But, in so far as she could lose herself in study, she was wonderfully placed to do so. Ascham described how the beginning of the day was devoted to the New Testament in Greek, followed by Greek literature and Latin literature, both carefully chosen to polish Elizabeth's style, and by oral studies in the modern languages. Ascham praised not only his pupil's aptitude but the 'simple elegance' of her personal appearance. With hindsight it seems odd to hear Elizabeth – Edward's 'Sweet Sister Temperance' – praised for her contempt for adornment (though plainness was the fashion in the advanced Protestant circles to which the Dudleys also belonged).

But in the January of 1550 Ascham left Elizabeth's service in a squabble that casts a slightly odd light on all his eulogies. He had, as he wrote to Cheke, been overcome by the 'court violence' that impinged on her circle. In the curious settlement left behind by King Henry – government by nobles, without clear division of authority, tough religious reform urged through by a King Edward who was still in his minority – neither court nor country was easy.

The rebellion which broke out in the summer of 1549 was, on the face of it, a poor man's revolt against poverty – against the enclosures and speculation of the landowning classes; against the inflation that made the lives of common people a misery. But the fact that it was led by a landowner, Robert Kett, shows that it cannot be seen so simplistically. The rebels hoped to appeal to the 'good duke' Somerset to right their wrongs; but it was Somerset, as Lord Protector and head of the government, who ordered Dudley to put down the rebellion. When Dudley rode towards the Midlands in August, his sons Ambrose and Robert (the latter little more than sixteen) rode with his army.

It was no toy soldiery. The armies that faced each other, government and rebel, were each perhaps ten thousand strong. When conciliation failed, and the battles moved into East Anglia, it came down to savagery. Robert was there as his father led the fighting through the streets of Norwich; there when his father used all his gifts of speech and drama to rally the quaking city.

Nominally, at least, the teenaged Robert was in command of a company of infantry; and though it would be Ambrose who first took on the role of the family soldier in the decades ahead, Robert did well enough in the military campaigns of his young manhood to be able to see himself as his father's son. Later, he could still see himself as a warrior, even when advantage and affection kept him home, at Elizabeth's side; and he still chose to have his likeness drawn with the gauntlet and helmet of armed chivalry.

As the victorious army rode back towards London, it became obvious that the young Dudley brothers were being blooded politically, as well as militarily. Perhaps they were already no strangers to this game, but this was to be politics with the gloves off. It has been speculated that it was the internecine bloodshed of the Kett rebellion that led Dudley to decide the time had come for Somerset's rule to end. But he did not go quietly. October 1549 saw a series of frightening and dramatic scenes, with Somerset effectively kidnapping his nephew and taking the young King by night to Windsor on a plea of safety. When the dust settled, Somerset was in the Tower, and government was in the hands of John Dudley.

Few political figures have been the subject of such diverse opinions as John Dudley. He has (under his last title, Northumberland) been vilified for more than four centuries as ruthless, cruel, in the end cowardly as well, and above all as over-weeningly ambitious. Yet some, recently, have seen him very differently – so differently that to reconcile the two opinions is impossible, in the context of this, the next generation's story. Even so, the problem itself casts a kind of pall over anyone attempting to follow the Dudley family through the early 1550s. Certainly, the question of his heritage would not be forgotten by Robert's contemporaries. His rise was watched by the hostile eyes of those who remembered the days when it was said that 'the great devil Dudley ruleth'. Yet despite the 'black legend' that has grown up around the Dudleys, John Dudley was a loyal as well as an able soldier and administrator; one who – faced with the dangerous challenges of a child king, and, in Somerset, a weak and untrust-worthy co-ruler – tried to educate that king for kingship as fast and well as possible, and to forge a collegiate relationship with even the most unpromising of colleagues. Many modern historians are inclined to suggest that while Somerset had been arrogating near-royal authority, Dudley ruled through council and in the name of the rightful monarch; and that if Edward had lived, history might have seen his mentor very differently.

Robert must have remembered his father, later, as powerful and, yes, ambitious. He must have felt he had large shoes to fill. But it seems possible (though Robert, like Elizabeth, seems hardly to have spoken of his disgraced parent) that he would also remember his father as fiercely loyal to the monarchy; as blamed unfairly. Here, then, may lie the explanation for Robert's odd blend of touchiness and fidelity.

As the star of the Dudleys rose that autumn of 1549, Elizabeth came up to court for the Christmas festivities. Her complete rustication had not lasted long. She was preferred to Mary by the new elite, being, as the Habsburg ambassador put it, 'more of their kidney'. Indeed, a year later it was reported that John Dudley was to divorce his wife and marry her. It was an extraordinary story and unlikely – but again, Dudley's motive was thought to be that through Elizabeth he could 'aspire to the crown'. One wonders at what stage she wearied of being regarded as a means to an ambitious end.

A few weeks later Elizabeth was finally granted possession of the formidable land holdings that should have come to her from her father's death, including a swathe of manors and lands to the north-west of London, and Durham House in London for her town residence. (In the spring of 1553 she agreed, rather reluctantly, to hand the latter over to the Dudleys in return for the recently refurbished Somerset House – the keeper of which was Robert Dudley.) It was, if not a kingdom, at least a fiefdom. But she had sole possession only for her spinsterhood, her virginity.

Of John Dudley, the Habsburg ambassador wrote home that he was 'absolute master here. Nothing is done except at his command.' And his command had altered life for King Edward – and for his entourage, presumably. There were still the intensive lessons, still the emphasis on the reformed religion; more emphasis than ever on statecraft, since John Dudley seems to have been trying to fit his charge to assume the real rulership. But there were also more shooting, more tilting, more water tournaments and military displays, mock battles and mastiff baitings recorded in the young King's journal. All these were fitting arenas to display the talents of the young male Dudleys; for John Dudley packed the royal apartments with his followers. Robert was learning another useful lesson – about the importance of proximity to the monarch's person.

But in 1550, for Robert, private life came to the fore. He was betrothed to the daughter of a Norfolk landowner, Amy Robsart, at whose Norfolk house the Dudleys had stayed on their way to put down the Kett rebellion. It is possible the two knew each other already; they were much of an age, Amy perhaps a year the elder. It would seem to have been a love match – a carnal marriage, as William Cecil (now John Dudley's secretary) would later put it disapprovingly. Certainly the eighteen-year-old Robert might have attracted any girl – many years later one observer, besotted with the 'proportions and lineaments of his body', called him 'the goodliest male personage in England'. As for his side of the bargain, although John Dudley could now have made far grander alliances for his children, Amy was her father's heiress, and by this alliance Robert would become a significant landholder in the contentious territory of Norfolk. They were married at Sheen on 4 June – the day after Robert's eldest brother John was married to the daughter of Somerset, now out of the Tower and restored to a seat in government, in a limited way. John's wedding was public and formal; Robert's seems to have been marked by bucolic festivity. A live goose was tied to a pole (as King Edward noted in his diary), and the young male guests competed to cut off its head. The elder John Dudley, plagued by ever-worsening bouts of ill-health, was too unwell to be present at the ceremonies.

Elizabeth, however, was in higher and higher visibility. The Christmas celebration of 1550 brought her to London 'with a great suite of gentlemen and ladies', escorted by a hundred of the King's horse and formally welcomed by the council – the point being, as Charles V's ambassador bitterly pointed out, to show that she who had embraced the new religion had 'become a very great lady', by contrast with her sister, who so obstinately clung to the old. Fourteen months later, in 1552, she was back with an even greater train: two hundred of the gentry on horse, besides the walking soldiery. As she rode through the park of St James towards Whitehall and the court, along a highway specially strewn with clean sand, John Dudley himself was among her escort. He was now Duke of Northumberland, his eldest son Earl of Warwick, the title the father had previously held. The younger sons automatically became 'Lord' Ambrose, 'Lord' Robert and 'Lord' Guildford Dudley; titles they used by courtesy even after their father's attainder.

On all these visits, if Elizabeth did not meet Robert – and why would anyone bother to mention it, if she did? – she certainly met Dudleys. And although Robert's marriage saw him spending some time on those Norfolk estates, he too was climbing the ladder of court in a more modest way, appointed gentleman of the privy chamber in August 1551 and one of the welcoming escort for the Dowager Queen of Scotland in October. In 1552 (the year when, in January, Somerset was finally executed for treason and conspiracy) he was Member of Parliament and Lieutenant of Norfolk, and Master of Buckhounds as well when his eldest brother John was upgraded from that position to Master of Horse.

In 1553 Robert, with his father-in-law, was charged with removing all superstitious objects from the churches in their part of Norfolk – and, more frivolously, with taking on the office of the King's carvery. Not that this was a sinecure, at a time when every piece of flesh, fish or fowl had its own techniques and its own special vocabulary. You would 'break that deer', 'trush that chicken', 'disfigure that peacock' and 'splat that pike'. You would 'undertranch that porpoise' – not a task many could contemplate with equanimity. All this had to be mastered – and then you had to add the appropriate sauce to each dish. Small wonder that this was regarded as no menial task: John Dudley's stepfather, Arthur Plantagenet, had been carver to his own half-nephew Henry VIII.

None of Robert's tasks made the wheels of government spin. Still, it was not a bad haul for a young man of only twenty.

But a time was soon coming when life would cease to be so easy for the Dudley clan – and when Elizabeth's interests would diverge from theirs, radically. So far Mary's loss of favour had been Elizabeth's gain (and when in 1553 Mary seemed to be back in favour it seemed, again, to Elizabeth's detriment). Nevertheless, when push came to shove, they were both the daughters of King Henry – and, as such, had a place in the succession; a place enshrined in their father's will; a place that now seemed significant, in view of King Edward's increasing frailty.

In the spring of 1552 Edward had fallen sick of measles and smallpox – from which, however, he seemed rapidly to recover. But that summer's progress was a demanding one; and by August, it was noted on all sides how ill he looked. By the autumn it was obvious within court circles that the feverish and coughing King was suffering from (probably) tuberculosis. The medicines available included spearmint syrup mixed with red fennel and turnip, and the raw meat of a nine-day-old sow. No wonder (so Hayward later reported) a rumour would spread that Edward was being poisoned – even, that his malady dated from the time Robert was first placed in close proximity to him. But in fact there was nothing John Dudley desired less than Edward's death. Upon Edward's life depended John Dudley's power and safety, and that of his family. He could expect only the harshest treatment from the Catholic Mary.

We should not exaggerate the degree to which the turmoils of the next year should really be put down to John Dudley's slate. As 1552 turned to 1553 and Edward's health worsened, the King himself, committed to his position as defender of the new faith, was determined his throne should not pass to Mary. It was in many ways a reasonable decision. Even to contemporaries, without benefit of hindsight, it was obvious that the clashes of Mary's will with that of her people were likely to bring dissent; and that her complete and proven reliance on Habsburg advice and interests made her a dubious candidate for ruler of an independent country. It remains less clear why it was decided that

Elizabeth had to be excluded along with her. Because Elizabeth was too much her father's daughter to consent to the overturning of his will? Because Dudley knew she would never be his puppet? Or because he knew he would be able to marry his son Guildford to Lady Jane Grey, and fulfil his enemies' worst suspicions by getting his blood onto the throne that way?

But Guildford did not marry Jane (or Dudley's daughter Katherine marry Lord Hastings, descended from a brother of Edward IV) until late May 1553. The paper in Edward's hand which bears the title 'My device for the succession' must have been written well before that; and Edward, by this point, was mature enough to be no mere puppet, even of a man as forceful as John Dudley.

Henry's will had ordained that after his daughters (or heirs of their body), the throne should pass to the descendants of his younger sister Mary, bypassing the senior Scottish line. Edward followed the basic principle of disinheriting the Catholic Scots – but there was still a measure of chicanery. If Elizabeth and Mary were ruled out, the throne should by right have gone to Lady Suffolk, Henry VIII's niece and mother of Lady Jane Grey (and of two other daughters, but no sons). But though England had no Salic law actually to forbid a woman's rule, a woman had never ruled England successfully.* So Edward's 'device' was that the throne should pass to the 'heirs male' of Lady Suffolk's eldest daughter, Lady Jane.

By the end of May the King was – as one young doctor recorded – 'steadily pining away. He does not sleep except when he is stuffed with drugs. The sputum which he brings up is livid black, foetid and full of carbon; it smells beyond measure. His feet are swollen all over. To the doctors, all these things portend death.' No-one could afford to wait nine months, even in the unlikely event that Lady Jane were already pregnant with a boy. While a desperate Dudley brought in a 'wise woman' – whose

---

* The only example of a woman ruler was Matilda, who in the twelfth century had contested the throne with her kinsman Stephen, and whose arrogance and ambition had almost torn the country apart.

potions for the dying King, probably containing arsenic, pro-
longed Edward's life but horribly increased his suffering – the
words about Lady Jane's heirs male were altered to read 'the Lady
Jane and her heirs male', so that Jane herself could ascend the
throne and a dangerous vacuum be avoided. It was Edward himself who, in the middle of June, put forward this plan to the chief
lawyers of the country; Edward who forced them reluctantly to
agree. The justification for the exclusion of Mary and Elizabeth
from the succession was to be that they were both bastards. They
could marry abroad, they would condescendingly be told. No
wonder Elizabeth looked on marriage as a poor consolation prize.

As it became clear that Edward's life was ending, the Dudleys
were clustered around the court. We do not know if Robert was
in the stuffy death chamber, but it was his brother-in-law Henry
Sidney who, in the fading light of an ominously stormy evening,
held the dying fifteen-year-old in his arms. Edward has gone
down in history as a chillingly inhuman boy, whose journal
recorded the death of his uncle Somerset with the most laconic
brevity; who was said once to have torn a pet hawk in pieces,
(and, as he did so, to have been seen to smile, twice). The
elevation of an anointed king would have set clear limits to
intimacy. But though sickness was the close companion of everyone in the sixteenth century – though Robert's and Elizabeth's
letters would be full of ailments – Edward's sufferings could
surely not fail to move those who had watched him so long and
so closely.

But there was no time for sentiment. Edward's sisters – kept
away from the court – should be given no chance to rally a party.
The King died on 6 July; the following day, the great stronghold
of the Tower was put into readiness. The officers of the City of
London were bound over to Queen Jane, and on 10 July she was
proclaimed. Long before that – possibly even before Edward was
dead – a party of guards several hundred strong had been sent
towards Mary's house at Hunsdon near Hertford to 'escort' –
effectively, to secure – the princess. Their commanders were
Robert Dudley and his eldest brother John. We simply don't
know whether they had any qualms to weigh against their family

loyalty; but Robert's later opinions make it possible that he was as committed to preserving the Protestant religion as even Edward himself could be.

But Mary had been warned, and had ridden north to Norfolk, the heart of her own lands, where many of the people owed her loyalty. When the Dudley brothers arrived at Hunsdon to find the bird had flown, Robert set off in pursuit with most of the troops, while John returned to London to consult with the council. But Robert, riding through the night, missed Mary, who had taken the back roads to Sawston. Arriving at Sawston Hall early the next morning only to find that Mary had left an hour before, in (one must suppose) a young man's frustration he told his soldiers to set the place on fire. Hearing that the gentry of East Anglia were turning out to join Mary as she rode, he fell back on Cambridge, where the Protestant faith had many friends, to await fresh troops, instructions, and his brother John.

The day after Jane was proclaimed Queen, Mary set up her rival banner, and many were now flocking to what they saw as the true Tudor monarchy. In other parts of England, too, the people were rallying to her standard. Robert rode north to his own and his father-in-law's Norfolk lands, where with Robsart help he made a brief stand for Queen Jane's authority, proclaiming her in King's Lynn on 18 July with the support of the mayor and several hundred of the citizens. But on that day, had he but known it, the councillors holding the Tower, where Jane was lodged for safety, turned it over to the supporters of Queen Mary.

Four days before, John Dudley senior himself had set out for East Anglia with his remaining sons and an army. But no-one cheered them as they rode through the sullen city streets. His troops slipped away from him; the ill-health of which he had complained for months meant that he himself was operating at only half his strength. He could not fight the will of the country. The council, left to its own devices, was only too relieved to abandon a policy of which it had never really approved. On 19 July, Mary was proclaimed Queen in London, and on the twenty-first John Dudley himself proclaimed her at Cambridge. In the Tower, the trappings of queenship were stripped from Lady Jane Dudley.

On the twenty-fourth John Dudley and two of his sons were arrested. Robert, in King's Lynn, stayed free (but isolated) a little longer. It must have been nearing the end of the month when he, too, arrived in the Tower to join the rest of the fraternity.

4

'This night I think to die'
1553–1559

VISITORS TO THE TOWER CAN STILL SEE THE CARVINGS THE DUDLEYS left on the thick stone walls. Near the locked door, in the lower chamber of the Beauchamp Tower, is a whole name: ROBART [*sic*] DUDLEY. The lines are faint – almost illegible – but no more imaginative effort could have spoken as eloquently. Each groove speaks of the frustration born of fear and anger; of the need for some activity to damp down panic and occupy the surface of the mind.

At first the five brothers were scattered around the Tower, but as the prison quarters became more crowded than at any time in the place's history, they were squashed together into the upper room of the Beauchamp Tower, hard by the Lieutenant's lodging, while their father was held in what is now called the Bloody Tower, under conditions of even stricter security. By the fireplace in their one cramped room is carved an entire four-line verse.

> You that these beasts do well behold and see
> May deem with ease wherefore here made they be
> With borders eke wherein [there may be found?]
> 4 Brothers names who list to search the ground

The positions of the various Dudley carvings suggest almost

that they may each have taken a corner, and it is tempting to envisage them each working away. It was the eldest, John, who made himself responsible for a representation of the Dudley devices – a bear and ragged staff, and a double-tailed lion – and his name in a border of leaves and flowers. But in the embrasure of the upper chamber window, looking inwards onto Tower Green, Robert himself is also represented by a deeply etched spray of sprightly oak leaves and his initials, R.D. Perhaps he, ever energetic, was the first of the brothers to pass time this way: the very few earlier carvings in the room are in the same window embrasure, while (from those inscriptions that are dated) it looks as if John, by the fireplace, was striking out onto fresh territory.

Below Robert's oak leaves someone has carved the name 'Jane' – written again, and larger, elsewhere in the room. Guildford, perhaps? It is unclear whether he was sometimes with his wife or – since the verse speaks of John's 'four' brothers – held always with John and Ambrose, Robert and Henry. It is certain that the Dudleys helped spark a positive craze for carving: the walls of the Tower are littered with carvings today. (It used to be thought professional help was called in for some of the Tower's myriad carved graffiti, but in fact it is easier than you might expect to make a mark in the soft Reigate stone.) In the Beauchamp Tower, by a strange irony, most are the work of Elizabeth's Catholic prisoners, held there in the last part of the sixteenth century.

On 18 August John was taken with his father to be tried, in Westminster, on charges of high treason. The verdict was a foregone conclusion even though – as the elder John Dudley pointed out – half the peers trying them were as guilty as they. They were sentenced to be hung; cut down before they were dead; their entrails dragged out and their private parts cut off while they were living; and the four quarters of their bodies stuck up on posts. They might reasonably hope that the sentence would be commuted to a mere beheading, as was usual for the aristocracy – but the events of the next few days produced a different, a wholly unforeseen, horror for the Dudleys.

On the twenty-first, the brothers were taken out to watch their father's public recantation 'from the bottom of my heart' of the faith which he had propounded so vigorously. He has gone down in history as a turncoat; as one whose apparent Protestantism can only ever have masked ambition or, alternatively, one who turned coward in the end. Eve-of-execution confession and recantation was par for the course in Tudor history. But John Dudley's letters show a long history of self-doubt and sickness. The day before his public change of heart, right after the Lieutenant told him to prepare for his 'deadly stroke', he wrote a letter to the Earl of Arundel that seems to suggest that his tumble into panic was a genuine one, whether you care to call it cowardice (odd in a professional soldier), or frank humanity:

> An old proverb there is and that most true that a living dog is better than a dead lion. Oh that it would please her good Grace to give me life, yes the life of a dog that I might but live and kiss her feet . . . Oh that her mercy were such as she would consider how little profit my dead and dismembered body can bring her, but how great and glorious an honour it will be in all posterity when the report shall be that so gracious and mighty a Queen had granted life to so miserable and penitent an abject.

It is possible that, in his recantation, Dudley was gambling not only for his own life, but for the life of his sons. If so, he lost only half the throw. The day after his abject letter he was taken out to Tower Hill. Blindfolded, he knelt – but the blindfold slipped, and he had to struggle up from his knees and put it on again, which all too obviously strained his nerves unbearably. He was beheaded; but, for the moment at least, all his sons lived on, in physical safety but in mental agony. Did Robert blame his father for his recantation? Or was it the Catholic faith he blamed more bitterly?

In the Beauchamp Tower the brothers must have been cramped indeed, even by Tudor standards. But the most crippling effects of their confinement were the fear and the boredom; for, though a later Beauchamp resident, the Catholic Earl of Arundel, complained of the 'unwholesome air', the actual living conditions of life in the Tower were not always too difficult. Prisoners could bring with them their own servants, pay for their own furnishings and food (the Dudleys certainly had bedding, and books) – even have their pets brought in. The daily diet of Somerset's widow in the Tower the year before had included a supper (after an even more substantial dinner) of beer and wine, mutton and potage, coneys, sliced beef, a dozen larks and roast mutton with bread; plate, mustard and salads to be provided by the Lieutenant of the Tower.

While the Dudleys and Mary Tudor had contested for the country, Mary's sister, by contrast, had stayed completely silent. Enclosed at Hatfield, Elizabeth took no part in the fray. To have staked a claim of her own to the throne would have been neither a practical nor, for her, an ethical possibility. Too many of the Protestant party might have followed Jane (though many were in fact supporting Mary, out of civil rather than religious loyalty). More important, by the dynastic rules to which Elizabeth herself subscribed, the throne did for the moment belong to Mary – their father had willed it so – even though she must already have hoped that Mary would not hold it for too long. Now she wrote to Mary, offering her congratulations, and herself rode into London just ten days after her sister had been proclaimed in the city. Her huge escort – some said as many as two thousand horse – constituted, perhaps, a silent reminder of what she might have done had she too cast her hat into the ring; a convoluted demonstration of loyalty. On 3 August she rode directly behind Mary when the new Queen formally entered the city. Family pride and practicality, this time, had set Elizabeth in direct opposition to any Dudley. Elizabeth and Mary had both alike been publicly declared 'illegitimate and not lawfully begotten in the estate of true matrimony'. But it would be interesting to know what was in her heart as – smiling and dressed in white – she watched her sister ride ahead, triumphantly; an apparently smooth moment in Elizabeth's fortune, at a time of fear and distress for the Dudleys.

Elizabeth can have had at best mixed feelings about John Dudley's death. He had tried to deprive her of her place in the succession. But the moment when it seemed Dudley loss was the triumph of both Tudor sisters proved to be brief indeed. And if it had seemed that, of the Dudley family and Elizabeth, one was in and the other out, like figures on a weather vane, then very soon it became clear that they were more like companions in adversity.

Elizabeth would later describe the relationship between queen and country as a marriage. In Mary's case the honeymoon was over almost immediately – as, too, was the brief community of interest between the sisters. Religion was the sticking point, needless to say. As early as September, Elizabeth felt it necessary to make the first move, begging an interview with her sister in which she pleaded mere ignorance of, rather than hostility to, the Catholic faith, 'having been brought up in the [Protestant] creed which she professed', and requested instructors. A few days later she duly attended Mary's Chapel Royal, but with an ostentatiously 'suffering air' that gave a coded message to her supporters; a typically Elizabethan compromise. At the end of September she rode behind the new Queen on the way to her coronation – but very soon, the Venetian ambassador noted that Mary was treating her sister with fresh hostility. As Mary painfully, obstinately, rerouted the past – causing Parliament to declare valid the marriage of Henry VIII and Katherine of Aragon – so old bitterness revived. Mary even contemplated having her sister removed from the succession, but that was not so easy. And she, like her advisers, must have hoped it would soon be unnecessary. When Elizabeth asked permission to leave court in December, her absence must have been the more welcome – to both sisters – for the fact that Mary was about to marry.

In the event, the repercussions of Mary's marriage to Philip of Spain would give Elizabeth as good a reason as anything in her childhood to decide that queens regnant (they, at least!) should never marry: a political, rather than a personal, urge to chastity. Some of the dangers inherent in the match were already obvious now, at the end of 1553. The Holy Roman Emperor Charles V had proposed his son Philip as Mary's husband almost before the ink was dry on the letters that announced her accession. At the end of October, Mary had agreed. Only a fortnight later Parliament (more unanimous than her divided councillors) had presented a petition that she reconsider, and marry within the realm. Mary's reply was singular, based less on the protection of a powerful Spanish alliance than on her personal preference. 'Where private persons in such cases follow their own private tastes, sovereigns may reasonably challenge an equal liberty.' Mary's sister Elizabeth, when the time came, would order her priorities differently.

From the start, the Spanish marriage met with the deepest public hostility: when an Imperial embassy arrived in London in the first days of 1554, even the schoolboys in the streets threw snowballs at them. Within weeks came news of the so-called Wyatt rebellion, the aim of which was to depose Mary, replacing her on the throne with Elizabeth. Its underlying impetus was the fear that if nothing were done, England would become a mere adjunct to the vast Habsburg empire. The Wyatt rebellion was in theory an impressive plan – a series of co-ordinated risings (with possible backing from France) to take place across Kent, the south-west, the Midlands and the Welsh Marches. But the plots were leaked in early January, and it was only Wyatt himself who, at the end of that month, marched on London with a Kentish army.

Some of the government troops, even, went over to Wyatt, rather than be ruled by 'Spaniards or strangers'. But Mary herself showed to advantage in this crisis, riding to rally her troops in the City. She loved her subjects, she told them, 'as the mother doth the child'. She would never marry 'but [unless] all her true subjects shall be content'. The subtext would prove to be that if you weren't content, you weren't true, but at the time it went down nicely. London stood; Wyatt surrendered his arms and was taken to the Tower, already a dead man walking. Within a few days of the rebellion's end, a stream of fresh prisoners were headed for the crowded fortress, there to join the Dudleys.

Wyatt's revolt brought a new climate of toughness. It may be no coincidence that in January 1554 Robert too had to walk through the streets with a headsman before him, and to give the automatic plea of guilty; had to hear a court pronounce the verdict that he should be hung, drawn and quartered, knowing that the sentence would not necessarily be carried out – or not immediately – and not in its full enormity . . . but that anything was still a possibility. Almost half a century before, in the same Tower, his grandfather Edmund, in the weeks between his arrest and his trial, had described himself as 'a dead man by the king's laws', and was then kept waiting for almost another year before the time came for him to die. Robert was the last of his family to come to trial. Henry and Ambrose Dudley had been tried and sentenced back in November, along with Guildford Dudley and his wife Lady Jane Grey. It is possible that since most of Robert's activities had been in Norfolk (and in an area that owed him loyalty), evidence could not easily be gathered against him.

Mary's councillors – and the Spanish ambassador – urged that there should be an end to mercy. On 12 February 1554, the death sentence was carried out on Guildford Dudley. He was beheaded on Tower Hill: his wife (and presumably brothers) saw his body brought back, 'his carcass thrown in a cart and his head in a cloth'. More was to follow. From their room in the Beauchamp Tower, the remaining brothers could have heard the thunk of the axe as Jane Grey too was beheaded, but this time within the Tower precincts, privately. Unless access was barred to them, the window of the Beauchamp Tower, where Robert stood to carve, would have given them a close, an immediate, a balcony view. But in any case, tales must have gone round the Tower, with all the details of the scene. How she struggled to adjust her clothing for the axe; how the executioner offered to help her until, revolted, she shrank away. How – with the scarf tied round her eyes, and panicking for a moment – she groped for the block, blindly. How (dignified still, but fearful at last) the seventeen-year-old had asked the headsman: 'I pray you despatch me quickly.'

Elizabeth had been much more closely implicated in the Wyatt rebellion than Jane. Older, guiltier, more dangerous – if she escaped punishment, it could only be by a miracle. On 19 March the fallout from the revolt also brought Elizabeth to the Tower; and if the traditional arrival at Traitor's Gate has proved to be a myth, the real drama was just as deadly.

On 9 February, two days after Wyatt's rebellion folded, three privy councillors and a troop of soldiers had arrived at Elizabeth's house at Ashridge to bring her to court. Her pleas of ill-health were not accepted, though her face and body were swollen with what might have been nephritis, or might have been a psycho-somatic illness, and when she entered London on the twenty-third it was with the curtains of her litter thrown back, to defy rumours (the French ambassador said) that the swelling was a pregnancy from 'some vile intrigue' – the anonymous lover with whom gossip so regularly credited her. The sound of the axe might have beat the time to her journey: Jane Grey died on the day Elizabeth set out, and Jane's father on the day she arrived. The Spanish ambassador had long reported that Elizabeth too would die, surely.

In Whitehall Palace, while the Queen refused to see her sister, the process of collecting evidence went on. There was no diffi-culty in showing that the rebels had suggested to Elizabeth trouble might be brewing; that members of her household had been in touch with Wyatt; even that she had kept the French informed of her movements. But had she known, specifically, that rebellion was planned? Had she agreed to it, specifically? Wyatt himself, throughout his trial on 15 March, played down all contact with her. On 17 March, a Friday, the council none the less came to Elizabeth and charged her with conspiracy. She denied it, passionately – but her servants were taken away. The next day the councillors came to take her to the Tower; Elizabeth implored, first, to be allowed to make a written plea to her sister – a docu-ment with desperation breathing through every line. (She even scored across the blank space below where her writing ended to prevent anyone's adding in any other matter that could be interpreted treasonably.) That letter bought her the turn of the tide, and it was Palm Sunday before her boat set off downriver in the rain.

We do, now, have to add a pinch of salt to the old pretty stories that once painted such a romantic picture of the captive princess. Elizabeth arrived not by water through Traitor's Gate, but by land past the roaring lions of the menagerie. She was held not in the fairytale turret of the Bell Tower, but more prosaically in the old royal palace – since the Tower was a royal dwelling place as well as a prison; and a mint, and a zoo, and an armoury. Physically, the terms of her imprisonment were not harsh; though the Tower had dark dungeons, they were not for such as her. She had four rooms; permission to walk in the privy gardens (though other prisoners, so her chronicler John Speed reported, were not even to look in that direction while she was there); and a dozen servants in close attendance. But when the councillors left her there, they turned the keys in the door – albeit with a few doubts as to whether it were really appropriate to her royalty. And there was a mixed message to be read even in the rooms themselves: rebuilt for Anne Boleyn's coronation, they were also those in which she stayed before her execution, and the omen cannot but have struck Elizabeth unpleasantly.

Other romantic stories about her imprisonment were told by the chroniclers of her own day – for Protestants like Foxe and Speed made much of Elizabeth's near-martyrdom in the Tower. One told of gaolers' children who brought her flowers, and an old bunch of keys, in the infantine belief that the pretty lady captive could use them to get away. Another story – a whole long-lived legend! – told that the romance of Elizabeth and Robert began here, on the high walkway that connects the Beauchamp to the Bell Tower; began with snatched meetings as they were allowed each to take the warming spring air, promises of allegiance exchanged as they gazed westwards on the forbidden city . . . Sadly, there is no evidence for this at all; and indeed the scenario on the walkway loses some of its point now we know that Elizabeth was held not in the Bell Tower, but the whole width of the fortress away (and that Robert had permission to be visited by his wife, Amy).

But to prick the romantic bubble is not to deny that there could be a powerful and enduring emotional punch in this common experience of captivity. When Anne Boleyn heard that her brother George was also in the Tower, accused of incestuous adultery with her, she had said: 'I am very glad that we both be so nigh together.' Is there any kind of echo in these words for Elizabeth and Robert Dudley? Whether or not they actually met there, each would have known of the other's presence and, if they already shared some measure of friendship, they could not fail to have felt an increased bond of sympathy. Both had now lost a parent to the headsman; and, even in the Tudor century, there were not many in that fraternity. But in some ways their experience of the Tower highlights the differences, as well as the similarities, between them. Elizabeth's time there was more comfortable than Robert's, as well as briefer; and her situation no more menacing. But through all these years she was wheeling and dealing alone. 'Help me now, O God, for I have none other friend but Thee alone,' she prayed. Those closest to her (like Seymour; like those servants who had been forced to tell damaging tales) served only to endanger her.

Robert, too, is credited with putting his pen to a religious writing in the Tower. In a prayer based on the psalms, he wrote of a time

> Where, when the wicked ruled / And bore the sway by might
> No-one would [preace] to take my part / or once defend my right
> So that for want of help / I had been sore oppressed
> If that the Lord had not with speed / my woeful plight redressed.

But, bad though Robert's situation might be, at least he was, as he had always been, wrapped in family companionship and loyalty. In the years ahead, it would often seem as though, in his relationship with Elizabeth, Robert had the emotional stability though she had the worldly authority.

In the end, Elizabeth was in the Tower for only two of the eighteen months the Dudleys spent in captivity. Though her nerve may have quivered as she entered the place, it held fast as she was questioned. She admitted nothing. What written evidence there was proved nothing, really. And when Wyatt was executed on 11 April, his speech from the scaffold exonerated her completely. The terms of her imprisonment became lighter. When fresh guards appeared at the Tower early in May, she was still in a state to be terrified – asked whether Lady Jane's scaffold had been taken away. But in fact, the guards were there to escort her away from the Tower, to house arrest in Woodstock. She left on 19 May.

No-one bounces back from a shock like that; not immediately.

London legends have her leaving the Tower in a burst of bravado, and going straight to the London Tavern. But in fact, after leaving the Tower she slept at Richmond Palace, telling her servants, '[this night] I think to die'. Assassination might have been a possibility; her enemies at court had hoped to send her to Pontefract Castle, where Richard II had disappeared. But the slow journey to Woodstock showed how difficult such a procedure would be. The women of High Wycombe, the schoolboys of Eton and the villagers of Oxfordshire all turned out to greet her. When she reached the rusty and rambling old palace of Woodstock, outside Oxford (in what are today the grounds of Blenheim Palace), it was clear that she would have a fighting chance of controlling the terms of this comfortable captivity – of a tenancy that would last for a year. The council's instructions had been that Elizabeth should communicate with nobody. But that was hard to enforce, when her own servants might come and go, and the Bull Inn in Woodstock ('a marvellous colourable place to practice in', in the bitter words of her gaoler) had become the headquarters of her trusted Thomas Parry.

As 1554 wore on, with Elizabeth at Woodstock and the Dudley brothers in the Tower, at the end of July Mary married Philip of Spain; and if the old Catholic marriage service she used had seemed to promise unqueenly compliance on her part, it seemed, too, as if Philip and his Spanish entourage were determined to prove that the worst fears of the English would not be fulfilled and to use his position as queen's consort tactfully. Parliament would never grant Philip a matrimonial crown, nor any official authority. It would become a bone of dissent between Philip and Mary. But for the moment, everyone strove to do their duty smilingly. In Mary's case there was no pretence. She loved her unenthusiastic husband passionately. In the autumn Mary, ecstatic, was convinced she was pregnant – with a child who would consolidate her marriage, confirm her husband's status and ensure a Catholic future for the country.

The time was right for some improvement in the lives of the Dudley brothers. All the months of their imprisonment, their widowed mother had been working frantically for their freedom, attempting to bring all her old family contacts with Mary, and with Mary's Spanish kindred, into play. No English courtier would help Jane Dudley – but the Spaniards proved more receptive, spurred thereto by the efforts of her son-in-law Sir Henry Sidney (married to Robert's sister Mary), who was one of the diplomats sent to Spain on the marriage negotiations. Philip of Spain even stood godfather to Sir Henry's new son, the baby who became Sir Philip Sidney. He arrived in England anxious to prove himself a friend to all the English nobility. Jane Dudley was allowed back to court; found friends in the Duchess of Alva and Don Diego de Mendoza, and other of Philip's advisers, who were remembered in her will as those 'who did my sons good'. 'I give my lord Don Diego de Acevado the new bed of green velvet with all the furniture to it . . . to the duchess of Alba my green parrot, I have nothing worthy for her else.'

Still, her sons' release was not easily won. In October John, the eldest, was set free to go to Sir Henry Sidney's home of Penshurst – but only because he was sick of Tower fever. He died three days later: yet another loss in the terribly depleted family. Perhaps this last death took the heart from Jane Dudley. At the house in Chelsea which was all that remained to her, she too fell ill. She died on 22 January 1555 – and by now at last, on compassionate grounds, the three surviving brothers had been set free, to pay their mother's debts and arrange for her obsequies. For the next few months they (and their wives) would live a strange half-life. Still under attainder, they were not allowed to enjoy the fruits of their estates, yet they had few other sources of income and no real employment; though it seems they were allowed some vestige of court life, since they were recorded as taking part in an Anglo-Spanish tournament that winter. It would not be surprising if they fell in with disaffected sections of society, as is suggested by the Venetian envoy's report that they had been ordered back to the country.

These were grim times in the city. That year of 1555 saw the worst of the burning of heretics at Smithfield. The martyrologist John Foxe's description of the burning of John Rogers who, when the fire 'had taken hold upon both his legs and shoulders . . ., as one feeling no smart, washed his hands in the flame as though it had been in cold water,' masked a hideous reality. Perhaps the Dudley brothers, with their Protestant background, hung out with the malefactors and miscontents who clustered around St Paul's, where coney-catchers waited for their gulls, and gallants loitered before their dinner (perhaps as fashionably late as midday). 'What swearing is there,' Thomas Dekker later wrote, 'what facing and out-facing? What shuffling, what shouldering, what jostling, what jeering, what biting of thumbs to beget quarrels . . . what casting open of cloaks to publish new clothes, what muffling in cloaks to hide broken elbows . . . ?' They might dice or drink the afternoon away; go to a bull or a bear baiting. (London had as yet no theatres, and fishing or walking in the fields around the city's edge was probably unfashionably healthy.) It sounds an aimless sort of life – but it seems possible that his time in the Tower, with all that he had seen there, had changed Robert in some way. In the years immediately ahead it was Robert, though he was not the eldest brother, who seemed to be taking the lead in the family – trying to act politically; trying, like his father, to take the long view (if not actually to have always three or four purposes in his mind, as people had said of that same father, not altogether admiringly).

Just as there can be a survivor's guilt, so there can be a kind of zest in the survivor – a determination to make the most of the life that has been returned to you so unexpectedly. Robert Dudley's adolescence had seen his family riding very high. Now the red carpet had been pulled out from beneath his feet, and did he determine to climb back on it, in some way? He would live his life fully, greedily – but now, perhaps, he also became the person who could be useful (as well as merely attractive) to Elizabeth; the person whose experience of loss and danger following after indulgence matched her own; her spiritual 'brother', as she called him so frequently.

When, in the second half of April 1555, Elizabeth was summoned from Woodstock to Hampton Court, it was that she might be on hand to witness her sister's triumph: the birth of a child who would finally sweep her out of the succession. Instead, she would watch – in horror, surely, and perhaps also in pity – one of the age's more drawn-out tragedies. There were rumours, at the end of the month, that the Queen had been delivered of a son. The bells rang out joyfully. But it was a mistake – or perhaps, a miscarriage. Or perhaps, as the French ambassador heard early in May, the whole thing, swollen belly and all, had been the result of 'some woeful malady'.

Hunched, with her knees drawn up to her chin in pain, but still, appallingly, in hope, Mary waited in her birthing chamber through May – through June – through July. Elizabeth, still at court, had ample time to reflect yet again on female destiny. In August, Mary quietly left her chamber; only to hear that Philip – faced with a choice between barren marriage in England and his duties in the vast continental realm from which his father planned to abdicate – had unsurprisingly decided to go away. Elizabeth was there for the parting; there too when Mary prayed for her absent husband. She witnessed Mary's humiliation; the crumbling of the pretence that Philip had sought anything other than political advantage in this marriage, that he had any interest in Mary personally. In October, Elizabeth received permission to leave court, not for a return to Woodstock but for her own estate at Hatfield; there to begin what, for the next three years, would effectively be a waiting game.

But Philip had left behind him a legacy. There is a story, from those months at Hampton Court, of a famous meeting between the sisters. Elizabeth, summoned from her rooms at ten in the evening, was taken to the chamber where Mary awaited what she still thought would be a happy outcome to her pregnancy. As Mary again pressed her sister to admit her guilt in the Wyatt conspiracy, there was – as Foxe later claimed – a hidden witness to the meeting: Philip, who, from behind an arras, was listening secretly. Legend says that as he listened, he looked; and as he looked, he lusted . . . More certainly, Philip now saw Elizabeth as a valuable pawn in Habsburg policy.

The spectre of royal death was ever-present in the sixteenth century. That Mary should die childless – and early – was beginning to look likely. If so, Elizabeth (suspect heretic though she might be) was from Spain's viewpoint the best candidate to succeed to the throne. The alternative – the right heir by Catholic rules: Mary, Queen of Scots – was a wholly committed Francophile, raised in that country and married to the heir of the French king. With England under French control, the Channel passage would be barred between Spain and Spain's Netherlands territories. Better a heretic; especially one who could be safely married to a Catholic prince, and converted that way.

So, for the rest of Mary's reign, Elizabeth would be protected by Philip against Mary's suspicions; and behind this shield she was able to move with increasing freedom. In theory, she was living retired. In practice, she was building her political support as surely as she studied to increase her Greek vocabulary. Nothing illustrates the strength of this shield better than the events of the next winter, 1555–6, when another plot aimed to replace Mary with Elizabeth on the throne; a plot of which Elizabeth almost certainly knew, in which she was almost certainly guilty. Yet it is less well known than the Wyatt rebellion, in part because Elizabeth suffered none of the same dramatic penalties. Indeed, she suffered none at all – because Philip (policy outweighing any passion for justice he may have felt) decreed that she should not.

It is interesting, to say the least, that the name of the leader in that conspiracy should be Sir Henry Dudley. Though a distant cousin only, he had been employed by Robert's father. Still, there was no trace of the involvement of any of Robert's immediate family. It was only ten years later, with Elizabeth on the throne, that William Cecil would make a list of those he considered to be close to Robert and there, one on a list of many plotters against the Marian regime, was the name of Henry Dudley. Perhaps it was just as well for Robert that Jane Dudley had taken such care to make friends among the Spanish clan, and that Philip, for his part, had every motive to forge links with the disaffected English nobility. It seems ironic that both Elizabeth and Robert should owe their rehabilitation to Philip of Spain – later, so famously, the enemy of both.

But the worst threat to Elizabeth's position came also through Philip of Spain, and it came in the shape of a possible marriage.

In November 1556 Elizabeth (bored in her country exile) received a welcome invitation to come to court for Christmas, where she was received with unexpected warmth – received very, very briefly; for in the first week of December she was on her way back to Hatfield. She had, almost certainly, been instructed to marry a suitor of her sister's choosing. And she had, almost certainly, rejected the instruction, frantically.

The proposed husband was the titular Duke of Savoy, a cousin of Philip of Spain whose dukedom, however, had been seized by the French. If he married where Spain suggested, he would effectively get the hope of a kingdom in exchange, since he and Elizabeth would be named heirs after Mary. If Elizabeth did not agree, Mary threatened, she would be punished with an official declaration of bastardy and the loss of any place in the succession. In her misery (or so the French ambassador recalled years later), Elizabeth even contemplated flight across the Channel. But that would lose her any chance of inheriting and ruling her own country, just as surely as enforced marriage to a foreign prince and a future of Catholic domesticity.

In the spring of 1557 Philip returned to England. After a brief truce, France and Spain had resumed active hostilities; he needed to secure both England's involvement on Spain's side and a marriage that would keep the Duke of Savoy – Spain's general in the north – happy. There was (so the French ambassador warned her) even a plot to carry Elizabeth abroad by force. But one can easily imagine that this very atmosphere of coercion and urgency reinforced her determination to refuse. Clearly she already hoped to rule, and contemplated doing so alone. Maybe she saw spinsterhood as a price she was prepared to pay for power. But perhaps everything in her life – even this latest attack on her autonomy – conspired to lead her to a more radical conviction; to make her view marriage as a punishment, a sentence, a second best.

Though the most pressing, this was neither the first nor the last of the marriage proposals made for her in Mary's reign. Other candidates included Don Carlos, Philip's mad pre-teenage son by his first marriage, and, later, the crown prince (soon to be king) of Sweden. Once Elizabeth 'said plainly that she would not marry' – 'no, though I were offered the greatest prince in all Europe'. Then she said she liked her single status too well to change it. (That she liked it so well 'as I persuade myself' there was no other comparable . . . One wonders whether the very fact of having endlessly to repeat refusals were not driving her into an entrenched position; whether she did not wind up talking herself into conviction, to some degree.) So now Elizabeth continued to refuse, saying, so the Venetian ambassador reported, that 'the afflictions suffered by her were such that they had . . . ridded her of any wish for a husband'. And Mary refused further to coerce her – less out of affection, it would seem, than because she did not want Elizabeth (even an Elizabeth transformed into Catholic wife) ruling her, Mary's, country.

Also in the spring of 1557, the three surviving Dudley brothers – Ambrose, Robert and Henry – were allowed access to the revenues of which their father's attainder had deprived them (though they would not be 'restored in blood' for another year). Coincidentally or not, Robert was among the young Englishmen who volunteered to sell some of his lands and raise troops to swell Spain's army. Parliament and council long opposed Mary's desire to send troops and money to her husband's war, a war they felt was none of their own. The French ambassador commented that she was on the eve 'of bankrupting either her own mind or her kingdom'. But French support for yet another minor rebellion helped persuade the English government, and in June a herald was sent to the French court, literally to throw down the gauntlet. All three Dudley brothers sailed to France the next month, with Philip's six-thousand-strong English army.

They sailed into battle, and into the horrors of the siege of St Quintin. It was considered a notable Anglo-Spanish victory. Robert in particular was judged to have done well, in charge of the artillery. But the game was hardly worth the candle; whatever praise it brought Robert in Spanish circles, the fighting at St Quintin also saw the death of the youngest Dudley brother, Henry, struck by a cannonball before Robert's eyes. Of the thirteen children Jane Dudley had borne, only four were now left alive: two sisters (Katherine, married to the Earl of Huntingdon, and Mary, married to Henry Sidney), and two brothers, Ambrose and Robert.

Even the campaign itself went sour when the French took Calais in January 1558. England's last remaining continental outpost, it had been in the country's possession for two centuries. Its loss was a humiliation for England abroad and a personal failure for Mary, widely blamed for taking the country into Spain's war. A few years later Sir Thomas Smith would recall: 'I never saw England weaker in strength, money, men and riches . . . Here was nothing but fining, headinging [sic], hanging, quartering and burning, taxing, levying and beggaring, and losing our strongholds abroad.' If Robert on the continent had at least had his first taste of personal military success – his first hint he might emulate his father on the real field of battle, as well as in the tilt yard – Elizabeth was learning that war was an evil to be avoided at all costs; a reason to be wary of foreign alliances, and foreign allies.

Philip had left England again in July 1557.* In the spring of 1558 Mary once again hoped to be delivered of a baby. But few this time thought the pregnancy anything other than an illusion. Elizabeth was in London briefly, at the end of February, bringing (so legend said) a layette long thought to be of her own making that is in Hever Castle today. But she did not stay around for an event everyone really knew to be unlikely. Possibly she had other concerns. For Elizabeth was not passive in these years (a point raised by the interesting question of what – since she was richly endowed, and prudent, and yet constantly in debt at this time – she was doing with her money). She was scheming, preparing, setting up a virtual shadow government. The Venetian ambassador had written the year before that 'all eyes and hearts' were turned towards her as Mary's successor; that she or her people were found behind every plot; and, most tellingly, that 'there is not a lord or gentleman in the kingdom' who did not seek

---

* Charles V had now retired to a monastery. He would die in 1558, leaving the Austrian empire to his brother; from now on the Spanish and the Imperial ambassadors need to be distinguished.

a place in her service for himself or his relations. The picture of a powerful and professional opposition politician is at odds with the more romantic vision of a red-headed, white-faced girl transported in an instant from poverty to power. But it explains how, when she did come to the throne, she was already politically involved with Robert Dudley.

When Robert came back from the continent, he probably spent a good deal of his time at the London houses of various family connections, having always an eye to the various Norfolk properties inherited by himself and Amy. Apparently, he was lying dormant; but a few years later Elizabeth would say – to the Duke of Saxony's envoy – that, personal liking apart, she would always be grateful to Robert because, in her time of need, he sold lands to raise funds for her. (Schemes and shadow governments cost money.) There is no other hard evidence – no evidence that he mortgaged lands, no evidence as to what he did with the proceeds; what went to Elizabeth, and what to buying the Dudleys' way into the Spanish army. But the Protestant circles with which she was in touch were the circles in which he moved; indeed, he was at the centre of a useful network to a striking degree. He had connections to William Cecil (who was in regular touch with the princess) and to the other Cambridge scholars; to the disaffected plotters who had followed Sir Henry Dudley; and, simultaneously, to the Spanish courtiers.

If we doubt that there were dealings done, in these days of waiting and watching – dealings too secret to leave a paper trail – we have only to consider the story of John Dee. The one-time tutor in the Dudley household, who had secretly cast Elizabeth's horoscope for her, was himself close to Cecil as well as to the old royal tutor Cheke. Dee's name crops up repeatedly in the chronicles of Mary's reign, appearing first as a suspected heretic – and then as a Catholic inquiry agent in the service of the regime! One might assume that he had simply turned traitor to his beliefs . . . but in that case why would Robert Dudley approach him, of all available astrologers, to select a propitious day for Elizabeth's coronation, when the time came? It seems more likely that Dee was playing an underhand role not towards his Protestant friends, but to the Catholic authorities, and that these covert dealings would be known to such an ambitious insider as Robert Dudley.

We have no surviving records to show exactly where Robert Dudley was in these months. There is nothing to place him at Hatfield itself – but what information there is suggests he may have been living in a family house not too far away. Near or far, he was clearly in close enough communication that when, in the late summer of 1558, it became clear that Mary was very ill, he was one of the network waiting, ready. In early October the Queen's condition worsened; and Elizabeth's ever-loyal Parry began contacting supporters, ever more openly.

On 28 October Mary added a codicil to her will. Acknowledging that she had as yet no 'fruit nor heir of my body', she conceded that in the absence of such she would be followed by 'my next heir and successor by the laws of this realm'. Ten days later, she was brought to acknowledge Elizabeth more specifically.

Philip's special ambassador Feria, travelling rapidly towards Hatfield, wanted Elizabeth to acknowledge that her throne would come to her through Spain's favour. Instead, he found an Elizabeth well mounted on her high horse; an Elizabeth who claimed that the throne would come to her through the affection of the people, who told him, moreover, that Mary had lost that affection 'because she had married a foreigner'.

Feria thought that he knew the men she would favour: William Cecil for secretary of state; the faithful Parry, Sir Nicholas Throckmorton, the Earl of Bedford, Lord Robert Dudley . . . But he added that 'she is determined to be governed by no-one'. It was not a bad prophecy. When, in the early morning of 17 November, Mary slipped quietly away, Elizabeth's inner cabinet were ready. In the first hours of the new reign, her new secretary William Cecil recorded in a memo that messengers should be sent to various ambassadors, to the kings of Spain and Denmark – and, again, to Lord Robert Dudley.

5

'The King that is to be'
Spring 1559–summer 1560

IN THE AFTERNOON OF THE DAY MARY DIED, ELIZABETH WAS ALREADY holding her first meeting with many of the men who would become her close advisers. There were changes to be made to the composition of the privy council: no surprises there, surely. The most aggressively Catholic of the Marian councillors were out, with the exception of a few whose rank gave them automatic passage into power. What made their dismissal less personal is that Elizabeth was reducing the number considerably. William Cecil was already beside her when she held that first meeting in Hatfield's Great Hall – the one that is rented out as a banqueting hall today. Now, it looks archaic: a vault of warm red brick, with carved heads on the corbels, and pigeons flying in; oddly domestic, too, as the setting for a piece of political history. But then – though the Great Hall as a centre for communal life was already fading into the medieval past – it would have seemed modern enough, and suitable for a regime that planned to ground its reforms on ancient authority.

There at Hatfield, with the new Queen's future councillors clustered about her, the big questions that would haunt the reign already loomed: questions about the Queen's marriage, and the succession; questions about the extent and the limitations of her (female) monarchy. In another one of those revealing early prayers, Elizabeth acknowledged that 'I Thy handmaiden am slight of age, and inferior in understanding of Thy law . . . Grant me faithful councillors, who by Thy counsel will advise me.'

The days when Robert would take official place among those councillors still lay some way ahead. But in the 38-year-old William Cecil – able administrator, bureaucrat of genius – there could already be plainly seen the germ of the venerably bearded Lord Burghley, Elizabeth's famous elder statesman and *éminence grise* of later days. His three strongest characteristics were his pragmatism, his Protestantism, and his patriotism. He had a long association with the Tudors, since his grandfather had fought for Henry VII at Bosworth, but his own background had lain among the Cambridge humanists (his first wife was a sister of John Cheke) and the lawyers of Gray's Inn, and he had been secretary to John Dudley before falling out with Robert's father over the plan to proclaim Jane Grey queen.

Throughout Mary's reign Cecil had veiled his Protestant beliefs, but had kept in touch with Elizabeth herself, officially in his capacity as surveyor of her lands. (He was a distant kinsman of Thomas Parry.) She appreciated his discretion as well as his rectitude. 'This judgement I have of you,' she told him now, ' that you will not be corrupted by any manner of gift and that you will be faithful to the State and that, without respect of my private will, you will give me that counsel which you think best.' But in moments of temper, inevitably, she would turn from him to those who took her 'private will' more seriously; above all, to the man who might have been cast as Cecil's temperamental opposite – Robert Dudley.

So mild-mannered that his potential for ruthlessness was hardly apparent, studious but shrewd, too secretive ever to have any 'inward companion', the commoner Cecil at first sang pianissimo around the more glamorous nobles of the royal court. But behind the scenes he would come to wield a formidable power in the role Elizabeth now bestowed on him – that of state secretary. He and Robert would be locked in a relationship as long as that of the favourite and the Queen herself: often, at first, in opposition, but finally in a kind of reluctant amity.

Others of those first appointments did credit to Elizabeth's heart as well as her head. Wherever sense permitted, she not only acknowledged the claims of her mother's family, but gave reward for loyalty. The appointment of Robert Dudley as Master of Horse was in no way surprising; his elder brother had held the post before him, under Edward VI. But when she came to give Robert political influence in the time ahead, Elizabeth could again feel she was following her father's tradition: had not Henry trusted John Dudley? In the policies he would promote, Robert, too, could feel he was living out his father's legacy. Robert's brother Ambrose Dudley was appointed Master of the Ordnance (doing the same job his father had, early in his career) and their sister Mary Sidney became lady of the bedchamber, and one of the closest of that select band.*

On 23 November Elizabeth, with a thousand people in her train, left Hatfield for her official entry into London, and all the stages of her ceremonial acceptance into monarchy. For five days she stayed at Charterhouse, hard by Smithfield. (The palace at St James was still occupied by her sister's body.) On 28 November she formally entered into the City, and passed through to the Tower. She wore 'purple velvet, with a scarf around her neck', and the trumpets blared a fanfare as she passed; but she cut the image of majesty with her famous common touch, stopping to speak, so it seemed, to everybody.

Prominent among the retinue, leading her caparisoned palfrey behind the horse litter in which she rode, came Lord Robert Dudley. As Master of Horse, he was responsible for many of the arrangements when the Queen made formal appearances. But often, with his pronounced flair for showmanship, he also took a hand in even the indoor pageantry. On 5 December Elizabeth moved by water from the Tower to her old home of Somerset House, where she stayed until after Mary's funeral on 13 December formally ended the late Queen's authority. It was two

---

* Much later, towards the end of Elizabeth's life, an observer would write that the Queen was 'governed' by Robert's other sister Katherine, the Countess of Huntingdon.

days before Christmas when she finally moved into Whitehall for the seasonal festivities, and more than merely seasonal revelry. Here at last – after the hard work at Hatfield; after the formal speeches in the streets – came the real, intimate celebrations. Here was the time to party.

Pleasure was important to the Elizabethan aristocracy – all the more so, perhaps, since so many of the country's traditional festivities had been swept away with the old religion. A tournament displayed chivalry, as well as martial ability, for an audience of London notables and foreign dignitaries; a pageant spelt out a message carefully. (Even a dance showed off the participants' fitness as well as their cultivation, not to mention opening up a worrying – to the killjoys – suggestion of sexual desirability.) Maybe the court festivities had not yet achieved the peak of hedonism they would reach later in Elizabeth's reign, when those present at one January masque in the 1570s saw tiny comfits representing hailstones – flavoured with cloves, with musk, with ginger – and snowballs scented with rosewater. But the dancing went on till after midnight; and the court entertainments were organized by Robert Dudley. Amid the more conventional balls and masques was one farce that horrified an Italian observer, already shocked at the general 'licentiousness' and levity, with crows dressed up as cardinals, wolves to represent abbots.

The coronation was to take place on 15 January, and by Christmas frantic work was well under way to alter Mary's coronation robes and produce new finery from the bolts of rare fabric imported from the continent. (Customs officials blocked delivery to any other client, until the Queen and her household had taken what they needed.) On the day before her coronation – the day she was to process through the city – Elizabeth stood up in twenty-three yards of cloth of gold and silver, trimmed with ermine and gold lace. Tradition decreed that she spend the previous night at the Tower, and as she left the place on the fourteenth she paused, so Sir John Hayward later said, and reflected that 'Some have fallen from being princes in this land to be prisoners in this place. I am raised from being a prisoner in this place to be a prince in this land.' Others remembered a different wording, but she must have thought something very like it. So – as they passed the chapel where her mother and his father lay buried with scant ceremony – must Robert Dudley.*

As Elizabeth rode through London, propped up by eight satin cushions in a litter drawn by two 'very handsome' mules, again came the pageants, the crowds, the singing. As Hayward says: 'It is incredible how often she caused her coach to stay, when any made offer to approach her.' All the way from Fleet Street to Westminster she kept in her hand the gift of one old woman – a sprig of rosemary, the nearest any Londoner could get to flowers in a sixteenth-century January. Richard Mulcaster, who wrote up the official description, quickly published for the benefit of those who could not be there, called the City that day 'a stage wherein was showed the wonderful spectacle of a noble-hearted princess toward her most loving people and the people's exceeding comfort in beholding so worthy a sovereign ... Out at the windows and penthouses of every house did hang a number of rich and costly banners and streamers' – that Tudor love of fabric, as ostentatious and elaborate as may be, that set silken colours rippling through the air on every royal festivity. At the upper end of Cheapside, they gave her a crimson satin purse containing a thousand marks in gold, and she took it in both hands; as she neared Paul's Gate they gave her an English Bible, and she pressed it to her breast, promising to read it diligently.

Again Robert Dudley rode right behind her; ahead of the thirty-nine ladies in crimson velvet with cloth-of-gold sleeves, ahead of the guards marching three by three. There can be no doubt that he – and Ambrose, leading one of the mules at the litter's head – watched with approval the Protestant message the worthies of the City had thus enshrined in their ceremony. (Dudley connections were all over this coronation ceremony: Katherine's father-in-law bore the Queen's spurs, and Ambrose's future father-in-law bore St Edward's staff.) Perhaps Robert read another message: for the

---

* St Peter ad Vincula holds also the headless bodies of Elizabeth's uncle George Boleyn, her kinswoman Katherine Howard and her first love Thomas Seymour, besides Guildford Dudley, Jane Grey and Robert's stepson the Earl of Essex.

great biblical queens to whom Elizabeth was being compared at this stage of her life – Deborah, Judith, Esther – may have been strong women in their own right, but they were known for their married status, rather than their virginity.

Elizabeth lay at the Palace of Westminster that night and the next day, over a light carpeting of snow, walked the small distance to the abbey. As she left again – after the vows, and the anointing with holy grease that transmuted a mortal woman into the epitome of enduring monarchy – she made no attempt to hide her joy, accepting the acclaim of the people, relishing every evidence of her popularity. 'In my opinion she exceeded the bounds of gravity and decorum,' wrote an Italian envoy sniffily. But even he could not fail to be impressed by the cumulative ceremonies of the past few days and a court so sparkling with jewels and gold collars that, he wrote, 'they cleared the air'. Behind the scenes, it is true, they had had trouble finding a bishop willing to crown Elizabeth; too many of those recently in office, of course, had been appointed under Mary. But there was no sign of that dissent in the massed ranks of the nobility, nor through the proclamations and the anointings, the banquet, the festivities and the jousts that filled the next days.

For all the rejoicing and merrymaking, though, there were more serious questions on everyone's mind. The business of having got Elizabeth into power once concluded, thoughts turned immediately to what would happen once she was out of it by process of mortality. After the past decade (and the wars of the previous century) everyone had had enough of uncertainty. They wanted that thing the Tudors had seemed to promise and then at last failed to deliver: a clear linear path of monarchy. Within four days of the old queen's death, on 21 November, the Spanish ambassador Feria had been writing to Philip that 'everything depends upon the husband this woman may take'. (Just so had the Emperor Charles V, Philip's father, written to the newly proclaimed Mary that she needed a husband 'in order to be supported in the labour of governing and assisted in matters that are not of ladies' capacity'.) Feria had no doubt who the new queen's husband should be: Philip himself. But the Spanish would have to move quickly. Both Elizabeth and 'her people', Feria warned, 'will listen to any ambassadors who may come to treat of marriage'; and he pressed the point three weeks later, on 14 December: 'Everybody thinks that she will not marry a foreigner, and they cannot make out whom she favours, so that every day some new cry is raised about a husband.'

Whosoever it might be, it was assumed she must and would marry someone. There was, Elizabeth herself would observe wryly, 'a strong idea in the world that a woman cannot live unless she is married'. Cecil would be one influential voice urging now and later that a husband was her and the realm's 'only known and likely surety'. The Holy Roman Emperor's envoy agreed that she should ('as is woman's way') be eager 'to marry and be provided for. For that she should wish to remain a maid and never marry is inconceivable.' But no-one, at this stage, was yet mentioning the name of Robert Dudley – who, apart from anything else, was of course a married man already.

On 4 February the Commons drafted a petition urging Elizabeth to marry quickly, in order to ensure the succession. Her instinct was not to take it kindly – and she might have taken it even less so, had she known that they had contemplated the impertinence of restricting the choice of whom she should marry, hoping that it would be an Englishman and not foreign royalty. If she should remain 'unmarried and, as it were, a vestal virgin', it would be 'contrary to public respects'. It is odd that her parliamentarians should, so very early in the reign, have figured, in repudiating it, exactly the course and image she would choose: as if her views, incredible though they must have seemed, were already clear to this presumably not over-imaginative body of men.

She answered them that 'from my years of understanding' – since she first was old enough to understand herself a servant of God – 'I haply chose this kind of life in which I yet live, which I assure you for mine own part hath hitherto best contented myself and I trust hath been most acceptable to God.' If ambition for a grand alliance, obedience to the ruler's will, or the fear of danger 'could have drawn or dissuaded me from this kind of life, I had not now remained in this estate wherein you see me; but constant have always continued in this determination'.

Over the next decade she would when necessary vary, even directly contradict, these protestations of determined virginity (albeit equally rapidly to reiterate her devotion to the single life). It would be almost twenty years before England would see the full flowering of the cult of the Queen's virginity; as if only then, when she was after all passing out of the reproductive years, could her advisers bring themselves to make the best of her decision. But none of her later statements is stronger than this first answer to Parliament's petition. In the end, she said, 'this shall be for me sufficient: that a marble stone shall declare that a queen, having reigned such a time, lived and died a virgin'. It looks as though any sort of romantic emotional satisfaction she would allow herself to take would be one that yet allowed her to maintain this publicly professed virginity.

True, it was at this vulnerable early moment in her reign that she most needed something to set her apart from other women – from those fallible female creatures who, it was assumed, were quite incapable of rule. Rather than accept her coding as the weak daughter of sinful Eve, she would do better to borrow from the banned Catholicism, and evoke the heavenly virtue of the Virgin Mary. But it is none the less extraordinarily interesting that she should be defending her virginity in such terms now, well before she was even thirty. It is all the more interesting if these first public professions of Elizabeth's virginity occurred at very much the time when she was falling in love with Robert Dudley.

These were the months when Elizabeth was most open, most edgy. In these months – when she and Robert were both high on the buzz of power and victory – the personal side of their relationship flowered. On the one hand, Elizabeth had inherited an uncertain throne (in France, Henri II was already proclaiming the rival Catholic claim of his daughter-in-law Mary, Queen of Scots) and an impoverished and vulnerable country. On the other, she had won. She had managed what had so often looked like an impossibility. And as a corollary, a perk, a minor pay-off, after all those years of closely watched constraint, she was free to speak and flirt with whom she pleased – all the freer, no doubt, for the fact that Robert was safely married already.

She was twenty-five years old, vibrant and lively, with an ability to spin from imperiousness to intimacy that would keep a man guessing, pleasurably. If she was not beautiful then she had, like her mother, the ability to project the idea of it. Later in life, she told an ambassador that she had never in fact been a beauty, but had had the reputation of it in her day. 'Comely rather than handsome,' the Venetian envoy had reported her a year or two before; 'tall and well-formed, with a good skin, although swarthy, she has fine eyes.' Robert too was 'of a tall personage', said the Venetian, who praised his 'manly countenance' though regretting his 'somewhat brown' complexion. He had hair and beard shading dark to auburn; the legs to stand up to the trying fashion for short breeches, with their padding and pinking, and their prominent codpieces; and the physique, when they danced together the daring Volta, to twirl Elizabeth high. Philip of Spain had made sombre colours fashionable for men's clothing, instead of the bright colours the English usually preferred. But Robert (who spent more than £800 on 'apparel and goldsmith's work' this first year; whose accounts show repeated purchases of rosewater and ribbon points, and black silk netherstockings) was always resplendent by the standards of the day. Most striking of all Robert's physical features were his dark, haughty eyes. Elizabeth would play upon them: called him her eyes, so that he signed himself with the symbol of eyes, a pair of circles with lines for eyebrows over them. It may have been a pun, too, on what he could do for her – look out for her interest, watchfully.

When exactly did their personal relationship begin to develop? Probably in the spring of 1559; during the first six months of the reign. On 18 April 1559, Feria was writing that in the last few days 'Lord Robert has come so much into favour that he does whatever he likes with affairs. It is even said that Her Majesty visits him in his chamber day and night.' It might, he said, be worth 'coming to terms' with Robert immediately; exchanging a reciprocal promise of favour.

Despite Elizabeth's nerve storms, her bouts of ill-health, she and Robert shared a relish for activity, the kind of eager physicality that made Elizabeth outride half her courtiers and use a bout of intensive dancing exercise to start each day. The whole outdoor world of horse, hunt and hawk represented a huge bond between them, and Robert's job as Master of Horse had an importance it is hard to grasp today. He was responsible for the breeding, purchase, training and provision of what was not only the chief tool of transport and communication, but in war still a vital piece of armoury; a crucial task for which he was paid a thousand marks a year, with perhaps half as much again in perquisites and his own table at court served with the food considered 'fit for lords'. It was a job he would keep most of his life, long after other duties might have tempted him away, and one he took very seriously. One of his pet projects would be the improvement of English bloodlines with the Barbary strain; and the recruitment of continental horsemasters, who had at their reins' end the latest continental tips on *manège* and cavalry training. On a day-to-day basis, Robert had to provide the kind of mounts suitable for ceremonial occasions – and for the times royal messengers needed to ride swiftly – as well as horses for the Queen's own personal pleasure and for the haulage of baggage necessary when the court went on its annual progress (in which the schedule records the ominous words 'from thence to . . .' almost every day).

But more telling than all that, at this particular moment, was that, as Master of Horse, Robert's trump card was physical proximity to the Queen. Having provided the horses, he would then ride with her, close as a royal bodyguard today. Even before they left Hatfield, Elizabeth, between the first meetings of state, was out riding with him every day. This privileged aspect of his position was the more valuable since the fact of a female sovereign upset all the usual paths to power. With a king on the throne, ambitious men would normally clamour for positions, like gentleman of the bedchamber, that allowed them to spend off-duty moments with the monarch, and have their voice in his ear that way. With a queen on the throne, of course, most of those other immediate attendants had to be women – except Robert

Dudley. As would become ever more apparent in the years ahead, the other men in her administration came before her with problems on their tongue and paperwork in their hands. Small wonder if the urge to shoot the messenger overcame her all too frequently. Robert alone (especially in these early days, before he had political office) appeared to her in the guise of an invitation to play.

They were always riding in these early years, and Elizabeth's intrepidity could frighten even Robert. Ordering some 'good gallopers' from Ireland, he added nervously that 'she spareth not to try as fast as they can go. And I fear them much but she will prove them.' Surviving accounts for Robert's early years as Master of Horse bring the animals themselves back to life (though sadly, only those who incurred some veterinary expenditure!) – Bay Gentle, with the dressing for his forefeet, Bellaface, Delicate, and Great Savoy, who had to be bathed when he came from the mares. But it is still hard to recapture the galloping magic of these springtime days; hard, too, to understand how much greater importance springtime – the return of light and warmth to the world – must have had in an age before electricity.* Small wonder that Robert adopted the cinquefoil, the five-petalled form of the green-white, soapy-scented hawthorn blossom, as yet another symbol.

> In the spring time, the only pretty ring time,
> When birds do sing, hey ding a ding, ding
> Sweet lovers love the spring,

wrote Shakespeare in *As You Like It*, and Robert's relationship with Elizabeth flowered now against the backdrop of an eternal May.

---

* Even the putative Hatfield oak is usually pictured in full bud-burst glory. Both *Elizabeth R* and the BBC's recent reprise, *The Virgin Queen*, reinforced the iconography, the latter showing a brand-new Queen Elizabeth – though the accession was in November – under another oak tree in full leaf as she waited for Robert Dudley.

In this early part of the reign – before it became apparent that Elizabeth's love of peace would be England's path to prosperity – there loomed slightly larger the militaristic aspects of her monarchy, and the question of which men would represent her in an arena where she, as a woman, could not compete. The chronicles of Elizabeth's early court are full of tournaments like the one that marked her accession, Robert prominent among the jousters. Though actual warfare was moving into a new age, the traditional armed clash of knight against knight had still a significance that went far beyond the courtly trappings, the role-playing and the pageantry. This was a world where Robert excelled. But he and Elizabeth also shared intellectual interests, to a certain degree.

His mind was not as nimble as hers. Few could be. But he had a wit 'capable at once of entertaining agreeably and of designing deeply', besides a 'Delivery and a Presence' that commanded respect. He was well grounded (acknowledged one of his future colleagues) in all the writings 'on the best used governments and chief laws that have been made in all ages'. It sounds almost like the specific training in statecraft that Elizabeth felt herself to lack. His scientific interests (as witness the men who enjoyed his patronage) ranged from mining to medicine, from exploration to alchemy; and as early as 1559 he patronized the troupe of actors who later became known as the Earl of Leicester's Men. Elizabeth was fond of late-night conferences with all her advisers, calling them in one after the other. Her sessions with Robert Dudley were not all dalliance, necessarily.

For Robert Dudley (who early resumed his seat in Parliament) was not just a pretty plaything. That's what has tended to be obscured, not only in the romantic, but in the traditional, the censoriously Victorian, version of this story. Born and bred into the world of politics, bound by ties of faith or family to many of the other nobles at the court, he had – even at this early stage – his own clear policies. In the end, they would not always be hers; but if he was able to influence her, it is probably because their underlying attitudes were so similar in many ways.

They shared a measure of hard-headed practicality; Elizabeth was probably grateful rather than otherwise that Robert had not taken active part in any of the abortive rebellions in the days of Mary. They shared a reverence for tradition, for established order, for England's history. While genealogists traced Elizabeth's supposed descent from King Arthur, Robert's pet poet Spenser would be only one of those to figure Arthur himself as Robert Dudley. Indeed, though his family profited from every swing to the new (like the Reformation, and the alienation of lands from the great northern Catholic families), his attitude was possibly more traditional than that of Elizabeth, whose natural conservatism warred with a desire to exalt the monarchy at the expense of that same aristocracy.

In April 1559 Elizabeth named Robert a Knight of the Garter: a remarkable elevation, since the other three men so honoured – the Marquess of Northampton, the Earl of Rutland and the Duke of Norfolk (who would emerge as Dudley's great enemy) – were all men of rank or seniority. The Garter knights, moreover, were supposed to be men of irreproachable fame and family; their motto, *Honi soit qui mal y pense* – shame on him who thinks evil – must have seemed all too apt when thinking of Robert's relationship to the queen. She made several grants to him of land and money, including Knole Park in Kent: a significant gift, this (though he did not long keep it); not only for the spacious sprawl of house and garden, but because the property had once been in the hands of Robert's father, before his disgrace. It was as if Elizabeth were trying to wipe out all that had happened under Mary.

If so, she had Robert's enthusiastic co-operation. But to contemporaries, for whom all his long years of service still lay invisible ahead, it must have seemed more as if he were working for his own and his family's interests than those of his queen. Indeed, those who remembered Edward's reign, not a decade before, must have been aghast at how much power clustered once again around Dudleys and those associated with Dudleys. It is true the Queen did not immediately move to place either of the Dudley brothers on the privy council, perhaps well aware that members of this family entered the new reign with ready-made enemies. But now, already, those enemies grumbled, the privy chamber was staffed mostly by Robert's 'creatures'. (Besides his sisters Mary and Katherine, Robert would later be extremely busy in placing Ambrose's wife at Elizabeth's hand.) In this same year of 1559, Mary's husband Henry Sidney was given the presidency of the council in the Welsh Marches and would go on to become Elizabeth's viceroy in Ireland; while Robert's other brother-in-law, soon to inherit his father's title of Earl of Huntingdon, besides being a possible heir to the throne would later become Lord President of the Council in the north. Within a very few years events would place Ambrose Dudley in charge of an English army; within months, the Spanish ambassador would be reporting that Robert himself was laying in 'a good stock of arms' for an unspecified purpose. (Such rumours of suspect private military might would continue throughout his career.)

There is a risk, in picturing Robert as a patriot and a loyal promoter of Elizabeth, of glossing over the huge personal ambition that ran hand in hand with his loyalty, and the lust for control that would be seen in contexts as diverse as his chancellorship of Oxford University (where he stripped power from the main body of teachers to concentrate it into the hands of his own appointees) and the Welsh town where he never forgave the burgesses who dared pass over his own candidate for their parliamentary representation. It is unlikely Elizabeth ever forgot his ambition and the breadth of the power base he would build up. (More than two decades later, in 1581, she told a Spanish ambassador, perhaps somewhat mendaciously, that she could not dismiss Robert Dudley even if she wanted to, since he had placed his friends and kinsmen in every port and stronghold in the country.) But it is also unlikely that she feared it – or that it diminished his attraction in her eyes. On the one hand, a good measure of his ambition was in a sense for her, or at least for her kingdom – for an 'incomparable British Empire', in the words of his protégé Dr Dee. On the other, perhaps the harsh politics of the Tudor court had taught her to despise those she could control too easily. Robert's heraldic symbol would be the bear; among the many significant jewels he would give her was a fan from which dangled 'a lion ramping, with a white muzzled bear at the foot'.

The years would prove that she was right not to fear; that Robert was her liege man, at the end of the day. Indeed, among this first generation of Elizabeth's councillors, it would not precisely be true to say that he was the only one devoted absolutely to her interest; but Cecil (to whom that accolade is more often given) arguably gave his loyal and surpassing service less to Elizabeth personally than to the Elizabeth who currently embodied a moderate and successful monarchy. Cecil wrote that he was 'sworn first' to God, but that because the Queen was 'God's chief minister here, it shall be God's will to have her commandment obeyed'. There is a suggestion here of 'first among equals' with which Elizabeth would hardly have agreed.

The broadly accepted ideal of government was 'the king counselled': the king (or queen) guided by the advice of a band of councillors, the majority of them still drawn from the ranks of the nobility; and sanctioned, ultimately, by the voice of the people as represented in Parliament (though Parliament still did not have the voice that it would do in later centuries – still did not meet as often, even). Contemporary belief that the ruler must be swayed by such counsel gained added impetus from that ruler's being a woman.* To some, indeed, the rule of the female Elizabeth seemed to present a problem almost comparable to that of the adolescent Edward. Even Cecil, in these early days at least, could be found reproaching a messenger with having taken papers directly to the Queen, 'a matter of such weight being too much for a woman's knowledge'. There is no record of any such sentiment from Robert Dudley. As a friend, as a sympathizer, and as what has been called the impresario of her public galas, his enduring efforts aimed to elevate Elizabeth, personally.

---

* Even Ascham's friend (and Jane Grey's tutor) John Aylmer, writing a refutation of John Knox's *First Blast of the Trumpet Against the Monstrous Regiment of Women*, had written that Elizabeth's sex mattered the less because England was not 'a mere monarchy', nor yet a mere oligarchy or democracy, but 'a rule mixt of all three' – in other words, that Elizabeth's gender did not matter, because she was not that powerful anyway.

Later in their long relationship, his ideas would come to diverge from hers. His religious beliefs, in particular, would set him on a different path – but his grumbles against her, when they came, would always be couched in practical and personal, rather than theoretical, terms; and in the end he would always do things her way. And the second important point here is this: there is no evidence that Robert thought theoretically (unlike Cecil, with his background among the Cambridge humanists). That very absence of formulated belief in Robert, while it has helped posterity to put him down as a mere masculine dummy, must have appealed to Elizabeth, herself no lover of unnecessary theory. On the one hand, promoting Robert Dudley must have felt like keeping an attractive man close, rewarding a proven friend, and ensuring the continued loyalty of a major service family, rather than buying into a system of political belief. On the other, it must at least have been possible for her to believe that he came closest of all her immediate advisers to sharing her own conception of her monarchy.

The question was, might he actually share that throne, that monarchy? Ambition as well as attraction must have led him to dream of marriage, when first the Queen began to display such extraordinary familiarity. His family had several times brushed with royalty – his widowed Dudley grandmother marrying 'My Lord the Bastard', Henry VIII's illegitimate uncle; his brother marrying Lady Jane Grey; perhaps he might fulfil the family's destiny, if only . . .

But it is hard to know quite what he was thinking – he, still a married man. For Robert, Amy Dudley was a known and once beloved quantity; not just an abstract (in)convenience, easily out of mind as she was out of sight, away in the country. Elizabeth had no such tie. Possibly he was not thinking clearly at all: from the few examples we have available, he seems to have been a man who, faced by a strong and attractive woman, was capable of being swept away.

Then again, in that despatch of 18 April Feria had written that 'they say' Robert's wife 'has a malady in one of her breasts' and that he and the Queen were simply waiting for Amy to die in order to marry. The Venetian ambassador to the Habsburg court likewise reported that Amy 'has been ailing some time', and that if she were to die, various persons believed 'the Queen might easily take [Dudley] for her husband'. But this may be no more than Chinese whispers; and the Venetian envoy in England, writing on 10 May, was maddeningly discreet: 'My Lord Robert Dudley is in great favour and very intimate with Her Majesty. On this subject I ought to report the opinion of many, but I doubt whether my letters might not miscarry or be read, wherefore it is better to keep silence than to speak ill.'

It is striking how quickly some observers seem to have come to believe that Elizabeth and Robert would – could! – marry, even while no further details appear on Amy Dudley's putative illness. But while rhetoric decrees that marriage was for life – while even Henry had had to resort to extreme measures and obscure legal byways to detach himself from his wives – a look around the late Tudor aristocracy shows a slightly different story. Lawrence Stone, in *The Road to Divorce*, describes how the religious Reformation had thrown canon law into confusion; and how, if you look at practice rather than theological debate, you find a picture even more 'obscure'. A decree of separation might – or might not, depending on opinion – allow remarriage for the innocent party, that is, the husband who had proved his wife's adultery. (Robert himself would later be instrumental in pushing through one such second marriage.) But although it is unclear just how this might have worked out for the Dudleys, the long and the short of it was that if you had influence enough, the thing might be manageable – especially if the marriage was childless. That Robert knew this well would be clear in his own later marital history.

But as 1559 wore on it was clear there were many other candidates for Elizabeth's hand; and better-placed ones, too. It has to be admitted Philip of Spain had made but a reluctant wooer, sighing that while Elizabeth thought over his proposal he felt 'like a condemned man awaiting his fate'. Nothing would make him contemplate marriage with another Tudor bride except the knowledge that it would gain England 'for his service and faith'. (March 1559 had seen the end of the negotiations, and thereafter, with unflattering speed, Philip offered instead for a French princess. Was Elizabeth piqued, as well as relieved? Is it a coincidence that right after Philip's offer was withdrawn she turned more openly to Robert Dudley?)

Other royal suitors waxed more attractively enthusiastic – such as Eric of Sweden, who returned to the assault he had begun in Mary's day. In the first February of Elizabeth's reign the Holy Roman Emperor (Ferdinand, who had inherited Austria from Charles V while Philip inherited Spain) had suggested one of his younger sons. But that proposal too foundered on Elizabeth's declared reluctance to marry a man she had never even seen. Mischievously, she had suggested that the archduke should come to England for inspection; something to which his father was never likely to agree. But she meant what she said. (Perhaps she remembered her father's experience with Anne of Cleves – or Philip's sour words about the too-flattering portrait sent him of Mary – for she swore she would never put her trust in portraits.) When the time finally came to dispose of her Swedish suitor, she would tell him that 'we shall never choose any absent husband'. Indeed, the chances for personal unhappiness in such a marriage were high. Perhaps many royal princesses would have turned down the alliances proposed for them had they been able to do so; had they had, as Elizabeth did, an alternative destiny.

There remained the question of an English marriage, with a man Elizabeth felt to her taste. Neither of the first highly public front-runners had been Robert Dudley. The 47-year-old Earl of Arundel (father-in-law to the Duke of Norfolk) had little to offer but his money and his long pedigree; still, he thought that might be enough. The diplomat Sir William Pickering had other qualities to recommend him to Elizabeth: the courtly manners she always relished, and a history of loyalty to her interests. When he appeared at court on Ascension Day, Elizabeth treated him with all the warmth she would show to subsequent favourites. He, who had long known Elizabeth, said (like Robert) that he knew 'she meant to die a maid'. But in any case it had soon become clear that neither of these – swagger, compete, and spend money on entertainments as they might – had the appeal of Robert Dudley.

That summer of 1559, at Greenwich, Robert was organizing for Elizabeth what sounds like an enchanting summer festivity: a tournament and picnic in pavilions decked with boughs of birch and 'all manner of the flowers of the field and garden' – lavender, roses, gilliflowers and marigolds. But Elizabeth could still, at the height of Robert's attraction for her, proclaim her openness to other offers when necessary. When the new young King of France (Henri having died in a tournament of his own) declared that the English throne belonged to himself and his wife Mary, Elizabeth would threaten: 'I will take a husband who will give the King of France some trouble.' She meant the Earl of Arran, Protestant heir to the Scottish throne after Mary, and a natural focus for the disaffected nobles of that country. But as the court moved on to Windsor she spent ever more time with Robert, riding and hunting by day, talking and making music by night.

Then comes a puzzle: early in September, the Spanish ambassador received a visit from Lady Mary Sidney, Elizabeth's favourite lady-in-waiting and Robert's sister, who told him as representative of the Habsburg interest that it would be worth reviving the archduke's proposal; that the Queen believed, in view of the French threat, that the marriage had now become necessary. This was confirmed to the ambassador by no less a person than Robert Dudley.

This was the first – but not the last – time Elizabeth would exhibit an odd Janus-face to set the claims of her other suitors against those of Robert Dudley: and the first, but not the last, time he seemed to be acting in a way one would not expect. This time, however, he may have felt that the thing of first importance was to counterbalance Arran's Scottish suit. That would explain why, the next month, he would be hosting a banquet for Eric of Sweden's proxy, his brother Duke John – even though, back at Whitehall, when he complained his rooms were too damp, too near the river, the Queen had given him apartments next to her own. It was as if she doled out measures of private reassurance as to her affection in return for his compliance in the public parade of her royal availability. And when the Spanish ambassador told Elizabeth it might after all be possible to have the archduke visit England for her inspection, she told him she had after all no plans to marry at this time; that members of her household often gossiped about her marriage without her authority. This prospect of a flesh-and-blood suitor actually appearing before her seemed to make her 'frightened', said the ambassador tellingly. Perhaps the Queen had just been making a subtle ploy for power and time against the Habsburgs, with Robert as her pawn and mouthpiece, fully cognizant of the role he was to play. He must, as a political animal and Elizabeth's close ally, have recognized the diplomatic importance of the marriage ploy.

In November, the Spanish ambassador worried that Robert was 'slackening' in the archduke's cause, and the Imperial ambassador wrote home: 'It is generally stated that it is his fault that the Queen does not marry'; that he and the Queen had 'a secret understanding', that they would marry when his wife were once sent 'into Eternity'. But England, he said, would not sit quiet under such a match: 'if she marry the said Mylord Robert, she will incur so much enmity that she may one evening lay herself down as Queen of England and rise up the next morning as plain Madam Elizabeth . . . it is a marvel that he has not been slain long ere this.'

The Duke of Norfolk charged Robert with being the impediment to the Habsburg marriage, whereat Robert (in marked contrast to what he had told the Spaniard) answered back that 'He is neither a good Englishman, nor a loyal subject, who advises the Queen to marry a foreigner.' Nor was the Duke of Norfolk the only one to look askance at the rise of Robert Dudley. William Cecil was eyeing his progress warily. And Kat Ashley (now First Lady of the Bedchamber) went down on her knees to beseech her erstwhile charge to marry and put an end to the rumours, 'telling Her Majesty that her behaviour towards the Master of Horse occasioned much evil speaking'. Coming from Kat, Elizabeth took it quietly; said that Robert had deserved much of her 'for his honourable nature and dealings', and that to talk scandal was absurd, when she was constantly surrounded by her ladies of the bedchamber, who would know if 'anything dishonourable' had passed – adding, as an illogical rider, that if however she had ever sought a dishonourable life ('from which may God preserve her'), she 'did not know of anybody who could forbid her'. When Kat, with her usual impetuosity, again urged that, whatever the facts of the case, the damage to her reputation could even lead to civil war, Elizabeth – emotional now – refused an appeal that she see less of Robert. She needed him, she said, because 'in this world she had so much sorrow and tribulation and so little joy'.

To some of the foreign ambassadors, this was indeed becoming a scandal that could even topple Elizabeth from the throne. The Emperor's envoy was instructed to institute enquiries lest the imperial Habsburgs marry their young archduke to a woman of proven immorality. The agent employed was, the envoy reported, someone on very friendly terms with the Queen's ladies. 'They all swear by all that is holy that Her Majesty has most certainly never been forgetful of her honour. Yet it is not without significance that Her Majesty shows her liking for Lord Robert more markedly than is consistent with her reputation and dignity.'

But it is important to realize that Elizabeth was by her very existence already a figure of scandal; not only the daughter of an infamous woman and a much-married man but a *femme sole* – at a time when the law of England did not recognize any status for the average woman beyond daughter, ward, wife or widow. She was a queen regnant and, what is yet more, queen regnant of a Protestant country. The sixteenth century saw a number of women hold the reins of government, among them the regents Mary of Guise in Scotland and Catherine de Medici in France, or Mary of Hungary and Marguerite of Navarre. But not only did most of the others hold their power as temporary substitutes for a dead husband, young son or distant emperor; they were (like Mary Tudor) formally subject – whatever their temporal powers – to the spiritual power of Rome. Elizabeth, then, was in an unprecedented position. Had she been chaste as ice and cold as snow, she would not have escaped calumny.

Increasingly, though, as time passed, observers took the threat of a King Robert more seriously. There were more reports that the only bar to the match was the life of Amy Dudley. In January 1560, the new Spanish ambassador de Quadra could write that 'If there be any other who knows the Queen's purpose it is my Lord Robert, in whom it is easy to recognize the King that is to be.' De Quadra saw no hopeful outcome for such a match: the English people themselves would surely 'do something to set this crooked business straight. There is not a man who does not cry out on him and her with indignation.' None the less, Elizabeth 'will marry none but the favoured Robert'.

At the beginning of March, Elizabeth, so de Quadra complained, was treating the Spanish envoy 'like a dog'. He was in no doubt of whom to blame. Forget Robert's earlier offer of himself as the Habsburgs' intermediary: Lord Robert, the Spanish ambassador wrote now, was 'heartless, spiritless, treacherous and false. There is not a man in England who does not cry out upon him as the Queen's ruin.' All the same, Robert appeared to be treating de Quadra with a measure of confidence: casting out lures to see what foreign backing he could recruit, probably. By the end of the same month, 'Lord Robert says that if he lives a year he will be in another position from that which he at present holds. Every day he presumes more and more, and it is now said that he means to divorce his wife.' On another occasion, the ambassador reported a different story: that Amy was to be poisoned, the gossip coming 'from a person who is accustomed to giving me veracious news'. The same tale was passed on by the Imperial ambassador, de Quadra's ally. But rumours of poison at sixteenth-century courts were two a penny.

To such a point were the names of Dudley and the Queen coupled that on 29 April ambassadors were writing from Madrid that the government there had given them warning of a plot to murder Elizabeth and Robert together. That summer, the chief opponent to their marriage was sent out of the way. Penmen were out of favour – the Queen said she wanted a swordsman to set against these scribes. And so William Cecil was sent north to the Scottish court, to try to establish more friendly relations with that country. (The close alliance between the Scots to the north and the French to the south had long posed a threat to England's security.)

It may well have been Robert who urged Elizabeth to send Cecil north, while the court set out on a summer progress that was more than usually pleasurable and heady. When Cecil returned at the end of the summer, he was horrified to find the Queen ungrateful for the very favourable terms he had managed to pull off, and Robert even more in the ascendancy.

On 13 August one Anne Dowe, of Brentford, was imprisoned for claiming that the Queen had borne Robert's child; on 27 August Cecil wrote to his friend Randolph, talking of resigning. It is in this context that the famous events of that September must be seen.

6

'So sudden a chance'
Autumn 1560

ON ONE DAY IN EARLY SEPTEMBER, SO DE QUADRA WROTE IN A letter of the eleventh, William Cecil had been speaking to him – the agent of a foreign power! – with what seemed to be a most extraordinary and uncharacteristic frankness.

> He [Cecil] perceived the most manifest ruin impending over the Queen through her intimacy with Lord Robert. The Lord Robert had made himself master of the business of the State, and of the person of the Queen . . . Of Lord Robert, he said twice that he would be better in Paradise than here . . . Last of all he said that they were thinking of destroying Lord Robert's wife. They had given out that she was ill; but she was not ill at all, she was very well, and taking care not to be poisoned.

Later in the same letter, de Quadra wrote something even more extraordinary. 'The day after this conversation the Queen, on her return from hunting, told me that the Lord Robert's wife was dead, or nearly so, and begged me to say nothing about it.' And the ambassador added a prescient rider: 'Assuredly it is a matter full of shame and infamy, but for all this I do not feel sure she will immediately marry him, or indeed that she will marry him at all.'

In other words, or so it has always seemed, at some time after

4 September (the date of de Quadra's previous letter) and certainly by the eleventh, Queen Elizabeth told the Spanish ambassador that Robert Dudley's wife was about to die. On the eighth, Amy Dudley was found dead or dying at the bottom of a staircase.

This is the conjunction of events that has served to blacken the reputation of Elizabeth and – far more strongly – Robert for posterity; damning, it seems, in that the conversation is usually assumed to have dated from the earlier part of the week between the ambassador's letters. But why – if murder were really what she meant – would Elizabeth announce it, and to the man most likely to send the damaging news straight to the heart of Catholic Europe? It is as unlikely as ... well, as Cecil's odd and uncharacteristic garrulity.

Who was Amy Dudley? There are no certain portraits, no contemporary descriptions of Amy herself to be found, and very little correspondence. Our mental image of her owes most to the enduring influence of Sir Walter Scott's novel *Kenilworth*, and that pre-Victorian piece of anachronism was of course pure fantasy. (Renamed after Scott's publishers rejected *Cumnor Place* as too unromantic a title, it conflates the death of Amy Dudley with Elizabeth's visit to Robert at Kenilworth Castle a decade and a half later.) So if we see Amy as meek – pale, perhaps; diminutive, maybe – we have to remember it is just as possible she was hefty, red-cheeked and fiery. Our sole piece of evidence comes from the Imperial ambassador who once said that Robert, despite his pretensions to Elizabeth's hand, had 'a beautiful wife' already. But he had probably not even seen Amy Dudley.

There is, nevertheless, a certain amount we can deduce about her relationship with her husband. Back in 1553 she had been granted permission to visit Robert in the Tower, and to tarry there as long as the Lieutenant thought suitable. The implication is, at the least, that at this point the two Dudleys might still be expected to crave each other's company. Only two years before his wife's death, in July 1558, Robert was to be found writing in detail about the proposed rental of a house in Norfolk, with its grazing lands and sheep pens, where he presumably proposed to live with

Amy. We cannot automatically assume that all vestige of marital loyalty had quite died away.

The plan to set up home in Norfolk had fallen through when the events of autumn 1558 made it clear Robert would soon have other matters to attend to, and since then Amy's life had been spent moving between the houses of friends and family: Hertfordshire – Lincolnshire – Bury St Edmunds – Camberwell. It was probably quite a cheerful life in the short term, nor was it so unusual in the sixteenth century, when most great aristocratic households were peripatetic. It was, on the other hand, possibly not a way of life she would wish to continue indefinitely.

True, Amy came rarely to court – but the Queen discouraged the visits of all courtiers' wives, not just those of Amy Dudley. (And to be fair to Elizabeth, aside from her wish to be queen bee, there was a very real question of overcrowding.) In the first months of Elizabeth's reign, Robert's account books show a steady stream of gifts and messages to his wife: 'certain hackneys for my lady', 10s for hose 'for my lady's boy', 20s to furnish a horse to carry Amy's own clothes, 35s for russet taffeta 'to make my lady a gown'; a hood, a chain – these were probably presents, since Amy (an heiress in her own right) seems to have herself paid the bulk of her household expenses; 100s 'delivered to my lady by your lordship's commandment'. (This last, rivetingly if irrelevantly, comes right after 5s to Lord Darby's [Derby's] servant 'for bringing your lordship puffins'.)

The two were clearly not often together at this time. 'Item to Johns for his charges riding to Mr Hyde's to my lady.' 'Item to Langham for ii days' board and wages attending upon my lady at Christchurch your lordship being at Windsor.' But there was obvious friendly contact – even personal contact. (In a separate account book: 22s 'for spices bought by the cook when your Lordship rode to my lady's'.) Recent researches into this period of their lives have revealed that Robert visited Amy at Mr Hyde's in the spring of 1559 (just when his relationship with Elizabeth first attracted comment!), and that she visited London some six weeks after that. There is, however, no evidence of their meeting after that summer.

One of the two extant letters of Amy's own is a note to a London tailor, with orders for a velvet gown 'with such a collar as you made my rose taffeta gown'. Even that serves to show that she had once a bustling and prosperous existence beyond her role as the pale and tragic ghost of legend. The only personal letter of hers that survives was written to her husband's steward and concerns 'the going of certain sheep' at their estate in Siderstern, the price of the wool to be had from the sheep, and her husband's desire to 'see those poor men satisfied' even at the cost of a less than profitable sale. The interest lies in Amy's admission that she had forgotten to speak to Robert about the matter before he left, 'he being sore troubled with weighty affairs, and I not being altogether in quiet for his sudden departing'. We have here a couple with problems on their mind – with diverging spheres of interest, perhaps – but yet, a wife who can order her husband's affairs with authority. And the 'sudden departing' may have been for any cause – even for his going to the French wars with Philip – depending on when, precisely, the (undated) letter was written. But if we do not know what Amy was thinking in those months, when the infrequency of his visits might be taken to reflect the waning of his interest, then we hardly know what her husband was thinking, either. It is possible that Robert Dudley did not clearly envisage his ideal future, or what would be necessary to bring it about, when he set out to court Elizabeth. (It sounds a little like the wilful blindness that spasmodically affected her father, King Henry.)

In the spring or summer of 1560, Amy moved to Cumnor Place near Abingdon and Oxford. The house had been leased (from the family of the former royal physician, Dr Owen) by Robert's treasurer and longtime associate Anthony Forster. The grey stone building, dating from the fourteenth century and once the infirmary and summer retreat of a monastic foundation, was subsequently bought by Forster – described on his tomb in the local church as 'a very amiable man, very learned, a great musician, builder, and planter' – and he had probably already started to give it a gloss of Elizabethan modernity. Allowed to decay over subsequent centuries, it was finally pulled down. What echoes of the

Dudley connection survive in today's Cumnor – like the legend that nine local priests were once called to exorcise Amy's restless ghost – probably owe more to literature than to history.* And information enough survives – an illustration displayed in the church, brooded over by a contemporary statue of Elizabeth that Robert may have commissioned, since he once owned the house where it was found – to suggest that, medieval or no, Cumnor Place was far from the lonely, echoing pile of popular mythology.

But of course, Amy Dudley's name is known not for anything about her life; merely for the manner of her death. Yet even on that, our sources of information are quite extraordinarily limited, considering the huge edifice of story that has been built upon them. The main piece of direct evidence has always been the letters exchanged, immediately after Amy Dudley's death, between Robert and a man called Thomas Blount – 'Cousin Blount' – Robert's chief household officer and longtime satellite of the Dudley family. It was he to whom Robert first turned when a messenger from Forster's household arrived at the court, then in Windsor, to tell him his wife was dead. As he wrote – on the evening of 9 September – Blount appears to have been already headed towards Cumnor; and it was upon him that Robert relied for as much news as could be gleaned.

> Cousin Blount, – Immediately upon your departing from me there came to me Bowes, by whom I do understand that my wife is dead, and, as he saith, by a fall from a pair of stairs. Little other understanding can I have of him. The greatness and the suddenness of the misfortune doth so perplex me [that] until I do hear from you how the matter standeth, or how this evil should light upon me, considering what the malicious world will bruit [gossip], as I can take no rest. And, because I have no way to purge myself of the malicious talk that I know the wicked world will use, but one, which is [that] the very plain truth be known, I do pray you, as you have loved me, and do

---

* The local pub is called The Bear and Ragged Staff – but this was not its name in Robert Dudley's day. It was renamed in tribute to the *Kenilworth* tourist trade in the course of the nineteenth century.

tender me and my quietness, and as now my special trust is in you, that [you] will use all the devices and means you can possible for the learning of the troth; wherein have no respect for any living person.

Robert has often been blamed that his first concern, with his wife dead, was for his own reputation. His wholehearted concern was for 'my case', when the woman he had once loved was dead and cold. But if he were as aware of image and spin as his career suggests (and few Elizabethan courtiers were ignorant of these matters), he would have understood instantly just how this blow would strike him most shrewdly. It has been seen as suspicious that he jumped instantly to the possibility of foul play. But he knew his world. He has been blamed for not instantly setting off for Cumnor; had he done so, of course, the allegation would have been that he wanted to supervise the cover-up in person. And since it was probably on Elizabeth's orders that he had left court and confined himself at Kew (where, the year before, Elizabeth had granted him 'a capital mansion, called the Dairy House'), there was little he could do except to send frantic word that there should be an inquiry into Amy's death, which he declared would vindicate him completely.

He urged Blount that the coroner should be charged

to make choice of no light or slight persons, but the discreetest and [most] substantial men, for the juries, such as for their knowledge may be able to search thoroughly and duly, by all manner of examinations, the bottom of the matter, and for their uprightness will earnestly and sincerely deal therein without respect: and that the body be viewed and searched by them; and in every respect to proceed by order and law ... For, as the cause and manner thereof doth marvellously trouble me, considering my case many ways, so shall I not be at rest till I may be ascertained [how the matter doth stand], praying you, even as my trust is in you, and as I have ever loved you, do not dissemble with me, neither let anything be hid from me, but send me your true conceit and opinion of the matter, whether it happened by evil chance or by villainy.

More convincing yet was the fact that (he added in a postscript) he had sent for Amy's half-brother Appleyard, 'and other of her friends' to go to Cumnor, 'that they may be privy and see how all things do proceed'.

In fact, much of Robert's letter to Blount was unnecessary. By the time it reached him, Blount knew of Amy's death already. On the eleventh (the day when, from Windsor, Elizabeth officially announced Amy's death, and put the court into mourning) he wrote to Robert: 'The present advertisement I can give to your Lordship at this time is, too true it is that my Lady is dead, and, as it seemeth, with a fall; but yet how or which way I cannot learn.'

The night after he left Robert at Windsor (and after meeting Bowes on the way), Blount lodged at an inn at Abingdon, 'and, because I was desirous to hear what news went abroad in the country, at my supper I called for mine host, and asked him what news was thereabout'. This was a little disingenuous, perhaps (like Polonius' advice, or the proverbial sprat to catch mackerel). And it has been thought odd that Blount's first concern, like Robert's own, was with what the people thought; odd how ready he seems to have been to behave like an agent in enemy territory. But his technique worked. The landlord told him a great misfortune had happened within three or four miles of the town: 'he said, my Lord Robert Dudley's wife was dead: and I axed how; and he said, by a misfortune, as he heard, by a fall from a pair of stairs; I asked him by what chance; he said, he knew not: I axed him what was his judgement, and the judgement of the people; he said, some were disposed to say well, and some evil.'

The greatest argument for a sheer accident, the landlord said, sprang from Forster's reputation for honesty. Blount went on pressing. 'Mythinks, said I, that some of her people that waited upon her should somewhat say to this. No sir, said he, but little; for it was said that they were all here at the fair, and none left with her.' Then, in response to Blount's astonished query (a great lady, left unattended?), the landlord came out with an intriguing piece of information. 'It is said how that she [Amy] rose that day very early, and commanded all her sort to go [to] the fair, and would suffer none to tarry at home; and thereof is much judged.' No-one spells out what is judged, precisely. But if there were any suspicion of suicide, then there would be this sympathetic veil of vagueness.

Indeed, Blount reports, he has now had this confirmed by the servants themselves. They 'affirmed that she would not that day suffer one of her own sort to tarry at home, and was so earnest to have them gone to the fair, that with any of her own sort that made reason of tarrying at home she was very angry'. She was even angry with Mrs Odingsells (a widow living in the house, and one in whose own family house Amy had often stayed), when she said that this day, Sunday, was no day for gentlewomen to go to the fair, and that she preferred the (presumably less crowded) Monday. They asked who would keep Amy company if everyone indeed went to the fair, and she said she would dine with Mrs Owen (who, having been wife to the house's former owner, Henry VIII's physician, was possibly too elderly for a fair's frivolity).

'Certainly, my Lord, as little while as I have been here, I have heard divers tales of her that maketh me to judge her to be a strange woman of mind,' Blount adds, significantly. He had talked with Pirto (presumed to be Amy's maid) and one who 'doth dearly love her'. Asking Pirto what she thought of the matter, 'either chance or villainy', Pirto swore 'very chance, and neither done by man nor by herself'. It is interesting that Pirto's mind seems to have leapt to suicide independently. Amy, she said, 'was a good virtuous gentlewoman, and daily would pray upon her knees; and divers times she [Pirto] saith that she hath heard [Amy] pray to God to deliver her from desperation'. That, said Blount, sounded as if Amy might have 'an evil toy' – a dangerous idea – in her mind. 'No, good Mr. Blount, said Pirto, do not judge so of my words; if you should so gather, I am sorry I said so much.' Given the treatment meted out to suicides in the sixteenth century – unsanctified burial and 'shards, flints and pebbles' in place of 'charitable prayers', as the priest says in *Hamlet* – Pirto's hasty backtrack is not surprising.

To unravel what had happened to Amy 'passeth the judgement of any man', Blount warned Robert, adding again: 'but truly the tales I do hear of her maketh me to think she had a strange mind in her; as I will tell you at my coming'. It is a tantalizing rider. He adds that the jury seem both wise (for countrymen) and able; and if anything rather enemies to Anthony Forster than the reverse, which speaks well for their impartiality. 'I have good hope they will conceal no fault, if any be.' Robert cracked back a reply the very next day: until he hears how the matter falls out 'I cannot be in quiet'. Again, he urges that the jury should 'earnestly, carefully and truly deal in this matter . . . so shall it well appear to the world my innocency'.

On the thirteenth Blount wrote again – promising, annoyingly, to bring Dudley a report in person, the very next day. So far the jury, he says, 'be very secret; and yet do I hear a whispering that they can find no presumptions of evil . . . mine own opinion is much quieted; the more I search of it, the more free it doth appear unto me . . . the circumstances and as many things as I can learn doth persuade me that only misfortune hath done it, and nothing else.'

Robert was hearing much the same thing, as he wrote in a last, undated, letter (from Windsor; clearly he was back at court, if briefly). 'I have received a letter from one Smith, one that seemeth to be the foreman of the jury . . . and for anything that he or they by any search or examination can make in the world hitherto, it doth plainly appear, he saith, a very misfortune; which for mine own part, Cousin Blount, doth much satisfy and quiet me.' But he does not want to leave it there.

> None the less, because of my thorough quietness and all others' here-after, my desire is that they may continue in their inquiry and examination to the uttermost, as long as they lawfully may; yea, and when these have given their verdict, though it be never so plainly found, assuredly I do wish that another substantial company of honest men might try again for more knowledge of troth.

The Queen would seem to have vetoed this idea of a second coroner's inquest. But Robert was right to fear that the affair would not die easily. Everyone, in fact, immediately latched on to one theory: that of Robert as murderer – or at the very least as instigator of murder.

The curious thing is that de Quadra seems not to have been among them. His reportage of the event, at the time, was quite singularly free of shock or horror. His long letter of the eleventh starts off on his conversation with Elizabeth about the question of an Imperial marriage and moves on to the conversation in which Cecil so unexpectedly voiced his fears. Then he reports the important conversation with the Queen: he had managed to have a word with her as she came in from hunting, and she told him Robert's wife was dead or nearly so, but asked him to say nothing about it. De Quadra then discoursed briefly upon the question of the succession in England before adding, by way of ending, 'Since this was written the death of Lord Robert's wife has been given out publicly. The Queen said in Italian *"Que si ha rotto il collo."* [She has broken her neck.] It appears that she fell down a staircase.' This is the first suggestion as to the nature of Amy's injuries.

Not 'Lord Robert's wife has died', note, but 'the death has been given out publicly'. Is it possible the whole edifice of guilt which has been constructed on the basis of de Quadra's letter was founded on nothing more than a misconception? It has always been assumed that his so-damning conversation took place before the eighth, before Amy's fall. But nothing in the actual letter of the eleventh compels this reading. It is just as possible that the conversation took place after news reached court on the ninth, when Elizabeth knew that something had happened, knew the construction that could be placed on it, but had not yet decided what her public response would be. (As for the 'dead or nearly' – do we know that Amy died instantly?)

If this were so, then Cecil, too, would certainly have known of Amy's fall; and would presumably have had to think very fast, in order to turn a potential disaster into an opportunity. Robert Dudley a blameless widower, free to marry, would be a catastrophe for him – and, he must have thought, for the country. But if Cecil could seize the chance to blacken the image of Robert Dudley, then disaster might be turned to advantage. It is worth remembering how successfully William Cecil (and in time his son) would later use this technique of taking an existing situation and giving it a 'spin' that turned it to their advantage; how skilfully they applied it against the gunpowder plotters, against the Scots Queen Mary.

Cecil had every reason to wish to persuade de Quadra of Robert's villainy. As he suggested to de Quadra that Robert was trying to poison his wife, he urged the ambassador that King Philip should throw all his influence against a match between Robert and Elizabeth. Later in the letter, de Quadra advised his king that if the two should marry, and Elizabeth lose her throne because of it, then – according to Cecil – 'the true heir to the crown' was the Earl of Huntingdon, whose heir was Robert's brother-in-law, adding that he was a determined heretic and a probable friend to the French . . . It is as if every single thing Cecil said had been calculated to set the Spanish against the idea of Elizabeth's marrying Robert Dudley.

There is another possibility, which also leaves Robert – indeed, anyone! – innocent of murder, but casts the blame for the smear campaign differently. De Quadra himself was not wholly an impartial witness. Not only were ambassadors at the mercy of a court rumour mill they never dared ignore and of Englishmen with their own agendas who might deliberately leak information, true or false; they might have also their own fish to fry. Urging on his master the case for military intervention – fearful lest England make an alliance with France – de Quadra had a vested interest in painting the situation there as black as possible; an interest so powerful as even to prompt him, perhaps, to fudge the timing of his various conversations . . . A century ago, several historians of repute were already suggesting that de Quadra himself set out to suggest Elizabeth and Robert's guilt 'by a deft economy of dates', though the idea seems to have disappeared a little from currency since.

On 22 September Amy was buried at the Church of Our Lady in Oxford (some reports say she had already been interred once, at Cumnor, and then dug up to be more ceremoniously put away). This time, at least, she was buried with all the ceremony of velvet and scutcheons, full processional and feasts for the mourners; of 'Rouge Crosse pursuivant' and 'Lancaster herald in his long gown, his hood on his head'. It cost Robert Dudley two thousand marks. He has, again, been blamed in the centuries since for not having attended the funeral himself; but in the sixteenth century personal mourners were usually of the same sex as the deceased. Nor were his movements entirely at his own command; he would have needed the Queen's permission to travel to Oxford, and exhibit himself thus publicly.

In his exile at Kew, Robert had received a few solicitous visitors (besides the tailor to fit him with mourning). Among them had been William Cecil, who came within a few days, to assure Robert of his support. To this rival, perhaps even enemy, Robert wrote, rather touchingly, his thanks, and pleas for his intercession with the Queen.

> Sir, I thank you much for your being here, and the great friendship you have showed toward me I shall not forget . . . the sooner you can advise me thither [the sooner Cecil could get him permission to travel to court] the more I shall thank you. I am sorry so sudden [a] chance should breed in me so great a change, for methinks I am here all this while, as it were, in a dream, and too far, too far from the place where I am bound to be. I pray you help him that sues to be at liberty out of so great a bondage.

Of course, support on Cecil's part for Robert would make his allegations to de Quadra sound a little oddly. Somewhere, there is hypocrisy. But certainly Cecil was now in a good position to ask for favours. Robert's disaster was his route back into the Queen's confidence; in this crisis, impelled by self-preservation to keep Robert at arm's length, Elizabeth turned immediately back to her secretary.

The news spread slowly through Europe. On 23 September Randolph, the English ambassador to Scotland, was writing to Cecil about 'the slanderous reports of the French' (Scotland's old allies); and on 10 October (news sent by Cecil on 20 September having taken almost a fortnight to arrive) came the first of many letters from Sir Nicholas Throckmorton, the English ambassador to the French court itself.

A busy correspondent, Throckmorton had a responsible position in these months, when England was trying to conclude an important treaty with France; and he was not the man to make the least of any responsibility.* An ambitious individual and an old ally of Cecil's, he, like Cecil, believed Elizabeth should be guided by wiser heads. A convinced and longtime supporter of Elizabeth's accession, he had none the less taken it upon himself to write her a detailed list of guidelines (instructions, even) for her behaviour in her new reign; having earlier been the one to warn Thomas Seymour off his pretensions. From the start, he clearly took the affair of Amy Dudley's death as evidence of just how far wrong a female monarch – left to her own devices – could possibly go.

His letter to Cecil on the tenth is full of lamentation about the rumour of foul play: 'which as it was strange indeed, so has it been and is yet discoursed of here at pleasure, and liberally enough of the malicious French . . . God forbid that the rumour thereof should prove true.' On the same day he wrote to another English correspondent of the 'dishonourable and naughty reports . . . which every hair of my head stareth at and my ears glow to hear'. People there were relishing the stories, he said, and 'Some let not to say, what religion is this that a subject shall kill his wife, and the Prince not only bear withal but marry him?'

Yet on the same day, Throckmorton also wrote to Robert himself of 'the cruel mischance late happened to my Lady your late Bedfellow, to your discomfort. But for that God hath thus disposed of things, the greatest of your . . . [grief? trouble?] being assuaged, and the remembrance thereof partly worn, I will no further condole with your Lordship, thereby to renew your grief.' The bulk of the letter is concerned with a horse Robert has given him, a coming tilt, and his urgent desire to be back in England, which he hopes Robert might promote . . . for Throckmorton was also on friendly terms with Robert Dudley.

* He had been the supporter of Elizabeth's waiting at Mary's court to bring word of the Queen's death.

In a letter to Cecil on the twenty-eighth Throckmorton writes his private opinion of Robert Dudley: 'I do like him for some respects well, and esteem him for many good parts and gifts of nature that be in him.' Yet 'if that marriage take place . . . our state is in great danger of utter ruin and destruction . . . the Queen our Sovereign discredited, contemned, and neglected; our country ruined, undone, and made prey'. He had already told Cecil, appalled, that Mary, Queen of Scots had joked that the Queen of England was about to marry her horsekeeper, who had killed his wife to make a place for her.

It is worth noting that the concern of all these men (like that of Robert himself) seems, throughout, to be with reputation rather than reality. They cared what was thought of Dudley; and, by implication, of the Queen. In their letters, at least, they show no concern with the fundamental question whether he really had done his wife to death. Was it matter too dangerous to be written? Were they really that cynical? Or were they convinced of his innocence?*

On 17 October Throckmorton wrote to Cecil that all men 'take it for truth and certain she will marry Lord Robert Dudley, whereby they assure themselves that all foreign alliance and aid is shaken off, and do expect more discontentation thereby among yourselves. Thus you see your sore, God grant it do not with rankling fester too far and too dangerously.' But at the beginning of that month, Cecil had told de Quadra that the Queen had informed him she would not marry Robert Dudley. She probably failed to say as much to Robert Dudley. In the face of his repeated pressure she agreed to raise him to the peerage. But when the time came, in one of her famous histrionic gestures, she took a knife and slashed up the letters patent.

We know of the incident from Throckmorton's secretary Robert Jones, whom the ambassador had sent back to London to

---

* A letter from a correspondent in England, Henry Killigrew, mentions the rumours but describes the death as an accident. Even when, on the twenty-ninth, Throckmorton wrote to Chamberlain, his fellow ambassador in Spain, he said his friends advised him that Lord Robert's wife was dead 'and has by chance broken her own neck'.

remonstrate about the same old matter. In a long letter back to the ubiquitous Throckmorton, Jones manages to convey something of the tense and puzzled atmosphere around the court. Robert himself quizzed Jones about what the Queen of Scots had said; it's hard to know whether it was tantalizing him, or galling him like a bite from a horse fly. When Jones had an interview with Elizabeth herself, in exasperation, or confusion, she tried to laugh the matter away, turning from side to side in embarrassment, as Jones reported vividly. She told him that the question of Amy's death had been tried in the country, and that the coroner's verdict showed it 'should neither touch his honesty nor her honour'. He added: 'The Queen's Majesty looketh not so hearty and well as she did by a great deal, and surely the matter of my Lord Robert doth much perplex her.' The marriage was never likely to take place, as being too widely opposed, 'and the talk thereof is somewhat slack'.

It sounds as though the death of Amy Dudley had left Elizabeth herself as perplexed as any. Perhaps she blamed Robert, for having been at least the inadvertent means of getting her into this mess. Her repeated refusal over the next few months to give him his earldom (even saying she wanted no more Dudleys – a family who had been traitors for three generations – in the House of Lords) smacks of anger and resentment, as well as mere concern for public opinion. But then, any pressure to advance a favourite to more power and independence would be enough to make her angry – and her impulses were often contradictory. It is hard to believe she really thought he had indeed murdered his wife. (If he had, then she herself was at least morally guilty.) Perhaps she saw Robert, like herself, as mere victim of a monstrous chance; believed that malign fate killed Amy Dudley. Or perhaps she suspected – even, conceivably, knew – that another person was guilty.

What did happen to Amy Dudley? There can at this date be no certainty. There is a good case for saying that it is impossible ever really to solve a historical mystery, that the task is akin to that of proving a negative. You just don't know what evidence is missing . . . and this mystery in particular is bricks without straw; a postmodern detective story where every piece of evidence crumbles to your touch. But let us at least try to clear the air a little; first, by examining the case for and against the most popular historical suspect, Robert Dudley.

Here the Blount letters are key. Unless these letters are to be taken as fakes, or as a subtle piece of double bluff intended to be 'leaked' to a sceptical third party, they surely exonerate Robert completely. It is perhaps unfortunate that the letters as they survive, in the Pepys Library in Cambridge, are not the originals, but contemporary copies, written in a hand that may be that of Blount but is not that of Robert Dudley. When the case came up for re-examination some years later, we hear that Blount has been asked to 'do' something by the investigators. To provide these copies? One cannot wholly exclude the possibility that the letters are forgeries; but if Robert and his supporters were going to the trouble of inventing a correspondence, surely they would have cooked up something that cleared him completely – and, for the sake of verisimilitude, have bothered to fake two different hand-writings!* There is in the end no more (and no less) reason to mistrust the Blount letters than any other piece of historical testimony.

Whatever faint question marks hang over them, the Blount letters still play a major place in the study of the case. The coroner's report was lost for centuries, along with the all-important depositions he received. Instead we hear that John Appleyard (that half-brother of Amy's who had been summoned to Cumnor) some years later queried the jury's judgement. He was rumoured to have been saying that 'he had not been satisfied with the verdict of the jury at her death, but that for the sake of Dudley he had covered the murder of his sister'. When haled before the privy council he denied having of his own volition said any such thing, and told instead a rambling story of a mysterious stranger who, the year

---

* Fewer letters from Tudor persons of importance than one might think survive in the author's own hand, so often was correspondence dictated to a secretary, or subsequently copied for file. Other letters quoted that survive only in copy include John Dudley's last despairing letter (p. 58); that of Edward Dyer quoted on pp. 221–2; and a good deal of the Netherlands correspondence (pp. 310–19).

before at Hampton Court, had taken him across the Thames to meet a third party, who offered to pay him a thousand pounds to spread a murder story. From the Fleet prison, Appleyard – told to produce any evidence he had – instead asked for a written copy of the coroner's verdict, and declared himself satisfied when he had seen it: 'Not only such proofs testified under the oaths of 15 persons how my late sister by misfortune happened of death, but also such manifest and plain demonstration thereof as hath fully and clearly satisfied and persuaded me.' Appleyard could have been under pressure to recant; but then he could indeed have been bribed to make the original allegation, at a time when Robert was beset by enemies.* Again, nothing is conclusive. We are left with supposition and suggestion merely.

One thing perhaps suggestive of Robert's innocence is his very passivity in the first days after his wife's death. He behaved like a man baffled, rather than one who had a response ready. But to the more pressing of his posthumous detractors, even this did not argue that he was not expecting Amy's murder. To them, it merely suggests that he was not expecting it to happen at quite this time or in quite this way.

It may be interesting to compare two authors on the subject: both writing in the nineteenth century, the heyday of speculation about Robert and Amy. Between them, they print virtually all of the documents quoted above; but the two make their selections very differently.

George Adlard, whose *Amye Robsart and the Earl of Leicester* was printed in London in 1870, gives the Blount correspondence in full, while discussing contemporary (and subsequent) reaction in curiously modern terms – as image-making rather than indictment. Adlard believes Robert Dudley innocent, and subscribes, with caution, to the suicide theory. He is the writer most often cited by modern historians in their source notes today.

By contrast, Walter Rye, whose *The Murder of Amy Robsart: A Brief for the Prosecution* was published in Norfolk (Amy's

---

* Appleyard took his mysterious strangers to be emissaries of the Duke of Norfolk and his party; see p. 177.

territory) in 1885, makes only passing reference to the Blount correspondence, which he takes to be a series of covert suggestions on Robert Dudley's part that Blount should lean on the jury. He does, however, quote Throckmorton's letters in detail (and repeatedly cites Cecil, whom he takes to be an unimpeachable authority). His work is much less considerable than Adlard's; indeed, it might hardly be worth discussing, except that it stands as a good exemplar of the other side's theory.

Amy was to have been poisoned (so this theory runs); but she was so careful that this attempt failed, and the assassins therefore turned instead to direct violence. Amy was indeed desperate, but not because she was suicidal in any way; because she knew her husband was trying to poison her. It all looks rather shaky if you remember that the only named source of the poison rumour is Cecil, and if you decide there is any reason to suspect Cecil's veracity. To Rye, Robert Dudley was a likely poisoner because he was alleged to have poisoned several other people in the years ahead; so many, indeed, that he takes four pages to run through them all. But these allegations were made in what came to be known as *Leicester's Commonwealth*, a scurrilous pamphlet, by an anonymous Catholic author, printed late in Robert's life with the patent intention of doing him harm;* and before that in another anonymous tract, the recently discovered *Journal of matters of state*, in circulation soon after Amy's death.

So what, then, about the other possible causes of Amy Dudley's death? I am inclined to ignore the possibility of complete misadventure – that a happy, healthy Amy simply happened to fall down the stairs so awkwardly that, against the odds, she broke her neck. It's not impossible, but it leaves every other oddity of the case unaccounted for. Still, natural causes are a possibility.

Reports described Amy as suffering from 'a malady in one of

---

* Adlard gives a very full exposé of how one source led to another: a paragraph-by-paragraph comparison of how the most popular source, long taken as both authoritative and impartial, actually plagiarizes *Leicester's Commonwealth* to an extraordinary degree.

her breasts' – presumably breast cancer. This may have been what Elizabeth meant, in saying Amy would soon be dead. Modern medicine has been co-opted to suggest that untreated cancer could have led to cancerous deposits breaking away from the original tumour to settle on Amy's spinal column, causing an abnormal brittleness. Not only could a short fall have been fatal, but even the slight series of shocks involved in a walk downstairs could possibly (according to the theory put forward by Professor Ian Aird in 1956) have fractured a vertebra. This image of a kind of spontaneous skeletal collapse – like the mummy in an old horror movie – may sound unlikely, but it receives more credence than the other medical theory: that Amy suffered an aortic aneurism. (According to this scenario, the increasing enlargement of an artery could have caused pain and swelling in the chest, the result-ing erratic blood flow to the brain leading to irrational fits of anger or depression, until sudden rupture caused death and, obviously, a consequent fall: no forensic medicine of the sixteenth century could tell whether, when Amy's neck snapped, she was dead already.) Aird's attention, he said, was first caught by a claim, made in *Leicester's Commonwealth*, that Amy's terrible supposed 'fall' had yet mysteriously not been violent enough to disturb 'the hood that stood upon her head'. Coming from that publication, the detail itself has to be treated sceptically. (The Spaniards, by contrast, had been told that Amy had been found with a dagger wound on her head – unlikely to be literally true, since a knife to the scalp is no way of killing anybody, but perhaps suggesting the mark of a fall.) None the less, if Aird's supposition were correct, Amy may simply have collapsed where she stood, and her fall been a less disruptive affair.

Faint circumstantial evidence of illness comes from a letter written to Robert after the event by his brother-in-law the Earl of Huntingdon. In a postscript added to a routine note, he makes surprisingly casual reference to 'the death of my lady your wife'. 'I doubt not but long before this time you have considered what a happy hour it is which bringeth man from sorrow to joy, from mortality to immortality, from care and trouble to rest and quiet-ness, and that the Lord above worketh all for the best to them that love him.' The 'long before this time' may refer to all the other deaths Robert had known, rather than specifically to Amy – but it is true that the tone is unsurprised, brisk and unfussy, as if her death had been foreseen within the family.

If Amy were ill but not suicidal, of course, we would have to assume that she sent her servants away because her condition made her desperate for that commodity so rare in Elizabethan times: privacy. Or we could dismiss her hysterical (and anachronistic) insistence on solitude as an irrelevance. But it may be helpful to see Amy's illness not as a primary cause of her death, but as an underlying condition that either gave her a reason to wish to end her life, or brought other factors into play.

Of the two theories that remain to us – suicide, or murder by a third party – both (given Amy's illness as a precondition) can be fitted to the evidence we have, entirely. They are the only two theories of which this is true.* The others may fit most of the facts, but they leave some ends hanging very oddly.

The fashionable theory of recent years has been death by the hand of that third party. But we have not returned to the old nineteenth-century assumption of Robert's guilt; the century whose perceptions were coloured by Sir Walter Scott's long-influential *Kenilworth* and its picture of blackest villainy. Though Robert Dudley can never conclusively be dismissed as the villain of the piece,† there is, as we have seen, one other candidate, to whom the natural death of Robert Dudley's wife would have represented a threat, not an opportunity. It is possible to read Robert's insistence that the jury act without respect of persons as reflecting his suspicion that there existed such another guilty party. Someone determined Robert Dudley should be blamed; someone who saw the prospect of his marriage to Elizabeth as disastrous for the country. The notion of William Cecil's guilt

---

* These are also the two theories propounded, respectively, by the two most recent fictional interpretations: the one by the BBC's *The Virgin Queen*, and the other by Philippa Gregory's novel *The Virgin's Lover*.

† And if he were guilty, this rather implies that Amy was not sick: why on earth should he have her murdered, if a few more weeks might see him a blameless widower?

became popular in the last part of the twentieth century. Perhaps that reflects the modern love of a conspiracy theory. Perhaps it is just that he makes so convincing a hate figure for our times: the faceless Whitehall mandarin, capable of any covert villainy.

Cecil had the best motive. One has only to think of Cecil's position before Amy's scandalous death; and his very different position after it. He was at once the person who seemed to have foreknowledge of Amy's death, and the chief beneficiary of it. He is a constant presence throughout the story: the Queen's comforter; Throckmorton's correspondent; the first leaker, before the event, of homicide rumours to Europe (so uncharacteristic, so stupid, if it really were a leak); the one known source of the poison theory. In his later, private, memo about Robert Dudley's unsuitability as Elizabeth's husband, he describes Robert as 'infamed' by his wife's death – not as guilty of it. An odd emphasis, since he was notching up every possible score against Robert – unless he knew Robert to be not guilty.*

But if Cecil actually had Amy murdered in order to damage Robert Dudley, the risks he ran were huge. He was gambling that Elizabeth's reputation would not be irreparably damaged by association, and gambling that her disgrace would not affect the status of the Protestant religion, of which she was the most visible exponent. On the other hand, if Amy were really terminally ill, then Cecil's motive becomes all the stronger. If she were going to die anyway, it was vital that she should die in such a manner as not to open the way for Robert's marriage to Elizabeth. Or did the thought that Robert might soon be a blameless widower frighten someone other than Cecil, someone for whom Cecil was an obvious tool and ally?

If Cecil were guilty of murder, the open question (as it is if Robert was the murderer) must be to what degree, if any at all, Elizabeth knew or guessed at what was going on. She would later

---

* It is worth noting in this context that Camden, the colouring of whose history of the reign owes a good deal to Cecil's patronage, though no friend to Robert Dudley, mentions Amy's death only in passing – writing of Dudley, 'whose wife (being heir to Robsart) had lately broke her neck'.

manage 'not to know' about a death – that of the Queen of Scots – even when she had herself signed the death warrant. Of course, this takes us straight back to the heart of the sixty-four-thousand-ducat question itself: did Elizabeth really want to marry – to marry even Robert Dudley? It has been said she had Amy killed because she wanted to make him available. It is conceivable that, on the contrary, she had Amy killed to put him out of court; so that she could avoid marrying him, without losing him completely. It would, perhaps, have been out of character for her to have acted alone in this, and directly. But a half-and-half position, of the kind Elizabeth always favoured? She would probably not have had to utter the words, to admit the actual intent. A hint, a half-breathed wish, might do it – the 'Who will rid me of this turbulent priest?' theory.

If Amy were gravely ill (or even amenable to a divorce) – if Robert told her he would soon be free – did Elizabeth see it as a promise, or a threat? It used to be assumed that her feelings about Amy's life and death were identical with those of Robert. That is a huge assumption – and unwarrantable, actually. We have here some benefit from hindsight. Elizabeth's contemporaries still, at this point in her life, assumed that she – that any natural woman – must and would want to marry. We have the great advantage of knowing what happened in the next four decades; knowing of her deliberate policy of single blessedness, her trumpetings of virginity.

But if Elizabeth were in any way aware of what would happen, then she was running even more of a risk than Cecil. And, even more importantly, she was crazy to have anything remotely resembling the conversation de Quadra reported. And although she was clearly distressed in the weeks afterwards, it was not quite the behaviour she usually exhibited when (as after the death of Mary, Queen of Scots) she felt herself guilty. In the end, there is nothing more than circumstantial evidence to suggest even Cecil's guilt, let alone Elizabeth's complicity.

It is interesting to see how things work out if one turns, instead, to the possibility of suicide. There is evidence beyond those rumours of breast cancer that *something* was wrong with Amy.

The reports of the ambassadors, of Blount, of Pirto-via-Blount and even of *Leicester's Commonwealth* all tend that way. Amy's insistence upon being left alone at Cumnor that day gives considerable weight to the suicide theory. *Leicester's Commonwealth* said that Dr Bayly, a noted Oxford physician, was called to prescribe because Amy was so 'sad and heavy'. The point the tract was trying to draw was that Bayly refused, since he was so afraid his medicine might be used as cover for poison, but the basic information contained is just this: that Amy was very melancholy. She had, of course, good reason to be – her husband's relationship with the Queen, quite apart from any malady.

The flustered statement of Amy's devoted maid tells us her mistress had been depressed in recent months; and though Pirto insisted Amy would never have taken her own life, she would say (even think) that, wouldn't she? Suicide was an appalling crime to the sixteenth century, punished by unsanctified burial at the public crossroads and damnation for all eternity. And the maid's initial point was that Amy was desperate, praying to God to deliver her out of her melancholy.

Against this has been offered the shortness and shallowness of the 'pair' of stairs concerned (a flight broken by a landing in the middle), which would have made death extremely chancy. That might have meant she would not die instantly . . . But, no-one has ever said she did die instantly. The staircase at Cumnor has long been destroyed, so no-one can measure it. And if Amy were ill then the state of her health, besides providing one motive for suicide, may indeed have come into play. A fall might have killed her that would not have killed someone healthy.

She cannot have been wholly sunk in melancholy that autumn. The letter to her tailor, ordering a velvet gown, was written only a fortnight before her death. But a fortnight is more than long enough for a dark mood to come upon one; nor would Amy have been the first or the last woman to turn to shopping in an attempt to cheer herself up. (A Spanish report has been cited alleging that Amy was 'playing at tables', gambling, when she left the room and went to her death, which if true would hardly sound suicidal – but that report was made only in 1584, in a document that may be the nucleus for *Leicester's Commonwealth*.) Hers may have been a half-hearted attempt at suicide rather than a determined plan – what Adlard, writing in the Victorian age when suicide was still a crime, elegantly glossed as 'an involuntary act of self-destruction' under the influence of 'an aberration of mind'; or what one modern coroner calls 'parasuicide'. (The coroner adds, moreover, that the 'ideation' of Amy's death, right down to the reaction of her friends and relatives, fits the pattern of suicide precisely.) If Amy were distressed by her husband's relationship with the Queen, there may have been the well-known element of 'then they'll be sorry'. Lastly, if Amy were ill and taking medicine, one might have to query the effect, on the mind as well as the body, of cordials, stored in leaden vessels, that combined red wine and laudanum; of medical treatments that, besides such arcane but probably anodyne ingredients as powdered crabs' eyes or pigeon dung, might involve arsenic or mercury. Without more information, we cannot really factor this possibility into the equation, but neither can we discount it entirely.

The more we read Blount's letters, the more it sounds as if he were edging around the suicide theory. And in an age when suicide was a mortal sin, Robert's repeated insistence that the jury should speak as they found, without fear or favour to any living person, might be read as a message they should not hesitate to record a verdict of suicide if necessary.

Clearly they did not do so; if they had, Amy could not have been given her lavish Christian burial. But sympathy for the deceased – or fear of the living – may have come into play; the Queen would not have enjoyed having it known Amy had been driven to act so desperately (which may have accounted for her uncertainty over what to say to de Quadra). And even in death, 'great ones' have more licence – as *Hamlet*'s Gravedigger said of Ophelia, so shrewdly:

> *First Gravedigger*: Is she to be buried in Christian burial that wilfully seeks her own salvation?
> *Second Gravedigger*: I tell thee she is, therefore make her grave straight. The coroner hath sat on her, and finds it Christian burial . . .

Will you ha' the truth on't? if this had not been a gentlewoman, she
should have been buried out o' Christian burial.

Though Shakespeare was not born at the time of Amy's death, his
birth in the area of Dudley influence, and his work with actors –
like James Burbage – who had been in Robert's own company, the
Earl of Leicester's Men, make it likely he would have been
familiar with the story.

If Amy Dudley committed suicide, then William Cecil was
guilty of nothing more than a little 'black PR'. And no-one in the
Elizabethan battle for hearts and minds ever baulked at fighting
dirty. But much, as always, depends on the real mystery that was
Elizabeth's mind. If one could evaluate that, then one might be
better placed to evaluate the scanty evidence as to the solution of
the Amy Dudley mystery.

That mind was never more incalculable than in the period
immediately ahead – the few years that followed the death of
Amy Dudley. The scandal fired by the affair did not quickly die
away. But just when one might have expected Elizabeth to
become more circumspect with Robert, she became less so. She
spoke of her affection for him more openly than ever, now that
the furore seemed to make him as unmarriageable as ever a living
wife could have done. There was always something of the bully in
Elizabeth, as there had been in her father. Those who had given
her an inch found themselves missing an ell, and she probably
never enjoyed her Robin more than when she had him at a dis-
advantage. Who knows whether he understood this clearly? He
did understand Elizabeth, perhaps better than anybody. But he
was also the child of his age – replete with the generic confidence
of the sixteenth-century male.

Robert's position had changed, superficially giving him more
freedom of action; in fact possibly far less. But something had
changed for Elizabeth, too. She had gained from her ability to
surmount this crisis; from the establishment of where her private
pleasures and her monarchical responsibilities came in her
priorities. She had, in this, demonstrated the difference between
her and her sister Mary. She behaved like someone who had

survived a dangerous situation (as she had, in that she was still on the throne), but, more, like someone who found herself freed from a problem. She had, in fact, the slightly dizzy confidence of someone who – whether or not she had actually done anything to achieve it – found she had been granted a victory.

7

'Maiden honour and integrity'
1560–1561

IN ONE OF ELIZABETH I'S ACCOUNT BOOKS THERE IS RECORDED THE
purchase of a bed. Its wooden frame was carved, painted and gilded;
its tester and valance of cloth of silver figured with velvet. The
curtains were tapestry, trimmed with gold and silver lace, and
buttons of precious metal. For the headpiece, crimson satin had been
brought from Bruges and capped with ostrich feathers shimmering
with gold spangles. At her palace of Richmond (so a later visitor
noted with wonder) Elizabeth slept in a boat-shaped bedstead with
curtains of 'sea water green', quilted with light brown tinsel; at
Whitehall, the bed itself was worked in woods of different colours
and hung with Indian painted silk. In the Elizabethan house, with its
scanty list of solid furnishing and extensive catalogue of textiles, the
bed was an important and emotive item – witness Shakespeare's
famous bequest of his 'second best bed' to his wife. But in
Elizabeth's case the question, of course, is whether she slept in
hers alone, or whether Robert Dudley ever shared it with her.

There was and is no categorical answer. In the 1590s, when she
was sixty, Henri IV of France would jest that one of the three great
questions of Europe was 'whether Queen Elizabeth was a maid or
no'. The question had practical import for contemporaries, and it
continues to fascinate today. There seems no doubt that she was
passionately in love with Robert Dudley; little that the pair

enjoyed a degree of physical intimacy marked enough to strike contemporaries. But knowing that only makes it harder to be sure at what point that intimacy stopped, precisely. Elizabeth herself, defending her honour, would later point out indignantly that 'I do not live in a corner – a thousand eyes see all that I do'. It is true that at least one court lady would habitually share her bedchamber, which opened onto the room of the ladies of the privy chamber. Had Robert passed whole nights under an earlier version of those painted silks and nodding plumes, it is unlikely the secret would have survived for centuries. But of course a queen might speak alone with a close adviser, and we have to remember that Elizabeth's consultations often took place late at night, and in her private chambers. If we accept that Elizabeth and Robert would have spent time alone, then we have also to accept that no third party can ever be sure precisely what they did or did not do in that privacy.

In many ways, sexuality was in the open in Elizabethan society. Shakespeare's bawdry had a ready audience. The language and letters addressed to the Queen habitually breathed an extravagance, a pleasurable sensuality, that might seem more suggestive to later ages than it would to contemporaries. Even a royal suitor, whose courtship was half ritual, could write some years later that he kissed her 'everywhere you can imagine', that he longed to share her big bed. The normal conditions of Elizabethan court life – the very lack of privacy, the living of life in public – itself presented both opportunities for and restrictions on a certain amount of sexual play. The Duke of Norfolk and the Earl of Arundel, Robert's enemies, would later complain of him not that he entered the Queen's bedchamber – as any other officer of state might have occasion to do – but that he pushed the privilege of doing so to its limits, appearing (like Thomas Seymour . . .) before the Queen was out of bed, and handing her the shift she would put on.* Likewise, Norfolk and Arundel complained not that Robert had been seen to kiss her – the English kiss of greeting full on the lips

---

* Though even here, since the act of putting on his shift had been singled out as signifying particular closeness to King Henry, the point made may just conceivably have been about status, rather than sexuality.

was much remarked by foreigners – but more specifically that he had been seen 'kissing the Queen's Majesty without being invited thereto'. The thing was a sliding scale, and Elizabeth and Robert played it with virtuosity.

In less rarefied circles, legislators at the church court in Havering decided that for two unmarried people of different sexes to share a bed was suspect. But to share a room was acceptable – inevitable, in most households. In terms of homosexual sex, sodomy was punishable by death, but open expression of affection between men might pass without remark.

Satirists and moralists, later in Elizabeth's reign, fulminated that public gardens were no better than brothels, that the theatres saw young men shamelessly 'wallowing in ladies' laps', that the 'forward virgins of the day' could hardly wait until their teens to shed that virginity. As many as one in five brides were pregnant on their wedding day. Pre-marital sex was comparatively acceptable *if* it were to lead to marriage. This might provide one explanation for the statement reported by the Spanish ambassador at the beginning of 1561. Robert's brother-in-law Henry Sidney told de Quadra that Robert and Elizabeth 'were lovers' – '*eran amores*', in the Spanish – but that nothing had happened that could not be put right with King Philip's help; that is, his support for their marriage. (A great deal can come down to precise points of translation and semantics; another rendering of the same phrase says that 'it was a love affair'.) If so, then we have to imagine that they did have full, penetrative sex, right back at the very start of their relationship – with the proviso that the liaison had been so scant, so secret, as to enable Elizabeth actually to perform a feat of self-hypnosis and subsequently, through all their long years, to put it from her mind entirely.*

* Polite euphemisms serve only to confuse the issue. We cannot ask whether 'anything was really going on': clearly, *something* was. Nor whether the two 'slept together': passing whole tranquil nights together is about the one thing we can be sure they didn't do. As I argued over the relationship – in the usual clumsy, guarded terms – with a historian older than myself, it finally transpired that we were envisaging precisely the same situation . . . But she, growing up before the sexual revolution, had counted that situation as 'doing it', while I, from a later generation, had not.

But there is still a problem, and it is hard to believe it did not loom very large indeed in Elizabeth's mind: the risk of an unthinkable pregnancy. An ordinary woman might risk pregnancy in the knowledge that marriage would surely follow, but a queen regnant, as closely watched and as vulnerable to scandal as Elizabeth was? Hardly. These early years when Elizabeth's relationship with Robert flowered most passionately, moreover, were the very years when it would have been hardest for them to rush into marriage if it became necessary: first because of Amy Dudley's living presence, and then because of the scandalous manner of her death.

The veiled nature of any contemporary discussion makes it hard to be sure about contemporary contraceptive practices beyond withdrawal. The uses of a physical barrier – half a lemon rind, strategically inserted, or a primitive condom made from sheepskin or the less reliable brine-soaked linen – were known in certain circles. Elizabethan medical writings, moreover, often describe herbs – rue, marigold, mandrake – that could be used to bring on a woman's 'courses', in what may or may not be coded references to an abortifacient. But anyone sophisticated enough to have known about such closet devices must also have known that they were far from trustworthy.

In some of her later prayers, Elizabeth would ask forgiveness 'for sin committed in youthful rashness', for her flesh that was corrupt, 'frail and weak'. Is it tempting to read into them a particular meaning? Maybe. But all the heirs of Adam and Eve were so weak, so corrupted. Eighteen months after this time, on what might easily have been her deathbed, Elizabeth (so the Spanish ambassador reported) would declare that 'although she loved and had always loved Lord Robert dearly, as God was her witness nothing unseemly [desconveniente] had ever passed between them'.

What can be gleaned from the reports of contemporaries? Throughout her life, those who spread scandal about Elizabeth would prove, on closer investigation, to be those far away from her – agents abroad, humble subjects who could never have met her face to face – rather than those in her immediate circle. You might argue that her own courtiers would not dare: the humbler souls who gossiped in the alehouses certainly paid the penalty, like the Marsham who was condemned to lose both his ears or a hefty sum of money for saying Elizabeth had borne Robert two children.

But even the ambassadors to her court, in their coded, privileged letters home, displayed a mixture of opinions. In 1560, the Swedish chancellor wrote that 'I saw no signs of an immodest life, but I did see many signs of chastity, virginity, and true modesty, so that I would stake my life itself that she is most chaste.' One Spanish ambassador, in the time immediately after Elizabeth's accession, had been quick to repeat every damaging report, yet one of his successors would 'doubt sometimes whether Robert's position is irregular as many think'. Her own ministers and spymasters – partial witnesses, but enquiring and not besotted ones – would in the years ahead show every sign of believing the great story of her virginity.

Perhaps there was a measure of 'forgive and forget' about Elizabethan sexual morality. Those of her maids who were caught out in affairs were damaged, but not always irrevocably ruined. Perhaps if Elizabeth did have sex with Robert, but then turned her face firmly away, her society would collude with the reinvention (in much the same way as, in the film *Elizabeth*, the formerly fully sexual heroine was allowed to remake herself as a virgin). But then again, do we think that for Elizabeth herself her chastity was only and entirely a question of her public reputation? Surely Elizabeth saw her 'virtue' in its original Latin sense of *virtus*, strength, and would not relinquish it easily.

All through her life, and far beyond it, the rumours would continue. There were rumours that she had borne children to Robert Dudley and to others; as late as 1587 a young man presented himself at the Spanish court claiming that his name was Arthur Dudley, and that he was Elizabeth's son.* There were rumours that her favourites treated her with all the freedom a man might a wife (as the imprisoned Mary, Queen of Scots would later put it). But there were always rumours about the rare public woman.

* See Appendix II for a full discussion of this claim, and the Afterword for the whole question of Elizabeth's sexuality as it has appeared in some recent fictional treatments.

Even Catherine de Medici – no sure friend to Elizabeth, but one who was herself in a position to know – once spoke supportively on the subject to Elizabeth's ambassador: 'we of all Princes that be women are subject to be slandered wrongfully'.

The evidence of her life is that Elizabeth saw some of the games of courtship and foreplay as fulfilling ends in themselves, rather than as precursors to the inevitable main event. It is possible that in putting the old, crude, question – in asking just: did they, didn't they? – we are seeing things too simplistically.

The romance of Elizabeth and Robert would be played out by the rules of a game that was old in their own day – the rules of courtly love, that time-honoured but still potent fantasy.* The cruel, superior mistress rules the lover, who eternally yearns, may never attain, but must always obey. It was a veritable religion of earthly love, modelled at once on the devotion man owes to God, and the service a feudal vassal owed his lord. Born in the courts of Provence, finding its English apogee in the days of that other desirable and powerful Queen of England, Eleanor of Aquitaine, this was the cult that would, centuries later, give a form and a vocabulary to Elizabeth's and Robert's long romantic loyalty. All the more so, as those years wore on, for the fact that courtly love, in essence adulterous and often of necessity chaste, was never meant to end in marriage; for the lady was already married, just as Elizabeth claimed to be married to her country. (And – usefully, as it would prove, for Robert and Elizabeth – the tradition allowed the man, in the end, to marry another lady of his own rank without its affecting his feeling for his more elevated mistress.)

Courtly love produced adoration unbounded but no heirs, sublimated ambition into desire unsatisfied . . . It gave respectability to the most lavish protestations of love made not just by Robert (who, after all, cherished real hopes) but even by Elizabeth's other courtiers. It meant that a man who spent his whole life publicly positioned in a posture of yearning for a woman he might never

---

* A centuries-long movement 'compared to which', C. S. Lewis wrote, 'the Renaissance is a mere ripple on the surface of literature'.

attain looked romantic – even heroic – rather than merely ridiculous. It gave licence, too, to Elizabeth's extreme delight in all the flattering games of flirtation: her eagerness to play and her reluctance to pay. Most writers of modern days have seen this lust for the simulacrum of love as a pathology, an expression of a miserably frustrated sexuality. But in terms of courtly love, it was something closer to artistry.

One song written to Eleanor, that earlier queen, neatly fits the romantic devotion Elizabeth demanded:

> Were all lands mine
> From Elbe to Rhine
> I'd count them little worth
> If England's Queen
> Would lie my arms between.

Robert Dudley would be the first and the greatest – but not the last – of those required to live his life according to this theory. You might say, what is more, that Robert's courtship, and that of her other suitors, would give point to the great mythology of Elizabeth's maidenhood. For, after all, if no-one assaults it, where is the virtue in virginity?

Writers in the courtly love tradition varied in their opinion as to whether the lover would or would not have full enjoyment of his mistress in the end, or whether the question should be left in decent obscurity. But one text at least lays down the rules precisely. In the late twelfth century Andreas Capellanus, author of the classic *De Arte Honeste Amandi* and chaplain to Eleanor of Aquitaine's daughter, wrote that *amor purus* 'goes so far as the kiss and the embrace and the modest contact with the nude lover, omitting the final solace, for that is not permitted to those who wish to love purely'. (Love being once constrained within these boundaries, he claimed that even a young unmarried woman should take a lover. Her husband, when she eventually marries, would understand that a woman who had followed 'the commands of love' showed more, rather than less, *probitas* than one who had not.) On a less elevated note, the satirist and playwright

Thomas Nashe wrote of a successful prostitute who takes her pleasure with a sex toy that 'will refresh me well / And never make my tender belly swell'. Some Elizabethans, at least, clearly understood sexual pleasure in a sense broader than the procreative act.

Some contemporaries certainly thought that Elizabeth was only technically a virgin.* After her death the playwright Ben Jonson claimed that 'she had a membrane on her, which made her incapable of man, though for her delight she tried many'. (He also claimed that when Elizabeth contemplated marriage with Alençon, a French surgeon 'took in hand to cut it, yet fear stayed her' – an image horribly evocative of female circumcision.) Jonson would hardly have been in a position to have inside information about the Queen's physique, but as a sometime Catholic he would have been in touch with all the scurrilous propaganda spread about her. He was not, however, alone in the basic assumption behind his slur.

Some of the contemporary observers suggested not only that Elizabeth was a virgin, but that there was something unnatural about the fact.† Soon after her accession the Spanish ambassador had reported that 'for a certain reason which [my spies] have recently given me, I believe she will not bear children' – a theory repeated by his successor, de Quadra (just before he also repeated the story that Elizabeth had borne several children illegitimately). The Venetian ambassador similarly reported that she was barren, a conclusion he had reached for reasons that 'I dare not write'. Envoys on the continent heard tales of her irregular menstruation

* Some modern historians, too, have surely hinted at that view. Milton Waldman, in the 1940s, elegantly suggested that Elizabeth and Robert exercised 'just enough continence to avoid the varied dangers of incontinence'. Elizabeth Jenkins wrote of 'a sexual relationship which stopped short only of the sexual act', and David Starkey suggests 'a Clintonesque formula' as one way of squaring the circle. Martin Hume, who just over a century ago wrote the classic *The Courtships of Queen Elizabeth*, was inclined to believe that Elizabeth's various relationships 'stopped short of actual immorality', but also hints that she was an exhibitionist in the most literal sense.

† In effect, while starting with a wildly different perspective from our own, they might be said to be voicing the twentieth-century, the Lytton Strachey theory. See Afterword.

– that (as the papal nuncio in France put it) 'she has hardly ever the purgation proper to all women'. Others heard that she had to be bled from the leg, or the foot, instead; and it is hard not to see this emphasis on Elizabeth's lack of the 'proper' womanly functions as an attack on her as an improper womanly ruler.

In the twentieth century, Michael Bloch gave a scientific gloss to this gossip by suggesting that Elizabeth (like the Duchess of Windsor, whose biographer he was) suffered from Androgen Insensitivity Syndrome: that is, that she was born with male chromosomes but, failing to produce also male hormones, developed outwardly as a woman. Such androgens, he claimed, are often handsome women – tall, long-limbed, with 'strident personalities' – but have no viable reproductive organs and, yes, only a shallow vagina. But it is notable that none of the prying ambassadors who questioned Elizabeth's doctors and ladies, nor even any of the laundresses who washed her bloodstained linen, ever actually concluded, in the end, that she was not a viable dynastic possibility. Even Philip of Spain, whatever tittle-tattle his envoys reported, went on negotiating for her as for a successful brood mare. A French diplomat in 1566 – rushing to Elizabeth's doctor in a fluster, having heard that the Queen herself believed she was barren – would be roundly told that the Queen was capable of bearing ten children, and claimed otherwise only out of caprice (or to give some rationale for a decision she herself could not otherwise explain?). In 1579, with Elizabeth entering the second half of her forties, William Cecil would institute enquiries with all the usual backstairs sources and expressed himself as wholly satisfied as to the 'probability of her aptness to bear children': that, in other words, she could if she would.

It was Elizabeth's will to marriage that was the real question; and never more so than in the months that followed the death of Amy Dudley. Whatever had passed between her and Robert, in her tortuous mind, as 1560 turned to 1561, the situation was still a flexible one. Nothing had been done that could not be undone. Or, from Robert's standpoint, everything was still to do.

Robert's aims at this point were simple. He had no conceivable reason – political or personal – not to desire marriage with

Elizabeth. She was the key to the attainment of every worldly goal. There is certainly no indication that he saw the scandal over Amy's death as putting that marriage outside his reach. He saw it as a passing threat, an obstacle he had triumphantly surmounted. And the fact that Elizabeth sometimes – though not always – behaved every bit as if their relationship were still in full romantic flame must have raised his hopes unbearably.

Elizabeth is less easy to gauge. She took the public reaction to Amy's death, at home and abroad, more seriously than he; understood that if she married him now, it would be widely assumed she had conspired with him to murder his wife. (And this would be murder for an ignoble, a wholly personal, motive. Perhaps few royal hands were wholly free of blood, but such a killing would confirm every suspicion about the frailty of her sex, the immorality of her religion.) The issue was not just whether Robert had been declared innocent of his wife's murder. The wildfire spread of the scandal had in itself shown the hostility such an alliance would provoke at home; the contempt it would draw down upon her internationally. The start of 1561 brought still more letters from Nicholas Throckmorton in France. On New Year's Eve he had sat down to pen to Cecil yet another lamentation on the dire consequences 'if her Majesty do so foully forget herself', when he was interrupted by the Spanish envoy who asked, as a piece of hot gossip, 'whether the Queen's Majesty was not secretly married to the Lord Robert, for, said he, I assure you this court is full of it'.

Cecil, in fact, shortly warned Throckmorton to leave matters alone. Attacking the Queen's favourite only made her defend him more protectively. Did it also attract her in some way? When her self-appointed guardians warned her off, the object of their warning acquired the savour of forbidden fruit. Robert was her rebellion.

But was that rebellion anything more than an empty gesture? The real question is how Elizabeth felt about the fact that, for the moment at least, she still could not marry Robert Dudley. The easiest and most common assumption is that she regretted the situation – that she, as much as he, was the victim of a kind of cosmic irony, the pair of them kept apart by the very event that should have set them free. But that assumes she did, still, truly want to marry Robert Dudley. We have come back to the question of whether she wanted to marry at all, on which historians never will agree.

In these dizzy months before Amy died, Elizabeth might indeed have been flattered, or rushed, or pressured into marrying Robert Dudley, had he only, at that vital moment, been blamelessly, unimpeachably, free. That much was evident to her horrified contemporaries. They objected to Robert, specifically, on the grounds that he brought no great alliance or foreign friends (had, indeed, many enemies among their own ranks); and that the elevation of one man so far above his fellows could not but shake the foundations of the small aristocratic society that governed England. They failed to realize that when Elizabeth's eyes were opened, it would not be to the personal unsatisfactoriness of Robert Dudley; it would be to the fact that, in the core of her being, she wanted to keep her own autonomy; to retain in her own hands the sovereignty which was at the core of her identity.

It is only hindsight that encourages us to ask whether marriage, for Elizabeth, was ever really an emotional possibility. With hindsight we see the many and varied nature of her excuses as having an almost unmistakable import. But at the time, in these early days, it can hardly have been obvious to her contemporaries. What must have been far more evident is that there were genuine problems with every choice.

Any marriage of a queen regnant offered an insuperable problem: whose would be the mastery? As John Aylmer had tried to argue in the first year of Elizabeth's reign, writing in answer to John Knox's *First Blast*: 'Say you, God hath appointed her to be the subject to her husband . . . therefore she may not be the head. I grant that, so far as pertaining to the bands of marriage, and the offices of a wife, she must be a subject: but as a Magistrate she may be her husband's head.' She could be his inferior in 'matters of wedlock', and yet his leader in 'the guiding of the commonwealth', he claimed. But such a distinction would be almost impossible to make, in practical terms.

More specifically, marriage to a foreign prince and marriage to a subject of her own carried each its penalty. It is easy for us to underestimate the difficulty Elizabeth would have perceived. We have the experience of those married queens regnant Elizabeth II and Victoria; of Queen Anne, even, whose breeding stallion of a husband nobody even remembers.* And at that, we are inclined to overlook the initial difficulty Victoria and Albert had in accommodating their different statuses; and the balance of power (so heavily weighted in his favour) between the joint sovereigns William and Mary. But sixteenth-century England offered no such even half-consoling stories.

If Elizabeth married a foreign prince, she risked the loss not only of her own independence, but of her country's autonomy. Edward VI's will (that disregarded but in one way prophetic document) put forward that possibility as one reason for cutting out his still-unmarried sisters: the 'stranger' husband of either would work to have the laws and customs of his own native country 'practised and put in use within this our realm . . . which would then tend to the utter subversion of the commonwealth of this our realm, which God forbid'. (Better the princesses should be 'taken by God' than that they should so imperil the true religion, thundered one of his bishops, supportively.) If Elizabeth married either a Habsburg or a Valois of France, she plumped England ('a bone between two dogs', as one of her own agents put it) irrevocably down on one side of the see-saw balance that dominated European politics. Although everyone agreed that in theory she should marry, to find one candidate who had the support of all her councillors would prove an impossibility.

The one immediate example, of Philip and Mary, was far from happy. Elizabeth would have only to remember how Mary's troops had gone over to Wyatt; how a mob of young Englishmen had marched on the Spanish at Hampton Court, so that the palace guards had to drive them away; how cartoons had shown Mary as a crone suckling Spaniards at her breast, below the

---

* He sired eighteen short-lived children on his royal wife, and yet who now recalls the unlucky Prince George, son to the King of Denmark?

legend *Maria Ruina Angliae*. She would have remembered not only her sister's personal unhappiness and humiliation, but that Philip (and his father) had patently entered into the marriage believing that – whatever lip service was paid to the authority of an anointed queen – it was he who would really rule; that England had been dragged into Spain's war and had lost Calais. Later, discussing the long-running proposal of the Habsburg archduke, 'With regard to the Emperor's remarks showing that he wishes the Archduke to be called King and to govern jointly with [the] Queen, Cecil thinks this would be difficult,' the envoy concerned wrote all too accurately.

If she married a subject, she had still to deal with contemporary belief that the dominance of a husband over a wife superseded the claims of her royalty; and with the diminution of Elizabeth's own royal status. Feria had boasted of having put it to Elizabeth that if she married a commoner, she would be setting her own value below that of her sister: he thought, he crowed, that he could get at her that way. 'Suppose I be of the baser degree, yet am I your husband and your head,' Darnley would tell his royal wife Mary Stuart. Such would be Elizabeth's dilemma if she married Robert Dudley. Moreover, the rise of this particular subject had been too far and too fast, and he had flaunted it too openly. He came from a family with enemies. Better, safer, to keep him as a favourite; as that mushroom, perennial figure of court stories, who could be enjoyed at will and then if need be put away.

But the question of the favourite itself comes loaded with a baggage of unease, and never more so than in the late sixteenth and seventeenth centuries. This has been called the 'great age' of the European favourite; perhaps because the whole question of power exercised by someone whose only claim to wield it came at second hand, via the personal favour of the ruler, focused an uncomfortable attention on the primary source itself, raising questions about personal rule and the powers and limits of monarchy.

The nature of the monarchy, and the limitations of its power, were hotly debated throughout this era. As one modern historian (Stephen Alford) writes, the 'Tudor polity of the second half of the sixteenth century was in a period of transition – from a royal estate, where the monarch was the kingdom, to "state", a polity conscious beyond the life of the king or queen'. And yet the Tudor age had seen the dynasty arrogate to itself and its central court more and more power and glory. Elizabeth herself believed that 'absolute princes ought not to be accountable for their actions to any other than to God alone'; had written in an early letter to her father of kings, 'whom philosophers regard as gods on earth'. Later in her reign she sent a sharp reproof to the Queen of Scots for having dared to write to her privy council rather than to herself. Although Elizabeth 'doth carry as great a regard unto her Council as any of her progenitors have done', yet 'they are but Counsellors by choice and not by birth, whose services are no longer to be used in that public function than it shall please her Majesty to dispose of same'. Everyone agreed that the worthies around the ruler should offer counsel. (They differed on whether those counsellors should be drawn from an aristocracy or a meritocracy.) Whether the ruler had to be bound by that counsel . . . That was less easy.

In this climate there would be a sharp focus of attention on, and equally sharp critical debate about, any person upon whom the ruler's favour lighted; especially one who could promote his ideas, his counsel, with all the power of personality; and especially one who, like Robert Dudley (and to his detractors, this just made it all the worse), showed no signs of being prepared simply to sit back and passively enjoy what the Queen gave him; to soak up the honours and spend the moneys. He did both of those things, certainly – but he also expected, as soon as opportunity offered (and it soon would), to play an active, practical, daily part in the running of the country. He believed in the ideal of the king/queen counselled; was, after all the son of a man who is now credited with having done much to elevate the power of the privy council, and the grandson of one who had written a book on commonwealth and morality.* The translation of the

---

* *The Tree of Commonwealth*, the political allegory he wrote in the Tower, reveals a good deal about Edmund Dudley's attitudes: a guilt that he had been tempted too far in the King's (and his own) interests; a concern that he had collaborated in the King's use of fiscal penalties to clip the wings of the nobility.

tellingly named *A very brief and profitable Treatise declaring how many counsels and what manner of counsellers a Prince that will govern well ought to have* was published under Robert's patronage. (And Thomas Elyot's influential *Book Named the Governor*, laying down the training that would enable a nobleman to act as the ruler's watchful adviser and ally, had described the ruler's 'friends' as his 'eyes and ears and hands and feet'. Her 'Eyes' would of course be the nickname Elizabeth gave to Robert Dudley.)

The question of the favourite was never more controversial than when the ruler was a woman and the favourite a man. Not only was an illegitimate sexual frisson added into the mix, but the accepted balance of power between the sexes seemed more than ever in jeopardy. A male ruler might have, on the one hand, his mistresses for personal recreation, and on the other his minister-favourites – men such as Richelieu or Wolsey. (Philip II in Spain used his childhood friend Ruy Gomez as effectively a mediator between his secretariat and his nobility.) But the two functions were treated as separate. There should not be this confusion, that strained the bounds of safety and decency.

Of course, the worst had often happened; and when a royal mistress got too much power or patronage, or when a king with homosexual leanings gave power into the hands of a male love object, it did indeed outrage the country. There were (even before Elizabeth's successor, James, gave far too much power to pretty George Villiers) well-remembered medieval models that provided the context for the fears of Robert Dudley. Edward II had sinned most conspicuously. After Elizabeth's death, Naunton would praise her not only for having given her favourites only limited power, but for having purposely kept several on the go; 'for we find no Gaveston, Vere, or Spencer to have swayed alone during forty-four years'. After his adored Piers Gaveston was murdered by his outraged nobles, Edward II had fallen under the sway of Hugh le Despenser, one of the most powerful magnates, and of his son. The Despensers were in turn brought down by Mortimer, another mighty subject, in alliance with Isabella, Edward's rejected queen; while Robert de Vere was the hated counsellor (some said lover) of Edward II's grandson Richard II. Just the one scurrilous pamphlet, *Leicester's Commonwealth*, would in time compare Robert Dudley with Mortimer (who, when Isabella came to rule for her young son, exercised almost total power behind the scenes); but by and large those who knew Elizabeth in her maturity, or who looked back with hindsight, tended to agree with Naunton. 'I conclude that she [Elizabeth] was absolute and sovereign mistress of her grace and that those to whom she distributed her favors were never more than tenants at will and stood on no better ground than her princely pleasure and their own good behaviour,' Naunton wrote.

In the early seventeenth century, too, Fulke Greville, comparing Elizabeth approvingly if tacitly with her susceptible successor, wrote that, 'in the latitudes which some modern princes allow to their favourites, it seems this queen reservedly kept entrenched within her native strengths and sceptre'. But Greville, like Naunton, was writing with the benefit of hindsight, having seen Elizabeth destroy her last favourite, Essex, when he grew too high. At this earlier date, no-one yet knew Elizabeth's strength. They were afraid she might let Robert Dudley exercise unlimited sway.

In fact, the striking thing would prove to be the versatility – and perhaps the callousness – with which Elizabeth made use of him. A favourite could be a useful and malleable tool; especially in this age, when the distribution of patronage was being increasingly centred on the court (away from the church, away from the regions and the nobility), where the clamour for office, territory, money was deafening.* The function of the favourite as scapegoat was known even in the figure's heyday. When James I's favourite George Villiers, the Duke of Buckingham, was assassinated in 1628, 'it is said at court there is none now to impute our faults unto'. Remember the Imperial ambassador, wondering that no-one had yet assassinated Robert Dudley? Less dramatically, it was noted in Elizabeth, her contemporary John Clapham wrote, 'that she seldom or never denied any suit that was moved unto her . . . but the suitor received the answer of denial by some other; a

---

* The most plausible explanation of the rise of the favourite in the late sixteenth and early seventeenth centuries, writes Ronald G. Asch, lies in his position 'as the ruler's patronage manager – often his original and most important duty'.

thankless office, and commonly performed by persons of greatest place, who ofttimes bear the blame of many things wherein themselves are not guilty, while no imputation must be laid upon the prince'. This did not make the favourite popular, needless to say – especially in so far as he was often brought in from outside the ranks of (and even used as a curb upon) the standing interests of the old nobility.

There were times when it seemed Elizabeth was using Robert Dudley as a stalking horse; flaunting her interest in him the better to conceal what her real intentions might be. There were times when he seemed to be more like her whipping boy. Her brother Edward, in the schoolroom, would have had a real 'whipping boy', to take the stripes protocol forbade a common schoolmaster placing on the royal posterior. Elizabeth's stripes, in the fragile early moments of the regime, were the lashes of bad publicity. But she too needed an alter ego. Just so had Anne Boleyn known she was blamed for decisions in fact taken by Henry.

It is interesting to compare the situation of Elizabeth *vis-à-vis* Robert Dudley with that of other women rulers and their favourites* – all the more so since the opprobrium heaped on one favourite could be used to reflect on others. When the scandal pamphlet of 1584, *Leicester's Commonwealth*, was reprinted in 1706 as the *Secret Memoirs of Robert Dudley*, it was meant as an attack on the Duke of Marlborough, famous or infamous as the 'single minister' of Queen Anne's day. Anne's prime favourite was, of course, less Marlborough himself than Marlborough's wife, Sarah Churchill, with whom Anne exchanged the most striking series of letters (in the awareness, apparently, that this relationship too could be taken to have a sexual element). Sarah took on the identity of 'Mrs Freeman', Anne (still a princess, when their friendship began) that of 'Mrs Morley'. Mrs Morley would write to Mrs Freeman, in tears, that 'tis no trouble to me to obey your commands'; or 'Let me beg you once more not to believe that I

---

* Or, for that matter, with the choices that confront the woman head of a Fortune 500 company. Do you marry a man of comparable status – and then spend every day of your life battling the assumptions that he will take priority? Or do you choose a consort of dramatically lower status – in effect, a boy toy?

am in fault, though I must confess you may have some reason to believe it'; that 'if you should ever forsake me, I would have nothing more to do with the world, but make another abdication, for what is a crown when ye support of it is gone'. One cannot imagine Elizabeth writing to Robert in such self-abasing terms.

But then – Sarah said – Anne 'would not take the air unless somebody advised her to it'. She is blamed for that very over-confidence in Anne's pliability; since their bitter falling-out came when she failed to realize the difference Anne's accession to the throne had made in their rapport: blamed by contemporaries for exercising too much power; blamed by Marlborough's biographers for not having been content to exercise it only in a private, domestic way. Had she been so content – the theory runs – Sarah might have kept influence longer, to the advantage of her husband and his political party. This ignores the fact that her husband's beliefs were not always altogether hers – and again, it raises the more general concern about the bounds within which a favourite can operate appropriately. Though Sarah was once in a position of emotional dominance over Anne that Robert never had over Elizabeth, her gender ultimately made it easier to side-line her.*

But move further into the eighteenth century and set Elizabeth and Robert side by side with Catherine the Great of Russia and Grigory Potemkin, and both the similarities and the divergences are extraordinary. A minor German princess married off to the Russian heir, Catherine was a woman who took the throne by coup; and this background of insecurity might have been expected

---

* Sweden's Queen Christina in the seventeenth century might seem an even better comparison. She certainly had her favourites – a French doctor/ adventurer, to whom she gave unpopular licence; her cousin; and two men, a powerful minister and, later in her life, an Italian cardinal, with both of whom rumour linked her, scandalously. But all Christina's relationships and decisions must be seen as those of a woman who, far from being determined to keep power, was determined to throw it away; to abdicate in favour of that cousin she had always favoured. By the same token, the widowed Queen Victoria had her John Brown, and her Munshi. But in fact – although gossip sneered at the Queen as 'Mrs Brown' – their status as servants was so far removed from hers as not to have allowed them political influence, even had real political power still lain with the monarchy.

to produce the same edgy, in many ways exploitative, relationship with her favourite that Elizabeth and Robert 'enjoyed'. Instead, Catherine and Potemkin appear in many ways to have had the pleasures without the penalties. ('General love me? Me loves General a lot,' she would write to him tenderly.) They were physical lovers; but then, her sexuality or the absence of it was never invoked as totem of her right to rule, and the question of the succession had already been settled by the birth of a son (albeit fathered by an earlier lover, rather than by her husband). Potemkin too showed no signs of wishing to go off and found his own dynasty – but then, he could hardly have done so, since it seems likely that, early in their relationship, he and Catherine had gone through some form of secret marriage ceremony. His ambition seems to have been satisfied by huge power and military success – but, as the years wore on, he admitted that he found relief in those distant reaches of the empire where he ruled like a monarch, effectively, and where Catherine allowed him to do so. They had more space to share between them, since Russia was a very much larger territory than England. Potemkin seems to have displayed few signs of sexual jealousy, selecting and training for Catherine younger lovers, who were required to address him as 'Papa', and whose existence gave him a measure of freedom without challenging him in any way.

And yet, and yet ... as you read the story of Potemkin and Catherine, you are struck by a thousand tiny echoes of the earlier pair: right down to the nicknames, to the increased religiosity as Potemkin grew older, to the belief that they were predestined to each other ('God nominated you to be my friend before I was even born,' Catherine told Potemkin) – and, inevitably, to the blame of him as an 'evil counsellor', though that is something both Potemkin and Leicester shared with every favourite through the centuries.

Where, then, did the magic difference lie? For there is a huge difference between the places Potemkin and Leicester hold in history. In Potemkin's far greater abilities, in his hold on the military power base that first brought him to Catherine's attention? Probably. In the different sexual attitudes – and the very different social and political systems – of the mid-eighteenth and mid-sixteenth centuries? Certainly. In the very flexibility of the Russian succession and monarchy, and the accepted tradition of empresses' favourites/empresses' lovers that was already in existence before Catherine's day? No doubt. But above all it must – must! – lie in the personalities of the two different rulers. Leicester could never have been a Potemkin, because Elizabeth didn't want him to be.

Elizabeth herself provided, over the years, a cloud of rhetoric to cloak her lasting reluctance to marry. 'I have already joined my self in marriage to an husband, namely the kingdom of England,' she had said when, in the first spring of the reign, Parliament had urged her to wed. More significantly, she said – even thus early, long before one might have expected her to be paranoid about a 'rising sun' – that children, if she had them, might 'grow out of kind, and become perhaps ungracious'. Only two years later, in 1561, she told the Scottish ambassador that 'Princes cannot like their children, those that should succeed unto them' – a chilling enough remark. She suspected that a male heir might usurp her throne. Perhaps her suspicion was a symptom of that throne's insecurity – but remembering the terms of her brother's scheme, whereby all the Brandon/Grey heiresses were to defer to their own 'heirs male', her fear was not such an unreasonable one.

But it is also a truism that *nothing* in Elizabeth's youthful experience could have taught her to view marriage without a shrinking of the flesh. None of Henry's wives failed to suffer from marriage; even Katherine Parr, who survived Henry, then suffered from another husband's roving eye, and from female biology. Camden wrote that Robert Huicke, one of Elizabeth's doctors, dissuaded her from marriage 'for I know not what womanish Impotency'. Any suggestion that she might not find childbirth easy could only be horrifying, for a woman two of whose stepmothers, as well as her grandmother, had died that way.* There had been her sister Mary, in political and emotional thrall to a husband who did not

---

* Her kinsman the Duke of Norfolk had lost three wives to childbirth before the first decade of her reign was out.

care for her; Jane Grey, married off to a boy for whom she did not care. There had been the women who had formed her circle at Hatfield, who had had in common a disastrous marital history: the Marchioness of Northampton, second wife to a divorced man, left in legal limbo when the Catholic Mary came to the throne and refused to recognize the divorce; the Countess of Sussex, who had entered Elizabeth's service after her husband had divorced her for extreme religious views, and for the practice of sorcery.

Elizabeth would later tell the Earl of Sussex that she hated the idea of marriage more each day, 'for reasons which she would not divulge to a twin soul, if she had one, much less to a living creature'. Is it just our prurience to envisage the 'reasons' physically? At the end of Elizabeth's life her godson, Sir John Harington, wrote of her that 'In mind, she hath ever had an aversion and (as many think) in body some indisposition to the act of marriage.' But by then, the mood of the times – the advent of a fertile new ruling family – dictated a need to puncture the mystique of her elective virginity.

When she tried to make up her mind to marriage, 'it is as though her heart were being torn out of her body', the French ambassador once reported her telling him, unforgettably. (She added that if ever she did take a husband, she would use his 'services' to procure an heir, but give him 'neither a share of her power nor the keys of her treasury'.) Pending medical evidence that is never likely to appear, it is to reasons psychological and political, rather than to physiology, that we should first look for Elizabeth's decision not to marry and, after the experiences of her youth, to retain control in this most personal of ways. But even the word 'decision' makes it sound too fixed and too conscious. Elizabeth's failure to marry (itself an even more loaded way of putting it!), and her courtiers' realization that this was not going to change, happened not in one giant stride but in a hundred tiny stages.

In the end, surely, the best proof that she did not really want to marry Robert Dudley was that she never did. True, the scandal of Amy Dudley's death would have made their marriage impossibly dangerous in the short term – but five, ten, fifteen years down the line? Does any scandal retain its white heat indefinitely? In the years that followed Amy's death, the 1560s, various ambassadors tried to recruit Robert to their countries' causes, and then to thrust him into a marital bed with the Queen. They at least clearly thought that after the first fuss had died down, a marriage would still be politically viable. And they should know, surely. As she herself would tell the Spanish ambassador in a few years' time: 'They said of me that I would not marry because I was in love with the Earl of Leicester, and that I could not marry him because he had a wife already; yet now he has no wife, and for all that I do not marry him.'

Again, we have here the advantage over Elizabeth's contemporaries. We know that Elizabeth chose never to marry – never to marry anybody. We know that she never bowed to what everyone assumed were the proclivities of her sex, determined not to throw her own rule away. But none of that was apparent to her courtiers, as a new year dawned after the end of 1560. They assumed, still, that she had to marry somebody. They could only hope it would not be Robert Dudley.

8

'Not yet towards a marriage'
1561–1565

IT SEEMED, IN THESE FIRST YEARS OF ELIZABETH'S REIGN, AS IF EVERY-
one was pressing her to marry. (Everyone, that is, who did not
believe her secretly married already.) Leaf through the *Calendars
of State Papers*, studying the reactions to her relationship with
Robert Dudley, and you find also a subsidiary story. Just a few
days in December 1560 produce several epistles all harping on the
same theme: the implications of the marriage of a queen regnant.
Elizabeth's own ambassador in Spain was writing to her of 'the
opinion in the Spanish Court about her marriage'. (True, she had
politely asked for Philip's own advice, but it seems Philip's
courtiers were also getting in on the act.) The Lords of Scotland
were writing to the English privy council also regretting that
Elizabeth 'is not yet towards a marriage' and again offering their
own Earl of Arran 'for the preservation of the whole isle'. And
Throckmorton (whose own outspoken Protestantism was becoming a threat to his diplomacy) was writing to the council – not, for
once, directly about Elizabeth's own actions, but about the newly
widowed Mary, Queen of Scots, whose husband Francis had
lasted a bare eighteen months on France's throne.

The question of Mary's remarriage immediately sprang to
Europe's mind – a marriage, for England, of import second only
to Elizabeth's own. Mary, Throckmorton wrote admiringly, 'more

esteemeth the continuation of her honor, and to marry one that may uphold her to be great, than she passeth to please her fancy by taking one that is accompanied by such small benefit or alliance as thereby her estimation and fame is not increased'. Compare and contrast, obviously. And yet, there was another lesson to be had from what the ambassadors wrote of Mary. As Throckmorton put it a few weeks later: 'During her husband's life there was no great account made of her, for that, being under band of marriage and subjection to her husband (who carried the burden of care of all her matters) there was offered no great occasion to know what was in her.' And this was the noose into which even her closest advisers wanted Elizabeth – the proud, the poised, the dazzlingly clever – to run her head? Small wonder that, as Throckmorton's secretary had reported to him: the Queen 'uses all means not to marry; the Council does the contrary'.

She must have felt both nagged and beleaguered. And in response to all that paternalistic pressure, it is not surprising if, in the time ahead, in the intervals of the most subtle diplomacy, she allowed herself occasionally to behave brattishly; childishly, almost, you might say. Not that the two aspects of her behaviour – the poise and the petulance, the assurance and the adolescence – were in fact even as divorced as two sides of the same coin. They were both aspects at once of her nature and of her technique. Elizabeth's greatest strength, as a female ruler in a male world, was that she managed the qualities of her defects so peerlessly.

These first years of the 1560s would see several of the more puzzling episodes in Robert's and Elizabeth's common history. The first arguably shows Elizabeth taking the widespread belief that Robert held sway over her and, inventively, using it to her advantage. Two of them at least may in the end show her treating him with calculated caprice – calculated for its effect on him, yes, but on others too maybe. Only when the chips were really down would the depth of her underlying affection show clearly.

Early in 1561 (when Cecil could write in confidence to Throckmorton: 'I know surely that my Lord Robert hath more fear than hope, and so doth the Queen give him cause') the Spanish ambassador was taken aback to be approached by

Robert's brother-in-law, Sir Henry Sidney, 'a high-spirited noble sort of person'. Sir Henry's message for King Philip was this:

> The marriage was now in everybody's mouth, he said; and the Queen, I must be aware, was very anxious for it. He was surprised I had not advised your Majesty to use the opportunity to gain Lord Robert's good will. Your Majesty would find Lord Robert as ready to obey you and do you service as one of your own vassals ... The Queen and Lord Robert were lovers, but they intended honest marriage, and nothing wrong had taken place between them which could not be set right with your Majesty's help. As to Lady Dudley's death, he said that he had examined carefully into the circumstances, and he was satisfied that it had been accidental, although he admitted that others thought differently ... He allowed that there was hardly a person who did not believe that there had been foul play. The preachers in their pulpits spoke of it, not sparing even the honour of the Queen, and this, he said, had brought her to consider whether she could not restore order in the realm in these matters of religion. She was anxious to do it, and Lord Robert to his own knowledge would be anxious to assist.

It sounds as if Robert, so often hailed as champion of the new faith, were offering to help return England to the old in return for Philip's support for the marriage. This has often been seen as proof of his venal cynicism – proof that he was a turncoat, like his father. But in fact Robert was far from the only English player in the affair. De Quadra prudently insisted on getting this extraordinary offer from a better authority than Sidney. In February he had an interview with Robert himself – followed by one with the Queen. Elizabeth, as ever, refused to speak out directly: 'she replied after much circumlocution that she would make me her ghostly father' – de Quadra was in orders – 'and I should hear her confession. It came to this, that she was no angel. She could not deny that she had a strong regard for the many excellent qualities which she saw in Lord Robert. She had not indeed resolved to marry either him or anyone; only every day she felt more and more the want of a husband ...' But the ambassador believed it was at least possible she too might be prepared to return to the Catholic faith – although it was also possible, he advised Philip, 'that she may be playing a game to keep in favour with your Majesty, and to deceive her Catholic subjects with hopes which she has no intention of fulfilling'.

There was, after all, good reason to hold out an olive branch to Spain at this time. Towards the end of 1560 the Council of Trent, herald of the Counter-Reformation movement, presented the threatening possibility that all Catholic Europe would at last ally against heretics. The sudden re-entry of Mary, Queen of Scots onto the marriage market only made the threat more acute. Early in 1561 Elizabeth had indeed every reason to show herself amenable to the possibility of a Spanish-backed marriage – but it would hardly be politic to do so too openly.

But there is another twist to the story. In March Cecil entered the fray, saying that Elizabeth wanted de Quadra to have King Philip write a letter supporting the marriage. This, he said, the Queen could show to Parliament and thereby gain their approval. But Parliament, of course, was highly unlikely to respond with approval to any such piece of Spanish interference. Cecil knew it; de Quadra knew it; and Elizabeth would certainly have known it too. The next month, April, all pretence of the Spanish sponsoring Robert to a matrimonial crown was at an end, when Cecil saw to it that de Quadra was accused (almost certainly without reason) of involvement in a Catholic conspiracy against the Queen. Word that Philip had promised to support the Dudley marriage, if Elizabeth would restore the Pope's supremacy, was used to whip up an anti-Spanish frenzy. Of course, it also whipped up a good deal of anti-Dudley feeling . . . It is possible that Cecil, once again, was manipulating events to ensure Robert's continued unpopularity. But it is also possible that Elizabeth herself had indeed all along been using Robert as a mouthpiece – whether or not what she said was sincerely meant.

There is no need to make Robert out as wholly the injured innocent here. He could, at this stage of his career, be *politique*, of course he could, and throughout the early 1560s he went on offering himself as Spain's advocate and as Elizabeth's potentially

Catholic consort, though the ambassadors approached did occasionally express doubts about his sincerity. Even decades ahead, after the Armada, English statesmen (Cecil's son among them) could be found calmly accepting Spanish pensions; and Robert's youthful experience would have encouraged him to regard Spain as a viable ally. But all the same, one might also wonder just how callously were Cecil and the Queen using Robert Dudley?

Certainly Robert's already battered reputation was further damaged by the affair. One report claims he asked Elizabeth, if she would not marry him, to allow him to move abroad, and serve as captain in the Spanish army. To this, of course, she was never likely to agree. That summer she was treating him even more warmly. Summer was always a time of fun and fantasy in their courtship, when Elizabeth might slip out with her ladies, all disguised, to watch Robert shooting in Windsor park; or when de Quadra, sharing a boat with the Queen and Robert to watch a water pageant on the Thames, was a little disgusted to find them talking 'nonsense' about marriage again. 'Lord Robert at last said as I was on the spot there was no reason they should not be married if the Queen pleased. She said that perhaps I did not understand sufficient English. I let them trifle in this way for a time . . .'

She was offering Robert alternately the carrot and the stick. In June she refused, again, to grant him a peerage; but she gave him rooms next to her own in all the palaces; a licence to export eighty thousand undressed cloths, to be followed by an annual pension of £1,000; and rights over the customs duties on imports of sweet wines, silks and velvets, oil and currants. The first alone brought him £2,500 a year; Robert was – not altogether to his credit – a leader in the unwelcome new practice that allowed a courtier to cream off a layer of profits from an industry. Among the lands she was to give him was the lordship of Denbigh in North Wales, hitherto kept within the royal family. In 1563 she would give him Kenilworth Castle in Warwickshire, representing not only – since Kenilworth had once briefly belonged to his father – a significant gift, but also recognition of his family's influence across a broad swathe of the West Midlands. At the end of the year Elizabeth restored Robert's elder brother Ambrose to the earldom of Warwick, which their father had held, with the mighty fortress of Warwick Castle, close to Kenilworth, and large land holdings. Soon Robert had estates in more than twenty counties; and he would develop and exploit them, not necessarily with the rapacity of which he has been accused, but with the fixed intent of restoring the territorial status of the Dudleys.

At the end of the year, too, Robert was admitted to membership of the Inner Temple in London's law courts, having supported its cause in a land dispute. Effectively he became patron of this exclusive association of professional men, and with them celebrated in legendary style the festive revels that ended 1561. A procession of a hundred gentlemen – noblemen and councillors among them – rode through the streets in gorgeous disguises, under the leadership of a lord of misrule, that old festive figure reinvented by John Dudley to cheer Edward VI's last Christmas. In his guiser's identity of Prince Pallaphilos, it was Robert who received the homage of his supposed army, the 'Knights of the Order of Pegasus'; he who was served with such 'tender meats, sweet fruits and dainty delicates' that the world wondered at it, while trumpets signalled his every course, as they did Claudius' carouse in *Hamlet*. The masque staged on this occasion was an allegory of Perseus (who but Robert?) ridding England of the many-headed monster; the play performed was *Gorboduc*, the tragedy of a king who died without heir. The message was clear . . . it was a rehearsal perhaps; a fantasy parade of kingship, certainly.

For a moment, in the summer of 1562, it looked as though fantasy might have become fact. Rumours were rife that Elizabeth had actually married Robert secretly, at Baynard's Castle, home to the Earl of Pembroke, a friend of his. Elizabeth teasingly told de Quadra that her ladies had been asking whether they should now kiss Robert's hand. One can only imagine the parade of unconsciousness, the mixture of tension and delighted hope, with which Robert himself must have greeted such stories. Perhaps they made him incautious in his optimism; weeks later, the

Swedish diplomat Robert Keyle was reporting the Queen as telling him 'in the Chamber of Presence (all the nobility being there) that she would never marry him, nor none so mean as he'. All this with 'a great rage and great checks and taunts'; a dreadful humiliation.

It was only a few months earlier that Elizabeth, speaking to the Duke of Saxony's ambassador, had made her famous explanation of the mutual fidelity that persisted between her and Robert. She

> was more attached to him than any of the others because when she was deserted by everybody in the reign of her sister not only did he never lessen in any degree his kindness and humble attention to her, but he even sold his possessions that he might assist her with money, and therefore she thought it just that she should make some return for his good faith and constancy.

Perhaps it was this sense of a long exchange of loyalties between them, of shared experiences, that in her mind lent a kind of legitimacy to their relationship. That would explain what happened next – something that made her games with him, her mixture of slaps and strokes, seem as frivolous a game as the Prince Pallaphilos parody of royalty.

There was neither feint nor fantasy about what happened in the autumn of 1562: Elizabeth caught smallpox, and caught it badly. The sickness that year was in especially virulent form, and Elizabeth's treatment for the first symptoms – a bath, followed by a chilly walk outdoors – drove up her fever. Dismissing her German physician Dr Burcot, who dared name to her the dread disease, she simply took to her bed and waited. Within a week she had lapsed into a semi-conscious state. As she herself put it later: 'Death possessed every joint of me.'

To her councillors, to her courtiers, to Robert Dudley, it seemed indeed as if she would die, and that shortly. To whatever personal agonies Robert felt must have been added the sharpest awareness of his own danger. His position depended upon her absolutely. Without her, he might find himself at the mercy of his many enemies. But to a lesser degree, his uncertainty was shared by the whole country. If Elizabeth did die, who would succeed her? One possibility was the Earl of Huntingdon, husband to Robert's sister Katherine, with his strongly Protestant sympathies. But though some of the council might have supported him, the earl himself had stood so aloof from politics, had so played down his Plantagenet blood, that even the jealous Elizabeth was always content to let him be, confining herself to the occasional 'privy nip' to squash the faintest hint of pretensions. Others (as de Quadra reported) spoke up for Lady Katherine Grey, younger sister to Lady Jane, currently in prison for having married and borne a son without Elizabeth's authority. Others wanted Parliament and the legal authorities to decide . . . No-one was fool enough to speak for the Catholic Queen of Scots, or at least not openly, for that was the most dangerous of all possible options; a recipe for strife, uncertainty, even civil war.

In this nightmare situation, with the court on the verge of ordering their mourning clothes, Dr Burcot was forced back into the bedroom of the unconscious Queen. The treatment he ordered was that she should be wrapped in red flannel and laid beside the fire, and given a potion of his own. Within two hours she was able to speak; and the words de Quadra reported were extra-ordinary. With the councillors gathered round her bed, with the Queen herself making no pretence that her situation was not still desperately dangerous, she demanded that in the event of her death they appoint Lord Robert Dudley, with a staggering annual salary of £20,000, Lord Protector of the country.

She was in no fit state to be argued with. The councillors promised everything that was asked – but, de Quadra added, it would not be fulfilled. He could say so with some certainty. What Elizabeth demanded was frankly ludicrous; a sick woman's fantasy. Not only was Robert at this stage not even a privy councillor (the power he wielded was considerable, but informal); a protectorship was no answer to the long-term question of who would head the government. Somerset had been Lord Protector for his nephew Edward, but that had been intended as a temporary measure, until a minor came of age. The real significance of Elizabeth's request lies elsewhere. It shows how much, in her moment of extremity, Elizabeth actually cared for Robert, how desperate she was to ensure his safety. It shows that she not only trusted, but respected him; that to her at least, when push came to shove he was no mere lapdog.*

The question was never put to the test. On Elizabeth's famously elegant hands appeared the pustules that showed the pox was moving into its less dangerous, though potentially disfiguring, phase. Elizabeth recovered rapidly. There was not too much permanent damage to her looks – and while her face *was* scarred, so the Spanish ambassador heard, only Robert of all the court had access to her. The real victim was Robert's sister, Lady Mary Sidney, who caught the disease herself through nursing her mistress, and was so lastingly scarred that she retired from court. Her husband was abroad at the time, and, having left his wife, as he put it 'a full, fair lady, in mine eyes at least the fairest', returned to find her 'as foul a lady as the smallpox could make her'. He voiced no regrets about the price of waiting on 'Her Majesty's most precious person' – and Elizabeth remained fond of her friend and attendant. But it seems a harsh payment for loyalty.

Shortly after her recovery Elizabeth did at last make Robert a member of the privy council. It looks rather suspiciously co-incidental that not long after this, the question of the Queen's marriage was once more on the council's table. But in fact, that can hardly have needed Robert's intervention. The smallpox, along with the return of the widowed and available Queen Mary to Scotland, had put the succession right at the top of the agenda; not that it had ever gone away. Scotland's ambassador had long been pressing Elizabeth to recognize Mary as her heir. (The point was, more or less tacitly, tied to the terms of that 1560 peace

---

* According to the Spanish ambassador (writing over a week after the crisis, by which time the rumour mill would have got busy), Elizabeth also insisted that 'a groom of the Chamber, called Tamworth, who sleeps in Lord Robert's room', should be given a pension of £500 a year. It has been taken for hush money. But John Tamworth – if this was he, or even a scion of the same family – while indeed a Dudley associate, was the Keeper of the Privy Purse and a man of status, rather than Robert's all-knowing body servant, as has sometimes been inferred, and Elizabeth had sworn to her innocence on the threshold of what she believed might be her own judgement day.

treaty of Edinburgh that Cecil had negotiated, but Mary had been reluctant to ratify.) Elizabeth resisted, pleading the stipulation of her father's will and Act of Succession, but adding more honestly: 'If it became certainly known in the world who should succeed me, I would never think myself in sufficient security.' There were many eager to press an heir towards the throne itself, as she had found in her sister's day. 'Think you that I could love my winding sheet?' she demanded rhetorically.

But the Parliament that met in January 1563 was determined Elizabeth should marry. Robert himself was behind some of the more vehement voices, like that of the Dean of St Paul's, who asked her bluntly, if her parents had been of like mind, where would she have been? Both Houses united in sending petitions urging on Elizabeth the delight of beholding 'an imp of your own'; the comfort to the kingdom, the discomfiture of her adversaries. The Commons refrained from discussing who the father of the imp might be. 'Whomsoever it be that your Majesty shall choose, we protest and promise with all humility and reverence to honor, love, and serve as to our most bounden duty shall appertain.' The Lords went further; and here perhaps Robert may have been at work. They urged her against Mary's claim, since as 'mere, natural Englishmen' they did not wish to be subject to a foreign prince. And they urged her to marry 'where it shall please you, to whom it shall please you, and as soon as it shall please you'. Whatever cocktail of desperation and determination had brought them finally to this point, it was an endorsement for Robert Dudley.

If Elizabeth truly wanted – still – to marry Robert Dudley, now was the moment, surely. But we are forced to wonder whether, instead, she saw this permission as a threat rather than an opportunity. When they pressed her to marry other men, she would flaunt her affection for him. When instead they indicated, through gritted teeth, that even Robert Dudley might be better than no-one, then, instead of announcing the wedding ceremony, she put the whole question away, fobbing Parliament off with one of her expert 'answers answerless'. Though she thought celibacy best for a private woman, 'yet do I strive with myself to think it not meet for a prince. And if I can bend my liking to your need, I will not resist such a mind . . .' And then Elizabeth did something far more extraordinary. She offered her own beloved Robert as a husband for the Scots queen, Mary.

When, in the spring of 1563, Elizabeth first suggested the idea to the Scottish ambassador, William Maitland of Lethington, he tried to pass it off as a joke. Yes, Lord Robert might – possibly – be a man in whom, as Elizabeth put it, 'nature had implanted so many graces that, if she wished to marry, she would prefer him to all the princes in the world'. But he was also damaged goods in several different ways. Mary, said Maitland, would never wish to deprive her sister queen of all the 'joy and solace' she had from Robert's company; and he asked, rather maliciously: Why did she not marry Robert herself, so that she could later bequeath both her husband and her kingdom to Mary? For 'that way, Lord Robert could hardly fail to have children by one or other of them'. It was a suggestion Elizabeth, with her sensitivities about death and inheritance, might easily have taken badly.

Cecil supported the plan with enthusiasm. Besides ensuring a friendly Protestant Scotland, it would be a great way to get rid of Robert Dudley. He wrote to Maitland with unconvincing warmth that Lord Robert was 'a nobleman of birth, void of all evil conditions that sometimes are heritable to princes, and in goodness of nature and richness of good gifts comparable to any prince born . . . He is also dearly and singularly esteemed of the Queen's Majesty.' Cecil had crossed out 'beloved' of the Queen's Majesty, but that of course was the rub; that, and the fact Robert was still not even a peer, let alone a prince. Maitland, when he returned to Scotland, dared not even pass on Elizabeth's proposal to Mary. But he had told the Spanish ambassador, who told the rest of Europe, who laughed heartily. (When de Quadra was among the many who died of the plague in England that summer, there were probably some who thought fate had dealt appropriately.)

Was Elizabeth genuinely trying to settle the vexed succession question by placing her own Protestant candidate beside Mary on the Scottish throne, preparatory to declaring them her heirs? In favour of this interpretation is the fact that, as an alternative to

Robert, she also offered Ambrose Dudley. 'Would to God the Earl of Warwick was as charming as his brother – we might then each have had our own.' (Not that Ambrose was 'ill-looking or ungraceful, but he is rough, and lacks the sweet delicacy of Robert [though] he is brave enough and noble enough to deserve the hand of a princess'. The romantic emphasis always placed upon Robert has rather obscured the memory of Ambrose Dudley. But 'the good earl' – as posterity knows him – had also grown up around the Tudor palaces; had shared that formative time in the Tower.)

Was Elizabeth trying to steer Mary away from a choice more dangerous to English security? Was she even, conceivably, with this frankly rather insulting offer, making a subtle mock of Mary – trying to needle the Scots queen into making a foolish choice, one that would threaten Scottish stability? (In which case, as events would prove, she succeeded spectacularly.)

To this day it is unclear what she was trying to achieve. Did she think Mary would find Robert as irresistible as she did? Was she really prepared to relinquish him, or did she never really mean for Robert to move north? Perhaps not: she actually suggested that she, Robert and Mary should live all at the English court (admittedly more important and more agreeable than the Scottish one) as an extended royal 'family', a virtual *ménage à trois*. There was always that strange near-flirtation, the thought – voiced by Throckmorton in a letter to Robert – that if only Mary and Elizabeth could marry . . .

Was Elizabeth trying to make amends to Robert for her own rejection by giving him another queen to marry? Or was she, in the end, indulging herself? Not 'simply' indulging herself, for Elizabeth did nothing simply. But was she permitting herself a gesture – insulting, incalculable – that would silence and baffle all those men who had so patronizingly urged and arranged for her to marry? One that, as a bonus, a personal *bonne bouche*, would offer a smiling snub to the queen with whom – especially now they were competitors on the marriage market – she already felt a personal rivalry? For Elizabeth did indulge herself, though only when it did not really matter. (One of her best gifts as a ruler was an unerring, if idiosyncratic, order of priorities.)

If we go back to that *Calendar of State Papers* in the British Library, it is certainly clear from the start how dangerous was the possibility of Mary's marrying to disoblige England, and allying her northern kingdom to a southern Catholic prince, who would then have England in the jaws of a nutcracker. Almost from the moment Mary's husband died, Throckmorton had been writing to the council his hope that her next husband might be 'not so prejudicial to us' as the French king had been.

But in that calendar, besides the political, you can also trace a personal story. That same letter was the one in which Throckmorton went on to sing the praises of the Queen of Scots, who set her honour so high and her personal desires so low. The very next day, the Scottish lords had been pressing Elizabeth to marry the Earl of Arran. Very well – in return for their Earl of Arran, she would offer them an Earl of Leicester (as Robert Dudley would shortly be). And it would annoy the French, who had mocked at her and stalled her over the treaty; and one way or another it might silence the demanding Robert. It would give a gratifying jolt to the Throckmortons of the world, and to Cecil too, they with their endless demands that she marry.

But from the outset it was clear there were insuperable problems, even beyond the plan's core improbability. Robert Dudley was far from keen. Whether from real love, or just real hopes, of Elizabeth herself, he had no mind to go to the wild lands beyond the border, however much he might approve of England's coming to terms with Mary. And keen, of course, is hardly the word to describe the proud Queen Mary.

Throughout the rest of that year, however, Elizabeth's ambassador in Scotland, Randolph, was told to keep urging Mary that if she married Elizabeth's choice, she might do well by it – without, however, mentioning who the proposed suitor might be. At least the ongoing negotiations helped keep Mary from putting Scotland's ha'p'orth into the French wars. The Huguenots, the French Protestants, were rebelling against the Catholic powers of France's regent, Catherine de Medici, and Mary's Guise relations. In 1562 Elizabeth (sweetened by a loan of the French port Le Havre, which the Huguenots commanded, until she could regain

Calais) had sent to their assistance a force of six thousand men. It was Robert's plan, fuelled by Robert's Protestant passion. But Elizabeth could not bear to let him go away from her, so the force was commanded by Ambrose Dudley.

Ambrose failed to hold Le Havre (Newhaven), hampered by plague that decimated his men – and still more by the fact that France's Protestants and Catholics negotiated a peace, before uniting against their old English enemy. When he returned to England in the summer of 1563, with a wound that would trouble him for the rest of his life, Robert rushed off without permission to Portsmouth, from 'natural care and love toward my brother', as he wrote in a self-exculpatory letter to the Queen, who was afraid he would catch plague from the returning army. Elizabeth did not blame the Dudleys for England's failure. During the siege of Le Havre she had written to Ambrose: 'If your honour and my desire could accord with the loss of the needfullest finger I keep, God so help me in my utmost need as I would gladly lose that one joint for your safe abode with me.' The careful lack of exaggeration may be typical (it would certainly be more conventional, now, to offer one's right hand!), but the letter again shows the regard Elizabeth had for the whole Dudley family. All the same, in the future she would show herself even less willing to be drawn into religious wars. The episode had shown both the strengths and the limits of Robert's influence on her – and the growing strength of his own conviction as leader of the Protestant party. Perhaps that helped foster his reluctance to marry the Catholic Mary.

When, in the spring of 1564, Randolph named Robert Dudley to the Queen of Scots as the husband Elizabeth suggested, Mary was as incredulous as angry at this suggestion that she should so far 'abase my state'. For one who had been wife to the King of France, the proposed comedown must have seemed extraordinary. In the meantime Elizabeth had been attempting, half-heartedly, to revive her own plans for a Habsburg marriage with the Archduke Charles, though braced for marriage only 'as Queen and not as Elizabeth', she said dauntingly. But there were many obstacles in the way: Charles's Catholic religion; the Emperor's suspicion as to

Elizabeth's motives in pursuing what she had formerly rejected; and Elizabeth's continued closeness to Robert Dudley.

Mary long avoided a direct refusal of Elizabeth's proposal, instead demanding as a condition that she be declared heir of England if she married Robert, with her rights duly ratified by Parliament. In the end, Elizabeth said bluntly that that was impossible, setting aside as it did the laws of England, her father's will, and Parliament's desire for a Protestant heir of her own body. The most she could do was to promise to work for Mary behind the scenes. In the end there was no price that Scotland would accept and England was prepared to pay.

Robert was no more willing than his prospective bride. Mary later said he even wrote to her, claiming it was all just a diplomatic ploy: Robert, for his part, told the Scottish ambassador that it was all a scheme of Cecil, his 'secret enemy'. He himself was not fit to wipe the shoes of the Scottish queen, he added definitively. Indeed, Randolph found, to his consternation, that 'Now I have got this Queen's goodwill to marry where I would have her, I cannot get the man to take her for whom I was a suitor.' He had, at Cecil's urging, to write to the reluctant bridegroom, that if he indeed put obstacles in the way of 'so good a cause', then 'as all men hitherto have judged your Lordship worthy to marry the greatest queen, so will they alter their opinion of you'. He had to urge, via Henry Sidney, the pleasure of having so famously beautiful a woman 'in his naked arms'.

But the Scottish match was never likely to happen. By the autumn of 1564, the Earl of Lennox was writing to Randolph: 'He has not descended from a great old house, and his blood is spotted. I fear we shall not accept him.' But Elizabeth would not give up the game so easily. In September Mary sent a fresh ambassador south, in the polished shape of Sir James Melville, who might at least, she hoped, ensure the negotiations ended amicably. Melville's later memoirs give glimpses of Elizabeth that live in the memory. Here at last was a Scotsman in whose courteous, consoling company she could give safe vent to her jealousy of Mary. She spoke to him in the different languages they both shared; dressed each day in the style of a different country.

Which did he prefer, she asked him? He said the Italian, knowing that that fashion showed off her red hair, 'curled in appearance naturally'.

For years, Elizabeth had heard all too much about Mary: her charm and her femininity; her passion for pets; her game of domesticity, whereby she and her maids made conserve in a toy kitchen; her exquisite embroidery – and her beauty (and the worst of it was, she had Elizabeth's own style of beauty: curling auburn hair, height, and an alabaster skin). The Scottish queen had even pre-empted Elizabeth's accession, earlier the same year, with a more traditionally female ceremony. When Mary wed the French Dauphin, clad in untraditional white, six mechanical ships had circled the party afterwards, each bearing a prince to claim his princess. Now Elizabeth plagued the ambassador with questions: which was the fairer, Mary or she? He seems to have handled his role as mirror, mirror on the wall with considerable tact; Elizabeth was the fairest queen in all England, Mary in all Scotland, he said diplomatically; Elizabeth 'was whiter, but my Queen was very lovely'. Mary, he said, when asked, played the lute and virginals 'reasonably, for a queen'. Elizabeth made sure he 'happened' to come upon her playing expertly the next day. (Elizabeth surrounded herself by such seeming accidents.) When she took Melville into her closet to show him Mary's portrait on which she 'delighted oft' to gaze, the wrapped miniature on top of the pile was inscribed 'My Lord's picture' in Elizabeth's own hand. Melville says it took all his powers to persuade her to unwrap it. It was of Robert, needless to say . . . Another accident? Maybe.

On the last day of Melville's visit, Elizabeth finally bestowed on Dudley the earldom intended to make him more acceptable to Mary. He joined his brother as one of the only two men Elizabeth raised directly to this rank. The title of Leicester had a resonant history, having previously been held by several royal princes, including John of Gaunt and Henry of Bolingbroke, the future Henry IV. It was said Elizabeth even considered making Robert a duke. Everything was in order: the motto, 'Droit et loyal'; the distinguished crowd of titled observers; the new earl behaving with perfect dignity, and indeed, said Melville, 'great gravity'. But as Elizabeth placed the earl's chain around Robert's neck, the watching ambassadors were taken aback to see that the Queen 'could not refrain from putting her hand in his neck to kittle him smilingly'. It is usually assumed that Melville was right in assuming that Elizabeth's feelings overcame her – that she couldn't resist tickling that neck, even if it lost her the proposed Scottish marriage. But one suspects Elizabeth could resist anything if she really wanted to.

In one of their conversations, Elizabeth had told Melville that 'it was her own resolution at this moment to remain till her death a virgin queen'. He told her the information was unnecessary. 'I know your stately stomach. You think if you were married, you would be only a queen of England, and now ye are king and queen both. You may not endure a commander.' But the point about Robert was, she could enjoy him without fear of mastery. The two were 'inseparable', Melville concluded firmly.

If she had ever wanted a husband, she told Melville, 'she would have chosen Lord Robert, her brother and best friend, but, being determined to end her life in virginity, she wished that the Queen her sister should marry him,' since the only way she could be free of the fear Mary might usurp her was to see Mary married to one 'so loving and trusty'. It sounds paranoid, or nearly. But Elizabeth had come out of this episode with her faith in Robert confirmed – though it may have tried him hardly. Maybe, given her jealousy of the younger queen, she had found a personal reassurance in Robert's reluctance to leave her for Mary. Maybe, just maybe, that was what she had really wanted.

9

'Majesty and love do not sit well together'
1565–1567

MELVILLE'S VISIT WOULD PROVE TO BE JUST A PARTICULARLY COLOUR-
ful interlude in a long, long story. In the tale of the relations of
Elizabeth and Mary – and of both women with Robert Dudley –
the prologue, at this stage, was barely under way. But at the
English court, the story was still a *roman à deux*. In January 1565
the Thames froze so hard that traders could set up stalls on it, as
if on a street. The bitter weather, wrote the latest Spanish
ambassador, de Silva, 'has found out the Queen, whose
constitution cannot be very strong'. But with the warmer weather
she rallied quickly; and as the spring wore on, a playful Elizabeth
was still allowing her affection for Robert to be seen, as coyly but
boldly as a flash of pretty lingerie.

De Silva was taken riding by Robert in the park at Windsor
early one summer's morning. As the party came home they passed
under Elizabeth's window, and a call from Robert's jester brought
Elizabeth to an open casement in her nightgown. The ambassador
was particularly horrified that the Queen seemed to see nothing
unusual in her state of undress; de Silva was clearly yet another
Spaniard fated to spend his time in England in a flutter of
outraged modesty.

Thoughts of a match with Robert were still very much on the
tapis; Elizabeth herself was fond of telling de Silva as much. As he

wrote in June: 'the Queen has always brought up the matter of the Earl to me and has frankly told me that she would marry him if he were a king's son.' But his lineage was a bar that would never go away, and Robert, in the spring of 1565, was far from the only marriage possibility. Not only was the archduke said to be on the verge of putting himself forward again, but in the beginning of the year the new King of France had also sent a proposal, via his mother, Catherine de Medici. On a personal level, Elizabeth had some difficulty taking this one seriously; Charles IX (who five years earlier had succeeded his elder brother, the Queen of Scots' husband) was fourteen years old to Elizabeth's thirty-one. People – said Elizabeth – might think she was leading her son to the altar, and Charles' proxy protestations of love were even less convincing than the usual diplomatic flummery. One of the chief supporters of the match, however, was the new Earl of Leicester – not, one assumes, because he really thought Elizabeth was likely to wed this stammering schoolboy, but because it provided a useful diversion from the far more plausible Habsburg match – with the useful corollary that if and when Elizabeth officially refused Charles, the French would throw their weight behind her marriage with Leicester, since the last thing they wanted was a Habsburg behind the English throne.

Meanwhile Robert may have been playing matchmaker in another direction. Hoping himself to evade the threatened Scottish marriage, he had urged Elizabeth, in February 1565, to allow young Lord Darnley to go north to Scotland. Darnley was son to the Scottish Earl of Lennox, and his family's interests in Scotland provided an excuse for the visit. But Darnley had through his mother (daughter to Henry VIII's elder sister Margaret) a potential place in the succession to the English throne, and it was because of this that Darnley had hitherto been forbidden to travel north by the English authorities.* Not yet twenty, tall, pale and interesting, he had always to be considered

---

* It was true that Henry VIII's will and the Act of Succession had specifically debarred Margaret's line from inheriting, preferring the line of his younger sister Mary. But the will at least was of dubious legality.

as a potential mate for Mary. The English were well aware of Scots interest in Darnley: Elizabeth had signalled as much to Melville during his visit the previous autumn. But from Elizabeth's viewpoint, Darnley was not entirely a safe candidate: too ambitious, too close in blood to the English throne, too allied to Scottish interests – and, damningly, reared in the Catholic faith.

Leicester's motive in forwarding Darnley's visit is fairly clear. He wanted to get himself off the hook (and perhaps to prove that a queen could marry a commoner?). When Mary rapidly fell for the handsome, swaggering boy, and in April sent south word of her determination to marry Darnley, Leicester was one of the very few privy councillors who did not sign a letter protesting at this 'unmeet, unprofitable, and perilous proposal'. But what was Elizabeth thinking, when she allowed Darnley to cross the border? Was she, too, secretly pleased by the result? It is hard to believe she did not see it coming. Was she relieved it was no worse – since Mary was clearly going to marry somebody? Was she even so Machiavellian as to be dangling in front of Mary a husband she knew would prove a liability?

At least now Elizabeth would not have to read any more commendations of Mary's prudence and virtue. In May Throckmorton himself, who in 1560 had so pointedly praised Mary's preference for 'honor' over 'fancy', was sent to the Scottish court to bring Darnley home. He arrived to find a queen 'seized with love in fervered passions than is comely' even for 'mean persons'. Indeed, so Randolph wrote to Leicester (who was by this point receiving his own reports from England's emissaries, and so had first-hand news every step of the way), Mary showed so much change in her nature 'that she beareth only the shape of the woman she was before'. 'What shall become of her, or what life with him she shall lead, I leave it to others to think,' Randolph reflected gloomily. As Throckmorton (long since reconciled to Robert's interest) quoted to Leicester and Cecil: 'Majesty and love do not sit well together, nor remain on one throne.' All three must have been aware how easily Ovid's words could have had a personal application for Robert Dudley.

There was starting to unfold in Scotland a situation that would offer a strange mirror image – hideously distorted, but all the more revealing for it – to that of Elizabeth and Robert Dudley. While Elizabeth's failure to marry may be seen as either her blessing or her curse, Mary was damned by her marital history. Indeed, she made poor choices in men (always excluding her first boy husband, the ailing French king Francis, to whom she had simply been contracted as a child). Two years before Darnley appeared on the scene there had been something of a scandal over the attractive French aristocrat Pierre de Chastelard, who had gratifyingly declared his love for her. He was beheaded after being found in her bedchamber; whether to speak to her, seduce her, or assassinate her was unclear.* A more fruitful source of scandal was the favour Mary had started to show to her Piedmontese secretary David Rizzio – a foreigner (like Chastelard) who (said Randolph) 'rules all'. Those who wanted the Queen's ear had first to bribe the ubiquitous Davie. 'To be ruled by the advice of two or three strangers, neglecting that of her chief councillors, I do not know how it can stand,' Randolph wrote disapprovingly.

But if the Scottish queen's infatuation with Darnley would do nothing to quiet the turbulence of that court, the English court had its own troubles of division and party. Robert's peerage and his position on the privy council had brought him a new sort of power base, and newly bitter enemies. Increasingly, the mistrust many nobles felt for the upstart Earl of Leicester attached itself to the hostility of England's premier peer, the Duke of Norfolk, in 1565 a young man just turning twenty-nine. And Norfolk's story would prove to be inextricably linked not only with that of the English queen and her new earl, but also with that of the Scots Queen Mary.

In some ways Thomas Howard, fourth Duke of Norfolk, had a good deal in common with both Elizabeth and Dudley – even ties of blood and family. He was the grandson of that third Duke of Norfolk famous, in Henry VIII's day, for having seen two of his

---

* Mary, like Elizabeth, was a constant target of calumny; would even later be suspected of 'over-great familiarity' with the young brother of her gaoler, an eighteen-year-old boy.

nieces marry the King (and then finding that the relationship between himself and those nieces in their queenship would prove to be one of enmity). The beheading of his father, the Earl of Surrey, had made Norfolk a member of that small, unhappy club to which Elizabeth and Robert also belonged. But among his father's legacies, Surrey had left his son a full share of the family pride, and when Elizabeth ascended the throne he expected his rank to make him first of her advisers.

As Earl Marshal of England, arbiter of all questions of precedence, and second only in precedence to the Queen herself, the young fourth duke, who had already inherited his grandfather's dignities, had had a huge part to play in Elizabeth's coronation. But he had left court during the first summer of Elizabeth's reign, taking his new bride home to his Norfolk estates; and when he had returned in the autumn of 1559, he had been horrified by the rise of Robert Dudley. As early as that October, the Spanish ambassador was writing that Norfolk was behind a plot to murder Dudley – surely a fantasy, but if Norfolk were really talking openly about the Queen's 'lightness and bad government' it was enough to give real concern to Elizabeth as well as to Robert. Small wonder that by the Christmas of 1559, with trouble brewing on the Scottish border, Norfolk had been appointed Lieutenant General of the North. But during his time away, he had heard the most lurid reports from his satellites: that Robert was 'laying in good stock of arms', that he was every day 'assuming a more masterful part in affairs', that he was 'ruining the country with his vanity'. When Norfolk returned to court early in 1561 he was reported to be 'on very bad terms with the Queen' as a result of his open enmity with her favourite. Nor were subsequent developments likely to improve things. The revival of the Habsburg proposal, which Norfolk passionately supported, brought him back into conflict with Robert Dudley, and by this spring of 1565 relations between the two men were as bad as they could be.

In March 1565 there was reported an incident which has gone down as an archetypal courtiers' quarrel. The duke and the earl (so Randolph in Edinburgh heard) were playing tennis while

Elizabeth looked on, 'and my Lord Robert being hot and sweating took the Queen's napkin out of her hand and wiped his face, which the Duke seeing said that he was too saucy, and swore that he would lay his racket on his face; whereup rose a great trouble and the Queen sore offended with the Duke . . .' Not that she was particularly pleased with Leicester either, as the year wore on – well aware that he was fanning the flames by boasting of her favour, and making a virtue of the fact that he was 'a man that never did depend upon any but merely Her Majesty'.

In the summer of 1565 the Earl of Sussex, Thomas Radcliffe, Norfolk's friend and kinsman, returned to court from five years' warfare in Ireland and, as Cecil recorded, 'all that stock of the Howards seem to join in friendship together'.* In the autumn of 1560 Sussex had written robustly to Cecil that Elizabeth should choose a husband speedily and 'therein follow so much her own affection as by the looking upon him she would choose *omnes eius sensus titillarentur* [her whole being may be moved to desire] which shall be the readiest way with the help of God to bring us a blessed prince'. (There was a contemporary belief that for sex to be productive, the woman too had to release a seed, to experience orgasm.) So Sussex wrote: 'if the Queen will love anybody, let her love where and whom she list and him . . . will I love serve and honour to the uttermost'. But a lot of water had gone under the bridge since then; and the Howards clearly did not feel the Queen's favourite improved on acquaintance.

Scandalized observers complained that the quarrels that ensued threatened to convert the court into an armed camp. Indeed, the different armies would soon be wearing what amounted to different uniforms: blue or purple for Leicester's friends, yellow for Norfolk's. 'I am told that Leicester began it, so as to know who were his friends,' wrote de Silva, 'and the adherents of the Duke did the same in consequence of some disagreements they had with them about the aid [that] the Duke and his friends had given to the Archduke's match.'

* A duke of Norfolk, this duke's grandfather, had presided over the trial of Robert's father, and a Sussex had presided over Robert's own.

This was the chief ground of the controversy. In June 1565 Elizabeth finally refused the French proposal, which left two immediate contenders for her hand: the archduke, and Robert Dudley (whose pretensions the French now supported, *faute de mieux*). Small wonder that Cecil, as well as Norfolk and Sussex, threw all his weight behind the Habsburg contender. A new envoy from the Holy Roman Emperor had arrived in May (a new envoy from a new emperor, to boot, since Ferdinand had been succeeded by his son Maximilian, the archduke's elder brother). His tasks were to decide, first, whether Elizabeth were serious about the match this time; and second, whether there were any truth in all the rumours about her and Robert Dudley. No point in the Emperor's allying his brother with a woman of proven immorality.

In the interests of reassuring the Emperor that there would be no more embarrassing put-offs, Norfolk now demanded of Leicester that he abandon his pursuit of the Queen, and give his support to the archduke's suit. In the end, so forcefully did the duke tackle Leicester on his opposition to the match that Robert, taken aback, had little choice but to agree, and promised to give it his support ... *if* Norfolk could guarantee that the Queen would not take his volte-face the wrong way; that is, would not believe her Dudley's affection had turned to distaste, since that 'might cause her, womanlike, to undo him'. Leicester found himself forced to make part of the team negotiating for the Habsburg marriage. Even if it were at Norfolk's insistence that he took part, Elizabeth did not protect her favourite from a position that must have chafed him unbearably. Perhaps she was sending him a message, for these two, in moments of anger, did speak to each other in deed and gesture, whatever verbal conversations they also had behind the closet door in the moments of their intimacy.

Leicester told de Silva he believed Elizabeth 'had made up her mind to wed some great prince, or at all events no subject of her own'. And Elizabeth herself, strolling with de Silva through the gravelled walks and carved heraldic beasts of the privy gardens, took care to assure him that no-one was 'more inclining and addicted towards this match' than Leicester; 'neither doth any person more solicit us towards the same'.* But she also reminded the Imperial ambassador that she had 'never said to anybody that I would not marry the Earl of Leicester'. It seems almost a reflex reaction in her to invoke Robert's name as talisman or stalking horse whenever the proposal of another suitor took on too much reality.

Around this time, William Cecil felt it necessary to set down a private memorandum comparing the archduke and Robert Dudley; to the latter's disfavour, needless to say. The one was 'an archduke born'; the other 'an earl made'. The one was in wealth 'by report 3000 ducats by the year'; the other 'all of the Queen and in debt'. In knowledge, the one had 'all qualities belonging to a prince – languages, wars, hunting and riding'; the other knew what was 'meet [suitable] for a courtier'. In age, and in beauty, he tersely conceded that Leicester was 'meet'; but against that was his failure to have children with Amy, while the archduke came from a prolific family.

Cecil made another version of the same memorandum, dwelling less on the personal and more on the political attributes of the pair. It may have been meant for discussion with the council, rather than the Queen. This was less of a point-by-point comparison than the first, but still the contrast was intended to be clear. If the Queen married Leicester: 'Nothing is increased by marriage of him either in riches, estimation, power.' 'It will be thought, that the slanderous speeches of the Queen with the Earl have been true.' 'He shall study nothing but to enhance his own particular friends to wealth, to offices to lands, and to offend others.' Against Leicester's name Cecil also put down, rather oddly, 'He is like to prove unkind, or jealous of the Queen's majesty.' Perhaps he was thinking of the arrogance and ambition

---

* Perhaps she protested too much. Camden, decades later, would describe at length how Leicester used his position at Elizabeth's ear to urge on her the evils of 'marrying out of the Realm': how a queen who married abroad found she had handed her realm to her husband; how the children of such marriages too often turned out ill; how dangerous it was to commit yourself to a man you had never seen; how it might be 'an extreme misery and grief, to be daily conversant with a man of strange manners and language'.

Robert displayed so frequently. Of course, wanting the Habsburg marriage to take place, he had no motive to put down the other side of the case: the archduke's Catholicism, and the probable hostility of the country to the match.

Now, as always, Cecil steered something of an independent course among the court parties of the aristocracy. Their shared experience in Scotland at the beginning of the decade had briefly bred in him an amity with Norfolk; but it had not lasted, though for the moment they found themselves allies again. By the same token, in the years ahead he would often be found working with, rather than against, Robert Dudley.

In the summer of 1565 Robert was flirting with another lady. The Spanish ambassador heard it was by Throckmorton's advice, to pique Elizabeth's jealousy. But if he were not merely trying to make Elizabeth jealous, then it is a sure sign that he at least was coming to see his situation with the Queen less hopefully. Perhaps her attempt to marry him to the Queen of Scots had taught him something about Elizabeth's feelings. Perhaps he knew already. Whatever the case, he now turned to Lettice Knollys, Viscountess Hereford, the Queen's kinswoman (her mother being Mary Boleyn's daughter) and sometime favourite: twenty-five years old, another redhead and a famous beauty. The flirtation seems to have passed off quietly, for the moment, with just a mention in Cecil's notebooks that the Queen had shown herself 'much offended'. Lettice was, after all, at this time a married lady.

That summer, too, Elizabeth had a flirtation of her own – with a court gentleman called Thomas Heneage, a man famed 'for his elegancy of life and pleasantness of discourse', who had come to public notice under Cecil's auspices. This was another relationship with clear boundaries on it: Heneage too was married (and one who had been at court for five years: plenty of time to catch the Queen's eye, had she had any serious interest in him). But Leicester quarrelled with Heneage and, furious, asked permission to leave the court at Windsor 'to go to stay at my own place as other men [do]'. The Queen refused even to answer; they fought violently. As Cecil wrote to a friend: 'The Queen was in a great temper, and upbraided him with what had taken place with

Heneage, and his flirting with the Viscountess, in very bitter words.' In 'many overt speeches', he noted, the Queen was letting it be known that she was sorry for the time she had wasted on Robert – 'and so is every good subject'. It seems likely Elizabeth was using Heneage to keep Robert in line, and display the fact that she would not necessarily always bend his way.

At Windsor that summer she wrote a verse on the flyleaf of her French psalter: Cecil noted she had written an 'obscure sentence in a book' at the time when she was much annoyed with Robert Dudley:

> No crooked leg, no bleared eye,
> No part deformed out of kind,
> Nor yet so ugly half can be
> As the inward, suspicious mind.

She took care to give Robert the occasional humiliatingly public reproof. Naunton describes one incident when a satellite of Leicester's was refused admission to the privy chamber, and the earl swore to have the official concerned turned out of his place. The man threw himself on the Queen's mercy, asking 'whether my Lord of Leicester were king or Her Majesty queen'. Elizabeth's response to this skilful goad was predictably savage. 'God's death, my Lord, I have wished you well,' she told Leicester, 'but my favour is not so locked up for you that others shall not participate thereof. And if you think to rule here, I will take a course to see you forthcoming. I will have but one mistress and no master.' A quarrel would end in a sulk – in Leicester's withdrawal from Elizabeth's presence – and then in a weeping reconciliation. Kat Ashley died that summer, to Elizabeth's great distress (Thomas Parry had died as far back as 1560), and she was less able than ever to do without her old friend. But each quarrel was another straw in the wind.

In Scotland (and did this heighten Elizabeth's sensitivity?) Mary married Darnley at the end of July. It would be just two headlong years until her abdication. The marriage was only months old when it became apparent that the worst fears would be fulfilled.

Darnley quickly proved 'wilful, haughty and vicious', in the words of one Scots counsellor. His overriding belief – fuelled by a mixture of arrogance and alcohol – that his gender gave him the right to rule his wife's kingdom was equalled only by his complete lack of any qualification for the task. Already furious that Mary refused to grant him the Crown Matrimonial, he became convinced that Rizzio (whom he blamed for Mary's obstinacy) was far more than her secretary; was, in fact, 'a filthy wedlock breaker', as a hostile Randolph described him. Randolph warned Leicester: 'Woe is me for you when David's son shall be a King of England.' Darnley's jealous suspicion of Rizzio was only heightened by the fact that he himself may have been sleeping with the Piedmontese secretary. But by the autumn Mary was pregnant. The marriage had to limp on as best it might.

That Christmas Leicester again asked Elizabeth to marry him. She said she could not answer him at once; that he must wait until Candlemas in February – which at least suggested she was giving it serious consideration. But Leicester's satisfaction – and arrogance – were given a much-needed check by the fact that Heneage was also much in evidence that Christmas. The Venetian envoy described how he was chosen, on Twelfth Night, as king of the revels, which allowed him to rule court for that evening and to give the direction to the festivities. In one of the games of wit and wordplay, Heneage in his new role of command instructed Leicester to ask the Queen 'which was the most difficult to erase from the mind, an evil opinion created by a wicked informer, or jealousy'. The Queen answered that both were difficult, but jealousy was the harder.

Afterwards, Leicester sent to Heneage threatening to chastise him with a stick. Clearly, he assumed that so pointed a question could only have been chosen pointedly. Heneage replied hotly (the stick, rather than the sword, was used only against inferiors), and finally complained to the Queen, who told Robert that 'if by her favour he had become insolent he should soon reform and that she would lower him just as she had, at first, raised him'. Robert flung himself into ostentatious despair, 'placing himself in one of the rooms of the palace in deep melancholy' until the Queen, 'moved by pity', restored him to favour. But the watching ambassadors – still waiting for Elizabeth to 'proclaim him duke and marry him', considered that he had misplayed his hand. And Candlemas passed without an answer, needless to say.

Robert left court in the February of 1566, by permission, and was not back until April, despite the Queen's sending to protest at his 'long absence' and desire his 'hasty repair'. He had, he said, been delayed by the need of his sister Katherine, who had been sick, or possibly suffered a miscarriage, and 'with whom I tarried continually, because I would do her all the comfort I could, for the time'. When he did return to court, he was there only a month before he received permission to go to his estates for a while. He was a courtier born, who wrote of the court as 'home'; but small wonder if he wearied of it occasionally, and sought permission to go to his own lands, where it was his will that held undisputed sway. He still gained considerable status from being ack-nowledged as even a possible pretender to the Queen's hand, but he had undoubtedly begun to suspect his suit would never lead to matrimony.

But relations around the throne of Scotland were far, far worse. On 13 February Randolph was writing to Leicester that 'I know now for certain that this Queen repenteth her marriage, that she hateth the King [Darnley] and all his kin.' Darnley (prompted by a disaffected Scottish faction) had driven himself into a jealous fury, convinced Rizzio was the father of the child Mary now carried. 'I know that, if that take effect which is intended, David, with the consent of the King, shall have his throat cut within these ten days,' Randolph predicted. It took a little longer, but on 9 March a party of nobles, Darnley among them, burst into Mary's chamber and hacked Rizzio to pieces almost before her eyes. Within the next few days she rallied enough to persuade Darnley that his life as well as hers would ultimately be in danger from these over-mighty subjects, and managed to regain a meas-ure of control over her monarchy. Elizabeth was genuinely and profoundly horrified at the insults heaped upon Mary, expressing to the Spanish ambassador her indignation that Rizzio's killers had broken into Mary's chamber 'as if it were that of a public woman'. If this could happen to one of the two queens in the isle, how much harder it might be for the other to preserve any sense of invulnerability. But she would have had to be more than human – and Elizabeth was very human – not also to enjoy her moral superiority. Mary had made mistakes Elizabeth would always have foreseen, and some of them included her misunderstanding of the role of a favourite. Her heedless reliance upon Rizzio had allowed him – a foreigner, and a Catholic – to be cast as the archetypal 'evil counsellor'.

On the surface, the Scottish royal marriage was patched up, after a fashion. With an heir in Mary's womb, it had to be. Mary's son James was born in June, but not even this could repair the breach, and by the end of the year it was with dismay that Mary heard there could be no legal way of freeing her from Darnley. (The Scottish ambassador took care to give Elizabeth all the gory details of the birth, telling the Queen his mistress had been 'so sore handled that she wished she had never been married' – in order, as he himself said, 'to give her a little scare' off any marriage of her own.) That October, when Elizabeth, in order to raise funds, was forced to call the first Parliament in three years, the members returned to London even more determined to tackle the question of the succession than when they had gone away. They let it be known, in fact, that some decision was the price of their voting her any more money. But to this infringement, as she saw it, of her prerogative, Elizabeth reacted angrily. Had she not told them at the outset that 'by the word of a prince, she would marry' . . . eventually?

When the Commons none the less began to put pressure upon her, having heard her vague promises before, the Lords backed them up every inch of the way. What is more, it was Robert who persuaded her to receive the Lords' deputation; and he, along with his erstwhile great rival, was prominent among those on the receiving end of her anger when the pressure did not abate. De Silva had accounts of the incident from Elizabeth herself, as well as from Norfolk, whose affection for the idea of a Habsburg marriage and half-Habsburg heir had never gone away.

The Queen was so angry that she addressed hard words to the Duke of Norfolk, whom she called traitor or conspirator . . . The Earls of Leicester and Pembroke, the Marquess of Northampton and the Lord Chamberlain spoke to her on the matter, and Pembroke remarked to her that it was not right to treat the Duke badly, since he and the others were only doing what was fitting for the good of the country . . . She told him [Pembroke] he talked like a swaggering soldier, and said to Leicester that she had thought if all the world abandoned her he would not have done so, to which he answered that he would die at her feet; and she said that had nothing to do with the matter.

Leicester, like Pembroke, was commanded not to appear before her. If Leicester and Norfolk appeared to be finding a kind of amity, then conversely Leicester too had – at least for the moment – become one of the enemy in Elizabeth's eyes.*

The Imperial marriage was going on the back burner, as Elizabeth took to complaining about the size of the archduke's 'dowry', and as the diplomats on both sides began to despair of compromise (though it would be the end of 1567 before the negotiations finally ran into the sand and Elizabeth definitively refused the archduke's proposal). Leicester – it was said – had been urging Protestant divines to inveigh from the pulpit against the archduke's Catholicism, and the plan that he should be allowed to celebrate mass in private. It was a bad time to suggest toleration for any Catholic practice, with Philip of Spain ferociously crushing Protestant rebels in the Spanish Netherlands just across the Channel, and diplomatic relations between Spain and England growing unprecedentedly chilly.

But attention was soon to be focused to the north, rather than the south, of England's bounds. Mary's reconciliation with Darnley was not working. 'Things are going from bad to worse,' the French ambassador warned. Darnley 'will never humble

---

* It was in the spring of 1567 that Appleyard, Amy Dudley's half-brother, made his allegations; and it had been assumed Norfolk's party, this previous year, had paid him to do so. But by then the two men were able to present themselves as victims, alike, of a slander campaign.

himself as he ought', while the Queen – understandably, after Rizzio's murder – suspected him of plotting with her nobles. In February 1567 came the shock of the explosion at Kirk o'Field, and Darnley's murder amid rumours of Mary's complicity. This is not the place to tell in detail the crowded story of the next months, far less to assess Mary's guilt or otherwise in the murder. (Most now believe, at the least, that the evidence against her was unreliable.) But the shock waves that followed showed up the events at Cumnor, and Amy Dudley's death, as a mere storm in a teacup.

Mary now compounded error with error, submitting herself in May to a marriage with the Earl of Bothwell, whom most at the time blamed for the murder of Darnley. Debate still rages as to whether his seduction of her was a rough wooing or a rape; either way, she turned to him because she felt herself so isolated. Scotland 'being divided into factions as it is', she said in self-exculpation, 'cannot be contained in order unless our authority be assisted and set forth by the fortification of a man'. If Elizabeth used faction at her court to her advantage, Mary was allowing the Scottish factions to make use of her.

Certainly Scotland could not be contained under this particular man. As Bothwell swaggered through the streets of Edinburgh after Darnley's death, challenging any man who believed he had killed the Queen's husband to a duel, he had also summoned the nobility to a dinner and, by way of dessert, produced a petition to which they were asked to put their names, imploring their queen not only to marry, but to marry the earl who had done Mary such 'affectionate and hearty service'. But his aggressive attempts to coerce support did him no more good than Leicester's comparative passivity had done. He dominated Mary – insisting she saw no adviser without his presence – but every sign of his power over her increased the hostility of her nobility.

In July, with Scotland openly at war with itself, and Mary's forces defeated by those of the Protestant lords under her illegitimate half-brother, the Earl of Moray, she was forced to abdicate in favour of her own infant son. The excuse her lords made for keeping her imprisoned after she had signed her throne away was that they feared that, if free, she might turn again to Bothwell, that 'notorious tyrant.' Truly, passion was dangerous for a queen regnant. For any woman, maybe.

The scene when a defeated Mary was brought weeping back into her own capital city was something from Elizabeth's worst nightmare. Where now were Mary's jokes about the Queen of England's marrying a man who had murdered his wife to be rid of her? Elizabeth could not but reflect on how much better she had behaved over the mysterious death of Amy Dudley; the instant distancing of herself from Robert, the formal inquiry – how much better, indeed, she had handled the whole matter of favouritism, handled Robert Dudley. In so far as he was, like Darnley, an ambitious commoner, she had enjoyed him but managed never to marry him. In so far as he was, like Rizzio, an employee and conduit to her, she had chosen more appropriately. (Ironically, the question of Mary was to set Elizabeth more sharply at odds with her ministers than the question of Robert Dudley had ever done.) And as for Bothwell, apart from anything else, he was another married man, whom only a patched-up divorce had set free. 'With what peril have you married him that hath another wife alive,' as Elizabeth wrote to Mary, from the moral high ground of outraged respectability.

On the one hand, Elizabeth had sought and would continue to seek to protect the position of a sister monarch. She was profoundly shaken at what was in effect a diagram of just how badly her own story might have turned out. But, as she adjured Mary to clear her reputation of 'a crime of such enormity' as a husband's murder – as she told her 'an honourable burial' was better than a soiled life – the sense of *schadenfreude* must have been extraordinary.

10

'The daughter of debate'
1568–1569

AT THE BEGINNING OF MAY 1568 ELIZABETH, NOW IN AMICABLE communication with the Scottish lords, had been only too happy to purchase from them some of the imprisoned Mary's jewellery. When a glorious rope of pearls arrived, she showed them off to Leicester and Pembroke: her offer of 12,000 *écus* had outbid Catherine de Medici. But the very next day, 2 May, Mary escaped from Lochleven, and from her lords' custody. Her attempt to rally supporters and to regain her throne lasted but briefly, and on 16 May she crossed the Solway Firth and fled across the border into England, taking refuge from humiliation and defeat in her own country.

Mary had believed all Elizabeth's protestations of sisterly solidarity; believed Elizabeth would restore her to her throne, and instantly. She had made the mistake of confusing what Elizabeth said and what she did. It was not a mistake that would ever be made by Elizabeth's own councillors, least of all by Robert Dudley.

In the short term, the situation might seem to have played into Elizabeth's skilled and manipulative hands. She had Mary, a royal pawn in the great political game, in her hands, to be held in reserve and deployed as necessary. But in the long term Mary would have her revenge; would prove to be a 'daughter of debate /

That discord aye doth sow', as Elizabeth would write of her ruefully. If Mary's life as a free woman was over, then life in the country of her cousin Elizabeth would also never be the same again. For almost twenty years to come, Mary would provide a focus for plot and rebellion; a romantic personification of the possibility of an alternative, Catholic monarchy; a bone of contention between Elizabeth and her ministers. Elizabeth always tended to prolong a situation beyond its real viability; witness her tenacious hold on Robert Dudley. But this time she found herself hoist with her own petard, caught in a stasis from which she could not break free.

No doubt Elizabeth talked over with Leicester the fate of the woman she had once suggested he marry. No doubt she had done so every step of the way. Melville in his *Memoirs* said that before he left England, having delivered news of James's birth, he tried to bring Elizabeth to the point of declaring Mary her heir: 'for my Lord of Leicester was become my queen's avowed friend'. Leicester certainly acted as Elizabeth's mouthpiece in explaining to Throckmorton (who had found his task of mediating between the different Scottish parties an unenviable one) why Elizabeth would not throw her weight more decisively behind the Protestant lords. 'She is most earnestly affected towards the Queen of Scots ... There is no persuading the Queen [Elizabeth] to disguise or use polity, for she breaks out to all men in this matter, and says most constantly that she will become an utter enemy to that nation if the Queen [Mary] perish.' When Mary wrote to Elizabeth in the early days of her captivity describing the harshness of her treatment, her 'bodily fear', and her particular terror of 'false reports', it must have reminded the English queen of her own youthful imprisonment, and perhaps drew her close to one who had shared that terrible experience.

For Elizabeth's first instinct was to assist Mary to regain her throne. Queenship called to queenship. This met with disagreement from most of Elizabeth's councillors, and from Cecil especially. To return Mary to her throne would have been to replace a friendly Protestant government with a Catholic one. Cecil was adamant Mary should instead be sent back to Scotland into the custody of the Protestant lords, but to this Elizabeth could not bring herself to agree. Mary could not be sent abroad, to become a puppet pretender to the English throne in the hands of France or Spain; nor could she be left to roam around England, penniless but at liberty. So she was to be kept fast as Elizabeth's 'guest'; and part of the compromise package was that Elizabeth should launch an inquiry into the rumours about Mary's conduct and her part in her husband's death. If Mary would agree to have her case heard by her 'dear cousin and friend', then 'I will send for her rebels and know their answer why they deposed their queen'. The inquiry began in the autumn, in York, moving south to London in the spring of 1569, where first Leicester and then also Warwick joined the list of commissioners. The production of the so-called 'casket letters', seeming to provide evidence of murderous adultery, ensured that Mary could not be found innocent; the fact that she herself never debated the implication of them meant she could not officially be found guilty.*

At the English court, another bout of internal strife was brewing, and events were soon to display Cecil and Leicester profoundly at odds in an episode intimately connected with Mary's story. We are only now beginning to guess that the slightly unsatisfactory tale we have always been told about this perplexing passage in late Tudor history may be no more than a veneer over a far more complex set of events, in which Leicester's role may well have been less venal than at first it appears.

The central figure in this episode was the Duke of Norfolk – cast, in the conventional story, not as Leicester's enemy, but as his ally. The duke had been one of the original commissioners on the inquiry into Mary's guilt as to the murder of Lord Darnley, and his reaction to the sight of the casket letters had been a disgust – 'such an inordinate [he crossed out 'and filthy'] love between her and Bothwell', he wrote – that one would expect not to be easily done away with. But very shortly afterwards, Norfolk went hawking with one of the Scottish lords, who suggested that the

---

* The most damning of the 'casket letters' are now believed to be fakes; and John Guy powerfully suggests that Cecil was a prime mover in the forgery.

best way of neutralizing and utilizing Mary (her marriage to Bothwell having been annulled) would be for Norfolk himself to marry her, thus keeping her safe under the authority of a loyal English subject, and co-opting her royal genes for a new dynasty which could reasonably inherit Elizabeth's throne one day.

The idea did not bear instant fruit. There was, after all, a clause in Norfolk's instructions as commissioner which said that anyone plotting Mary's marriage 'shall be *ipso facto* acknowledged as traitorous and shall suffer death'. But it was an idea that, once mooted, no scion of the ambitious Howard clan could ever entirely forget. It was in part Norfolk's dawning partiality towards Mary that had seen the commission moved south, to be under Elizabeth's eye. When Elizabeth taxed Norfolk, half jokingly, with the rumours she had heard, he protested he had no desire for marriage with 'so wicked a woman, such a notorious adultress and murderer'. Elizabeth declared herself satisfied, and there, for the moment, the matter seemed to die.

Soon, however, it was reborn, as bastard love-child to another conspiracy. Norfolk and those around him resented Cecil's implacable hostility to Mary and the severity with which he proposed to pursue the anti-Catholic laws. More subtly, they saw him as a new man intent on the overthrow of the old regime, and were concerned that the general trend of his policies would throw England and Spain into conflict. These were not, surely, fears likely to recruit Leicester's support. Yet it seems on the face of it as though his ambition, or his famous hostility to Cecil, weighed more heavily in the balance than his fervent Protestantism.

There is now good reason to suspect the version of events we have always been told. The trouble is that the veil of secrecy still holds, and there is simply not the evidence to offer a complete alternative narrative for the events of this spring and summer. So let us stick with the old tale for a moment longer. The story goes that at a meeting of the council, with the Queen not present, Cecil (like Thomas Cromwell, in Henry VIII's reign) was to be charged with being an evil adviser – enough to dismiss him to the Tower. But soon after Leicester finally decided to throw his weight in with the plotters, Elizabeth – ever less easy to hoodwink than was fondly supposed – got wind of the plan. On Ash Wednesday, with Cecil, Norfolk and Northampton also in her chamber, she taxed Leicester first with his folly. Leicester gave his complaints against Cecil; most of her subjects, he said, were in despair because affairs were being so badly managed by Master Secretary. Norfolk spoke to Northampton in an audible aside. 'You see, my Lord, how the Earl of Leicester is favoured so long as he supports the Secretary [Cecil], but now that for good reason he takes an opposed position, she frowns upon him and wants to send him to the Tower.' 'No, no,' replied Northampton, 'he will not go alone.' Elizabeth, standing firm behind Cecil, had shown her position clearly. Leicester was perhaps embarrassed by being thrust into the position of leader, but pleased by the novel popularity with his peers.

But it is notable that three times in the following weeks Leicester stymied fresh anti-Cecil moves by threatening to tell the Queen (aided by conciliatory moves from Cecil himself, and by Sussex's urging on Norfolk that this quarrel was the worst thing possible for the country). And it is notable, too, that the famous scene in the privy chamber comes to us from one very particular source – from the French ambassador, de la Mothe Fénelon, a recent arrival in the country who was complaining how hard he found it to get a handle on English affairs and who this spring was being force-fed a picture of England in disarray, with dissent in the government ranks and widespread support for Mary. His informant was a man of whom more would shortly be heard: a Florentine banker called Roberto Ridolfi who used this method to persuade both Fénelon and the Spanish ambassador to join a Catholic alliance with plans for an invasion of England.

As spring wore on, several strands to the broad conspiracy became discernible. The first proposed merely Norfolk's marriage with Mary; and here Leicester assured Norfolk of his support, with Throckmorton acting as go-between from him to Norfolk's party. Robert may indeed genuinely have felt that 'there could be no better Remedy to provide for so dangerous a Woman'. And he had arguably a personal reason to comply, since with a tamed Mary ratified as heir presumptive, the pressure on Elizabeth to make a dynastic marriage would be relieved. But others in this vague alliance, particularly the nobles of the north, were plotting more dangerously. It is unclear whether even Norfolk, let alone Leicester, was in on their plan from the beginning. They envisaged Mary and Norfolk deposing Elizabeth immediately, and (with Spanish support) restoring Catholicism to the country. Mary herself – negotiating incessantly on her own account, with nobles both sides of the border – was willing to go with each and any plan that would set her at liberty. For her, concern for Elizabeth's safety was far from a priority.

It was Leicester's supposed power to persuade Elizabeth against her will that made him a figure of such importance in the plan for a marriage between Norfolk and Mary. But, just as the plotters perhaps over-estimated his influence here, they may also have played too many games with his loyalty.

The summer of 1569 could hardly be other than uneasy. The conventional story runs thus: that Norfolk's aspirations were something of an open secret, known even to Cecil, who urged Norfolk to speak to the Queen and confess his position honestly. Leicester, by contrast, was in negotiation with Maitland in Scotland, so that the marriage should seem to be suggested by Mary's own Protestant lords. If this failed, Leicester would broach it to the Queen himself – in which case, he insisted, he must be able to wait for the right moment to do so . . . At the end of July the court moved to Richmond, and Leicester was occupied fishing in the Thames, near his house at Kew, when Norfolk came upon him. The earl told the duke that the Queen had heard some gossip of the matter, and that it was more than ever incumbent upon them to open the subject only carefully. Perhaps that is why when, a few days later, Elizabeth asked if he had no news of a marriage to tell her, Norfolk baulked at the subject and scuttled away. Like a schoolboy looking for help in trouble he went straight to Leicester's rooms; finding that the earl was out stag-hunting near Kingston, he waited there until Leicester returned at the end of a long day.

On progress a few days later, Leicester kept his promise, finally. Norfolk himself described the scene in one of the many 'submissions' or confessions he was compelled to deliver later. The court was staying at Loseley near Guildford, the home of Sir William More, and as Norfolk came into the Queen's room one morning, he found one of Sir William's children 'playing upon a lute and singing, Her Majesty sitting upon the threshold of the door, my Lord of Leicester kneeling by Her Highness'. Leicester told him the news of Norfolk's aspirations had gone down 'indifferent well', and that Elizabeth would speak to him later in the progress. However, when Elizabeth gave Norfolk a tetchy, but not unforgiving, nudge upon the subject, again he let the opportunity to come clean slip away; and when opportunity arose for him to leave the progress he did so, still silent, leaving Leicester and a wary Cecil to do whatever they could for him.

By early September, with Norfolk summoned back to court, the best thing Leicester could think of to do was to give the whole story to the Queen, under conditions that would ensure her sympathy. At Titchfield Abbey in Hampshire he took to his bed (so Camden later heard), and when a concerned Elizabeth came to visit he told her of the marriage plan, protesting his own loyalty. When she told him she thought that the marriage, had it happened, would have seen her in the Tower, he could hardly fail to have responded with genuine contrition. Elizabeth rated Norfolk angrily, and charged him on his allegiance that he should 'deal no further with the Scottish cause'. He could expect no less. He had got away lightly. But still, the other courtiers shunned him – Leicester among them – and when he got permission to retreat to his own house in London, he did so gratefully.

Might it perhaps have ended there, had the plotting of that summer been limited to the comparatively innocent plan that Norfolk should marry Mary, and – long term – secure the succession that way? But the situation, as Norfolk left court, can hardly have struck Elizabeth, or her ministers, as one of safety. The religious malcontents in the north – they who had planned to replace Elizabeth with Mary – still posed a threat (even without Spanish support). So the ports were closed, the militia alerted, and the Queen of Scots removed to a place of greater security. Leicester and Cecil, on Elizabeth's instructions, wrote to Norfolk ordering him to come to Windsor immediately. Leicester also wrote him a warning, privately, and this frightened Norfolk so much that, instead of obeying the summons, he set off immediately in the opposite direction. He was in fact heading for the imagined safety of his own estates; but to the authorities it looked as if he were setting out to recruit his forces, planning to return at the head of an army. The whole court 'hung in suspense and fear lest he should break forth into rebellion', wrote Camden later. Instead, Norfolk stayed at home, sick and quaking – ruined, as the latest Spanish ambassador, de Spes, put it, by his 'pusillanimity' – and it is no wonder the crown seized its opportunity. A messenger was sent to take Norfolk to the Tower – in a litter, if necessary.

Before he left for London, Norfolk sent a messenger northwards, to his brother-in-law, the Earl of Westmorland. The message begged that Westmorland and his allies call off the projected rising; but it had the opposite effect. When they too were summoned to court, they feared for their own safety. Sussex (at once Norfolk's friend, and Elizabeth's Lord President of the Council in the north, before Robert's brother-in-law Huntingdon took over that role) urged them that this was folly, and their best course was to comply. But on 9 November the so-called 'northern earls' rode with their supporters to Durham, where they proclaimed that 'to whom of mere right the true succession of the crown appertaineth' should be determined by themselves, 'the ancient nobility'. At Ripon they stated their main aim more clearly: 'evil-disposed persons about the Queen's Majesty', they said, had 'overcome in this our realm the true and Catholic religion'. The wording of the proclamation implicitly recognized that Elizabeth, at least for the moment, was 'the Queen's Majesty'; none the less they planned to free Mary. From Ripon they rode south to Selby – near to Tutbury, where Mary had been held until a hasty removal to Coventry. But as November turned to December, as an army led by Elizabeth's kinsman Hunsdon advanced to meet them, as the weather worsened and they squabbled about what to do next, their forces melted away. They withdrew north (still unaided by the Spanish), the leaders fleeing into Scotland in time to allow Christmas to be celebrated at the English court with all festivity.

Leicester's brother Ambrose, the Earl of Warwick, was one of the leaders of the royal forces mustered against the rebellion, and one of those who presided over a suppression so punitive as to damage the north for many years ahead. Some 750 rebels were executed under martial law, many more later tried and fined; clergy were deprived of their livings, great estates alienated from their previous owners and redirected into other, more loyal, hands. It is a glimpse of the harsher side of the Dudley family.

No dramatic reprisals were taken among the courtiers in on the plot. But Throckmorton was questioned in the Tower, and Leicester was the only one who went quite scot free. If he really had betrayed the Queen, even to the extent of keeping quiet about Norfolk's marriage plan, would she not have been more angry? At what stage and from what source did he become aware that there was a more dangerous aspect to the marriage fantasy?

Or . . . should we be thinking more adventurously? It is interesting that Robert's brother played so large a part in putting down the revolt; and that Elizabeth had contemplated placing Mary in Huntingdon's charge, for greater security. Interesting, too, that Norfolk's family ever after felt that if Leicester had not actually been an *agent provocateur*, then at least he had behaved provocatively. Is it possible that Leicester had been tipping Elizabeth off – even that she had been the puppetmaster who placed him as a spy in the camp of the enemy? That the whole tale of his huge enmity towards Cecil that summer had been to some degree a made-up story, so that England's enemies, at home and abroad, were being lured into showing their hand by a false display of division and vulnerability?

In the autumn of 1569, as the revolt was brewing, Roberto Ridolfi, source of many of the rumours about this famous enmity, was arrested and remanded to the house of Francis Walsingham, a notable ally of Leicester's. It now seems likely that, while Ridolfi was imprisoned, he was persuaded to 'turn' and, while still apparently orchestrating plans for a Catholic invasion of England, also keep England informed as to their progress. The instructions for Ridolfi's arrest, his interrogation – and his surprising release 'under certain conditions' – were all forwarded from the court by two particular councillors: William Cecil, and Robert Dudley.

It is hard accurately to gauge the nature of relations between Leicester and Cecil, so universally has the picture of their hostility been accepted – a hostility that even split the council into factions. Of course there is plenty of genuine evidence of quarrels and rivalries. In the spring of 1570 Fénelon reported that Leicester had been complaining that Cecil was trying to get him ousted from the council; that summer, Sir Henry Neville wrote to Cecil that 'My Lord of Leicester sings his old song unto his friends, that is, that he had the queen in very good tune, till you took her aside, and dealt with her secretly, and then she was very strange suddenly.' A year later the Spanish ambassador wrote that 'The Queen's opinion goes for little, and Leicester's for less; Cecil rules all, unopposed, with the pride of Lucifer' . . . but then again, in that crucial autumn of 1569, the Duke of Alva had heard that Leicester and Cecil, together, 'entirely govern the Queen'. Even Leicester's far more convincing enmity with Sussex was not such as to prevent him, this autumn, writing Sussex a respectful letter laying out his reasons for advocating a measure of friendship towards the Queen of Scots. 'In worldly causes men must be governed by worldly policies,' he said, albeit with the proviso that he would not forget 'my duty to God'. (Leicester would long continue trying to stay on terms with Mary – but many other nobles also did so. While she remained the next heir, it was an essential insurance policy.)

There is no reason to doubt that Leicester and Cecil did indeed sometimes disagree; that each could be made uneasy by the mounting influence of the other. (And at least one letter from a Spanish ambassador suggests that Spain had actively been fanning any visible spark of enmity.) But the trend of recent scholarship is to feel that any antagonism has been greatly exaggerated; that, in essence, over the years they achieved a fairly amicable working relationship. Reading three decades' worth of often warm and chatty letters between and about them, it is hard to disagree. As Cecil himself had written to Sir Thomas Smith earlier in the 1560s, he may hear 'that things are not sound betwixt my Lord Robert and me, but surely all is well . . . although either of us do understand well enough, how busy many be to move the contrary'. And again, on another occasion: 'all the Lords are bent towards her Majesty's service, and do not so much vary among themselves, as lewd men do report'. Leicester himself, for what it is worth, would claim repeatedly to be not 'a peace breaker but a peace maker'; to have 'never loved or favoured factious dealing', nor been 'willing to make quarrels in the court'. If it is true that Elizabeth, seeking often to play her courtiers off one against the other, found material ready to her hand in Leicester and in others, it may also be true that these were often no more than sibling rivalries among the courtly family.

Though Leicester had been kept with Elizabeth at Windsor while the revolt of the northern earls was in progress, after Christmas he went home to Kenilworth, and the surviving letters he wrote to Elizabeth in the early weeks of 1570 do not suggest that he felt any particular need to curry favour. They lack the particular tone of abasement that all her courtiers – himself included – felt necessary to assume when they had offended her in any way. Despite his grumbles about the 'cold and scarcity' of the place and the times, there is a note almost of cheerful optimism in the letter of 10 January, which he sends 'only to hear of your good estate, which I pray to continue longer in this world than ever earthly prince has done'.

He reminds Elizabeth that she had promised to send him a treasurer, 'although in respect of the weather, I shall pity his travel in so hard a time as I never found the like' – perhaps, he suggests in a malicious joke, she should amuse herself by choosing a man who really wouldn't want to come. He says his brother the Earl of Warwick has but just arrived, on horseback despite that same hard weather, jokes that Ambrose 'has left his gout behind him among the northern worse-natured subjects', but emphasizes that he plans to take only a few days' rest before returning to his duty again. A postscript is taken up with the repercussions of the rebellion: the letter is to be brought south by one Richard Topcliffe (later famous or infamous for the sadistic zeal with which he persecuted Catholics), who had brought thirty horsemen to join Warwick at his own expense, and Warwick had advice about the examining of two prisoners.

A few days later Robert (on behalf of both Dudley brothers), was penning a punning metaphor on the Dudley emblem of the bear and the ragged staff: 'We two here, your poor thralls, your *ursus major* and *minor*, tied to your stake, shall for ever remain in the bond chain of dutiful servitude, fastened above all others by benefits past, and daily goodness continually showed'. The stake itself prevents 'curs from biting behind', and therefore, 'so long as you muzzle not your beast, nor suffer the match over hard, spare them not; I trust you shall find they fear not who come before'.

It was a rather laboured effort at courtly wordplay, and it is with some relief that Robert warns the Queen he will now 'return to my wonted manner' in offering the best prayers for her safety of himself and his brother, of 'Sister Mary', and of Sister Kate, 'who is here with me'. It sounds as if the Dudley siblings felt a need to be together at this time. Perhaps, even, they were making a highly visible show of solidarity, a firebreak in a part of England that had so nearly been contested territory. In the years ahead Robert as well as Ambrose would be both active and aggressive in enforcing the Protestant party political line through the Midland territories where they held sway. The earl was in the process of making Kenilworth into a pleasure palace; but it was also a highly defensible stronghold, should that have proved necessary. (The Spanish ambassador certainly thought that he had gone north to fortify it.) The Norfolk matter, the northern revolt, could all have gone so very badly.

11

'The great Lord'

The 1570s

IN A PORTRAIT PAINTED IN THE MID-1560S, ROBERT DUDLEY CUTS A resplendent figure. His left hand rests on the hilt of his sword, the other haughtily on his thrusting hip. His tawny suit, embroidered and pearl-encrusted, matches the feather in his cap. His collar, with its small, discreet ruff, is so high he can hardly have been able to move his head. It is the picture of a lover, a swordsman, a grandee – but these were no longer the only roles Leicester had to play.

From the time of his appointment to the privy council, he had taken avidly to its powers and duties. As the Spanish ambassador wrote, later in the 1570s, though there were seventeen councillors, 'the bulk of the business really depends upon the queen, Leicester, Walsingham and Cecil'.* This – an active part in government – was what he felt was expected of him; the purpose for which he had been bred and indeed educated. Leicester (so one grateful scholar reported) was one who 'accepted the practical help of the historians' in the problems of ruling a country.

---

* Derek Wilson points out that in 1565, for example, Leicester had been present at four-fifths of the council's hundred or so meetings: more than any other councillor except Cecil or Sir Francis Knollys.

In one sense, his political importance was now an established fact; something that had to be recognized, whether or not the Queen's romantic interest seemed to be turning away from him. If the strength of her feelings was waning, then perhaps that is what encouraged him, over the years ahead, to operate more autonomously. For Leicester had his own information networks, bringing in reports from Europe and from Scotland, transcripts from the interrogations of state prisoners, letters from the embassies. He was a JP in several counties, Steward of Cambridge University and of several towns, Chancellor of Oxford University. And though Elizabeth discouraged all the old badges of allegiance that had shown the strength of a great lord's following, it was said that in every shire there were many JPs who openly wore Leicester's livery.

But all this, in a sense, was secondary. It was Leicester's special ability to persuade his royal mistress which made him especially useful to the council as a whole – an asset his colleagues increasingly recognized, once they had ceased automatically to regard him as the enemy. It was his handling of Elizabeth that 'amounted almost to a separate function of government', as Milton Waldman put it memorably in the 1940s. And here lay both his strength and his weakness. For whatever efforts he made to win himself an independent power base, his whole life and status had still been built upon the suspect foundation of that one relationship. His enemies would not forgive him that. Neither would posterity.

As a favourite, he was of necessity the ultimate courtier, with all that implied. 'He was very graceful in behaviour, of a liberal diet, and much addicted to sensual pleasures. He was commonly accounted a good courtier, which in other terms is called a cunning dissembler,' wrote Clapham after his death, dismissively. Castiglione (in his book on the courtier, of which Leicester possessed a copy) had written that the courtier's role was 'to be attractive, accomplished, and seem not to care, to charm and to do so coolly'. In asking a favour, the courtier 'will skillfully make easy the difficult points so that his lord [sic] will always grant it'. This is the way women have traditionally exercised influence: no wonder that Froude, the great Elizabethan historian of the nineteenth century, who despised Elizabeth's favourites and mis-trusted her femininity, wrote of Robert Dudley that he had 'the worst qualities of both sexes'. It was another reason to regard a queen's favourite suspiciously.

The most lucrative single gift Elizabeth gave Leicester was that of influence; every penny he was given or sent enhanced his prestige among other, minor, courtiers, hopeful for their own lesser share of royal bounty. He was at the top of the patronage tree; and he was consistent in his efforts to do his best for his clients, albeit also fierce in his demand for their loyalty. (A series of letters he wrote to Francis Walsingham, then in France, show him pursuing a servant he felt had done him wrong, even when the man had fled the country. He could be both vengeful and territorial, clearly.)

Surviving letters between Leicester and his many contacts show the hothouse atmosphere of this perfervid world, where all rights and revenues emanated ultimately from the Queen herself, diffused through her favourites and officers; and where power and personality were thus inextricably intertwined. They show the anxiety of the client: when to chase up a favour promised, and when to hold back; how to keep yourself in mind without being obnoxious, through a gift of a pair of gloves, a cash present, a pie. But they also show the pressure on the great men approached: their tetchiness at the unending demands – and their wounded anger when an impatient client showed signs of following another star. The favourites were pikes among minnows, to be sure; but still themselves dependent on the Queen's favour, a position of responsibility without power.

On the one hand (like any other great noble) Leicester kept what was in effect his own court. The bill of wages he paid shows that he had not just his grooms and huntsmen, his watermen, cooks and laundresses, but his gentlemen servants and his offi-cers, his grooms of the chamber. In this he was, like Elizabeth herself, seated in dramatic state at the very tip of a huge antheap of industry. (Like Elizabeth, he might sometimes dine alone when away from court, apart from the huge main company of his entourage, on the grounds that there was no-one present of rank high enough appropriately to eat with him.) On the other hand, when Elizabeth herself entered the picture, he himself joined the busy throng, rushing to make arrangements for her court and her convenience, her party or her journey; became, in effect, another worker bee.

And if, in this pyramidal structure, the great Earl of Leicester was subservient only to Elizabeth herself, then she could be cruelly dismissive. A French ambassador, telling her that his master approved the idea of her marrying Robert Dudley, and wished to meet him, had been told that 'It would scarcely be honourable to send a groom to meet so great a king' – and, laughing, 'I cannot do without my Lord Robert [as then he was], for he is like my little dog, and whenever he comes into a room, everyone at once assumes that I myself am near.' Robert was standing there, and one can imagine how he had to laugh politely, and how anyone else there probably laughed sycophantically, and how, yes, he probably did go away and kick the cat – or the nearest client, anyway.

True, he was a very great man in the country (and, indeed, beyond it – to half Europe he was now 'the great Lord'). He swam the teeming waters of the court and court politics like a leviathan. To crowds of minor satellite gentry – to hordes of others hoping for employment, or for his intercession with some hostile authority – it was his momentary attention that was the prize; his smile or frown that set the climate for the day. But faced with Elizabeth herself, he was still – in public at least – just another subject who had to address her on his knees; as Elizabeth herself had had to address her brother Edward in his day. (Even Bothwell, after he had married Mary, found it more politic to doff his cap in his wife's presence, though his new rank would have entitled him to keep it on.) Robert's power came from positions and properties the Queen had given; and what the Queen had given, she could take away. His only counterstroke could be armed revolt, and even if she had ever feared that, Elizabeth now – with her long knowledge of Leicester, with the confidence of a decade's successful rule – knew it was extremely unlikely.

There is a story from April 1566 that dramatizes Leicester's position, and that of Elizabeth, as clearly as if they were set out in a problem play. The Queen, being at her palace in Greenwich, agreed to travel up to Southwark to meet Robert returning from a journey. Robert entered the City in staggering splendour; with a train 'all in their rich coats and to ye number of 700'. From Temple Bar, he passed Ludgate and St Paul's on his way to the rendezvous at Lord Oxford's house, just north of London Bridge. Meanwhile the Queen was being rowed across the Thames in a wherry with a single pair of oars, accompanied only by two ladies. By the time they had stepped out of the boat, and into their 'coach covered with blue', Leicester – finding neither the Queen, nor any rumour of her coming such as his own grand arrival had made – had left Lord Oxford's house, and ridden over the bridge.

The chapter of accidents had a happy ending: Elizabeth's coach, in its turn, set off in pursuit of Leicester's party, who had halted on the road back to Greenwich where he knew she would pass. On overtaking him, the Queen 'came out of her coach in the high-way and she embraced the Earl and kissed him three times', as the beady-eyed spectators noted carefully. But the story has a complex moral. On the surface, it is true, it was the Queen who had been forced to chase the over-impatient earl. But look at the reason for all the confusion – Elizabeth's desire for privacy. The earl would arrive with a splendid retinue: it was in his interest that as many people as possible should know the Queen was coming to meet him. The Queen, by contrast, had no reason at all to broadcast the fact she was meeting the Earl of Leicester; her private pleasure, her Robert Dudley. That same year, the French ambassador had reported a conversation with Leicester who 'confessed to me, smiling and sighing at the same time, that he does not know what to hope or fear'.

Small wonder, then that as time passed Leicester would demonstrate an increased dissatisfaction with the court and its world. His letters to Elizabeth show a mounting distaste for London, with its 'corrupt air', urging 'exercise with open air' as the best remedy for 'those delicate diseases gotten about your dainty city'. To a young man, the court was opportunity – 'the nurse of dignity', as Sir Nicholas Throckmorton's nephew later put it. But

a man in his mid-thirties might begin to tire of the foetid atmosphere. ('Go tell the court it glows, and stinks like rotten wood,'
Walter Ralegh would write, famously.) In one letter to the Queen,
Leicester wrote with obvious feeling of the failing health of one
elderly nobleman, and of the distress and concern of the man's
wife. It sounds as though he were beginning to appreciate the
domestic virtues. His circle by now included his nephews – son
and son-in-law to his sister Mary – the young Philip Sidney and
the Earl of Pembroke. But he had still no heir of his own.

If he wanted to absent himself from the court's peregrinations,
he had the London base of Leicester House: one of those great old
noble houses whose courts and gardens stretched between the
Strand and the river (the latter being by far the more important
highway). He had his newly purchased retreat of Wanstead, to the
east of London but still accessible, and eminently suitable for
hunting trips up the Lea Valley. And he had Kenilworth, where his
programme of building work and improvement was just getting
under way. One letter, to Anthony Forster (he of Cumnor fame),
written before the Queen's first visit to Kenilworth, shows the
earl's concern for even the minutiae of his showpiece. He had sent
£12 'to buy trifles withal for fireworks and such like'; and
demanded in return a provision of spices, to be obtained at the
Queen's own, presumably lower, price. Furthermore,

> I willed Ellis to speak with you and Mr Spinola again for that I
> perceive that he hath word from Flanders that I cannot have such
> hangings thence as I looked for for my dining chamber at Kenilworth
> ... deal with Mr Spinola hereabout for [he] is able to get such stuff
> better cheap than any man and I am sure that he will do his best for
> me. And, though I cannot have them so deep as I would, yet if they
> be large of wideness and twelve or thirteen foot high it shall
> suffice ...

His papers show evidence of a huge range of interests, of affairs
both large and small. It was clearly a matter not just of
practicality, but of personality.

Leicester could write to Shrewsbury as enthusiastically as a boy about the new voyage of the Muscovy Company, 'and I am sorry your lordship is no deeper an adventurer'. Some of those activities aimed primarily at increasing his revenues – for Leicester 'lived always above any Living I had' – would prove also to have implications for the nation: his support for the great mariners (and great privateers); his backing of Hawkins's first voyage to the West Indies and of Drake's circumnavigation, of the Merchant Adventurers and the Company of Kathai. He and Ambrose would be the chief supporters of Frobisher's search for the north-west passage. Other activities would be to do with keeping his huge client base happy, and justifying the regular 'presents' they gave him; whether they were the Corporation of Yarmouth, the Dean and Chapter of Norwich, or mere members of the minor gentry. (White bears and white gerfalcons from the trader Jerome Horsey; fourteen pounds of marmalade from Southampton's worthies.)

But his interests extended far beyond the practical concerns of a landowner and a politician. There were considerable charitable concerns – to be expected of a great man, maybe; but there is surely something unexpected in his detailed suggestions to the local burghers for the cloth industry in Warwick: 'I could wish there were some special trade devised wherewith having a good stock both reasonable profit might arise and your poor set on work. Whereunto I would be glad to help . . .' One of his most enduring building projects was the old soldiers' hospital in Warwick, still in use today. Nor were his involvements, whether charitable or ruthlessly commercial, confined to the West Midlands; he was also lord of a huge tract of land just over the border in North Wales. It was there, at Denbigh, that he would in the decade ahead begin to build a church which, had it been completed before his death, would have had an honoured place in ecclesiastical history: for while existing church architecture reflected the pattern of the old Catholic service, this vast building was to be constructed on ardently Protestant lines, suitable for the popular preaching that was so important a part of the new theology. We have to understand his religious beliefs if we are ever to see the mature Robert Dudley clearly.

The Earl of Leicester, with his gaudy clothes and his grandeur, his self-indulgent appetites and the irregularities of his private life, seems a far cry from what we think of as a puritan today. But that is probably an anachronistic perception. The fact is that, even from the very start of Elizabeth's reign, the 'hotter' wing of the Protestant party had had their eye upon Robert Dudley. In that first winter of 1558–9 John Aylmer, dedicating his response to John Knox, had singled him out as one of the two courtiers endowed 'with a singular favour and desire to advance and promote the true doctrine of Christ's cross'. (The other was Lord Bedford, Ambrose Dudley's father-in-law.)

Those works dedicated to Robert Dudley or published under his protection early in the reign included: in 1561 a treatise against the doctrine of free will, by a Protestant writer; in 1562 a translation of *The Laws and Statutes of Geneva* (Switzerland being home to the most advanced wing of the Reformation); in 1564 a translation of Peter Martyr's influential *Commentaries on Judges*; and in 1572, a refutation of the papal bull against Elizabeth by the important Zurich reformer Henry Bullinger, the publication of which, given the importance of a clear answer to the Pope's threats, amounts to an official recognition of Leicester's status as guardian of Protestantism. Early in the reign, the writer of an anonymous note of recommendation had clearly chosen Robert Dudley as the best man to find places in the church for twenty-eight 'godly preachers which have utterly forsaken antichrist and all his Romish rags'. In the 1560s he was reported by the Spanish ambassador as having ordered the removal from the Queen's private chapel of several old-style furnishings; it was one of the things that made the ambassador doubt the sincerity of his offers of friendship.

The religious settlement Elizabeth had chosen back at the start of her reign was Protestant in essentials, but sufficiently familiar in its trappings (the colourful riches associated with the Catholic Church) to give some comfort to ordinary people. It was in many ways the plan that had been laid out under Robert's father – but times had moved on since then, and in measure as it soothed the traditionalists, so it came to give considerable concern to the real reformers; indeed, it risked being seen, as one anonymous author claimed, as 'a cloaked papistry or a mingle mangle'. Robert himself had once been prepared to make conciliatory gestures towards Catholicism, if urged by political necessity. But by 1568, the French ambassador wrote, Robert 'was totally of the Calvinist religion'.

It used to be assumed that his was merely a faith of convenience – that the puritans, as they were now coming to be called, were strongly against Elizabeth's marrying a Catholic prince, and so was he – or even that his first motivation was the chance to grab further church lands. But it is hard to square that view with a letter which, in August 1576, Leicester would write to a noted puritan, Thomas Wood, a longtime satellite of the Dudleys. Wood had written to the Dudley brothers, complaining that Leicester seemed to have played a leading part in suppressing the puritan practice of 'prophesying' in Southam in Warwickshire, an area of Dudley influence. The puritans were devoted to these sessions of communal study, but the conservatives, and Elizabeth herself, viewed them with mistrust as forums for public dissent. Leicester (and the rest of a largely supportive council) had been acting on royal orders when the prophesyings were put down.

But the point that strikes any modern reader of this letter is not that Leicester seems, in this case, to have failed the puritans. It is not even the degree to which they had thought of him as an 'earnest favourer and as it were a patron', as Wood acknowledged: one who had nudged their men into office (bishops, deans, heads of house at Oxford), pressed for further reforms, protected puritans whose practices laid them open to attack and smoothed the path for the French Protestant refugees who, in the 1560s, had begun trickling into England. What is most striking is the tone in which Leicester chooses to justify himself, in an extremely long and personal letter, to this apparently unimportant man.

There is, he wrote,

> no man I know in this realm of one calling or other that hath showed a better mind to the furthering of true religion than I have done, even

from the first day of her Majesty's reign to this . . . I take Almighty God to my record, I never altered my mind or thought from my youth touching my religion, and you know I was ever from my cradle brought up in it.

Perhaps he wrote in the memory of his father's apostasy.

Not that he himself was actually in favour of the most extreme puritanism. 'He that would be counted most a saint I pray God be found a plain true Christian,' he said.

I am not, I thank God, fantastically persuaded in religion but, being resolved to my comfort of all the substance thereof, do find it soundly and godly set forth in this universal Church of England . . . which doctrine and religion I wish to be obeyed duly as it ought of all subjects in this land . . . For my own part, I am so resolved to the defence of that [which] is already established as I mean not to be a maintainer or allower of any that would trouble or disturb the quiet proceeding thereof.

Leicester warned that internecine strife among the different wings of the Protestant religion was not helping anybody except their Catholic adversaries. 'I found no more hate or displeasure almost between papist and Protestant than is now in many places between many of our own religion.' He stood fast behind Elizabeth's position, when it came to it. Elizabeth is famously quoted as saying that there was one Jesus Christ and the rest was 'a dispute about trifles'. So here he too spoke of 'dissension for trifles'. Their phrases did still often echo each other's to a notice-able degree.

It would be possible to find in Elizabeth's writings, as well as in Leicester's, the strong religious rhetoric that strikes modern ears so forcefully. In a prayer published for the edification of her people, Elizabeth had written: 'Thou seest whereof I came, of corrupt seed; what I am, a most frail substance; where I live, in the world full of wickedness, where delights be snares, where dangers be imminent, where sin reigneth and death abideth. This is my state. Now where is my comfort?' It is something to set against those more familiar statements, suggestive of an easy pragmatism, that sit so agreeably with our own century; something that may perhaps suggest another strand in the bond she shared with Robert Dudley.

What is more certain, however, is that the faith which had in Mary Tudor's day united Robert and Elizabeth would in the years ahead help to divide them. In those times to come, in a world increasingly polarized by religious division, Leicester would declare as the Protestant champion while Elizabeth, on the contrary, would draw further away from the radical reformers, as the demands of their faith clashed with the functions and prerogatives of her monarchy.

The political *froideur* between them gained impetus from the personal. Leicester's relationship with the Queen – baulked likewise of any natural fulfilment and of a natural end – seemed to be foundering into sterility. Up with the rocket, down with the stick. And up, and down again . . . On one of his absences from the court, the Queen had sent after him a communiqué which evidently shocked him. Elizabeth's letter is long lost, as is whatever response Robert finally felt emboldened to send to her directly. But the letter he wrote to Throckmorton paints the situation vividly. He had 'never wilfully offended', he wrote plaintively; and even if he had done so inadvertently,

> Foul faults have been pardoned in some; my hope was that only one might be forgiven – yea, forgotten – me. If many days' service and not a few years' proof have [not] made trial of unremovable fidelity enough, what shall I think of all that past favour, which [when] my first oversight [brings about] as it were an utter casting off of all that was before . . .

The shock had been all the worse for the fact the letter had been written in the Queen's own hand: an honour, but one he could have done without, for 'then I might yet have remained in some hope of mistaking'. No need for him to make haste home to court – a 'cave in a corner of oblivion, or a sepulchre for perpetual rest' would be more suitable, Leicester added in a postscript, bitterly.

In these tetchy years we find the Chancellor, Sir Walter Mildmay, writing that he cannot do Leicester's bidding for fear of displeasing the Queen, 'who is in no wise disposed to hear anything that may do you good'. The Queen (Mildmay said once) could even be heard telling her cousin, Lord Hunsdon: 'My lord, it hath often been said that you should be my Master of the Horse, but it is now likely to come true.' One has the strong sense that both Elizabeth and Robert, while each communicating nominally with a third party, were actually speaking for each other's ears – as is clearly evident in a letter Throckmorton wrote to Robert towards the end of the 1560s. (There was more than one occasion on which Leicester, having clearly offended the Queen in some way, used Throckmorton as the conduit to make his peace.)

The Queen read Leicester's letter thrice,

and said you did mistake the cameleon's property, who doth change into all colours according to the object, save white, which is innocency . . . Then she willed me to show her what your lordship had written to me. She read my letter twice and put it in her pocket. Then I demanded of her whether she would write to your Lordship. She plucked forth my letter and said, 'I am glad at the length he hath confessed a fault in himself, for he asketh pardon.'

Throckmorton, correctly assessing the climate of her mood, saw that she was eager to picture Leicester as repentant, and dared charge her with harshness. The idea of her favourites being dismayed by her frowns always went down well with Elizabeth, for now she smiled: pleased, clearly.

So far, it is true, their estrangements had never lasted long. But there was an increasingly strained note about the squabbles and the reconciliations, as if each tug were stretching the elastic of their affection a little more taut; each release revealing it to have grown a little more slack. It could be suggested that Elizabeth – like a temperamental top seed throwing tantrums on the tennis court – fuelled herself by these teacup tempests. But there is no reason at all to suppose Robert Dudley felt the same way.

Backwards and forwards, in favour and out of it: it was (to use a later idiom) enough to exhaust a cow. Of course, Robert was not just the victim here. He, as much as Elizabeth, had his own game to play: supporting a foreign match proposed for her, and then turning against it; speaking favourably in public, but perhaps taking a different tone in private, in those conversations to which we never will be privy; taking what he could get from her, even while baulked of the thing he couldn't: a relationship of patronage that shaped and warped their bond. (Leicester's enemies said of him that he made money out of every quarrel – 'was never reconciled to the Queen under £5,000', in one account from the eighteenth century.) On the other hand, it is hard not to see Robert as the greater sufferer. Such, over the next few years, he increasingly felt himself to be. It was becoming apparent that Elizabeth had no interest in altering the status quo. If she could hold everyone and everything in stasis then she would be happy: foreign suitors proposing; Robert Dudley adoring; the country complaisant; and the years at bay. It was he who wanted to move the game on – by marriage to Elizabeth, if that were possible; but, if it were not, then maybe another way.

Again, perhaps Robert's feelings, his attitude towards Elizabeth's other suitors, bear looking at more closely. In the years ahead, he would seem not to be automatically opposed to all possible foreign alliances. It was partly pretence, but not entirely. As his own hopes began imperceptibly to fade, a measure of pragmatism was a self-preserving necessity. Best, if it really came to that, for Elizabeth to marry a foreign prince who had some reason to be grateful to him, Robert, because a hostile royal husband would have a mere subject at his mercy.

Robert's real position was becoming clear. Whenever another marriage possibility came too close, whenever the calls for her marriage became too pressing, Elizabeth could brandish his name at the aggressor. In these terms, Robert was as much a lay figure – 'The Suitor', the ever-ready – as a puppet in a Punch and Judy show.

Once he began slowly to realize Elizabeth would never marry him, then what did Robert Dudley think? Did he subscribe to the old courtly story, the credo that 'the Queen can do no wrong'? Again, it is extraordinary just how many points of connection can be found between the rules of courtly love and the relationship between Elizabeth and Robert Dudley – right down to the Queen's 'two bodies': her dual identity as a flesh-and-blood woman and as a genderless, presumed masculine, epitome of monarchy;* right down to the repeated rivalry, in the literature of courtly love, between the knight and the clerk – Robert Dudley and William Cecil? – for the favour of the lady.

The links extend to the relevance of courtly love to the Arthurian fantasy, which attracted both Elizabeth and Robert; to the importance of courtly love as a gesture against (in the words of one expert) 'the harsh authoritarian world of masculine kingship' in general, and the Holy Roman Empire in particular; to the habitual use of symbols (like Robert's sketched 'Eyes'); and of course to the fact that no history of the literature of courtly love can be complete without the afternote of *The Faerie Queene*, the long poem written by Robert's protégé Spenser and perhaps intended by the poet's patron (before his untimely death put paid to the idea) to buy his way back into Elizabeth's wandering favour.

But alongside the long devotion to lost causes that belonged to the old tradition of courtly love, there was a sharper strand in Elizabethan poetry. It spoke of cynicism:

> My sovereign sweet her countenance settles so
> To feed my hope, while she her snares might lay.
> And when she saw that I was in her danger,
> Good God, how soon she proved then a ranger.
>
> (lyric, anon.)

And it spoke of resolution:

* The courtly lover addressed his lady as *midons*, Lewis pointed out, 'which etymologically represents not 'my lady' but 'my lord'.

Since there's no help, come let us kiss and part:
Nay, I have done; you get no more of me;
And I am glad, yea, glad with all my heart
That thus so cleanly I myself can free.

(Michael Drayton)

Whatever Robert Dudley's sexual relationship with Elizabeth had been, it was surely fading away. In 1565 the Imperial ambassador – having made the most 'diligent enquiries' concerning her 'maiden honour and integrity' – had felt able to reassure his master that Robert was 'a virtuous, pious, courteous and highly moral man whom the Queen loves as a sister her brother in all maidenly honour, in most chaste and honest love. She speaks publicly with him as with a dear brother, but that she desires to marry him or entertains any but the purest affection is quite out of the question.' Suggestions to the contrary were 'the spawn of envy and malice and hatred' merely. Now, five years later, the French envoy likewise concluded that Elizabeth was 'good and virtuous', adding that with so many watching her it were impossible she could be so admired if she were anything else.

Did Robert, as the years wore on, as his first high hopes flagged, bring himself to the pragmatic position: that he had done pretty well out of the situation, even if he had not got the biggest prize? If so, perhaps he had also arrived at this proviso: that though he too could do worse than maintain the status quo, he would not allow it to keep him from another relationship, fulfilled and fruitful, indefinitely. And perhaps he had come to realize that a foreign marriage for Elizabeth – to the right person, under the right circumstances – could even set him free.

12

'Our estate requireth a match'
1570–1572

FOR ELIZABETH TOO, THE NEW DECADE OPENED ONTO THE FAINT rumours of change. One way or another, the possibility of the Queen's linking herself to a Valois prince was to occupy much of the 1570s, though the full impact of the latest set of proposals – the moment when the purely political turned to the personal, when the fantasy of marriage nearly became reality – would not come until almost the end of that decade.

But already, in 1570, there was clear and pressing need for England to find allies, and France (ancient enemy though it might be) was the obvious ally against the ever-growing might of Spain; a might that threatened to upset the precarious balance of power in Europe. At home, too, Elizabeth was feeling vulnerable. In February 1570 Pope Pius V issued the bull *Regnans in excelsis*, depriving Elizabeth, in the eyes of all loyal Catholics, of 'her pretended right to her realm'. The fact of the Queen of Scots' presence in her country put her under ever more pressure to marry. And so the year that first saw Elizabeth's Accession Day celebrated as a public holiday – that first saw the worship of the Virgin Queen, you might say – saw also the start of the long negotiations with the French royal house of Valois; negotiations that did at last come close to ending her virginity.

In the September of 1570 the French sent a proposal that

Elizabeth should marry the Duke of Anjou, brother to the French king Charles IX. Henri was nineteen to Elizabeth's almost forty; but the age gap that had worried Elizabeth so much when negotiating for Charles seemed not to concern her this time. But then, it is possible that the alliance was theoretical on both sides, anyway. Anjou was certainly reluctant. His fervent personal Catholicism was bound to prove a major problem; so indeed was his promiscuous bisexuality.*

Perhaps the conspicuous complications explain why Leicester himself sounded a note of cautious optimism about the potential match. On a personal level, he must have known Elizabeth's heart was never likely to be engaged; on a political one, he had learnt the usefulness of a marriage negotiation from his royal mistress. As he wrote to his ally Francis Walsingham, then serving as ambassador to the French court: 'I concede our estate requireth a match, but God send us a good one and meet for all parties.' (An exile for his faith during Mary Tudor's reign, Walsingham would become ever more important in the years ahead. The man who became the organizing genius behind Elizabeth's network of spies and informers – 'a most subtle searcher of secrets', as Camden said – would also be bound to Leicester and his family by a number of ideological and personal ties.)

For their part, the French – as Walsingham wrote in response – were understandably sceptical about England's apparent welcome of their approach. 'They think here you do but dally,' Walsingham explained to the Queen, and Leicester must have understood their feeling precisely. He himself felt, he wrote to Walsingham, that the match should be agreed or abandoned: 'that either upon very good deliberation it may be embraced, or in time, and in best sort, put from too much entrance; for neither is our cause meet to dally nor [Anjou's] person to be abused'. Nevertheless, Elizabeth, Leicester said, was 'more bent to

---

* Henri has to be distinguished from his younger brother François, at this time still the Duke of Alençon. Confusingly, François subsequently became the Duke of Anjou when Charles's premature death brought Henri to the throne, but for simplicity's sake I shall continue to call François 'Alençon'.

marriage than heretofore she hath been'; though still insisting on conditions the French would find it hard to meet, still complaining of princes who 'would rather marry the kingdom than marry the Queen'. Over the next few months he would harp to Walsingham on the same theme: that 'assuredly I do verily believe her Majesty's mind herein is other than it has been, and more resolutely determined than ever yet at any time before'. He wrote of Anjou's strong suit in terms that showed he now accepted the weakness of his own. When it came to the question of 'estate', he said, Elizabeth 'is of mind to marry with the greatest and he [Anjou] is almost alone the greatest to be had. The conditions will be all . . .'

Leicester was ready, Walsingham was to assure the French, accurately or otherwise, 'to allow of any marriage we shall like'. Everyone seemed to feel he had effectively a measure of veto, or at the least that his support would be well worth having. (At one point, the French commissioners were even instructed to sweeten him with the hand of a Valois princess if necessary.) But Leicester seemed to have abandoned all thought of sexual jealousy. Indeed, in December it was he who ushered Fénelon into Elizabeth's private rooms for the all-important discussion. And when in January 1571 Elizabeth told the French ambassador she was worried that Anjou would always be younger than she, Leicester quipped 'so much the better for you', with hearty bonhomie.

Anjou, on the other hand, was publicly grumbling that his brother the King and his mother Catherine de Medici wanted to marry him off to 'an old creature with a sore leg'. The French terms were as demanding as the English (at one point Elizabeth even demanded the return of Calais!): that Henri should be crowned king, should rule England jointly with his wife, and should be allowed to practise his own religion freely. Most of Europe reckoned it would never happen; but the English ministers and the French queen mother between them were determined to drag the two reluctant principals to the altar – and the threat that if Elizabeth did not take him, Anjou might instead seek to marry the Queen of Scots provided a powerful disincentive to the English to abandon the proposal too quickly. 'Of all impending perils that would be the greatest,' Leicester was warned, ominously.

Contemporaries, understandably, seem to have found it hard to grasp Leicester's own policy. The Spanish ambassador claimed that while on the surface he was all for the match, *'por tercera mano'* ('with the third hand') he was telling the Queen that Anjou was infected with loathsome diseases. Cecil was grumbling to Walsingham that 'It was strange any one man should give comfort to the Ambassador in the cause, and yet the same man to persuade the Queen's Majesty to persist.' The one man was surely Leicester – but such behaviour is not at odds with his convictions. He could not but applaud the Queen's cavils, in so far as they sprang from her 'true zeal to Religion', since the strength of his own conviction was increasingly coming to colour his public as well as his private life. But he could still send a private piece of advice that the French should not press their point (that Anjou should be allowed to practise his own Catholicism) before the signing of an agreement. The Queen was more likely to 'yield to reason' afterwards, to the persuasions of one 'that shall be her husband', than to a formal treaty.

In the spring of 1571, as the negotiations wore on, William Cecil was elevated to the peerage as Lord (Baron) Burghley. Leicester stood at his right hand during the ceremony; and the next year he deputized for the Queen at the Garter ceremony at which Cecil was accorded that honour, too. In February 1571 Throckmorton died, after falling ill at Leicester's house – after eating salads, so Camden said – and though it would later be rumoured Leicester had poisoned him, the fact is the earl had lost his subtlest political ally.* And early that same year, there came yet another story of political chicanery that shows Leicester acting equivocally.

Back in the summer of 1570, Norfolk had been released from the Tower into a form of house arrest on the pleas of Leicester

---

* Throckmorton died at his house on a Monday, Leicester wrote to Walsingham, 'being taken there suddenly in great extremity on Tuesday before; his lungs were perished, but a sudden cold he had taken, was the cause of his speedy death'.

and of Cecil and the promise of good behaviour. He was still hoping to regain a measure of favour; and the letter Leicester wrote on 2 January 1571 sounds (though of course his sincerity has been questioned) as if he were genuinely trying to help him. 'I know not almost with what face I may in this sort write to you, my good Lord,' the letter starts out. Leicester had tried to get the Queen to accept a New Year gift Norfolk had sent her; had persuaded her to read the accompanying letter, which she admitted to be 'very wisely and dutifully written', and then to examine what was inside: 'she took the jewel in her hand, and, I perceive, did not think before it had been so rich or so fair as it was indeed till she had seen it. Then did she commend it beyond measure, and thought there had not been such a one to be got in all London, and valued it with the pearl at least £500.' She looked at it for almost a quarter of an hour and, said Leicester shrewdly, seemed sorry to have to refuse it; but – 'contrary to all my know-ledge and expectation', Leicester writes, and in spite of 'all the persuasions' – refuse it she did. To accept the gift was to accept the giver; and Elizabeth had by now little belief in Norfolk's loyalty.

The very month after this proffered gift, Mary, Queen of Scots wrote to Norfolk with details of what has become known as the Ridolfi plot: the Florentine banker's plan for the Catholic powers of Europe to invade England, and set Mary and Norfolk on Elizabeth's throne. Ridolfi's touting of the plan round the European courts would have been bound to attract the attention of Cecil's agents, even had they not almost certainly had inside information early. In the Parliament that met in May 1571 (a Parliament at which Leicester held the proxies of seven of the absent peers), three acts were passed to raise the level of national security. All the potential conspirators were closely watched. By the summer, in fact, it had become apparent that Ridolfi's plan was unworkable. It was Philip of Spain's general in the Netherlands, the Duke of Alva, who sounded its death knell, refusing to order his troops on an invasion he knew would fail. But it was too late for the conspirators to retreat successfully. A courier reported the suspicious communications issuing from the

Duke of Norfolk's house; and the dawn of 8 September saw him back in the Tower.

There is still considerable debate as to just who betrayed the Ridolfi plot. Ridolfi himself is the likeliest; but he may have had among his allies one or more double agents as expert as he. One such was the sailor and freebooter John Hawkins; another was Hawkins's shipmate George Fitzwilliam. These two were supposedly prepared to bring English ships over to an invading Spanish enemy, but in fact handed Spanish plans over to the English authorities, triggering Norfolk's rearrest. That Fitzwilliam really owed ultimate allegiance to Spain was always the less likely for the fact that he was related to William Cecil, as well as to Leicester's brother-in-law Henry Sidney.

The full revelation of just how far an anti-England Catholic coalition had gone increased the need for a defensive alliance. But the very tension in the air perhaps heightened Elizabeth's instinctive reluctance to marry, her fear of putting herself and her realm in the hands of another power. In July Leicester had been writing to Walsingham: 'For her desire to marriage, I perceive it continueth still as it was, which is very cold, nevertheless, she seeth it is so necessary, as I believe she yieldeth rather to think it is fit to have a husband, rather than willing to have any found indeed for her.' By late September he was even less hopeful: 'surely I am now persuaded that her Majesty's heart is nothing inclined to marriage at all . . . For my part it grieveth my heart to think of it seeing no way, in so far as I can think, serveth, how she can remain long quiet and safe without such a strong alliance as marriage must bring.'

While various contacts were interrogated, while the Queen of Scots tried to excuse herself and while Norfolk languished in the Tower, the French negotiations wound towards their weary end. First it was Elizabeth who blew cold: Cecil told the Queen at the end of August that he would try to find another route to safety for her, and for her isolated kingdom; Leicester told Walsingham that clearly, after all, 'Her Majesty's heart is nothing inclined to marry at all, for the matter was ever brought to as many points as we could devise, and always she was bent to hold with the difficultest.' Then, as the revelations of the Ridolfi plot forced Elizabeth to realize just how much she needed allies, it was the French who drew back. In December, Leicester was writing to Walsingham that 'I find now a full determination in her Majesty to like of marriage . . . So she earnestly and assuredly affirms to me.' But Anjou made no secret of his distaste; Elizabeth, besides being a heretic, at thirty-eight was losing her looks. Her hair was thinning behind and she had taken to a front of false curls: 'The more hairy she is before, the more bald she is behind,' said England's ambassador Sir Thomas Smith ungallantly. No portraits of Elizabeth reflect her age accurately. She took care they should not; that they should broadcast, rather, the image of unchanging glory. But the grumbles of her ministers reveal the backstage story – that the cracks were beginning to show, in her aptitude as well as her appearance. Elizabeth was becoming more dilatory (a development which perhaps made Leicester's ability to handle her all the more valuable). Her natural bent had always been to procrastinate: to dislike innovation, to resent those who forced her to contemplate problems which, ignored, might go away. She preferred always to keep her own counsel, to reserve her judgement in her own heart, as her motto *Video et taceo* (I see all and speak nothing) might suggest. But now secretary after secretary complained (as Sir Thomas Smith put it in 1574) that 'The time passeth almost irrecuperable, the advantage lost, the charges continuing, nothing resolved.'

She was about to show just that character trait yet again. In January 1572 the Duke of Norfolk came to trial before a jury of his peers. (Almost the only witness called was a man of Leicester's, the writer Richard Cavendish, whose daughter would later marry Leicester's 'base son'.) The verdict of guilty, and the death sentence, were foregone conclusions. The execution itself, however, was another matter. The Queen vacillated almost hysterically, the enormity of Norfolk's repeated and incorrigible offences weighing against his nearness of blood, his 'superiority of honour'. In March she was ill, with 'heavy and vehement pains' that 'straightened her breath and clutched her heart'. For three days and nights Leicester and Cecil sat up with her. The doctors believed she had eaten bad fish – the idea of poison was ever-present – but her emotional distress must surely have played some part. She signed a warrant that Norfolk should be executed on 9 April; then cancelled it just hours before the time. Members of the Parliament that met again this May declared themselves unable to sleep in their beds at night for fear of more conspiracies. Great suit was made for the execution, Leicester told Walsingham, 'but I see no likelihood'. But this time he under-estimated Elizabeth. Another warrant was signed, that Norfolk should die on 2 June, and this time, it was carried out: the first beheading of Elizabeth's reign.*

England, meanwhile, had more reason than ever to pursue the safety of a French alliance against the increasing power and aggression of Spain. If not the reluctant bisexual Henri, then per-haps another Valois brother might do? In December 1571 had come the first suggestion that Elizabeth might marry François, the Duke of Alençon, instead of Anjou. François was (so his mother observed coolly) 'much less scrupulous' than his brother in matters of religion; sympathetic, even, to the Huguenots – altogether less 'like a mule', as Smith chimed in enthusiastically; and 'more apt than th'other' when it came to getting children. Not being heir presumptive to the French throne, he would be free to live in England. Against that, he was seventeen, small, and pockmarked. In April 1572 England and France concluded the Treaty of Blois, whereby they agreed to support each other against the Spanish enemy. Leicester arranged the celebratory banquet at Whitehall – the greatest, he boasted, in memory. It now seemed more desirable than ever that this alliance should be cemented dynastically.

In June came the formal offer of Alençon's hand, on the lips of a special envoy. Though the Queen remained non-committal, Walsingham was instructed to compile a report on the prospective

---

* The letter Norfolk wrote to his children after his sentence is one of the most touching in the period's history, warning his thirteen-year-old heir that, 'though very young in years', he must strive to become a man; that it was all too likely his brothers would be taken from him, as courtiers squabbled for their wardship; that he should, above all else, 'Beware of high degrees!'

bridegroom. The pockmarks on the end of Alençon's nose were the worst of it, he reported; that, and his general lack of beauty: 'when I weigh the same with the delicacy of Her Majesty's eye, I hardly think that there will ever grow any liking'. All the same, when the court set off on progress that summer, things looked as hopeful as they had ever done where Elizabeth's marriages were concerned – which is to say, moderately.

The July progress took her to Warwick, to stay as the guest of Ambrose Dudley. She watched a display of country dancing from the window, 'and made very merry'; herself played on a spinet to delight the company. The highlight of the visit – besides a mock water battle – was a spectacular firework display. Unfortunately, a spark from one firework set four Warwick houses ablaze, but the Queen organized a whip-round, raising £25 to be given to the residents in compensation; probably unusual consideration in the sixteenth century. But as Elizabeth moved on to Leicester's house at Kenilworth, nearby, an event was brewing across the Channel that would put an end to all festivities.

The summer before, Walsingham had written to Leicester that 'if neither marriage nor Amity may take place, the poor Protestants here do think their case then desperate; they tell me so with tears, and therefore I do believe them'. They were right to worry. On 24 August came what has gone down in history as the St Bartholomew's Day Massacre.

It is remembered, perhaps, as just another atrocity in the religious tussles of the sixteenth century, which had already seen the dungeons of the Inquisition and the fires of Smithfield. But in fact, at the time, it was one of those days that do shake the world; one of those days (and it is not hard to think of modern parallels) when an act of aggression so dramatizes an ideological or religious conflict that suddenly a polarity of conviction is set forth for all to see.

It started as the attempted assassination of a single man. The intensely Catholic Guises (the Queen of Scots' family), with the support of Catherine de Medici, who had been persuaded the French Protestants might draw the country into a war with Spain, set out to murder the Protestant leader, Admiral Coligny. The attempt failed, but it provoked riots in Paris, and from there the violence escalated sharply. Soon the Catholics of the capital were killing every Protestant they could lay hands on. As the Spanish ambassador to France sent home in a vivid, if horrifying, despatch: 'While I write, they are casting them out naked and dragging them through the streets, pillaging their houses and sparing not a babe. Blessed be God, who has converted the Princes of France to His purpose. May He inspire their hearts to go on as they have begun!' Three to four thousand died in Paris alone. As the violence spread to the provinces, the death toll rose to some ten thousand. When Philip in Spain received his ambassador's despatch, it was said that he danced for joy; as did the imprisoned Queen Mary.

Elizabeth was out riding when the despatches bearing the news arrived, still on horseback as she read them. Instantly, she turned back towards Kenilworth Castle. There could be no further thought of pleasure on this or many a subsequent day. As the court set off back towards London it was not until several days later, at Woodstock, that the Queen at last consented to receive the French ambassador. Not a courtier would speak to or look at him as he approached the presence chamber. There he found the Queen, her ladies, and her privy councillors all dressed in mourning black. What the Queen said to Fénelon was mild compared to the reproaches of the councillors. Cecil told him it was the greatest crime since the crucifixion. No-one on the English side, now, could think of a Valois marriage. If the French king had been 'Author and doer of this Act, shame and confusion light upon him', Leicester wrote to Walsingham. The question was whether anything could be saved of the Anglo-French treaty.

As Elizabeth wrote to Walsingham – a message for the French king – the murder of the supposed Huguenot conspirators, without 'answer by law', was bad enough: 'we do hear it marvellously evil taken and as a thing of a terrible and dangerous example . . . But when more added unto it – that women, children, maids, young infants and sucking babes were at the same time murdered and cast into the river . . . this increased our grief and sorrow.' Those of the reformed religion in France were driven now 'to fly or die'.

To the Queen's Protestant councillors, to the Earl of Leicester, the question was whether the massacre had been mere mob violence – bad enough – or the fruit of a deep-laid Catholic conspiracy. Opinion (though probably wrong) tended to the latter theory; and this fear was to fling Europe's beleaguered Protestants into a defensive frenzy. As Leicester wrote to the Earl of Morton (representing the Protestant lords of Scotland) on 7 September, the events in France

> be good warnings to all those that be professors of the true religion to take heed in time . . . seeing it to fall out as we do, we are to look more narrowly to our present estate. We cannot but stand in no small danger except there be a full concurrence together of all such as mean faithfully to continue such as they profess.

One of the goals of his life, from now on, would be the formation (in the teeth, if need be, of the Queen's reluctance) of an alliance of all Protestants wherever they might be: in England, Scotland, among the Huguenot community of France or in the Netherlands.

Amid all the fallout of the massacre, one thing that could be seen was a new consensus among Elizabeth's ministers as to the danger represented by the Scots queen, Mary. Back in March 1571, Mary's agent the Bishop of Ross had written that the Queen of Scots' life had been in great danger, with Cecil and others urging she should be put to death; 'and, of all the ministers whom Elizabeth admitted to her confidence, Leicester only had opposed her execution'. But there was no more talk now of Leicester's secret sympathy. Now, Elizabeth's councillors were almost united in believing that Mary (so recently the Catholic focus of rebellion) should be at the very least excluded from the succession, if not actually put to death. Now, Leicester and Cecil were united in urging a *rapprochement* with Scotland's Protestant powers, and in fearing that some around the Queen were too tender to Mary. In November Leicester wrote to Cecil: 'You see how far this Canker has passed. I fear a fistula irrecoverable.' In December, when the Queen was proving reluctant to face up to the Scottish question, Leicester wrote summoning an absent Cecil to the cause:

. There will little be done while you are away; if I saw plainly as I think, your Lordship, as the case stands, shall do her Majesty and your country more service here in an hour than in all the court there will be worth this seven years; wherefore I can but wish you here, yea to fly here if you would, till these matters are fully despatched.

The tone could hardly be more different from his 'old song' – the resentment of Cecil's authority. And here, surely, we need not accuse him of hypocrisy. It was rather a case of 'now is the time for all good men to come to the aid of the party' – the cause of international Protestantism.

It sounds as though Leicester and Elizabeth were beginning to draw apart a little on questions of policy. The political and religious tussles of the years ahead have often been presented as a tug of war for Elizabeth's attention between Leicester's hawkish faction and the more moderate policies best represented by Cecil. But more recently several historians have pointed out that in these years of Elizabeth's reign (before the genuinely divided and divisive 'second reign' and the fractious 1590s, by which time most of the old guard were dead), Elizabeth's advisers tended to be broadly united on what should be done. It was the Queen herself with whom they were all in disagreement.

If Leicester were no longer quite so closely tied to the Queen politically, then, did he need to stick quite so close to her personally? The answer, in a sense, is yes: all her ministers (as increasingly they understood) needed him to do so. He had the best chance of persuading her over to their way. But is the personal shift of tone he now started to take entirely coincidental? Which is the chicken and which the egg?

Already, before the massacre, those letters of Leicester's to the Queen which can be provisionally dated to 1571 (and since they bear no year, it can only be provisional) had been breathing great closeness, indeed; but closeness of a calm, almost a marital kind. The Queen and the earl speak much about health, as couples do, in what was by contemporary standards definitely middle age. One February day Robert scolds Elizabeth, as he has scolded her before, about her 'overlong sojourn in that corrupt air about the city; but you have so earnestly promised remedy as I hope to see you in time this year put it in practice, respecting yourself before others'. He thinks that Grafton, where he is, could be ready for her by May. (Meanwhile he is keeping her messenger with him for a time, after the 'painful journey' he had had: 'he came in such speed as I think he did fly, and therefore deserves some rest'. Leicester himself could sign a letter 'in haste and in bed', and it is rather touching to see how often, as the years wore on, Elizabeth's henchmen mention the need to secure some rest for each other, as well as for themselves. They were clearly all beginning to find the demands of the Queen's service exhausting to a degree.)

In another letter, Robert has to satisfy Elizabeth about his own health: 'your over great care of my present estate'. Though he 'departed away in some pain, yet in no suspicion at all of what you feared, only it seems, for lack of use, my late exercise wrought some strange accident, through my own negligence, to take more cold than was convenient after such heat. I was well warned by you . . .' He had been 'driven to use the commodity of a bath, to ease the pain' – but really, Elizabeth need not worry. It is warm, it is lovely – but it is not the tone of an ardent suitor. That, Elizabeth would now find elsewhere.

At court, a new rival had been competing for the Queen's attention: Christopher Hatton, who had been 'Master of the Game' in those Christmastime revels at the Inner Temple where Robert had presided as Prince Pallaphilos, some years before. Third son of an undistinguished Northamptonshire gentleman, Hatton had been born in 1540 and succeeded to the family estate in his minority, on the deaths of his father and elder brothers. After a spell at Oxford he had been sent by his guardians to the Inns of Court, but it is possible he caught the Queen's eye, still in his early twenties, before he ever had occasion to practise the law he had studied.

The first date of his coming to court is not recorded. He was not important enough for that, until the Queen's favour made him so. But Naunton wrote that he came there 'of a galliard', since it was his dancing first caught the Queen's eye; while Camden, more surely, says that 'being young and of a comely tallness of body and countenance, he got into such favour with the Queen that she took him into her band of fifty Gentleman-pensioners'. From there he rose to be a gentleman of the privy chamber (thanks, Camden says, to 'the modest sweetness of his manners'), and the few years that changed the 1560s to the 1570s saw a steady stream of grants and offices coming his way. The gifts were certainly enough to arouse the jealousy of Leicester, who is said to have offered to bring in a dancing master who could dance even better than Hatton, since that – he insinuated – was the young man's only claim to fame; the attribute that had attracted Elizabeth so powerfully. By the coming year, 1573, Christopher Hatton would be captain of the Gentleman Pensioners, that famously tall and good-looking band whose duty it was to provide a ceremonial guard for the Queen's person.

It has often been speculated that to Hatton – if not to Leicester – Elizabeth at last gave herself physically. It has been said that the tone of his letters is so frenziedly lover-like that no other interpretation is possible. Sending her a ring said to ward off the plague, he wrote that it was meant to be worn 'between the sweet dugs [breasts]'. Forced to leave court for his health in the summer of 1573, he wrote her a whole series of letters so extravagant in their terms that a delighted Elizabeth could be forgiven for concluding that here was a man who really might die for love of her.

> No death, no, nor hell, shall ever win of me my consent so far to wrong myself again as to be absent from you one day. God grant my return. I will perform this vow. I lack that I live by. The more I find this lack, the further I go from you . . . Would God I were with you but for one hour. My wits are overwrought with thoughts. I find myself amazed. Bear with me, my most dear sweet Lady. Passion overcometh me. I can write no more. Love me, for I love you.

And in another letter later in the same month, June, he urged her: 'Live for ever, most excellent creature; and love some man, to shew yourself thankful for God's high labour in you.' Certainly, the tone is more extravagant than what had by now become the rather domestic (and increasingly religious) tone of Leicester's notes.

The real 'evidence', though, comes not from Hatton's own words, but from those of a friend, Edward Dyer, who in the autumn of 1572 wrote warning him about his comportment with the Queen: 'who though she do descend very much in her sex as a woman, yet may we not forget her place, and the nature of it as our Sovereign'.* If a man 'of secret cause known to himself' were to challenge that established order, Dyer told Hatton, he should be very careful, for if the Queen were to mislike it – to 'imagine that you go about to imprison her fancy' – he would be wholly undone. He would do better 'to acknowledge your duty' to the Queen; 'never seem deeply to condemn her frailities, but rather joyfully to commend such things as should be in her, as though they were in her indeed'.

In a letter that serves as a manual of instruction for a favourite, Dyer goes on to warn Hatton against too much importunity, against criticism and jealousy. Particularly, he should beware of displaying his jealousy of 'my Lord of Ctm'; and though the reference is not explicit, this is possibly the young Earl of Oxford, Edward de Vere, who had come to court in 1571. As handsome and talented as he was erratic and untrustworthy, Oxford's career saw him bobbing on successive waves of scandal that might have overwhelmed someone less well born than himself. Elizabeth (and Cecil, who rued the day he had ever become Oxford's father-in-law) came to see that Hatton spoke no more than the truth when he warned Elizabeth to beware of the 'Boar' – for so she named Oxford – whose tusks might raze and tear. Better the Sheep (Hatton was often her 'Mutton'), for 'he hath no tooth to bite'. But for a brief time in the early 1570s, Oxford put everyone else's nose out of joint.

The key passage in Dyer's letter is this one: that 'though in the

---

* Dyer – who had recently been in Leicester's service – is better known now as the poet who wrote 'My mind to me a kingdom is'. When he found himself excluded for years from Elizabeth's favour, he made a successful comeback by staging a pageant in which he cast himself as a minstrel, singing his 'tragical complaint' from the branches of an oak tree.

beginning when her Majesty sought you (after her good manner), she did bear with rugged dealing of yours, until she had what she fancied, yet now, after satiety and fullness, it will rather hurt than help you . . .'. The modern age has been quick to read 'satiety' in a sexual sense; and indeed it is tempting to do so. But that reading falls into question as soon as we consider Elizabeth's character. Do we believe that she would have given herself to Hatton, if she had not done so to Leicester? Or that she could have done so without attracting far more comment, not just in the court, but in her own and other countries?

Yes, a few rumours would always crop up that Hatton, like Leicester, had (in the hostile words of one Mather, a plotter against Elizabeth), 'more recourse to Her Majesty in her Privy Chamber than reason would suffer if she were so virtuous and well-inclined as some [noiseth] her'. Yes, Hatton, like Leicester, was blamed for some of those supposed illicit pregnancies that Elizabeth was rumoured to have concealed so successfully. But it is notable that Elizabeth's statesmen did not seem rattled by Hatton to the degree one might have expected if he, alone, had indeed gained that kind of ascendancy over the Queen. And it is worth noting, too, that some of his most impassioned declarations of apparent love come cheek by jowl with what on the face of it are pleas that Elizabeth should marry him – hardly a possibility. (If marriage with an Earl of Leicester, son of the Duke of Northumberland, might have devalued her status around Europe, then marriage with a mere Christopher Hatton – not even 'Sir' Christopher until 1577 – would have been an absurdity.) What Elizabeth 'fancied' was less sex than adulation; and it was the knowledge that there were firm bounds set on Hatton's aspiration – that he could never realistically even dream of being king consort, nor could his colleagues suspect him of it – that allowed the flirtation to be indulged in all its delicious folly.*

---

* Josephine Ross, in her 1970s book on Elizabeth's suitors, made the point that the very extravagance of Elizabeth's flirtation was not the expression of a consummated love, but a substitute for it. The extravagant attitude of her admirers was of course characteristic of the unconsummated passion of courtly love.

If Hatton does as Dyer says, then 'your place shall keep you in worship, your presence in favour, your followers will stand to you, at the least you shall have no bold enemies, and you shall dwell in the ways to take all advantages wisely, and honestly to serve your turn at times'. Hatton has gone down in history as something of a political lightweight. (There was considerable comment when, in 1587, Elizabeth made him Lord Chancellor – this, when he had no more than the barest legal training.) That reputation is probably unfair. He served Elizabeth's turn not only in a personal capacity but as a privy councillor from 1578, inclining to conservative policies and tolerance of Catholics, and as a gifted parliamentary orator. Certainly men like Cecil came to regard him too as a valuable cog in the wheels of government; and not only because of the kindliness, the sweetness of disposition, that was conceded to him even by his enemies. Even Leicester's letters to him – about an exchange of news, the sending of a buck to court, a message from the Queen, or the royal comings and goings – show a half-mollified prickliness that reflects the combination of his own jealousy and Hatton's amiability.

In the mid-1570s it seemed, after the shocks of the past few years, that the council's internal rivalries had lost their edge. Perhaps the blood-red glow of St Bartholomew's Day made it seem temporarily a little less important whose light at court was shining more brightly. Or perhaps one should see, rather, Leicester and Cecil – and soon, to some extent, Hatton – as prominent figures in a senior group who would join forces against any new pretender to their dignities.

At the start of 1573 it was Cecil's turn to fall out with Elizabeth, and Leicester's to intercede for his old rival, and then to write encouragingly.

For your own matter I assure you I found Her Majesty as well disposed as ever . . . and so, I trust, it shall always continue. God be thanked, her blasts be not the storms of other princes, though they be very sharp sometimes to those she loves best. Every man must render to her their due, and the most bounden the most of all. You and I come in that rank, and I am witness hitherto [to] your honest zeal to perform as much as man can . . . Hold and you can never fail.

By the same token, Leicester in a later letter might grumble that Hatton has found a servant for Elizabeth, when he already had 'a very tall and good footman' of his own in mind – but, increasingly, even he came to trust Hatton to be his intermediary to the Queen in time of need.

Leicester, in Elizabeth's language, was her 'Eyes'. Her eyes were vital, in order that she should see her kingdom. But Hatton (besides being her 'Mutton') was her 'Lids' – lids that perhaps enabled her, when she needed to relax, not to see too much. Perhaps Leicester recognized that this was a role he himself was no longer so well able to play. One of the compensations in the years ahead for both Leicester and many of his erstwhile enemies would be their growing ability to live in increasing amity. As the chance of Elizabeth's marrying Leicester began to look slimmer – as all her councillors, Leicester included, began to feel she would never marry – it was as if they were able to relax with each other, at least to a degree; to work out a kind of *modus vivendi*. This first generation of Queen's Men would achieve, in the years ahead, a kind of collegiate relationship – the chief men in Elizabeth's suite covering for each other in the face of her anger, and consoling each other for her snubs, even when they clashed on policy. (A different analogy might be drawn with the women in a harem, or the wives in a polygamous marriage, who, it is said, may draw considerable support from each other.)

And in any case – something that may well have encouraged the Queen to turn to Hatton – Leicester's own eyes, in the early 1570s, were beginning to turn another way.

13

'I have long both loved and liked you'
1573–1575

court to his father, the Earl of Shrewsbury. The Queen, he said, was as fond of Leicester as ever, and

> of late he hath endeavoured to please her more than heretofore. There are two sisters now in the Court that are very much in love with him, as they have been long; my Lady Sheffield and Frances Howard; they of like striving who shall love him are at great war together, and the Queen thinketh not well of them, and not the better of him; by this means there are spies over him.

But Talbot's news was old; the love was indeed 'long'; and if Leicester was showing himself more assiduous to Elizabeth than had been his recent habit, it may have been because his conscience was pricking him. That same month Leicester and Lady Sheffield went, so she later claimed, through a form of marriage. And though that claim has often been disputed, a letter he wrote to her this spring shows a relationship of real though not unmixed affection; and one that by 1573 had mileage on it.

The Lady Douglass Sheffield was some ten years younger than Robert and Elizabeth, and kinswoman to the Queen through her father, the late Lord William Howard of Effingham, who had been half-brother to Anne Boleyn's mother.* She had married Lord Sheffield when she was seventeen – a decade before Gilbert Talbot's letter – and for several years, in Sheffield's Midlands home, they seem to have lived in reasonable amity. But she may have first been attracted to Leicester as far back as 1566, when Elizabeth went on progress through Northamptonshire and stayed at Belvoir Castle. All the nearby gentry came to pay their respects, the Sheffields among them – or that, at least, was the tale of a distant family connection of the Sheffields, Gervase Holles. The beautiful Douglass, he wrote from the romantic distance of the next century, 'shone like a star' in that gathering, and Leicester, 'being much taken with her perfection, paid court to her and used all the art (in which he was master enough) to debauch her. To be short, he found her an easy purchase, and he had the unlawful fruition of her bed and body.' But to throw a little cold water on the story, Elizabeth is not known ever to have visited Belvoir Castle, though an alternative venue might have been Oxford, where, in honour of the Queen's visit and that of the university's Chancellor, Leicester, Lord Sheffield was one of several gentlemen created Master of Arts.

Lord Sheffield being 'a gentleman of spirit', so Holles claimed, Douglass was terrified he would find out; and Leicester wrote her a cryptically incriminating letter, saying that he had 'not been unmindful in removing that obstacle which hindered the full fruit of their contentment'; that he had endeavoured to do so 'by one expedient already'. One inference is that the goal he was trying to encompass was Lord Sheffield's death. The letter came into Sheffield's hands, who 'that night parted beds, and the next day houses', and set off for London in pursuit of 'just and honourable revenge'. In Holles' version, Leicester bribed an Italian physician to poison the irate husband before he had time to accomplish his fell design . . . In fact, Gervase Holles (a ward of one of Sheffield's nephews) can have got only a garbled word-of-mouth version of

---

* Her somewhat disconcerting name can also be found written as 'Douglas', but I have chosen to keep the more unusual spelling as being less firmly associated with masculinity.

the tale, passed down through a family that viewed Leicester with hostility; and he was writing at a time when tales of poisoning, and particularly of Leicester's part in them, were standard currency. The story is worth recounting because, like many of the slanders on Leicester, it has stuck. But there is not the faintest hint of corroboration; and indeed, in a letter Leicester later wrote to Douglass, he recalls a time 'after your widowhood began, upon the first occasion of my coming to you'.*

Lord Sheffield did not die until 1568, and there was none of the outcry there would have been if someone of his status had expired suspiciously. And frankly, it does not look as though Leicester felt strongly enough about Douglass Sheffield to have gone to any extraordinary lengths to set her free. After she came to court as a widow, to serve in the privy chamber, it seems to have been she who was making the running, as Gilbert Talbot clearly saw. The lengthy letter Leicester wrote at some time during this period sets out very clearly the reasons why, fond though he might have been of her, he did not feel able to marry her.

> I have, as you well know, long both loved and liked you, and found always that earnest and faithful affection at your hand that bound me greatly to you ... after your widowhood began, upon the first occasion of my coming to you, I did plainly and truly open to you in what sort my good will should and might always remain to you ... It seemed that you had fully resolved with yourself to dispose yourself accordingly, without any further expectation or hope of other dealing. From which time you have framed yourself in such sort toward me as was very much to my contentation.

It is the familiar note of the aggrieved male, finding that the comfortable, no-strings arrangement he thought convenient all round is no longer enough for the lady; that, though she cannot bring herself to break off (a separation that he, by the sound of it,

---

* This letter, extensively quoted below, is addressed to an unnamed woman who has been identified as Douglass from internal evidence – see Conyers Read's article of the 1930s, cited in the source notes to this chapter (p. 384 below).

could have contemplated with remarkable equanimity), she is not prepared to set him free. To be fair to Leicester, emotions apart, he did indeed have compelling reason for not making a public commitment. The woman who could force him to risk the loss of Elizabeth's whole favour would need to be a strong character indeed – far stronger than Douglass proved herself to be.

A year back, he reminded her, Douglass had begun to press him 'in a further degree'; and though he 'did plainly and truly deal with you', as he protests indignantly, 'an unkindness began, and after, a great strangeness fell out'. It might have been better had it ended there: instead, she seemed to accept his conditions; they continued to meet 'in a friendly sort and you resolved not to press me more with the matter.'

They quarrelled again; separated for five or six months. He said he still cared for her; she cried out that instead, 'the good will I bare you had been clean changed and withdrawn, in such sort as you did often move me by letters and otherwise to show you some cause or to deal plainly with you that [what] I intended toward you'. So they had continued, through reconciliations and estrangements (like his with Elizabeth!), until now he desired Douglass clearly to understand that 'to proceed to some further degree' would mean 'mine utter overthrow', and that therefore 'no other or further end can be looked for'.

Earlier historians called his letter 'ungallant', and it is true that on one level he is just another man trying to wriggle out of marrying his mistress. But at least he gave her (and, by the sound of it, had always given her) the respect of treating her like a rational creature – took the trouble to explain the position fully, and had the courage to admit his own flaws. 'For albeit I have been and yet am a man frail, yet am I not void of conscience toward God, nor honest meaning toward my friend; and having made special choice of you to be one of the dearest to me, so much the more care must I have to discharge the office due unto you.'

He is, he says, 'no competent judge' of what Douglass should do now. Accept him on these terms or leave him; it is not for him to say. He shows a readiness to have her take the latter course that reflects either a certain lack of interest or a genuine sense of responsibility. He tells her to avoid 'your casual depending on me' (since all men are mortal) – a hint that Douglass (to whose character we have few independent clues) is perhaps a little clinging; perhaps a little like the popular perception of Amy. She should take care lest her 'youthful time be consumed and spent without certainty'. She should beware 'the daily accidents that hap by grieving and vexing you, both to the hindrance of your body and mind; the care and cumber of your own causes ungoverned; the subjection you are in to all reports to the touch of your good name and fame'. The lady has other suitors, 'of the best', who can offer her marriage, 'and as it is not my part to bid you to take them, so were it not mine honestly, considering mine own resolution, to bid you refuse them . . . to carry you away for my pleasure to your more great and further grief were too great a shame for me'.

The letter shows a certain amount of conflict in Leicester himself. It is not, perhaps, that he is so strongly drawn to Douglass, as that he is drawn to the idea of marriage in itself; to the chance of heirs for his dynasty. His friend Lord North had heard him say how much he wanted to be able to have children with some 'goodly [or godly?] gentlewoman'. He admitted as much to Douglass, wrote that the same situation that forced him to keep her at arm's length 'forceth me thus to be the cause almost of the ruin of mine own House; for there is no likelihood that any of our bodies are like to have heirs; my brother you see long married and not like to have children, it resteth so now in myself'. It had been with huge pomp and the highest hopes that Leicester, eight years before, had arranged his brother Ambrose's marriage to Anne Russell, daughter to the strongly Protestant Earl of Bedford, and a favourite with the Queen. But of the four Dudley siblings, only Mary was able to leave legitimate heirs behind her.

The problem now for Leicester is that if he should marry, as he has told Douglass, 'I am sure never to have favour' from the source he cares for above all, Elizabeth; 'yet is there nothing in the world next [apart from] that favour that I would not give to be in hope of leaving some children behind me'. Perhaps it was

that thought – more even than Douglass's pressure – that persuaded him to agree to marry her, secretly. If so, of course, he
must have hoped that the secret marriage could later be acknowledged. (Conversely, if he had not gone through some sort of
ceremony with Douglass, then he could have exercised no rights
over any child.) We will never know what hints Elizabeth received
as to the importance of the relationship; what private hints she
dropped to him. (Remember those 'spies', of whom Gilbert
Talbot wrote?) But then, the whole affair is shrouded in confusion. We have only Douglass's much later word for it that,
having formally contracted to marry in 1571 (perhaps under
pressure from the Duke of Norfolk, as head of the Howards?),
they wed secretly at Esher in Surrey, as 1572 turned to 1573.

We are told that the bride was given away by Sir Edward
Horsey, a soldier and supporter of Leicester's own. The other
witnesses included the skilled royal physician known to everyone
as Dr Julio,* who features as the Italian poisoner in all the anti-
Leicester stories, and Robert Sheffield, a connection of the bride.
To mark the occasion (Douglass said), Leicester presented her
with a ring 'set with five pointed diamonds and a table diamond'.
This ring had been given to him by a former Earl of Pembroke
(predecessor of the then earl, who had married Leicester's niece),
with instructions that Leicester should bestow it upon none but
his wife.

But this story, like others in Leicester's life, has been the subject
of long-running controversy. It's not in dispute that the two were
involved, and when, fifteen months later, Douglass had a child,
Leicester acknowledged the boy and would continue to do so;
would enter him at university with the rank of an earl's son, and
leave him all the property which (unlike his title) was his to
dispose of. He would write of this offspring later, however, as 'my
base [i.e. illegitimate] son'. Was he right to do so? Or had there
indeed been a ceremony, which only the fear of Elizabeth kept
shrouded in secrecy?

---

* Dr Giulio Borgarucci, or Borgherini – even Borgarutius, in one Latin
document.

To weigh the evidence, it is necessary to skip forward a few years; and then forward again, to the beginning of the seventeenth century. To cut a long story short (for the longer one, see Chapter 14 and Appendix I), within a few years this passion had run its course and Leicester married someone else – without, apparently, any serious fear he might be accused of bigamy. The Queen, in anger, raised with Douglass the rumour that she and Leicester had been married, and swore that if it were true, Douglass should have her rights; but Douglass denied there had ever been a ceremony and, more significantly, herself married someone else shortly afterwards. It was not until 1604, after Elizabeth and Leicester were both dead, that that same 'base son', seeking to prove his legitimacy, put his mother into the witness box to swear that she and Leicester had indeed married; to give those details of rings, and witnesses; to describe a letter from Leicester signing himself 'your loving husband', and thanking God for the birth of their son, who 'might be the comfort and staff of their old age'. Her earlier denial had been from fear, she said; of what Leicester might do if she proclaimed the match.

The Star Chamber, where the case was tried, found against the son's claim; but in a way that leaves the question open for posterity. The court did not pronounce directly on the question of his legitimacy; merely rejected the evidence by which he tried to prove it.* But then, in an impossibly vicious twist, the Star Chamber accused the 'base son' of *lèse-majesté* in having raised the question at all. The relations who might otherwise claim the Leicester inheritance had the ear of the new King James, and fiercely contested the case. But abroad – when he had left England in disgust – the supposedly bastard scion would be known by his grandfather's title of Duke of Northumberland. More tellingly,

---

* The only witness Douglass could provide who claimed to have been present at the ceremony was a gentlewoman servant called Magdalen Salisbury. But the prosecutor protested that she at first declared she could not remember anything about it, later putting her name to two contradictory stories. A Mrs Erisa, staying with Douglass when her baby was born, was also called upon to support Douglass's claim that Leicester's letter of congratulation was signed 'your loving husband'. She remembered the letter – but not those words.

later in the seventeenth century, Charles I formally declared his belief that the 'base son' had a legitimate claim; and a nineteenth-century court would refuse to grant to a Dudley descendant titles that could only be given if the 'base son' were bastard indeed. The burden of proof was on Douglass, and she failed to provide it; none the less, an uncertainty as inevitable as it is unsatisfactory endures.

But if Douglass and Leicester were married to each other, what were they thinking of, when they subsequently married other people? Perhaps of that unexpected (and, to most of us, little understood) flexibility of Tudor marriage – perhaps particularly relevant in this very period, after the Reformation had done away with one set of rules, and before the new situation first began to be regularized in the early seventeenth century. For all the talk of 'holy wedlock', marriage was not actually a sacrament of the Anglican Church. Though banns, a church ceremony and the presence of a clergyman were all desirable, not even the last was actually essential. A couple were bound if they simply declared before witnesses that they took each other as man and wife (or even if they declared that they intended to marry, and then slept together). The logical consequence was that if they subsequently both declared they were not married, then in effect, though not in law, they had undone the ceremony.

Douglass Sheffield (confronting the judges of the Star Chamber) declared that she had been married by a clergyman, and that he had shown a licence (presumably a special licence, used then as now to avoid the publicity of banns). Unfortunately she never knew the clergyman's name, nor could the issuing of a special licence be found among church records ... but again, neither clergyman nor licence was necessary.

Contemporary parallels throw some light on the story. Bigamy was not a felony until the start of the seventeenth century. A witness to Leicester's 'marriage', Dr Julio, had himself three years earlier married a woman who was married already; and when in 1573 his case came up before the ecclesiastical courts, it was stalled for another three years before judgement was given against him; nor did he then suffer any diminution of royal favour by way of penalty. Marriages could be airbrushed away. A decade earlier, in 1561, Katherine Grey, the Queen's near relative and putative heir, had secretly married the Earl of Hertford (finally, pregnant and desperate, imploring a horrified Robert Dudley to break the news to the Queen for her). On that occasion the story had ended unhappily; again, the witness had died and the priest vanished by the time the matter came under investigation, and Elizabeth seized the excuse to declare the union null and void, and any children illegitimate.

Douglass's baby was born at Sheen, while Leicester was away with the Queen, on progress in the west. A member of the household rode with the news to Bristol, returning to act as proxy for one of the godparents, Sir Henry Lee, at the baptism; the other sponsors were Ambrose Dudley, and Lady Margaret Dacre, for whom Mrs Erisa stood proxy. There seems to have been no particular upsurge of gossip. But then, unsanctioned births were not unknown among the nobility, and scandal came only when the parties concerned proved inept at hushing things up (as when, in 1581, the Earl of Oxford's mistress, Anne Vavasour, gave birth in the palace, near the Queen's own chamber).* By contrast, Douglass lay low for a couple of years – at Leicester's property in Esher, or at Leicester House in London – with her baby, visited by Leicester when the court was nearby. Since their relationship was an open secret, all they really needed to conceal from the Queen was the question of a marriage ceremony. Douglass later told the Star Chamber that she had herself served as a countess, privately, but that Leicester reproved her, lest the Queen should come to hear of it.

It is hard to get much of a reading on Douglass's character; not one of any great firmness, one might hazard, surely? But it certainly seems a strange coincidence that the two huge uncertainties in Leicester's life both have to do with wives; both

---

* Rumour said Douglass had borne Leicester one child already: a daughter delivered in deepest secrecy at Dudley Castle in Staffordshire, home to a kinsman of Leicester's and his wife, Douglass's sister. The baby dying within a few hours, it was said, Douglass was rushed back to court, and the matter concealed successfully.

absent, both shadowy. One might speculate that neither of them was entirely real to him compared to the vivid court and its dynamic, demanding queen.

Still things between Robert and Elizabeth continued outwardly as before. When he gave her a present of a fan of white feathers, its gold handle was engraved with her symbol of the lion and his of the bear. In 1575 Federico Zuccaro was commissioned to paint twin portraits of Elizabeth and Leicester. And in 1575 their official position towards each other was still such that Leicester was able to make the great, grand gesture of hospitality that has often been taken as his last bid for royal matrimony.

That summer – as was usual, in the first part of her reign – Elizabeth took her court on progress. The bald words, today, give little hint of the terrifying scale of an operation that would have been hideously familiar to her contemporaries. True, great households of the sixteenth century were by their nature peripatetic, moving from one house to another, so that crowded rooms could be aired and cleansed. So perhaps the basic concept of the Queen's taking her own furnishings with her – so that she might dine off silver plate, and sit on a suitably stately seat, even if forced to overnight in the home of a mere member of the minor gentry – would not seem remarkable. Any great lady travelled almost like a snail (and at about the same pace) with her home on her back, encumbered by and enclosed in a protective parade of personal baggage, provisions, and the ever-present parasite throng of servants and minor gentry. But when the lady was the Queen, taking with her the whole apparatus of both state and ceremony, the resemblance to the hordes of Midian spreading over the plain must have been quite extraordinary.

Besides the Queen and her own attendants, there travelled also a baggage train, sometimes of more than three hundred carts, each drawn by several horses (which the Queen's grooms had the right to requisition from the locals when necessary): a caravan of clothes and bed-linen, books and cooking pots, so cumbrous it could travel only ten or twelve miles in a day. If the Queen were to stay a night in the house of any but the grandest nobility, then one team would have moved in a few days ahead of her in order to get the house ready – putting up hangings, putting better locks on the doors – and would stay on after she left to close the temporary establishment down again. Meanwhile another team would have moved in to the different house where she would spend the next night; and (if a picnic were not on the menu) a third establishment might have to be readied for use in a single thirty-six-hour span: a 'dining house' where the Queen could stop to eat along her way.

Few houses, of course, could even begin to accommodate anything like the whole retinue. Leicester would be found a room in the same building as the Queen wherever possible; otherwise, even he would be at another house in the vicinity. The accommodation officer who lamented the year before that he could not tell 'where to place Mr Hatton, and for my Lady Carew there is no place with a chimney' – this at an archbishop's palace – must have had his counterpart on every journey. But in fact Hatton and Lady Carew were lucky: only the Queen's ladies, the heads of departments, the great officers and leading favourites could hope the Lord Chamberlain's officers would even try to find them a room. The rest had to cram into inns, to call in favours from nearby friends of friends, or, in the case of the lower orders, simply resort to canvas.

Each department of the royal household, from the bakehouse to the spicery, and the cellar to the laundry, sent its representatives on progress. The Queen's own cooks must be on hand to prepare her dinner; a matter of security against poisoning as well as of practicality. The royal factotums might have less to do when the Queen was staying in the house of a major member of the nobility; or sometimes, as at Sandwich once, the Queen might compliment the wives of the local burghers by sampling the dishes they had prepared for her without having them tasted first, and then by asking that the remains should be taken back to her lodgings so that she could enjoy them properly. But she herself (and the state visitors, the ambassadors, who might travel down to have an audience with her) were not to be at the mercy of possibly incompetent local cooks. And as for feeding her court, surely not even a noble's household, unassisted, could have contemplated feeding as many as five hundred extra people.

Some of the staff of the Queen's own chamber came along, inevitably: ushers, grooms and pages; the royal ladies and maids, all with their own servants. She was escorted by the Yeomen of the Guard – perhaps the whole body, some 130 strong – and a double handful of the ceremonial mounted bodyguard, the Gentleman Pensioners, with their distinctive gilt armour.

Then there was the official wing of this extraordinary parade. Except on the shorter, informal progresses – a hunting trip up the Lea Valley, say – the practical business of governing the country happened wherever the Queen was, and it was hardly practical to stop government for months on end, summer though it may be. So there were always enough of the privy council present with the Queen – individual members coming and going; Leicester, when present, a regular attendant – to make up a viable quorum to deal with whatever business came their way. Appeals against the justice system; auditing of officials' books; matters as elevated as messages from ambassadors and as mundane as authorizing the expenses of the messengers who brought them: all followed the court, and the councillors, around the country.

The privy council, obviously, required its own set of attendants, besides the personal retinues of those great lords who were also councillors. Arrangements had to be made not only for secretaries and officers – for a council chamber with 'paper pens ink wax and other necessaries' – but for the couriers bringing the raw fodder of the council's debates, and taking their decisions away again for implementation by local sheriffs and JPs. In remoter areas this could involve not only a relay of horses stationed every ten miles along the route back to London, but even the clearing of cross-country roads where necessary.*

Her councillors did not always find it easy to get the Queen's attention while she was in holiday mood. As Leicester once wrote to Walsingham from a progress: 'Our conference with Her

---

* Sometimes the mails were used for less elevated errands. Along with the despatches, Leicester's servants once sent him doublets, 'boot hose' and samples of patterned velvet for a new nightgown.

Majesty about affairs, more than by necessity urged, is both seldom and slender,' she being 'loth to trouble herself'. His role, probably, was to cajole her; but on this occasion even he had to break off his letter 'In much haste, Her Majesty ready to horseback'. (Cecil, on the same progress, had to take down a letter on a topic as important as authorizing Walsingham to agree help to the Dutch rebels 'in haste' while the Queen was 'making ready to horse'. One has the picture of her desperate to get away.) It was the job of her councillors to scrabble about, and ensure the work got done, as best they might.

Was it worth it? For the Queen, of course, a progress was the visible and audible reassurance as to the success of her monarchy. As the Spanish ambassador wrote once: 'She was received everywhere with great acclamations and signs of joy as is customary in this country whereat she was exceedingly pleased.' For the people – besides being a once-in-a-lifetime spectacle – it was a chance for institutions and even individuals to put their petitions and problems to her directly. Elizabeth might have argued that a progress was a vital mechanism in her publicity machine (had she ever felt the need to argue such a point with, say, a Cecil, whom the cost – some £2,000 a year – caused to groan dismally). It was true – though possibly the less true for the fact that her progresses over the years often tended to tramp over much the same ground: an area that ranged from Bristol to Warwick, and Southampton to Stafford, but that none the less represented only perhaps the south-easterly quarter of the entire territory she governed. Still, even in an age before mass media, the ripples of a progress perhaps spread beyond those routes and towns where the Queen's cavalcade might actually pass by. There was indeed a measure of organization to ensure it should do: when, for example, the Queen visited Norwich for six days in the middle of August 1578, two of the men responsible for setting up the entertainments quickly published accounts of them under the auspices of powerful London patrons. (Leicester had probably had a hand in planning the anti-French masques and politically pointed festivities.) The report of Thomas Churchyard, a professional entrepreneur seconded from the court, came out on 20 September.

Bernard Garter went one better. His version came out on 30 August, barely a week after Elizabeth had left the city.

The Queen would expect an expensive present, or several of them, at every visit, and so would courtiers in their different degree. (At court, so Spenser wrote in 'Mother Hubbard's Tale', 'nothing there is done without a fee / The courtier must recompensed be.') Elizabeth might be presented with a dress, a hanging, an agate cup from a noble host; leading courtiers might get embroidered gloves from a city. (At Saffron Walden in 1578 the Queen got an engraved silver gilt cup worth some £15 – well over £2,000 today; Leicester got sugar loaf worth 17s 8d – which sounds slight, but was not so bad, considering that the visiting French ambassador had to be content with a gallon of wine at 2s; coals to Newcastle, surely.) The costs of entertaining the Queen were immense and various, even though the royal household would bring their own provisions when necessary. At Lichfield, the host's expenses included such charges as 5s to a nearby house 'for keeping Mad Richard while her Ma[jesty] was here'; 3d 'to Gregory Ballard's Maid for bringing chickens'; 19s for painting the market cross the Queen would pass by; 6s for salt fish; 12s for a bear (presumably to be baited); 10s to the trumpeters and 3s 4d to the slaughtermen. The largest sums were to officers and scholars: £3 to the Sergeant of Arms, £1 to the Herald, and £5 to 'Mr Cartwright, that should have made the Oration'; a mere 3s 4d, however, to 'them of the Privy backhouse', who presumably had to handle toilet facilities.

The cost was all the more unbearable if the Queen changed her plans, from necessity, or mere caprice, and all that expensive preparation was wasted. For every great man who rebuilt his house with the incomes the Queen had granted him, every lesser light who ardently hoped the Queen might honour him with a visit, there were many who wrote in panic to their friends at court when they heard the Queen might be headed their way. The Earl of Bedford, back in 1570, had pleaded to Cecil that the notice given was not nearly enough to ready his house for 'so noble a guest and so large a train'. Later in Elizabeth's reign, in 1601 – when her subjects had perhaps become less inured to progresses, after the stay-at-home years of the eighties and nineties – the Earl of Lincoln simply decamped from his house, so that the offended Queen found only a locked door. (Two of her courtiers were instructed to pursue the earl with the information that she would be back next week, and that meanwhile they would be ordering in the necessary provisions on his behalf . . . farewell any hopes of economy.) Even so senior a man as Sir Henry Lee, at the same later period, could write to Cecil's son on hearing 'that her Majesty threatens a progress . . . My estate without my undoing cannot bear it.' In a sense the smaller people whose houses were requisitioned for a bare overnight stop got off more lightly. They were required merely to let the professionals get on with the job, having moved their own goods and chattels out of the way. But even for them, it must have been like having your home requisitioned by an only marginally friendly army.

Leicester, though, was not of this ill-prepared company. As Master of Horse – besides his informal role as impresario – he was in any case one of the most important officials in arranging a progress, and had often entertained the Queen. She had visited his Warwickshire seat of Kenilworth before (in 1566, 1568 and 1572) but this two-week visit of 1575 is the one that became a legend even in its own day (as attested by a tapestry depiction in nearby Baddesley Clinton); the one against which other Elizabethan entertainments were measured – and the one from which Leicester's finances never entirely recovered.

'For the persons, for the place, time, cost, devices, strangeness and abundance of all . . . I saw none anywhere so memorable,' wrote one contemporary. It had been at Kenilworth that Elizabeth had received news of the massacre in Paris. Did Leicester want to take the taste away? Or perhaps to remind her, subtly, that a marriage to the Valois was now a policy with which he, and many others, could no longer agree?

The oldest parts of the Kenilworth Leicester received had been built in the twelfth century, by which time the estate (first given by Henry I to his chamberlain, Geoffrey de Clinton) had become crown property. In the thirteenth century, in the Barons' War, Simon de Montfort, that earlier Earl of Leicester, had defended it against the forces of Henry III, and the threat of overweening royal authority. John of Gaunt remodelled the buildings in the fourteenth century; Henry V added a lakeside banqueting house, and Henry VIII a new range of lodgings. Robert's father, John Dudley, had briefly taken possession of the castle just months before his death and depossession in 1553.

Leicester spent a fortune on improvements to the property. By 1575, John of Gaunt's medieval palace, already one long step away from its martial origins, had further developed into an Elizabethan showpiece – without, however, changing its essential character. While other Elizabethan nobles only a very few years later built modern and symmetrical houses (Hardwick, Longleat) – while Leicester's own father had sent an architect to Italy to study the principles of classical style – at Kenilworth there arose a new tower above the old keep, and a block of lodging joining it to the medieval hall and chambers; stables; a tilt yard; and a gate-house to make a grand new entranceway.

The result was asymmetrical (his architect despaired) but charming; traditional, but admitting the newfangled indulgences of glass and light: 'every room so spacious, so well belighted, and so high roofed within . . . a day time on every side so glittering by glass, a nights by continual brightness of candle, fire, & torch-light, transparent through the lightsome wind[ows], as it were the Egyptian Pharos'. These transports come from the extensive descriptions of the place, and a precise chronicle of the visit, published under the name of Robert Laneham, a minor court offi-cial and one in Leicester's service (though it has been suggested that someone else wrote it in mockery).

Much of Leicester's money must have gone on the furnishing. The Queen even slept under a hanging spelling out the re-assurance that Leicester was *'Droit et loyal'*. An inventory of his possessions made a few years later includes carpets (then so expensive they were often used to cover tables rather than floors) of crimson velvet 'richly embroidered with my Lord's posies, bears, ragged staves, etc. of cloth gold and silver'; eight tapestry pieces of Judith and Holofernes; seven of Jezebel; five of Samson; seven sets of hangings in the newly fashionable gilt leather;

'instruments of Organs, regalles and virginalles covered with crimson velvet'; and portraits that included not only Robert himself 'with Boye his dog by him', but several nobles of the Spanish court – families his mother had once known as friends, and whom he would later face in enmity.

That family emblem, the bear with ragged staff, recurs repeatedly. You find it on a chair, of 'crimson velvet in cloth of gold, and the bear and ragged staff in cloth of silver'; on a 'fair, rich, new, standing square bedstead of walnut tree, all painted over with crimson and silvered with roses, four bears and ragged staves all silvered standing upon the corners'. The staves alone even featured on the crimson satin quilt and the 'pillowbeeres'. It was as if Robert, by stamping the family emblem on the place his father had had to vacate, were emphasizing that this time – they hoped – the Dudleys were here to stay.

The complete terrain of parks and chase stretched for nearly twenty miles from the castle walls; but within those walls, the garden boasted 'a pleasant terrace' and stone carvings – obelisks, spheres, and those ubiquitous white bears. There were 'fine arbours redolent by sweet trees and flowers', fragrant herbs, apples, pears and cherries; alleys of grass, or else of sand, 'pleasant to walk on as a sea shore when the water is avaled [ebbed]'.

A great aviary was decorated with painted gems; Elizabeth loved the sound of birdsong. The figures of two athletes, supporting a ball upon their shoulders, made a fountain eight feet high, while carp and tench swarmed in the pool below. With 'the Birds fluttering, the Fountain streaming, the Fish swimming: all in such delectable variety, order, dignity', this, Laneham said, really was worth the name often bestowed on medieval gardens – that of a Paradise. The story goes that when the Queen rather ungratefully complained to Leicester that she could not see the garden from her own apartments, he brought in an army of workmen at dead of night to make a precise duplicate, so that when she awoke, she was delighted to see it under her window. One may take leave to doubt the story, on looking at the terrain (and these workmen must have laboured very silently), but the magical piece of extravagance has become part of Elizabethan mythology. There is always, to modern eyes, something of the stage set, the fantasy, about Tudor houses. When a royal visitor moved into even so old and seemingly immovable a building as, say, Dover Castle, a temporary ceiling might be put up and painted, walls rehung, to change the appearance of the place considerably. But Kenilworth was the home of fantasy. Even the Gothic style Leicester chose suggests, like his pageantry, an Arthurian theme; that his aim was to evoke the once and future age of chivalry.

The Queen arrived at eight o'clock at night, on Saturday, 9 July. The dusk must have lent an air of unreality. Kenilworth lay by the side of spreading water, a hundred-acre lake curling round the castle (long since drained away). Over this, Leicester had built a 600-foot bridge, its pillars adorned with symbols of bounty. Across the dark water there now floated, on a 'moveable island, bright blazing with torches', the Lady of the Lake, claiming that she had kept the lake since Arthur's day, but now wished to hand it over to Elizabeth. (The Queen was heard to say that she thought she owned it already.) She entered to a 'great peal of guns and such lighting by firework' that the noise and flame 'were heard and seen twenty mile off'. The Italian expert in pyrotechnics had, happily, been dissuaded from his original idea of firing into the air live cats and dogs.

The Robert Laneham account gives her programme. Sunday, a church service, 'excellent music', 'dancing of Lords and Ladies', more fireworks; 'streams and hails of fiery sparks, lightings of wild fire on water and land, flight and shoot of thunderbolts; all with such countenance, terror, and vehemence, that the heavens thundered, the waters surged, the earth shook'.

On Monday, she stayed indoors through the heat of the day before going out hunting: 'the swiftness of the Deer, the running of footmen, the galloping of horses, the blasting of horns, the halloing and shouts of the huntsmen . . . in my opinion there can be no one way comparable to this, and especially in this place, that of nature is formed . . .' Leicester himself had once written to Cecil from another progress of how they were all 'altogether hunters and do nothing but ride about from bush to bush with a crossbow in our neck'. A contemporary illustration from Turbeville's book on hunting shows the Queen, before a chase, being presented with a bowl of fewmets (droppings) that she might judge whether the beast was worthy of her pursuit. Every so often a deer would prove its ingenuity by taking refuge in the lake, and Laneham admires 'the stately carriage of his head in his swimming', like the sail of a ship; the hounds following after like skiffs in the wake of a larger vessel. One such swimmer put up such an admirable fight that: 'the watermen held him up hard by the head, while, at her Highnesses commandment, he lost his ears for a ransom and so had pardon of life'.

Elizabeth was 'surprised' on her way home by another of the staged set-pieces she might, in fact, expect to find along her way. The 'wild man' she encountered was the soldier-poet George Gascoigne, a member of the minor Bedfordshire gentry whom Leicester had recruited for the occasion and who now, dressed up in moss green and ivy leaves, engaged in a rhyming dialogue with his companion player, 'Echo', before breaking his staff over his knee in token of his submission to the Queen's authority. He snapped, alas, a little too vigorously, and one of the pieces flew near enough to the Queen's horse to make it rear in terror . . . but she called out 'No hurt! No hurt!', and the horrified Gascoigne could live to recite another day.

Tuesday saw dancing, and music on the water; Wednesday hunting again. Thursday saw thirteen bears baited by a pack of mastiffs.

> It was a sport very pleasant, of these beasts: to see the bear with his pink eyes learing after his enemy's approach, the nimbleness and watch of the dog to take advantage, and the force and experience of the bear again to avoid the assaults . . . with biting, with clawing, with roaring, tossing and tumbling, he would work to wind himself from them: and when he was loose, to shake his ears twice or thrice with the blood and the slobber about his physiognomy, was a matter of goodly relief . . .

Thus Laneham's report. (Perhaps it really was a satire . . .) There were more fireworks, reflected in the water and some even burning below it, and the tumbling of an Italian acrobat whose limbs seemed to be made 'of lute strings', so that Laneham 'began to doubt whether he was a man or a spirit'.

Friday and Saturday were wet. Perhaps, confined indoors, the Queen found time to catch up with more serious business. The council had been meeting when necessary all this time, and Laneham as council porter had his duties. (His 'letter' gives a nice picture of court life at the middling level: up at 7 a.m. and to chapel; bread and 'a good bowl of Ale' for breakfast in my lord's chamber; and 'if the Council sit, I am at hand' to watch out for interruptions or interlopers. Sometimes the visit of an ambassador or his servant would give him the chance to show off his French, his Spanish, his Dutch and his Latin. 'Dinner and supper I have twenty places to go to and heartily prayed to.' Afternoon and evening he spends among the gentlewomen; a time of eyes and sighs. 'Sometimes I foot it with dancing; now with my Gittern [guitar]', now with a song, or at the virginals, 'they come flocking about me like bees to honey . . . it is sometime by midnight ere I can get from them'.) Inside the house on those wet days, Elizabeth herself would have found both luxury (for Leicester had had her rooms specially furnished, in silver fabric of peach and purple, as well as his favourite crimson) and diversion.

When the Queen's progress took her near Cambridge in 1578, Cecil presided, in Leicester's quarters, over a formal three-hour debate on mercy versus severity in a prince. The Queen had withdrawn to her own chambers, possibly feeling that she had heard enough on that theme already. She was perhaps unlikely to get quite such intellectual fare at Kenilworth. But there might have been, besides her daily exercise of dancing, the games Robert Burton describes in his *Anatomy of Melancholy*: 'cards, tables and dice, shovelboard, chess-play, the philosopher's game, small trunks, shuttle-cock, billiards, music, masks, singing, dancing, ulegames [*sic*], frolicks, jests, riddles, catches, purposes, questions and commands, merry tales . . .'

When Sunday came round again she watched a rustic wedding:

novel in its very crudity. The bridegroom was lame from an old injury got playing the rough and downmarket sport of football.* Rather incongruously, he carried pen and inkhorn on his back, 'for that he would be known to be bookish'. The bride was in her thirties: 'ugly, foul ill favoured; yet marvellous fain of her office [proud of her role] because she heard say she should dance before the queen'. The wedding party was joined by 'certain good-hearted men of Coventry' who, while the 'bold bachelors of the parish' were still tilting at a quintain, began to perform, in dumb-show, a battle between King Ethelred and the Danes.

At around four o'clock the Queen, watching from her window the 'great throng and unruliness', told the rustic actors to come back and perform again on Tuesday – either because she wanted to see it all again, or because she simply couldn't face any more that day. In its comedy and confusion the scene resembles the rustic play in *A Midsummer Night's Dream* (just as Laneham's lyric descriptions are sometimes evocative of phrases from the plays); and it has been speculated that his father may have brought the eleven-year-old William Shakespeare over from Stratford to see the fun.†

The finale to the day was 'a most delicious ambrosial banquet' of three hundred dishes. A banquet in sixteenth-century parlance was not a heavy main meal but specifically the dessert course that followed it, often taken in a garden bower or roof-top pavilion: a course of fruits and marmalades, of sugar-wrought 'subtleties' and flavoured spirits of wine; of candied peel and gilded ginger-bread; of sweetmeats with names like 'kissing comfits' and little mounds of sweetened cream called 'Spanish paps' [breasts]. The

---

* Football, in contemporary opinion, was 'a beastly fury and extreme violence; wherof proceedeth hurt, and consequently rancour and malice do remain with them that be wounded . . .'. Leicester inveighed against its popularity at Oxford University.

† By the same token, Oberon's 'mermaid on a dolphin's back' echoes the pageant with a swimming mermaid and Arion seated astride a dolphin that Elizabeth saw one evening. The man playing Arion suddenly pulled off his mask and exclaimed that he was really only Harry Goldingham . . . just as Shakespeare's Snug the Joiner does in the rustics' play. See Jenkins, *Elizabeth and Leicester*, pp. 208–10.

twin themes of a banquet were the ostentatiously expensive key ingredient, sugar – the very drinking vessels were often made of a stiff sugar paste – and sex; for most of the ingredients (almonds, ambergris, spices and wine) were thought to inflame lust. But even savoury foods could convey a hidden message, as in a salad recipe for the 'salatte of love' (asparagus meant the renewing of love; cabbage lettuce, your love feedeth me; rosemary, I accept your love; and radish, pardon me). At this banquet the Queen, as was her custom, ate 'smally or nothing'. But it is not inconceivable that Leicester – who sent 'a young man brought up in my kitchen' to spend a year with a Paris cook – could have coded even the dishes, carefully.

On the second Monday (after yet more hunting: a sport of which the Queen rarely tired), she knighted five gentlemen and touched nine people for the King's Evil, scrofula, and then saw a water pageant. Triton blew his horn to summon the Queen to the shores of the lake – and this is when she saw Arion riding on the back of a 24-foot dolphin with six musicians concealed in its belly. A song came softly through this 'evening of the day, resounding from the calm waters, where presence of her Majesty, and longing to listen, had utterly damped all noise and din'. And so it continued – but the prime piece was planned for the penultimate day.

Leicester had commissioned George Gascoigne to write a masque concerning the fate of 'Zabeta' ('Eli-sabeta'), one of Diana's favourite nymphs. Diana, chaste goddess of hunting, debates with Juno, wife to the king of the gods, as to which is Zabeta's best destiny: marriage, or virginity. Marriage was to win the debate, needless to say, with Iris descending from the skies to remind the modern Elizabeth (rather pointedly) that Diana had not helped her in the days of her youthful captivity. Alas, rain forbade the performance, which was to have been carefully staged on a site several miles away. Leicester – so the story goes – was confronting the failure of his entire expensive plan; seeing the money he had spent on the whole extraordinary visit simply trickle damply away.

He instructed Gascoigne, overnight, to write some farewell

verses that might yet salvage the scenario, since the Queen was determined to leave the next day; and in his character of the god of the woods, Gascoigne duly accompanied her down the drive the next day, boasting his readiness to keep pace with her for twenty miles as she, heedless, spurred away. Gascoigne prated of another of Diana's nymphs, Ahtebasile (which means Ah, thou queen), served by two brothers, Due Desert and Deep Desire; the latter, Leicester, changed into a holly bush to reflect 'the restlesse pricks of his privie thoughts' – and his worry that the Queen's favour towards him had abated in some way. The nominal message was that the Queen should stay at Kenilworth, 'among your friends'; hardly a point to affect her life-choices in any way.

One or two historians have postulated, dramatically, that per- haps England would yet have had King Robert, if only the sun had shone the day before, and Gascoigne been able to perform his Zabeta story. But surely by now, fifteen years into her reign, Elizabeth had thought enough about the issue. She was not going to be persuaded by a bit more bad poetry. It is elsewhere we need to look to understand the real drama enacted that day.

Was the Kenilworth entertainment, as has usually been speculated, Leicester's final throw, his last desperate bid to persuade Elizabeth to marry him (in which case, presumably, Douglass would have stepped silently aside)? It does, on the surface, look that way. Laneham reports that he had the clock dials on the keep stopped at two o'clock, to signify 'twos, pairs, and couples'. But in fact Leicester must long since have lost real hopes of the Queen's consenting to marry him.* Yes, the prize was worth a final throw of the dice. He might still have been a winner, even at this late day. But he was tiring of the game itself – tiring of the pretence that he would be a suitor indefinitely.

The dramas enacted at Kenilworth have been viewed more threateningly. One historian has noted that the entertainments Leicester commissioned tended to promote not only marriage, but

---

* Potemkin threw a spectacular party for Catherine, at the quarrelsome end of their long liaison, which replicates the mixed messages of the Kenilworth scene almost exactly.

militarism – his own hopes of leading an army to the Netherlands; that they tended to show women in jeopardy, in need of being rescued by a protective masculinity. The detailed analysis made by Susan Frye shows the Queen (who preferred to be both the hero and the heroine of the show) either redirecting or refusing to watch those entertainments that pushed the point most strongly; and one can accept the basic point without following Frye entirely.*

But it does seem clear that the entertainment at Kenilworth – whatever the host originally intended – wound up by dramatizing the increasing distance between Robert and Elizabeth. It might be possible to argue that he knew it would do, and to see the enormous sum he spent as a farewell gift; as guilt money. Because in the time immediately ahead, the real-life protagonists, queen and courtier, would openly be changing partners with the matched precision of a dance, or a French play. In those terms, of course, we might more appropriately see the whole extraordinary Kenilworth entertainment as the beginning, rather than the end, of a story.

---

* 'Elizabeth recognized Dudley as being dangerous,' Frye writes, even though she knew 'she had the power to check him'. But surely the Earl of Leicester she describes is more like Kenilworth's earlier owner, Simon de Montfort, than the protagonist of the relationship we see between the mature Elizabeth and Robert Dudley?

This portrait of Robert from the mid-1560s is attributed to Steven van der Meulen. The dark, haughty eyes gave Leicester his nickname of 'the Gypsy', while the fabulous embroidery and jewels on his clothing reflect his expensive taste in dress.

Like Leicester, the other
men Elizabeth singled
out as favourites, such
as Christopher Hatton
(above left) and Walter
Ralegh (right),
tended to be of a
different physical
type from her
royal suitor the
Duke of Alençon
(above right).

The Earl of Essex (right) was Leicester's stepson and in many ways his successor. Leicester brought him to court to counterbalance the influence of William Cecil and his son Robert (below left and right respectively).

This copy of a seventeenth-century fresco painting (above) shows Kenilworth in its heyday.

The still-standing ruins of 'Leicester's Building' (below) show the apartments Rober built to entertain Elizabeth.

The portrait of Lettice, Leicester's wife, probably painted by George Gower, shows the ragged staff of the Dudleys among the emblems embroidered on her dress.

The German painting above shows Elizabeth receiving the Dutch ambassadors, with Leicester among the councillors in the background. By the time England became embroiled in the struggle of the Netherlands against their Spanish overlords, Leicester (right) was an ageing man.

The allegory on the left shows Philip of Spain riding a cow that represents the Netherlands while the Spanish general milks it, the Duke of Alençon attempts to pull it backwards, and Elizabeth feeds the beast. The 'Armada portrait' of Elizabeth (below), painted to celebrate England's legendary victory, shows her with her hand on the globe, while the sea battle is depicted behind her.

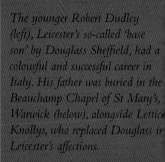

The younger Robert Dudley (left), Leicester's so-called 'base son' by Douglass Sheffield, had a colourful and successful career in Italy. His father was buried in the Beauchamp Chapel of St Mary's, Warwick (below), alongside Lettice Knollys, who replaced Douglass in Leicester's affections.

14

'Dishonorable brutes'
1576–1579

LEICESTER'S EVER-TANGLED MARITAL AFFAIRS WERE ABOUT TO TAKE
another turn. Just a year after the great Kenilworth gala, he found
himself caught up in a web of rumour. It was in August 1576
that the puritan Thomas Wood was writing to Ambrose Dudley
about the many 'very ill and dishonorable brutes' – rumours
– concerning Leicester, 'which I do often hear to my great grief'.
Wood was concerned first and foremost that the puritans' erstwhile patron and protector seemed to have turned against them –
but 'common report', he said, offered other tales of Leicester's
'ungodly life', and if all this rest were true, then 'God's judgement
in the opinion of all godly men without speedy repentance is not
far off'.

Ambrose replied indignantly – and Leicester too, when the
accusations were passed on to him, defended himself
hotly.

I will not justify my self for being a sinner and flesh and blood as
others be. And besides, I stand on the top of the hill, where I know
the smallest slip seemeth a fall. But I will not excuse my self; I may
fall many ways and have more witnesses thereof than many others
who perhaps be no saints neither, yet their faults less noted though
someways greater than mine ... And for my faults, I say, they lie

before him who I have no doubt but will cancel them as I have been
and shall be most heartily sorry for them.

I have many ill willers, and I am none of those that seek hypo-
critically to make my self popular . . . And he had need be a perfect
saint that should escape in any place slanderous tongues.

True enough – but by 1576 (perhaps even as he fêted the Queen
at Kenilworth the year before) Leicester seems, if we interpret
Wood's hints correctly, to have been giving material to slanderous
tongues. Back in 1565, Leicester's name had been linked with that
of Lettice Knollys, and it seems the old feeling had never entirely
gone away.

The exact timing of their affair is crucial here – both crucial
and, alas, uncertain, like several pieces of timing in Leicester's
story. Wood's 'common report' might seem to suggest that an
affair was already established by the summer of '76. Report since
has even suggested that the old attraction *really* never went away
– that Lettice's son, the second, the famous Earl of Essex, who
was born in November 1567, could, besides becoming Leicester's
stepson, also be his natural son. But there is no real evidence to
support this (unless one counts the assertion of the slightly later
courtier Sir Henry Wotton that Essex's supposed father had had
'a very cold conceit' of this one of his offspring) – and, for what
it is worth, the notably fresh complexion and gingery hair of the
father's portrait at Baddesley Clinton do seem to bear a certain
resemblance to portraits of his supposed son. But if either fact
were true, it was indeed a scandal. For back in the early 1560s –
even before Lettice's first flirtation with Robert Dudley – she had
married Walter Devereux, whom Elizabeth subsequently created
first Earl of Essex. When Wood wrote his letter in the August of
1576, Essex was still alive, and a relationship between Lettice and
Leicester would thus have been adultery; certainly on her side,
perhaps also on his.

A letter written by a Spanish agent in December 1575 had been
far more explicit than anything Wood ventured. It mentioned 'the
great enmity that exists between the Earl of Leicester and the Earl
of Essex in consequence, it is said, of the fact that, while Essex

was in Ireland, his wife had two children by Leicester. Great discord is expected.' The two children seem to have been just two more of the anonymous phantom infants rumour was so fond of crediting to the Tudor nobility; all Lettice's named and visible offspring had been born well before her husband went away. But the relationship was 'publicly talked of in the streets', the agent said, explaining why he felt discretion on his part unnecessary.

The pair would not have lacked for opportunities to meet. Lettice may have been present at Kenilworth for Leicester's grand entertainment of 1575; may even have been the cause of that tussle of wills, that anger of the Queen's, at which the tale of the final festivities seemed to hint.* Another tale sets their important encounter as occurring at the same time, but at Sir George Digby's house at Coleshill, just a dozen miles away. It may have been at the Essex seat of Chartley itself that they renewed their interest in each other; for when the court visited on that same progress, Lettice acted as the host, since her husband was away. But we cannot know for sure the single most important fact: whether Robert and Lettice were already indeed 'an item' by the time Essex went to Ireland on military service in 1573; by the time that (after a return home in the autumn of '75) he was sent back to Ireland in July 1576; or even by the time he died there, at the end of September 1576, in circumstances that struck the gossip-mongers as suspicious.

Leicester has been blamed for his part in sending Essex to Ireland – sending him to what proved to be his death. But in fact Essex's career there is hard to assess without some knowledge of the Irish situation, that perpetual running sore in the side of the English body politic. The project – crusade, almost, one might say – to impose a Protestant and, it seemed, civilizing influence upon

* One Edward Arden, Catholic and probably distant kin to Shakespeare's mother, had refused Leicester's demand that all the local gentry should show up wearing his livery; and, according to Dugdale's seventeenth-century report, added an unflattering rider touching Leicester's 'private access to the Countess of Essex'. Eight years later, Arden was executed for treason – some said, by Leicester's agency.

the wild and Catholic Irish was one beloved of the bulk of Elizabeth's leading counsellors: of Essex himself and in time of his son; of Sir Henry Sidney (Lord Deputy of Ireland to Essex's Earl Marshal) and his son, Sir Philip Sidney; and of Leicester himself. Though Cecil (and in the years ahead, his son too!) are usually identified with all Elizabeth's more pacific policies, even they had no sympathy with the Irish cause, but rather feared unrest in a country that could so easily become a back door into England, and let through a Catholic conspiracy. To the Irish, English policy looked more like a piece of pure colonial oppression, often conducted with extreme brutality . . . But that was a perspective with which English nobles like Leicester were hardly likely to agree.

So if Leicester – with his broad interest in promoting the Protestant religion, in pushing England's frontiers, in supporting the Tudor ideal of an imperial monarchy – supported Essex's missions to Ireland, it does not have to have been from personal enmity. Essex, back in 1573, had volunteered for the task of crushing the Irish rebellion. And he looks a little less like a sainted victim if one remembers this was the man who once invited Irish leaders to a feast, on pretext of discussing peace terms, and then had them massacred; feeling, no doubt, that it was no crime to treat a barbarous people with barbarity. There is a hint of fanaticism about the eyes of the Baddesley Clinton portrait. All the same, when Essex died at Dublin Castle on 22 September, the rumour mill was bound to be busy.

Those who stood around his deathbed – the Archbishop of Dublin among them – made a martyr's story out of it, telling how Essex took the news of his approaching end with a bearing 'more like that of a divine preacher or a heavenly prophet than a man'; how he 'never let pass an hour without many most sweet prayers'; and how he 'prayed much for the noble realm of England, for which he feared many calamities'. But in fact, to modern ears, the narrative is more horrifying than uplifting. The dying Essex saw around him nothing but 'infidelity, infidelity, infidelity; aetheism, aetheism; no religion, no religion'. He repeated the angry words as his breath began to run short and, lamenting 'the frailty of women', prayed that his daughters should not learn too much of 'the vile world'.*

In the first days of his illness, at the very end of August, Essex had himself suspected poison – 'some evil received in my drink': the more so, since his page and a third person who drank with him were taken ill in the same way; though the others recovered. He suspected some of the Irish – none of his own household – he said. His doctors, after a week passed with no improvement, dosed him with unicorn's horn, that well-known specific against poison, which just made him vomit violently – though the men available there in Ireland were 'of small experience', wrote his secretary dismissively, summoning a better-known physician with the vivid description of the earl's '20 or 30 stools every day', bloody or else 'black burnt color'. It sounds like dysentery, and it almost certainly was. But whenever any well-known person died, the rumours of poison spread; and would have done, even if there hadn't been friction between Essex and Sir Henry Sidney, his close colleague and Leicester's brother-in-law.

Sir Henry ordered an immediate post-mortem, which found that Essex had died of natural causes.† But the following February, 1577, Sidney still felt the need to offer Leicester further reassurance in a private letter about the 'false and malicious bruit'. The man responsible for spreading the rumours had now himself died of the same disease, Sir Henry said, 'which most certainly was free from any poison; a mere flux, a disease appropriate to this country and whereof there died many in the later part of the last year, and some of mine own household, and yet free from any suspicion of poison'. But why did Leicester need the

---

* He would hardly have been consoled had he seen their future destiny. Penelope – famous as Philip Sidney's poetic idol 'Stella' – was equally notorious for her political meddling and for her infidelity. Dorothy's first disgrace came from an elopement with an adventurer, and her second marriage – to Henry Percy, the 'wizard' Earl of Northumberland – saw the couple quarrelling so bitterly she threatened 'to eat his heart in salt'.

† The signs, according to Camden, were that his body did not change colour, that he showed neither spot nor infection, nor did his hair or nails fall out; these being the infallible stigmata of poison.

reassurance? Concern for his own reputation, as after the death of Amy Dudley? Perhaps – but not necessarily. The lasting slur, that Leicester may have had his rival murdered, in fact springs chiefly from a slanderous pamphlet not published until the 1580s. Right then and there in 1577, the worst canard seems to have been rather that it was Lettice – Essex's 'wellbeloved wife', as she was described in a will just three months old – who had had her husband put away. (Froude says that a few years earlier, Mary, Queen of Scots, had been warned to beware of Lettice, for precisely her facility with poisons.)

But whatever Lettice, guilty or innocent, may have hoped might follow her husband's death, in fact, in the short term at least, it left her almost destitute, since her husband's debts were enough to crush his heir and sink his estates, and her attempt to get some maintenance from the Queen did not prosper quickly or smoothly. If she had already been involved with Leicester, could he not have helped her in some way? In fact, as with the death of Douglass Sheffield's husband, the best evidence for the fact that Leicester did not kill Lettice's husband in order to marry her is that he showed no signs of wishing to do so the minute she was free. Instead, Lettice drops out of the picture for a year or two. In 1577, as far as the sources are concerned, it was the same old Robert and Elizabeth story.

That summer, on physicians' orders, Leicester went north to take the cure at the springs of Buxton in Derbyshire, newly developed and made popular by his friend the Earl of Shrewsbury. (Shrewsbury's famous 'guest'-cum-prisoner, the Queen of Scots, herself took the waters when the authorities allowed. A few years previously Cecil had met her there, as would Leicester, and had spent his time ever since trying to convince Elizabeth that they had not become too friendly.) Patients at the spa took the medicinal water both externally and internally. The place was fully equipped with a specially built accommodation block; chairs around the hot springs; waterside chimneys where your servant could build a fire to air your clothes; and healthful games, for the evening, of bowling or archery. Leicester wrote to Cecil that he and Ambrose were taking great pleasure in bathing in the waters, and drinking them too: dining off 'one dish or two at most, and taking the air afoot or on horseback, moderately'. The regime was probably a good detox after the rich diet of the Elizabethan aristocracy; and Leicester was not usually abstemious even by the standards of the day. That emerges clearly from two letters (or rather, a letter and the draft of a letter) that Elizabeth wrote, during his visit north, to his hosts the Shrewsburys.

The more formal letter expresses Elizabeth's thanks for all the kindness the Shrewsburys had shown to 'our cousin of Leicester' – the hospitality at Chatsworth, the stay at Buxton, the 'very rare present' they had given him. (The next year Shrewsbury's son Gilbert Talbot was writing that Leicester again 'threateneth' a visit to Buxton. A visit of his, by now, must have been almost as expensive an honour as one of Elizabeth's own.) She wanted them to understand that 'holding him in that place of favour we do', she took this lavish hospitality 'not as done unto him but to our own self, reputing him as another ourself'. Any debt incurred by him would find her a grateful debtor. The formal letter sent goes on to thank the Shrewsburys for their 'loyal and most careful' care of Mary, their dangerous charge – but the draft, which seems never to have been sent, continues very differently.

Mischievously, the Queen suggests that the Shrewsburys should reduce Leicester's diet, lest the debt should grow too great; should 'allow him by the day for his meat two ounces of flesh', and just 'the twentieth part of a pint of wine to comfort his stomach'. On festival days they might enlarge his diet by 'the shoulder of a wren' for his dinner and a leg of the same for his supper; ditto for Ambrose (who was obviously with Leicester) – except that he should do without the wren's leg, since 'his body is more replete than his brother's' and 'light suppers agree best with rules of physic'.

A modern dietitian would have agreed – and approved the Queen herself, who was famously 'temperate' in her diet, 'as eating but few kinds of meat, and those not compounded', as Clapham put it, and mixing her wine with three parts water. But more even than Leicester's lusty appetite, what emerges from the draft letter is his enduring, cosy, almost marital closeness to the Queen. Perhaps, in the end, Elizabeth hesitated to expose this note of playful intimacy even to such friends as the Shrewsburys. But it is no wonder that Shrewsbury (and his wife, the famously thrusting Bess of Hardwick) thought Leicester's friendship so well worth having that he sent back to the Queen his ecstatic thanks for her thanks, stressing his fondness for 'our dearest friend, my kinsman, my Lord of Leicester'. (No wonder, too, that when Leicester later proposed a marriage tie between his family and theirs, they were only too delighted to agree.)

Charles Stuart, the younger brother of Lord Darnley, had fathered a child on Bess of Hardwick's daughter, Elizabeth Cavendish – having married her in defiance of Elizabeth's authority. The child, Arbella Stuart, was a promising toddler when Leicester went into Derbyshire; and the scarcity of Tudor heirs meant the claim to the throne she had inherited from her father had to be taken seriously. From the start, the Shrewsburys had recruited Leicester's aid in promoting the cause of their infant heiress and securing her a pension from the Queen. He had already been called on to mediate between the couple (whose quarrels were legendary), and it would be fascinating to know whether, in return, he confided anything at all about his own marital history – or his future plans.

For Leicester was about to embark on the third and final chapter of that odd, muddled marital history. In the spring of 1578, at Kenilworth, he underwent a secret marriage ceremony with Lettice Knollys. Or so she later claimed . . . It was probably only thanks to firm action by her father that this situation, unlike that of Douglass Sheffield, was subsequently regularized; that there was, later, another ceremony; one even the Queen could not ignore indefinitely.

There remained, of course, something else to be regularized: Leicester's relationship with Douglass Sheffield. That year – or so she declared a quarter of a century later – he had a meeting with her in the gardens of Greenwich Palace where, in the presence of two witnesses, he told her their relationship was at an end. He offered her an annuity of £700 if she would 'disavow marriage' and surrender custody of her son. When she, in tears, refused, then he swore that 'he would never come at her again' and shouted that the marriage had never been lawful anyway. Douglass said that her compliance – now and later, when she denied her marriage and gave up her child to Leicester – was down to fear; that her hair had begun to fall out, and she thought she was being poisoned.* But then, by the time Douglass made that statement, at the start of the seventeenth century, Leicester was safely dead, and his reputation already blackened by the slurs of the 1580s. He could be impugned quite safely.

One does not have to subscribe to the full theory of his villainy, to the poison slurs, to believe that a good deal of pressure was put on Douglass Sheffield. Leicester would hardly have needed to threaten her directly. It would have been sufficiently obvious that he could either help or hinder the future careers of herself, and anyone close to her: obvious, too, that there would be no refuge in a queen whose instinctive reaction would be to regard any rival claimant to Leicester's loyalty with extreme hostility.

If Lettice had not bowled Leicester over, would he now have admitted to his relationship with Douglass – a relationship which, whether or not he was aware of a formal marriage tie, had already produced what he longed for, a healthy and promising baby boy? We do not know enough about her, or about their (scant) life together to know if he would in any way regret losing her. But he must have regretted the son – as an heir, and for the boy's promise – as is evident from the future affection he showed him. Maybe the longer he failed to announce that he and Douglass were married, the harder it had become? Maybe he wanted to break a deadlock in some way? He was taking a gamble, but he had the temperament of a gambler – and after all, he must have assumed he and Lettice would have more heirs. Although she was by now in her late thirties, they had both proved their fertility.

---

* By the same token, several sources claimed that Bothwell's deserted wife had similarly been offered a choice between divorce and poison – though others suggested that her family pushed her into co-operation, in hopes of currying Bothwell's favour.

Did he simply fall in love with Lettice, and decide that a marriage with Douglass, where love had died, was hollow mockery? It sounds anachronistic and oddly modern. But so, of course, do the actions of Henry VIII, if we accept the view voiced by many historians, new and old – that what Henry did, he did in search of love – above the more political explanations for his 'six wives' history. Does the answer to Leicester's actions lie purely in the attractions of Lettice? Certainly she was a forceful woman, we must infer from her later history; and, from a wonderful portrait of her, equally certainly a beauty. The portrait is thought to have been painted almost a decade later, when Lettice was forty-five. If it were, then she shared the ability of her kinswoman Elizabeth to hypnotize the viewer into ignoring her real age and frailties. Lettice gazes out, smooth-faced, luscious, faintly smiling; her hair a shouting auburn, while the magnificent embroideries of her padded dress show the ragged staff of the Dudleys.

If Douglass Sheffield's pliability makes it tempting to postulate a similarity between her and Amy Dudley, then Lettice must have had more in common with her kinswoman Elizabeth. She would prove the wife to whom Robert remained in lifelong thrall. We do, thankfully, have more information about Lettice than we do about Douglass, let alone Amy – and if much of it comes from later in her extraordinarily long life, then time can have had little impact on her forceful personality.

Like Elizabeth, she had a physical vigour. It was after Leicester's death that a courtier wrote of Elizabeth's normal exercise as being six or seven galliards of a morning; Lettice was over ninety when it was reported of her that she 'can yet walk a mile in the morning'. Her career rings with a lust for grandeur and a longing for court life. (No country mouse, no Amy Dudley, she.) In her letters to her son we can see the strength of her clinging; begging that other 'Sweet Robin', as she called him, 'to bestow some time a few idle lines on your mother who otherwise may grow jealous that you love her not so well as she deserves'. This at a time when Robert Devereux, Earl of Essex, was not only a prisoner in danger of his life, but a man of more than thirty. It sounds a little like

Elizabeth's own unseasonable demands for reassurance and flattery.

That same fierce possessiveness could show itself as a determination to take what Lettice felt was hers – as in her trying, after Leicester's death, even to seize by force the property, Kenilworth, he had left to his 'base son'. And in her third marriage (made in widowhood and in haste, to a much younger man of lesser rank) we can trace the strength of her appetites. Yet despite that subsequent marriage she would choose to be buried with Leicester in Warwick, the chapel that is resting place for so many of the Dudleys; and a verse on the nearby plaque written by her great-grandson Gervase Clinton, glossing over the many controversies of her life, describes the tomb as being that of an 'excellent and pious lady':

> There may you see that face that hand
> That once was fairest in the land
> She that in her younger years
> Matched with two great English peers
> She that did supply the wars
> With thunder and the court with stars
> She that in her youth had been
> Darling to the maiden Queen
> Till she was content to quit
> Her favour for her favourite

It might be possible, however, to trace a less personal, a more political, element to Leicester's marital history. Lettice had been born a Knollys, a family (like the Howards) that 'appertaineth to us in blood', as Elizabeth wrote. Her mother was Katherine Carey, Anne Boleyn's niece – but, almost more to the point, her father was Sir Francis Knollys, a fellow privy councillor and Leicester's close colleague. (Apart from anything else they were two of the three household officers most responsible for organizing those shattering progresses.) Knollys was also a leading and an ardent Protestant, high on the Catholic hit list in the rebellions of 1569. It had been he who escorted the Duke of Norfolk to the

Tower. As for Lettice's first husband, the Devereux Protestantism was evident not only in Essex's Irish career, but in his choice of guardians for their children: Cecil, and Leicester's brother-in-law the Earl of Huntingdon, whose wife Katherine took a number of girls into her house and boasted of her ability 'to breed and govern young gentlewomen'.

By contrast Douglass, while another of the Queen's relations, had been a Howard; member of a family notorious for their crypto-Catholic inclinations. Leicester's relationship with Douglass Howard must have begun at the time he was flirting with the crypto-Catholic causes of the Howard clan. One of the godfathers of Douglass's and Leicester's son was Sir Henry Lee, whom Norfolk embraced on the scaffold. Douglass's next marriage would be to a man, Sir Edward Stafford, whose Catholic sympathies may have led to his being recruited, while England's ambassador in Paris, as a Spanish agent; and when Douglass's son by Leicester grew up, he would himself later convert to Catholicism, reproving those who assumed he had done so only to facilitate his new life in Catholic Europe.

One cannot take this theory too far. Lettice too would later marry a man from a noted recusant family, while Douglass's brother, later Elizabeth's Lord Admiral, does not seem to have had his career blighted by any rumour of Catholic sympathies. But it does look a little as though Leicester's marriage to Lettice, personal attraction apart, both signalled and reflected the clear new trend of his position and his religious convictions. He was effectively moving from one wing to another of Elizabeth's maternal family. If it came to slighting Douglass and her child, or Lettice and – potentially – hers, then it is easy to see why his face would have turned the Knollys way.

For this looks very much like a shotgun wedding. In September, Francis Knollys insisted that his daughter and Leicester should be married properly and formally, whatever half-baked ceremony they may have gone through before. The chaplain who married them – Humphrey Tyndall, one of Leicester's staff – later recalled the event that took place at Wanstead, with just sufficient privacy that the Queen would not need to know about the ceremony. Leicester, Tyndall said, told him that he had 'a good season forborne marriage in respect of her Majesty's displeasure', but wished now to marry the Countess of Essex 'especially for the better quieting of his own conscience'. The wedding took place between seven and eight on a Sunday morning, in the presence of Ambrose, of the Earl of Pembroke (who had recently married Leicester's niece, Mary Sidney) and of Lord North – to whom Leicester had earlier confided his desire to marry 'some goodly gentlewoman', and the 'hearty love and affection' he felt for Lettice. His version of events confirmed Tyndall's. Lettice's brother Richard was there too – standing half inside the doorway, perhaps to keep a lookout? – while Sir Francis gave his daughter away, Tyndall binding them together 'in such manner and form as is prescribed by the communion book'. The bride was dressed 'in a loose gown', Tyndall remembered – taken as coded reference to a pregnancy. But, if there were a child in Lettice's womb, then this one died stillborn and Elizabeth, officially at least, continued in ignorance of the whole story.

Or did she? As so often, it is hard to be sure of exactly what Elizabeth allowed herself to know. But looking back across this summer of 1578, to the spring when Leicester first committed himself to Lettice, one can (as so often!) trace a version of events different from the traditional story; see successive layers of wilful blindness, layering over the (to Elizabeth) unpalatable truth as effectively as the oyster covers the irritating grain of sand in layers of mother-of-pearl.

In that April of 1578 – right after his first secret ceremony with Lettice – Leicester came south to London; but to his own Leicester House, rather than to the court. He pleaded illness, perhaps with truth; his doctors did send him to Buxton again that summer. But it may also have been a ploy, at once to provoke Elizabeth's sympathy and to speak to her privately. As the Spanish ambassador, Mendoza, reported at the end of April,

> the Queen had fixed the 28th for my audience with her, but as she was walking in the garden that morning she found a letter which had

been thrown into the doorway, which she took and read, and immediately came secretly to the house of the Earl of Leicester, who is ill here. She stayed there until ten o'clock at night, and sent word that she would not see me that day as she was unwell. I have not been able to learn the contents of the letter, and only know that it caused her to go to Leicester's at once.

Our chances of discovering the contents of the letter are no better than Mendoza's were – but it seems at least possible that on that visit, which clearly shocked Elizabeth greatly, Leicester confessed the whole story; whether forced to do so by an anonymous letter from a third party, or by his own contrivance.

If Leicester did confess his attachment to Lettice, then Elizabeth, in the end, brought herself to take it comparatively calmly. (And if Elizabeth had to any degree accepted Leicester's attachment to Lettice as a *fait accompli*, then the pressure on Douglass not to stake her claim would have been that much greater.) Perhaps the nature of her own attachment to him was changing – or perhaps, after all, he told her part but not quite all of the story. She must long have come to a tacit agreement that he would have relationships with other women; can hardly have expected to keep him, like herself, in perpetual celibacy. It was only the public attachment that would provoke her to fury.

That May, when she went on a 'little progress' hunting through the Lea Valley, she stayed at Wanstead; Leicester himself being absent, his place as host was taken by his nephew Philip Sidney, who wrote 'A Contention between a Forester and a Shepherd for the May-Lady', for the occasion.

> Like sparkling gems her virtue draws the sight,
> And in her conduct she is always bright.
> When she imparts her thoughts, her words have force
> And sense and wisdom flow in sweet discourse.

The masquers surprised the Queen walking in the woods of what was still a rural setting; the tale was of a lady asked to choose between her suitors. The generalized, ritualized air of courtship was still being nominally sustained. And maybe Leicester did make only half a confession; told of the attachment, but could not bring himself to admit to anything about a wedding ceremony. For in June, while Leicester was still away, Christopher Hatton, from the court, wrote to his one-time rival that Elizabeth had been dropping odd hints.

> Since Your Lordship's departure, the Queen is found in continual and great melancholy; the cause thereof I can but guess at, notwithstanding that I bear and suffer the whole brunt of her mislike in generality. She dreameth of a marriage that might seem injurious to her: making myself to be either the man, or the pattern of the matter.

The Elizabethans took dreams seriously, but the Queen (in many ways, of necessity, a very private woman) was not in the habit of posting news of hers off to all and sundry. This was a warning – but to whom? Poor Hatton felt understandably a little aggrieved at this blame by association. He had no plans to marry (and, despite some rumours, never did), whatever other favourites might do.

But Hatton was prepared gently to suggest that Elizabeth was being unreasonable in denying a man the right to find elsewhere what she would not give him.

> I defend that no man can tie himself or be tied to such inconvenience as not to marry by law of God or man, except by mutual consents on both parts the man and woman vow to marry each other, which I know she hath not done for any man, and therefore by any man's marriage she can receive no wrong. But, my Lord, I am not the man that should thus suddenly marry, for God knoweth, I never meant it.

It sounds very much as if Hatton had some little idea of what was going on; but it sounds, too, as though Elizabeth and Leicester were, as so often, hovering in a limbo, somewhere between deliberate deception and frank sincerity.

In August, during the summer progress, when the Queen was as usual vacillating about the question of whether to send aid to the beleaguered Protestants of the Netherlands, Leicester (so a scandalized but admiring Thomas Wilson reported to Walsingham) 'dealt so plainly, so boldly, so faithfully with our sovereign against delays and unnecessary used allegations as I never heard councillor take the like upon him'. He was, however, 'heard with great patience' by the Queen. It sounds as though his influence had not diminished – unless his poor health were affecting his temper, and she making allowances. Elizabeth herself was unwell much of that summer and autumn; depressed and ill-tempered, and tormented with the toothache that was to plague her later years.

Still, that summer's progress through East Anglia was in many ways a triumphant one, with a visit to Norwich that became a legend in the city. It was 23 September when the Queen arrived at Wanstead, where she was to dine on her way back to London; less than thirty-six hours after Leicester and Lettice had gone through that second, only semi-secret, marriage ceremony. (It was in theory to prepare the house, and the splendid feast, that Leicester had been allowed to slip away from the progress early.) But there must have been many tensions simmering under the surface at that meal.

A picture of Elizabeth at Wanstead was painted a few years after this. She stands beside her chair of state, on an expensive carpet spread luxuriously on the ground, the lawns and pavilions of a formal garden just visible behind her. One hand elegantly clasps at glove and fan; in the other is an olive branch, figuring her as 'Pax'. One foot treads the hilt of a formal, allegorical, sword, and a small dog gazes upwards adoringly. Perhaps that is Leicester's sign of loyalty. Alternatively, two of the figures glimpsed in the background may be him and the triumphant Lettice. There are pearls in Elizabeth's hair, and the inevitable ransom's worth of embroidery on her mantle – but between them this time Marcus Gheeraerts has set something a little different from the usual ageless mask of majesty. It is hard to know whether the expression on the Queen's face was of pensive relaxation, or of melancholy.

15

'The greatest prince in Christendom'
1578–1582

IT MAY, POLITICS APART, HAVE BEEN THE KNOWLEDGE OF LEICESTER'S desertion that in 1578 prompted Elizabeth to renew her interest in the Duke of Alençon. (Mary in her imprisonment heard so, anyway.) But Elizabeth tended to mix business with pleasure; and the political situation was certainly enough to justify her decision. The brother of the French king remained the route to a useful alliance to hedge England's lonely vulnerability.

Alençon had begun agitating for the marriage plans to be resumed as far back as 1573, barely a discreet interval after the infamous massacre; and in the middle years of the decade Elizabeth's own lengthy letters to her envoys had shown an almost frantic uncertainty. She would love to see Alençon before she decided whether to marry him, yet she feared 'that if upon the entrevue satisfaction follow not, there is like to ensue thereby instead of straiter amity, disdain, unkindness, and a gall and wound of that good friendship that is already between us'. Yes, her ambassador was discussing a meeting with the French, but now, heaven forbid, the French seemed to have heard she was eager for such a thing, 'Whereof we had much marvel' . . . at which point – as once before, immediately after the massacre – it had all seemed to go away.

But what did not, ever, go away was the need for a European

ally. In England, the mid-1570s had seen the start of the great Catholic infiltration of England – committed priests sent under cover from the European seminaries, to remind English Catholics of the papal bull against Elizabeth, 'the pretended Queen of England, the Servant of Wickedness', and persuade them of where their loyalties should lie. (The exiled Cardinal William Allen heard that 'the numbers of those who were daily reconciled to the Catholic church almost surpassed belief'.) Across the Channel, one of the least tractable problems of the 1570s and beyond – another that showed no sign at all of going away – was that of the Netherlands, where the northern Protestants under William of Orange had long been in rebellion against their Spanish Catholic overlords. The Spanish general Alva and his 'reign of blood' had battered but not broken the Dutch rebels. Elizabeth was for ever urging them to negotiate with the Spanish; but if they must fight, then religious solidarity and a regard for her own borders – the security of the Channel passage, with a vast Spanish army camped just over the waters! – forbade Elizabeth to let them fight alone. She was constantly being urged to give them open support, and money.

Leicester's was one of the most insistent voices in favour of intervention; as far back as 1567 the Spanish ambassador had reported he was 'very sorry' that the Spanish cause in the Netherlands was going so prosperously. (His own commitment to the cause of the Dutch Protestants would come to provoke his sharpest ever disagreement with his Queen.) He had an ally in the increasingly important figure of Francis Walsingham, whom at the end of 1573 Elizabeth had appointed as her principal secretary of state, and in the years ahead Walsingham would support Leicester whenever he promoted a more aggressively Protestant and militant policy in the privy council debates than that to which Elizabeth inclined. One of the Queen's problems with Walsingham – to whom, though she respected him, she never really warmed – was that his vehement religious beliefs represented in her mind the unpalatable facts, silently urging her towards more active involvement in the Low Countries.

Just to cap it all, the disaffected Alençon, always a Huguenot sympathizer, had himself become embroiled in the Netherlands. In 1574 the death of the French king Charles (probably from congenital syphilis) had placed the violently Catholic Anjou on the throne, and set Alençon more than ever at odds with his country and his family, wandering about Europe with all the irresponsible readiness to take up any convenient cause characteristic of stateless royalty.

While Elizabeth had been at Norwich, that summer of 1578, news was brought to her as she toured the cathedral that Alençon had actually invaded the Spanish Netherlands and struck an alliance with the Protestant rebels, accepting the title of 'Defender of the Liberties of the Low Countries against Spanish Tyranny'. (And this just when she had spent a year repeatedly patching matters up between Philip and the Dutch Protestants; now, instead of Spain, she was faced with the hardly more welcome prospect of France controlling the Low Countries.) Her immediate reaction was to send a message of solidarity to the said tyrant, King Philip. Philip's rights in the Netherlands were those of blood – his father Charles had been born there before inheriting, through his mother's line, the more prestigious throne of Spain in addition – and the kinship of monarchy was more present to her imagination than the kinship of religion, especially a religion with which, in its more violent extremes, she actually felt little sympathy. But the reactivated possibility of a glittering marriage would turn Alençon's thoughts another way.

So another story of greater weight had been running in tandem with Leicester's; and indeed, the two juggle each other in a letter Leicester wrote to a court official then away in the Netherlands. 'I perceive the matters there goeth not well, which I am right sorry for ... touching the other matter at home here for Monsieur [Alençon], which you desire to understand of, for that many speeches are of it, I think none but God can let you know yet.

'Only this I must say,' he added, disconcerted if slightly unbelieving. 'Outwardly there is some appearance of good liking ...' If Leicester 'should speak according to former disposition', he would hardly believe an actual marriage could take place, but on the other hand ... It was worrying for all her councillors that they knew so little of what the Queen was really thinking; and perhaps for Leicester especially. After Elizabeth received the French envoys on progress, he wrote to Walsingham: 'no man can tell what to say; as yet she has imparted with no man, at least not with me, nor for ought I can learn with any other'. This time (almost for the first time) he had been cut out of the loop; and it was poor consolation that no-one else fared any better. No wonder that, in the incident Wilson described, he had spoken to her angrily.

By October, when Philip sent a new Spanish army to the Netherlands under the command of the great Duke of Parma, a secret correspondence between Elizabeth and France was well under way – secret in the sense that Elizabeth did not take anyone fully into her confidence. This fresh outbreak of the Queen's marital plans was to divide her councillors, who had recently been living in comparative harmony. Cecil was theoretically for the match, albeit without any great conviction it would really happen; Leicester was most prominent among those who believed that Elizabeth's response to the Netherlands crisis should, instead, be open aid, immediate and military. Already the year before there had been rumours he would himself shortly be sailing to the Netherlands at the head of an English army.

If he had his secrets, so too did the Queen. At times it seemed to her councillors as if (with the French Guise family intriguing in Scotland, with Philip of Spain eyeing opportunities in Ireland), she no longer merely walked a tightrope, as she had often done before, but trod blindly towards her country's doom. 'The more I love her, the more fearful I am to see such dangerous ways taken,' Leicester had written to Walsingham. 'God of his mercy help all, and give us all here about her grace to discharge our duties; for never was there more need, nor never stood this crown in like peril. God must now uphold the Queen by miracle: ordinary helps are past cure.'

But amid the militaristic preoccupations of her menfolk, Elizabeth herself was not prepared to see Alençon's renewed interest in her as merely political; and in this insistence, perhaps her hurt over her growing distance from Leicester did come into play. So, perhaps, did her age; she may have felt this was her last chance, that she was letting love slip away. In the spring Alençon had written his devotion, and invited her to share the joke of how odd it was 'that after two years of absolute silence he should wake up to her existence'. It was indeed odd, but when Walsingham said as much, and suggested that Alençon 'entertaineth her at this present only to abuse her', she lashed out in fury. Leicester wrote to Walsingham warningly: 'Surely I suppose she is persuaded he hath more affection than your advertisement doth give her hope of . . . I would have you, as much as you may, avoid the suspicion of her Majesty that you doubt Monsieur's love to her too much.'

Though his prime concern was probably to protect Walsingham from Elizabeth's anger, it sounds, again, as though at this stage he could at least seem to regard the possibility of the match with equanimity. The Spanish ambassador reported that the King of France had, after all, sent Leicester a special message, promising that his 'authority and position should not be injured in any way', that he should be Alençon's 'guide and friend'. Perhaps, having married himself, Leicester felt a certain compunction about standing in Elizabeth's way. Or perhaps, knowing the Queen so well, he simply doubted whether the project would ever come to fruition.

But the match took a leap forward towards actuality as 1578 turned to 1579 and Jean (or Jehan) de Simier arrived in England. Alençon's personal envoy, his close friend and Master of the Wardrobe, was (as Camden put it) 'a most choice courtier, exquisitely skilled in love toys, pleasant conceits and court dalliances'. The 'chief darling to Monsieur', as Thomas Wilson had described Simier to Leicester, was just Elizabeth's type – a polished man with a smudgy past,* with whom she could flirt in safety. In February Gilbert Talbot was writing to his father that 'Her Majesty continues to have very good usage of Monsieur Simier . . . and she is the best disposed and pleasanteth when she talketh with him.'

Soon – and with Elizabeth, a nickname was always an

---

* He had recently murdered his brother, for having an affair with his own wife.

important sign – Simier became her 'monkey'. More formal gestures of amity were not lacking; in return for the 12,000 crowns' worth of jewels Simier brought to distribute around the court, Elizabeth gave a ball, with a masque in which six ladies gave themselves to six lovers. The language of the letters she exchanged with Alençon was that of high romance: Alençon's, so Elizabeth told him, should be carved in marble, rather than just written on parchment. As spring turned to summer, Leicester took fright – less perhaps at the perfervid prose of an absent Alençon than at the visibly charming presence of Simier. The monkey made a playful sally into Elizabeth's bedroom to snatch a night-cap to send to his master. Elizabeth visited him in his bedroom, catching him clad in no more than his jerkin. Englishmen might (and did) chunter about filthy French ways of wooing, but in fact it was all looking a little like Leicester's heyday.

Leicester even claimed, says Camden, that Simier was using 'amorous potions and unlawful arts' to bring Elizabeth to this pitch. She for her part was delighted (after the events of the previous year) to seize the opportunity to snub her old favourite, when one of her ladies spoke out for him. 'Dost thou think me so unlike myself and unmindful of my royal majesty that I would prefer my servant whom I myself have raised, before the greatest prince in Christendom, in the honour of a husband?' She seemed prepared even to consider, albeit dubiously, granting Alençon a concession she had denied to every former suitor: the right to practise Catholicism privately. But Simier's demands that his master should be crowned king ('a matter that greatly toucheth our regality', Elizabeth said) and an income of £60,000 a year went a step too far; the more so since they gave the Queen cause to think (she said several times over) that 'the mark that is shot at is our fortune and not our person'.

She had, she continued in this letter of spring 1579, always in the royal plural, 'just cause to think ourselves in this action not so well dealt with as appertained to one of our place and quality, having not without great difficulty won in ourself a disposition to yield to the match'. All the same, it seemed to be the council, rather than the Queen, who were putting on the brakes, while

Elizabeth, in any conflict, sided with Simier. (She had, she said of him, great reason to wish 'that we had a subject so well able to serve us'!) He had 'very good hope' of the draft treaty he put to the council in March, and though Londoners were betting three to one against the marriage's coming off, Leicester was not the only courtier who was laying in a stock of new clothes (velvets and silks as well as gold and silver tissue 'or such-like pretty stuffs', ordered from Davison in Flanders). He must have hoped it was only for Alençon's promised visit, and not for Elizabeth's wedding day.

For it was Leicester, so Simier became convinced, who was his greatest enemy. He begged Elizabeth to protect her monkey 'from the paw of the bear'. It was Leicester, he believed, who dissuaded Elizabeth from signing Alençon's passport. There had been an incident a few weeks earlier when a shot was fired as Elizabeth, Leicester, Hatton and Simier were travelling in the royal barge down the Thames. Simier was assumed to be the target – but of whom? Of an ordinary Englishman – for the English were as hostile as ever to a match with France, the traditional enemy? Or of an assassin in the Earl of Leicester's pay? These were the thoughts, so the theory goes, that at the start of July led Simier to move against his adversary; to exploit what must by now have been a semi-open secret; to tell Elizabeth that Leicester was married.

As Camden reported it, the Queen 'intended to have [Leicester] committed to the Tower of London, which his enemies much desired. But the Earl of Sussex, though his greatest and deadliest adversary, dissuaded her. For he was of the opinion that no man was to be troubled with lawful marriage, which estate among all men hath ever been held in honour and esteem.' A decade later, when Walter Ralegh secretly married Bess Throckmorton, Elizabeth did send them both to the Tower. But that case was a little different, since the young Bess was one of Elizabeth's maids, and bound over into the Queen's parental custody. (Ralegh had, in effect, stolen the Queen's and the Throckmorton family's property, while Lettice had the independence of the widowed lady.)

Camden's Tower story loses much of its point if we accept that Elizabeth had known even something of what was happening a year before, at the time when Hatton had voiced the 'lawful marriage' theory. But it is still possible that Elizabeth had not known quite the whole, and reacted accordingly. One tale runs that she ordered Leicester to keep at first to his rooms,* and then to Wanstead. One slightly unreliable report (wrong in some other important details) describes how the Queen boxed Lettice's ears when she came to court with a countess's train of servants: 'As but one sun lights the East, so I shall have but one queen in England.' This may be exaggerated hearsay, but the anonymous writer may well have seen the Lettice he described, riding through Cheapside 'drawn by four milk-white steeds with four footmen in black velvet jackets and silver bears on their backs and breasts, two knights and thirty gentlemen before her, and coaches of gentlewomen, pages and servants behind': like the Queen herself, the writer suggested, or else some foreign princess. Colourful details apart, it was understood that the earl would in the end have to show his face at court again – but his countess was, indeed, banished, though Leicester would persuade even Cecil to intercede for her. (A few years later, Leicester would be sending Cecil effusive, almost grovelling, thanks for having dealt 'so friendly and honourably with my poor wife. For truly my lord, in all reason she is hardly dealt with') It was Lettice's son, not her second husband, who would finally, twenty years later, win her a small measure of acceptance again – and that only with extreme difficulty.

It may have been now that Leicester wrote a tetchy letter to Christopher Hatton. He had been sent for to the council, but as it was clearly a general summons, rather than a particular, he hopes they will

> excuse me that I forbear to come, being, as I wrote to you this morning, troubled and grieved both in heart and mind. I am not unwilling,

---

* A more romantic version says he was confined to a tower in the gardens of Greenwich, called 'the Tower Mireflore', where Anne Boleyn had once lodged.

God knows, to serve her Majesty wherein I may, to the uttermost of my life, but most unfit at this time to make repair to that place, where so many eyes are witnesses of my open and great disgraces delivered from her Majesty's mouth.

Then again, Mendoza reported that it was Leicester who had chosen to retire to Wanstead, angry that Alençon's passport had been issued against his wishes, and that the Queen went to visit him there, secretly, and 'remained two days because he feigned illness'. One would give a great deal to know of what they spoke, so privately.

In August 1579, at last, Alençon arrived on the long-discussed visit – so while Leicester (with whatever qualms and regrets) could divide his time between everyday business and his newly public bride, Elizabeth could console herself with the attentions of a new wooer. This was the first time she had met one of her foreign suitors (unless you count Philip of Spain); the first time she had been able to play the game of royal courtship on a level of near-equality.

From the start, the visit was conducted on a note of amorous high fantasy. Alençon arrived at Greenwich early in the morning of 17 August, after travelling through the night, and had to be dissuaded (Simier said) from going instantly to Elizabeth to kiss her hand. Instead, so Simier told Elizabeth in a note, he had forced his master to go to bed: 'Would to God it was by your side.' When they met, later that day, Elizabeth declared that she had 'never in my life seen a creature more agreeable to me' – and though she would in any event have had to say something polite, though she would have found it hard to reject him on personal grounds having encouraged him to break with protocol and come on approval, she probably was relieved by what she saw. Though much had been made in reports of the pockmarks on his face, and of his lack of height, the Venetian ambassador in Paris once gave of him a cool but not wholly unattractive appraisal: 'his stature small but well set, his hair black and curling naturally'.

The French ambassador was of course delighted, reporting to Catherine de Medici that Elizabeth had only 'with difficulty been able to entertain the Duke, being captivated, overcome with love', that she 'had never found a man whose nature and actions suited her better'. The Spanish ambassador Mendoza reported much the same, albeit less happily. Soon Alençon was Elizabeth's 'Frog', the recipient of her presents and her promises of eternal love. This parade of instant affection, however, did not please everybody. Alençon's visit was shrouded in a thin veil of official secrecy – he was not supposed to be known to be there at all – and while the frisson of stolen meetings lent zest to Elizabeth's games, Mendoza reported that Elizabeth's councillors were giving the court a wide berth, aware that almost anything they did, in these odd circumstances, was bound to annoy Elizabeth in some way. 'It is said that if she marries before consulting her people, she may repent it,' Mendoza warned. 'Leicester is much put out, and all the councillors are disgusted except Sussex. A close friend of Leicester tells me he is cursing the French, and is greatly incensed against Sussex.'

Elizabeth seemed determined to flaunt the fact that another man admired her. When she arranged for Alençon secretly to watch a court ball, she not only showed off every dance step she knew, but waved excitedly towards his hiding place behind a tapestry. Describe it coldly, and it sounds as if Elizabeth were making a fool of herself – or, alternatively, playing the ongoing political game of passionate promise with scant regard for her personal dignity. (The more so, of course, since there were rumours not only about his brother's but about Alençon's own sexuality.)

Two days later Leicester, in what was described as 'great grief', arranged an interview with Elizabeth, from which he emerged clearly disturbed. That evening the opponents of the match held a council of war, as a result of which Leicester withdrew from the court, as did his sister Mary Sidney. Their chief hope now was that public opinion would put an end to Alençon's pretensions; the public opinion that had once stood in his, Leicester's, way. But circumstances came to their aid. Just ten days after his arrival, the death of a friend summoned Alençon back to France; and it may have been now that Elizabeth wrote a poem, 'On

Monsieur's Departure', which reflects a genuine confusion of emotion.

> I grieve, yet dare not show my discontent;
> I love, and yet am forced to seem to hate,
> I dote, but dare not what I meant;
> I seem stark mute, yet inwardly do prate.
> I am, and am not, freeze, and yet I burn,
> Since from myself my other self I turn.
> My care is like my shadow in the sun,
> Follows me flying, flies when I pursue it,
> Stands and lives by me, does what I have done.
> Oh, let me live with some more sweet content,
> Or die, and so forget what love e'er meant.

It sounds almost like a younger Elizabeth speaking – one with an adult ruler's responsibilities, true, but beset by the fears and conflicts she must have felt in the dangerous days under her brother Edward and her sister Mary. It sounds almost as though something – the imminence of the menopause? The loss of Robert? – had thrown her back into girlish uncertainty. Elizabeth, now in the second half of her forties, may well have found that it was one thing to dismiss the idea of marriage and children when her mind could be changed another day; another to give a final negative when the last chance was slipping away.

Perhaps she was persuading herself into love, but she wrote to Alençon now with all the intimacy she might have written to Leicester. 'My dearest, I give you now a fair mirror to see there very clearly the foolishness of my understanding . . .' 'I muse as do those on night watch, dreaming, not having slept well.' 'See where the love that I bear you carries me – to act against my nature.' At one point in their relationship, she compared herself to a beaten dog he could not turn away. Perhaps it is significant that she did so only after she had sent him away – the familiar pattern of push-pull. But all the same, would she ever have abased herself to a subject in this manner? (Although, as they might have done with Leicester, her letters turn in the end to a note of reproach. 'It seems to me that in commemorating the history of the dealings between us, it pleases you to tell me at length of the hazards, losses, and machinations that you have endured for my sake . . . I think that the king will repute me for such a one as goes a-wooing, which will always be a fine reputation for a woman!', she would write in 1582.) Not to be outdone, Alençon claimed to say his prayers before her portrait; wrote letters (so the French envoy Castelnau claimed proudly) 'ardent enough to set fire to water'.

But Cecil was quick to take advantage of her yielding mood while it lasted, and of her insecurities. 'If your majesty tarry till all the clocks strike and agree of one hour, or tarry till all the oars row the barge, you shall never 'point the time and you may slip the tide that yet patiently tarryeth for you.' Elizabeth, he flattered her, was a woman of high aspiration. She had found much delight in 'the morning of your time'; now she sought not just still to reign, but still 'to reign and rule honored, pleased, and contented; and to have the morning dew all the whole day of your life'. Even putting all considerations of policy aside, would the pleasure of rule seem always as fresh, unless she added a new delight to the mix? Would she still feel the morning dew?

Some, Cecil wrote, found all they needed in 'a good dinner, a supper, a soft bed, a carpet and a cushion, coin and crowns'. But she was not such a one. 'Is it mirth, meat, or music, honor, duty, and service done by your servants, that doth satisfy, if there be not some partner of the delight, honor, and pleasure, and that your majesty may love and esteem above the rest? Or lives the man and speaks he English that you highly esteem and love at this day?' Subtly, he needled her again and again with the fact that (with Leicester married) she now had no such companion, unless it were her Frenchman; and 'without that person you are alone though a hundred be about'.

Of course, he agreed, there were those who spoke against the marriage – some out of fear for their religious freedom; some from political motives; some 'for loathness and doubt lest such as have had the highest credit should come down'. The last group would be reassured when they find their leaders 'take no hurt' –

and 'doubt not, lady, for when lions make a leap, the bears and other beasts lie down'. It is a clear reference to Robert Dudley.

But the fact is that neither Leicester, nor any other man who mattered in the kingdom, could ignore the question of the French marriage. Indeed, this was an affair on which everyone in the kingdom felt entitled to have their say: the great problem the pair faced, as Elizabeth wrote frankly to her potential betrothed, was how to persuade the public to cede their Virgin Queen to a man who was, after all, the embodiment of England's traditional enemy. Though once they had longed for her to marry, the English had come to identify their unmarried ruler with peace and prosperity. The popular mood was vehemently against the French match, and voiced by the patriotic and puritan John Stubbs, who in September, with Alençon barely gone and Elizabeth feeling all the pangs of loss, published a pamphlet entitled *A Gaping Gulphe wherein England is like to be swallowed*.

Stubbs's motives were of the purest. He spoke as most Englishmen felt, but his words had the unpalatable bluntness of John Bull, uttered with all the appalling honesty of one who felt himself within the national family circle. To the fundamental problem he stated – that the English equated a foreign marriage with subjection, and a Catholic prince with tyranny – he added more personal facts of the sort Elizabeth (at this moment, with the public humiliation of Leicester's defection still fresh) must have been particularly unwilling to hear.

The Queen was too old to face childbirth for the first time, he wrote: 'how fearful the expectation of death is to mother and child'; and Alençon's motive in seeking to marry a woman so much older than himself could not be other than mercenary. This was the very spot on which Elizabeth was most sensitive – as Leicester had had occasion to warn Walsingham recently. Even the paternalism of Stubbs's tone (England's dear Elizabeth, he wrote, was being 'led blindfold as a poor lamb to the slaughter') could not but grate on a woman who increasingly felt herself at odds with the majority of her councillors.

While the council, in a flurry of meetings throughout October, debated the very same points Stubbs had raised, Elizabeth turned on the author himself with fury. Stubbs was arrested on a charge of seditious libel; and though the law forbade her to impose the death penalty, what happened was almost as horrible. On Westminster Palace Green, a shocked and silent crowd of spectators saw a cleaver slice through flesh and bone to sever Stubbs's right hand. With his remaining arm, Stubbs swept off his hat and cried 'God save the Queen!' before he fainted. A ballad popular in the middle years of Elizabeth's reign had figured itself as a love song, with Elizabeth holding out her hand to 'my dear lover England'. If the relationship between Elizabeth and her people were indeed a marriage, this was perhaps her one striking act of real infidelity.*

But politics as well as personal liking conspired to drive the French marriage negotiations onwards. The Protestant rebels in the Netherlands were by October suffering the full force of the 'Spanish Fury' as Parma was carried in a litter through the streets of Maestricht over a rubble of mutilated corpses. The times when Leicester and Elizabeth had joked of their marriage with a Spanish ambassador seemed very far away.

When the Queen asked the council for advice in October, it was Leicester and Hatton who mustered a majority of councillors against the match, Cecil who led the smaller party in favour. Never can Elizabeth have felt more profoundly at odds with her Robert. For years, she had wanted nothing more than permission *not* to marry. Now, when at last most of her councillors were urging her to refrain, she displayed uncertainty. Perhaps we may wonder what would have happened if her councillors had not opposed Alençon; what part their and the country's hostility played in allowing her to indulge her domestic fantasy? But certainly she sounded like a woman in love, a woman who did truly want to marry. After that meeting of 7 October, when the council debated from eight in the morning until seven at night,

---

* Leicester's nephew Philip Sidney, with all the arrogance of youth, wrote even more pointedly than Stubbs against the match. But he was never likely to suffer a comparable penalty – the more so since his words, at least, were confined to a private and courtly circle, rather than being published for all the blunt Londoners to see.

'without stirring from the room, having sent the clerks away', a deputation of four councillors – Cecil and Leicester, Lincoln and Sussex – waited on her to know 'the inclination of her mind'. Cecil had persuaded them to return an open verdict on the match. It was for the Queen to say.

Elizabeth marvelled that 'her councillors should think it doubtful whether there could be any more surety for her and her realm than to have her marry and have a child to inherit and continue the line of Henry VIII'. She had anticipated – so she said, in tears – 'a universal request made for her to proceed in this marriage'. The council returned the next day, duly vowing their commitment to the furtherance of the match, 'if so it shall please her'. For years, she had hammered home the point that her marriage was a decision for herself alone. Now, when she wanted real support, if not guidance, she must have wondered if she had done so too successfully. She spoke bitter words against those who had opposed the match, and thus incited the tolerant majority. After the conversation, so Mendoza noted, she remained 'extremely sad'; prohibitively 'cross and melancholy'. On 10 November, dressed in an embroidered cloud of French *fleurs de lis*, she told her councillors 'she had determined to marry'. Who could say whether it was her real purpose, or her hope that useful negotiations should be spun out indefinitely?

On 24 November she agreed that she and Simier (as Alençon's proxy) should sign the marriage articles – which, however, gave her two months to convince her people to 'rejoice and approve' (as she wrote to Alençon, 'my dearest'). If they failed to do so, the contract would be rendered null and void . . . Was Parliament ever likely to approve? Did Elizabeth really think it would? It seems extremely unlikely. Effectively, Leicester and his party were being used as her stalking horse again; though this time without their complicity. At the end of November Simier returned to France, taking some splendid presents with him and sending in return a series of ardent love letters tied up in ribbon of pink silk.

That same month Douglass Sheffield also left for Paris, as bride to Sir Edward Stafford, who accompanied Simier to lay the English position before the French king. (Stafford's father, though a prominent Catholic, had long been Leicester's friend; and Leicester assured Sir Edward, on his departure, that he would take care of his interests, though Sir Edward came to feel that the earl reneged on his promise when Douglass was once safely out of the way.) Elizabeth took the opportunity to launch an inquiry into the question of whether Douglass and Leicester had not, as was rumoured, secretly married. If it were found that they had, then the triumphant – and now pregnant – Lettice was a bigamist. The Earl of Sussex (kinsman to Douglass, and no friend of Leicester) was appointed to look into the matter; but all questions foundered on the rock of Douglass's inability or unwillingness to stake her claim. Stafford later recorded that Elizabeth told him 'to importune his wife whether there had been a contract between her and the Earl of Leicester, which if it were, then she would have him make good her honour with a marriage, or rot in the Tower'. Douglass 'answered with great vows, grief and passion that she had trusted the said Earl too much to have anything to show to constrain him to marry her'. She said she had 'told her husband the truth' – that she was free – 'when she married him'.

Probably Douglass knew that, once she had served her turn, Elizabeth was unlikely to treat her with any more favour than she showed Lettice, should she be once securely established as the woman who had stolen the Queen's Robin away. She would, moreover, have incurred the wrath of Leicester and the powerful Knollys clan . . . better, surely, to escape away to Paris and be happy. And if she had no documentary evidence to produce, far safer not to launch what was likely to prove an abortive inquiry, which might leave her stranded indefinitely in the limbo of the unsuccessful claimant.

But being thwarted in this attempt at revenge is unlikely to have made Elizabeth feel more warmly towards Leicester. Throughout the early autumn the pressure of events had forced them to work together, and the presence of the French – an urge to keep friction under wraps in the family – had perhaps put a lid on any open display of hostility. But in November Leicester wrote a painful letter to Cecil, excusing himself from coming to court.

I perceive by my brother of Warwick your lordship hath found the like bitterness in her majesty towards me that others (too many) have acquainted me lately withal. I must confess it grieveth me not a little, having so faithfully, carefully and chargefully served her Majesty these twenty years as I have done. Your lordship is a witness I trust that in all her services I have been a direct servant unto her, her state and crown, that I have not more sought my own particular profit than her honour.

Cecil, besides himself, has been 'best acquainted' with all their dealings: 'I have ere now broken my very heart with you . . .' Leicester had carried himself, he said, 'almost more than a bondsman many a year together, so long as one drop of comfort was left of any hope . . . methinks it is more than hard to take such an occasion to bear so great displeasure for. But the old proverb sayeth, they that will beat a dog will want no weapon.'

In the new year of the new decade it was noticed that Elizabeth was 'not showing as much favour as formerly to the Earl of Leicester'. And yet, gradually observers noticed that Elizabeth was beginning to relent once more; the most maddening thing for Leicester's many opponents must have been that the bond between him and his royal mistress never, ever, quite went away.

She continued to cast it up to him, whenever she was out of temper, that he had stood in the way of her marriage. 'Better for me to sell my last lands than to fall into these harsh conditions', he said. But when the French ambassador blamed Leicester for having raised the question of Alençon's religion, he found, as so many others had done, that it was never safe for anyone else to attack the Queen's dear 'brother'. That was a privilege she guarded jealously to herself.

Probably, Leicester had ceased to parade his opposition to Alençon – or his affection for Lettice. The tacit deal between him and the Queen would be 'out of sight, out of mind' (and Lettice would never again be a star of the court in Leicester's lifetime). Possibly, now that a little water had gone under the bridge, Elizabeth found that his marriage did not make so very much difference to what, after all, had long ceased to be an ardent love story. Possibly, too, now that Alençon was no longer there to charm her with all that youth and potential, the real problems with the match – the national hostility for which Leicester might be seen as the mouthpiece – loomed ever larger in her mind. Perhaps, even, her old aversion to marriage, her turning to Leicester as a shield against it, began to hold sway. She had been glad to play – but not necessarily to pay.

For his part, Alençon was reluctant to press his suit. (Suspiciously so, maybe.) The two-month deadline laid down in the articles of marriage came and passed without commentary. He seems to have decided that his best technique was to play Elizabeth's waiting game, and meanwhile to try to endear himself to the English nobility. He wrote to Elizabeth (so Mendoza said) asking that Stubbs should be released from gaol, so that people should see this marriage with a foreign prince would not signal a return to Catholic tyranny. Elizabeth complained to Cecil that she was 'between Scylla and Charybdis'; but Cecil for one was beginning to suspect that her real objective was just to keep the French on a string for as long as possible, and was appalled at the danger of such a policy. If she did not intend to marry she should undeceive Alençon at once, since 'those that would trick princes, trick themselves'. Walsingham chimed in to the same tune; if Elizabeth did not soon declare some resolution, then 'greater dishonour than I dare commit to paper' would soon be heading her way. (After all, people, so the French ambassador said once, trying to put pressure on her, were convinced she had slept with Alençon already.)

But Elizabeth continued to pursue the course of procrastination – that hallmark of her policy and personality alike – that for years had worked so well. She wore the frog jewel Alençon had presented to her; she kissed the gloves that he had given her, frequently and publicly. In a stream of letters she lavished Alençon with praise for his 'constancy'; insisted her people needed more time to come to terms with the idea, but that their souls would be united – eventually. In August 1580 (with a fresh papal bull issued against Elizabeth; with James VI in Scotland assuming his own rule and upsetting a well-established *modus vivendi*; with Philip of Spain increasing his empire by the annexation of the Portuguese throne), Elizabeth was rattled enough to invite France to send commissioners to discuss the marriage treaty. Dismayingly, they did not instantly respond. Alençon may simply have set his sights on another kingdom – in September he accepted the Netherlands crown – but the Venetian ambassador in Paris heard that he was remembering, too, Elizabeth's 'advanced age and repulsive physical nature'. The French court, moreover, was at least as divided as the English one, with brother pitted against brother; at one point there were even rumours Leicester was being bribed by the French king *not* to help his brother to an English crown!

In January 1581, to Elizabeth's relief, came news that the French commissioners were on their way. (Alençon's Netherlands campaign had run out of money.) But his necessity was her and her subjects' greatest fear: that England would be drawn into a war of her husband's, of the sort that had lost them Calais.

In March 1581 the commissioners arrived, to be greeted by a flurry of fêtes designed to prove England's (if not Elizabeth's) desirability. Once again the fantasy of love was resumed – though the game was getting a little threadbare, surely? The commissioners offered Elizabeth a symbolically unwithered posy of flowers plucked, they said, by Alençon's own hand ('the hand with the little fingers that I bless a million times' as she wrote to him, in an effusive thank-you note). She wore a gold tissue gown to the banqueting house especially built in the gardens of Whitehall. (The creation of wood and canvas, painted to resemble stonework outside, and the heavens within, took 375 men to build it and cost £1,744.)

When she took the French envoys to dine on board the *Golden Hind*, less than a year back from Drake's epic circumnavigation of the globe, she dropped one of her gold and purple garters, which the Frenchman begged as a prize for his master. Not then and there – she had nothing else to keep her stocking up, she said. But she sent it round later. The banquet was the finest that had been seen 'since the time of King Henry'. Drake's crew danced for the Queen in Red Indian dress; the captain himself told stories of his adventures (for a solid four hours . . .); and one of the French envoys was himself asked to act as the Queen's proxy and knight Drake on the deck of his ship. No wonder Mendoza (who had signally failed to get either Drake or Elizabeth to disgorge the £80,000 of Spanish treasure the adventurer had liberated along his route) sniped that she seemed more interested in 'ostentation and details of no moment' than in the serious conclusion of a marriage treaty.

May saw an allegorical Triumph in the tilt yard, where the 'Fortress of Perfect Beauty', defended by knights who were really the Knollys brothers, was beset by Desire and his foster children, as impersonated by Philip Sidney and his friends. The identity of the participants suggests that this was Leicester's show. Cannons fired balls of scented powder and toilet water and the foot soldiers threw flowers, while the fortress – the Queen's un-assailable virtue – refused to yield. At the end of a two-day spectacle, Desire's party sent to the Queen a boy 'clad in the ash coloured garments of humble submission'. Ironically – or tellingly? – the imagery of Elizabeth's virginity flowered in these very years when her maiden status was under assault.*

The frolics and the feasting went on throughout the ambassadors' long visit. But when it came to the serious negotiations, Elizabeth herself proved unassailable; just like the Fortress of Perfect Beauty. She said she was still concerned about the age gap, about the Catholic question, about being sucked into war against Spain. She said – after all that pageantry – that she wanted a marriage-free treaty, a simple league of alliance between the two countries. In June she apparently changed her mind, telling the commissioners to go ahead and draw up terms for a marriage – but also that Alençon would have to come himself to ratify them. But in one of her letters to the duke, she warned him that, though her soul was 'wholly dedicated to him', 'her body

---

* The so-called 'sieve' portraits, for example, showed Elizabeth holding a sieve, in reference to the story of a Roman virgin, the miraculous power of whose chastity was such that she was able to carry a sieve full of water from the Tiber without spilling a drop.

was hers'. Perhaps she was piqued into it by news that, at the beginning of that month, Lettice's son had been born into the security of legitimacy and with the honorary title of Lord Denbigh. He was named Robert after his father, and his parents doted on the 'noble Impe'. Leicester may have been out of the Queen's favour, and pained by it personally as well as politically. But at last he had an heir. In one sense, in the first years of the 1580s, emotionally he must have been in the money.

Walsingham, meanwhile, when sent back to France to persuade the French of Elizabeth's sincerity, said that he would count it 'a great favour' to be sent to the Tower instead; and if Leicester and Hatton joined him in begging her to end the pretence, who can blame them, really? 'When Her Majesty is pressed to marry she seemeth to affect a league,' Walsingham wrote to Cecil, 'and when a league is proposed then she liketh better a marriage.' It was the same old story.

As October turned to November Alençon arrived back in England, clutching a diamond ring for Elizabeth. (She gave him a jewel-encrusted arquebus, and a key that fitted every room of the palace.) They moved back instantly into the private language of lovers: rumour said she took him a cup of broth in bed each morning. The ever-jealous Mendoza noted that they spent hours together each day. 'I cannot tell what the devil they do.' By November he reported that the French 'look upon marriage as an established fact', but that the English 'scoff at it'. When they were alone, he heard, Elizabeth would pledge herself to Alençon 'as much as any woman could to a man', but she would not have anything said publicly. Again, it was the pattern familiar long ago to Robert Dudley. But the Valois prince was no traitor's son on his preferment: was it to placate him that she staged the famous scene of late November? Was it consciously a charade, or an expression of her real inner uncertainty? The French ambassador came to her as she was walking with Alençon in the gallery of Whitehall Palace; Leicester and Walsingham trailing behind. He said the King his master wanted to know the Queen's intention from her own lips. 'She replied, "You may write this to the King: that the Duke of Anjou [Alençon] shall be my husband," and at the same moment she turned to Alençon and kissed him on the mouth, drawing a ring from her own hand and giving it to him as a pledge.' She then called her ladies and gentlemen, and repeated to them her intention. Word spread like wildfire. The Spanish ambassador put the tale into a despatch. The Venetian envoy in Paris passed on a description given him by a servant of Alençon. The French, of course, rejoiced; but (as Camden put it), Leicester, Hatton and Walsingham 'fretted as if the Queen, the Realm and religion were now undone'.

Leicester's opposition to the French match he had once, long ago, promoted was based on sincere political and religious principles. But it is not implausible also that, just as Elizabeth blew hot and cold on him, so he felt more threatened by the proposal once it began to look more likely – and once it seemed it might involve her heart as well as head.*

But by the next day Elizabeth had changed her mind – though that is a cold way of stating one of the puzzles that have intrigued her biographers for centuries. If Camden is to be believed, it was her ladies who managed to 'terrify her from marrying', 'wailing and laying terrors before her', primed by Leicester and Hatton to do so. And so it was after a sleepless night that she sent for Alençon and told him that two more such would see her in her grave and that she could not marry him.

Over the next few weeks Alençon still hung around the court, perhaps hoping her mind would change yet again (as indeed it did – and back – and back again). But politically, things seemed to have worked out – as they so often did, despite or because of Elizabeth's baffling machinations. Spain was forced to be more conciliatory, which gave England more security. The parade of marriage had done its job. The French king unwittingly played his part by rejecting the admittedly excessive terms Elizabeth had sent him on the day she promised to marry. And Alençon for his part was something less than heartbroken; muttering about 'the

---

* It was said that he asked her whether she were a maid or a woman – which suggests, of course, that he did not already himself have the best of reasons for knowing she was no virgin.

lightness of women and inconstancy of islanders', he recovered sufficiently rapidly to convert his demand for Elizabeth into a demand for money.

A contribution of £60,000 to Alençon's Netherlands campaign was the agreed price, and Elizabeth thought it cheap: Mendoza heard that in her own bedchamber she danced for joy (also – in another echo of her relationship with Leicester – that she assured Alençon she would be happy for him to stay on in England as her brother, friend and good companion – anything but her husband). But by the end of December Alençon's continued presence in England, his declaration that he would rather die than leave England a bachelor, looked like an attempt to up the stakes: Leicester said that £200,000 would not be too high a price to get rid of him. (People said that Robert Dudley exploited Elizabeth. But he was not alone by a long way.)

It was the spring of 1582 before Alençon finally set out towards the south coast, accompanied as far as Canterbury by Elizabeth herself, and across the Channel by Leicester and several other prominent nobles. Gilbert Talbot wrote to his father: 'The departure was mournful betwixt her Highness and Monsieur, she loth to let him go and he as loth to depart.' (He also reported that Leicester had taken over with him '50 bives [beefs] and 500 muttons for his provision during his abode'.) But it was also said that the earl carried a secret message from the Queen, asking William of Orange to ensure Alençon never returned to England. Leicester stayed in the Netherlands feasting a little too long: Elizabeth began commenting ominously to Hatton that men never knew how fortunate they had been until fortune had left, which caused Hatton to summon Leicester hastily home again. Leicester described the Alençon he had left behind him as stranded like a hulk upon a sandbank – and Elizabeth, having once despatched her froggy wooer to Flushing, began sighing how much she would give to have him swimming in the Thames again.

16

'In times of distress'
1582–1584

THERE IS A PAINTING THAT HANGS AT PENSHURST PLACE IN KENT, described as Elizabeth and Leicester dancing the Volta. It is said to have represented one of the many stops Alençon's farewell party made along the way. As the two central figures leap, musicians play; and the watching throng of lavishly dressed ladies, gentlemen and court dwarves gaze on admiringly. In fact, it was never likely to have been a simple representation – more like a propaganda piece using a set of established images and designed (since the figure meant to be Alençon is ignoring the central spectacle, and slyly squeezing another woman's waist) as a final thrust of the Dudley faction against a marriage Leicester so vehemently opposed.

Its reproduction is placed, dampingly, in the box file labelled 'Elizabeth I: borderline false' in the archives of the National Portrait Gallery. A note says that a larger version can be found in the Musée de Rennes, labelled 'the ball of Henri III'. But Penshurst has a copy of an old *Country Life* article (23 January 1973) arguing that it forms one of a series of French-inspired marriage ball scenes (and that the lecherous figure does indeed represent Alençon, whose short doublet and tights were then characteristic, though not common, wear), albeit that it is likely to be less a straight depiction than a sort of allegory . . . Perhaps it is the youthful vigour of the central pair, bounding athletically – almost aerobically! – straight up into the air, that gives the game away. True, the Queen was always painted as youthful, or at least ageless. But the same consideration was not extended to Robert Dudley.

As the 1570s edged towards the 1580s – with Elizabeth's Robert transformed, past all denial, into 'Benedick, the married man' – the two seemed to be leading very separate lives in a way they had not done for twenty years. For the first time since Elizabeth came to the throne, we are telling two very different emotional stories. Where Elizabeth is concerned, we have been reading her intimate, revelatory letters to a man other than Robert Dudley. Leicester, meanwhile, was preoccupied with his new wife and baby. Even Camden admitted that – after all those years, after all the rumours, after the two wives who had had little joy of him – when finally committed, he was uxorious, 'a good husband in excess'.

It is a lucky chance that among the stray survivals of Leicester's papers is the 'disbursement book' that, albeit patchily, covers his expenditure for these very years. It gives an extraordinary insight into his daily life at this point, just when the records of court life feature him less prominently; and gives also, perhaps, a picture of the man. There are many records of sums lost 'at play', but more records of smaller sums given out in tiny acts of charity: 12d 'to a poor woman of Leighton', 6d to another poor woman of Knightsbridge, 5s to one of Stepney and 10s for one who had come all the way from Devonshire; £30 to a sick gentleman servant; £10, handed over to Leicester's chaplain, to be distributed among the London prisons; the odd 20s 'in small money' delivered 'to your lordship own hands' for distribution that same day; 5s given 'by your lordship's commandment' to 'the blackamoor'. Every such casual gift or payment – as opposed to the regular wages given to the keepers, to the French cook (and, less obviously to our eyes, the French gardener), to 'Jesper that mends instruments', to Roger Gillions the bargeman and the laundress his wife – bears that magic, grandeur-affirming phrase 'by your lordship's commandment'. Three pounds to the musicians who came to Wanstead from London, more than a guinea to four gardeners who made a 'knot' in the garden there; money to those who gravelled its walks or tended its ponds.

Leicester obviously loved his gardens and his garden produce. Just one six-month period (October 1584 to March 1585) shows a 'reward' to 'young Adams' for making a dial in the garden at Leicester House; 20s to a gardener who gave pink seeds and 'philbud' [filbert] trees; money for transporting a basket of violets to Wanstead; and then again ten days later, money to the servant of William Hunnis (master of the famous child players) for picking more violets for Leicester's benefit. Later in the year there would be pots of gillyflowers, and hyssop and thyme, and radish seeds brought to him at Nonsuch; oranges and lemons, rosewater and peas. Leicester appears to have paid a retainer to 'Edyth Eryth a poor woman that follows the Court' to keep his chamber there supplied with flowers and boughs, and one of the most frequent rewards, as the year wore on, would be for the man who brought artichokes.* Luck the fool got 6s 8d for presenting Leicester with a basket of apples, the keeper of the gatehouse at Westminster 3s 4d for presenting grapes. When spring came the same keeper offered vine slips; sadly, we don't know whether or not Leicester's gardeners grew them successfully.

His household now comprised something like a hundred to a hundred and fifty people, as opposed to the thirty to fifty he had had at the start of Elizabeth's reign. When not on the road, or following the court, Leicester joined his wife, dividing his time between Wanstead and Leicester House (where rooms were set aside for his stepchildren's use), and many of his servants moved with him. One of the most often recorded costs was boat hire for transport along the Thames: 6s for Leicester's servant to transport his clothes from Oatlands to London; 10s to the Queen's watermen for taking Leicester home from Arundel House. Everything went by water where possible, from Leicester's yeomen of the wardrobe and his groom of the chamber, travelling from Leicester

---

* Which newly fashionable vegetable, it was said, 'provoketh lust in women so it abateth the same in men', according to Turner's *Herbal*.

House to the court at Greenwich, to a brace of does, and a servant headed the other way carrying 'a short gown furred with sables to show the skinner'.

Travel further, by land – to Oxford, in this instance – meant paying for the dinners of dozens of retainers on the journey. Six of Leicester's servants, sent on as an advance guard, had to be bought dinner at Henley; Mr Clinton and Mr Devereux had to have their 'horsemeate' paid when they came to see Leicester at Woodstock; and 'Paid more the same day for the charges of your lordship's servants being xxx in number for Saturday night and Sunday breakfast at Henley as appeareth by a bill.' Then as now, travel threw up a myriad odd expenses. There is even a payment to the man who washed Leicester's linen along the way.

Clothing himself and his retinue in appropriate style absorbed a good deal of money. Four pairs of 'dry perfumed gloves' at 3s 4d the pair; 24s for two pairs of large gloves, lined, perfumed, and trimmed with black silk and gold. There were stomachers, and scarlet to line them; girdles and 'hangers' trimmed with gold lace to hold short swords. Black silk nightcaps at 6s the piece were a present for the Earl of Shrewsbury. Shortly before Christmas time, £22 bought two doublets for Lettice. The mentions of Lettice are less frequent than one might at first expect: one occasion when Roger Gillions was paid for 'carrying my lady from Leicester House to Putney and back again'; a mention of shirts that Lettice bought for Leicester; one item of money delivered to her when she was clearly losing at play. But the bulk of Lettice's personal expenses, and the salaries of the women who served in her chamber, seem to have been paid out of her own income as the Earl of Essex's widow.

Robert clearly attended to his family. There is a present of £20 to Lettice's daughter, and his stepdaughter, Dorothy; £30 went to the schoolmaster who taught 'Mr Robert Dudley', while on the same visit to see young Robert in his schoolroom in Oxfordshire, Leicester gave the boy himself a 10s tip. (The young Robert probably spent most of his time in Sussex, however; and indeed another bill records his transport from there.) On another occasion the boy is getting a hat; on yet another a gilt rapier and dagger with a velvet scabbard. Other donations are more curious. Lady Stafford – the former Douglass Sheffield, or her mother-in-law? – was given £5. Another equally puzzling item records payment for transport of 'the bathing tube [tub?]'; another is to the baker, for 'horse bread'.

A new coach; dozens of towels. Reams of paper; a looking glass. Wine from abroad; three bottles of Warwickshire water. Lots of payments to 'your lordship's spaniel keeper', who seems to have been paid per day, per dog. To the lark catcher, 2s 6d; to Robert the trumpeter, £40 – but he did have to buy a new trumpet out of that. And there is a whole handful of items, all together, about the purchase of cases of pistols, and dozens of crossbow arrows – sign of the edgy times, maybe.

Messengers got money, like the man who brought letters from Sir Francis Drake (in whose projected West Indies voyage Leicester was to be an investor; and who features occasionally as a fellow card player). More money to the men who held torches to light the earl from 'the Bishop of Canterbury's', or the Scottish ambassador's, and home to Leicester House again. Servants attached to noble friends, and to Leicester's own client gentry, had also to be rewarded. The keeper of a royal park might get several shillings just for opening a gate. Six shillings and eightpence went to Hatton's coachman for carrying Leicester from Syon to Colbrook; 5s 'to the cooks of the Star Chamber when your lordship passed through the kitchen there'; more than £5 to the Queen's officers, when she dined with him; 5s to his own gentleman usher's man 'for presenting a dozen and a half of partridges to your lordship'; 2s 6d to Sir Horatio Palavicino's man for presenting Leicester with dried peaches; 20s when he made the same gift to the Queen. (Leicester supervised the sending of presents of horses, in the Queen's name, and hounds, and a bow, to King James in Scotland, whom the English were trying to woo.) But at least he also got many gifts himself, even if there were always this indirect payment to be made.

Venison was a favourite gift to send him. Fat coneys, 'two swans and a lamprey pie', even 'two fat wethers', or a boar, or a peacock. The French ambassador offered wine and cheese. He got dogs, and hawks, and horses (a 'pyde nag'); and glasses – still a luxury. Occasionally it was a book; though Leicester himself was prepared to pay out good money for a book of martyrs and one of Psalms, and Calvin's *Sermons on Job*: standard reading for the ardent Protestant.

By and large, the disbursement book records the story of a personal life. It is the letters of the period that reflect the political one, and they still show Leicester and his queen as bound together, willy nilly – Leicester instrumental in promoting new anti-Catholic measures; sending congratulations on the putting down of a minor outbreak of disorder; warning Heneage that the Queen still held him out of favour and the time for an approach was not yet ripe – show, in other words, business as usual among the court's inner circle. And they show, more specifically, Leicester concerned still for the Queen's business and the Queen's image . . . It was in this period that he wrote the letter that most clearly shows him as consciously promoting that image, building Elizabeth's support base; acting in effect as campaign manager in the constant popularity parade that was Elizabeth's monarchy.

Elizabeth was on progress, and Leicester was writing from the house of one 'hearty noble couple', Lord and Lady Norris, at whose home she had been expected, but where she had failed to appear. Leicester had had, he writes to Hatton, to pretend that they two had been the chief 'dissuaders' – that they were responsible for the disappointment, having told Elizabeth that the weather had made the roads too bad. Lady Norris had taken the excuse poorly: 'Trust me, if it had not been so late, I think I should have sought me another lodging, my welcome awhile was so ill.' He had 'more than half' won the irate hostess over – especially by offering the Norrises his own rooms at Elizabeth's next port of call – but her Majesty herself 'must help somewhat' in placating Lady Norris, 'or else we have more than half lost this lady'. In another incident at this time, a sailor arrested in the Queen's presence was, by Elizabeth's order, carried to Leicester's chamber. The man was accused of being part of a Spanish plot, in what looks rather like a darker kind of PR exercise.

Clearly, Robert was still travelling the country on the Queen's business. (Horses and hounds feature largely in the disbursement book.) No doubt he was still an active man: he went with the court to the races; drew out 9s 'to put in your lordship's pocket' when he went on a fishing trip. But he was getting older, and less fit. The book shows a payment of £30 to 'Ezard your lordship's bonesetter', and six pairs of 'spactakells' at 12d the pair. There is repeated mention (though paid only at 10s) of 'one that did cut your lordship's corns'. In one of his bouts of what was probably a malarial fever, Leicester wrote of himself to the Queen as 'your old patient, that has always from [your] holy hand been relieved'. ('I have no more to offer again but that which is already my bond and duty: the body and life, to be as ready to yield sacrifice for your service, as it has from you received all good things . . .')

As Leicester got older, he was getting more difficult. John Aylmer wrote of some 'unhappy paroxysm' that had rocked their friendship. He wished only, he wrote, that he could 'appeal from this Lord of Leicester', whom something has 'incensed with displeasure', 'unto mine old Lord of Leicester, who in his virtue of mildness and of softness . . . hath carried away the praise from all men'. A Catholic divine who had fled the country in 1582 wrote to Sussex that he had done so through extreme fear of Leicester's 'cruelty'. Indeed, Leicester could now be less tolerant of the foibles even of his queen. In July 1583 Leicester was 'in great disgrace about his marriage', having dared to refer to it more openly than before, wearied perhaps by Elizabeth's almost hysterical insistence on her wilful blindness. He was believed, too, to have been indulging in a spot of dynastic scheming – one of the offences Elizabeth found it hardest to forgive.

Leicester had proposed to Bess of Hardwick a match between his son Lord Denbigh and Bess's royal granddaughter Arbella Stuart. Such an alliance could (if Arbella ever inherited the crown) have made him the power behind England's throne. If that failed, it was rumoured Leicester hoped to marry his stepdaughter – Lettice's younger daughter Dorothy – to James of Scotland, though Dorothy foiled any such scheme when she made a runaway match with adventurer Thomas Perrot. Elizabeth was inclined to blame Dorothy's whole family both for the *mésalliance* with Perrot and for the ambition of an alliance with Scottish royalty; Lettice was a 'she-wolf', and Dorothy the wolf's cub. When Leicester invited the French ambassador, Mauvissière, to dine with himself and his wife, he lamented that he had lost the Queen's favour. (Mauvissière wrote that Lettice had 'much influence' over Leicester, and noticed that Leicester seemed 'much attached' to his wife; whom, however, he introduced 'only to those to whom he wishes to show a particular mark of attention'. One wonders how the ambitious Lettice relished the retirement that implied.) Yet by the end of the summer it was observed once more that Leicester had 'grown lately in great favour with the Queen's Majesty, such as this ten years he was not like to outward show'. Still, always, he bounced back. Earlier in the summer of 1583, Leicester's old enemy Sussex had died, warning from his deathbed: 'beware of the gypsy [Leicester]; for he will be too hard for you all. You know not the beast as well as I do.'

A letter Leicester wrote to Elizabeth and dated September speaks of his prayers 'that God will long, safely, healthfully, and most happily preserve you here among us, and as He hath begun, so to continue in discovering and overthrowing all unloyal hearts towards you'. As so often, no year is given, but the letter would fit with the events of 1583. By September the Queen's inner circle would have been aware of what has become known as the Throckmorton conspiracy. One Francis Throckmorton – Catholic nephew to the dead Sir Nicholas – had been paying secret visits to the French embassy. Through the spring and summer of 1583, he had been carefully watched, and the mischief was clear. 'This is the goodness of God, my sweet lady, that hath thus saved you against so many devils,' wrote Leicester ecstatically.

> You may see what it is to cleave unto Him; He rewardeth beyond all deserts, and so is it daily seen how He payeth those that be dissemblers with Him. Who ever, of any Prince, stood so nakedly assisted of worldly help as Your Majesty has done these many years? Who has had more enemies in show, and yet whoever received less harm?

The long letter breathes sincere belief, as well as the consciousness of a great danger passed. True, Robert's letters, by the standards of the age, were never flowery. But this was very far from the usual vein of courtly flattery. By the end of the month, after all, both he and Elizabeth had turned fifty.

When Throckmorton was finally arrested in November and racked, he revealed that it was predominantly the Spanish king whose 'Enterprise of England' had planned to set Mary on the English throne – but that the four separate invasion forces would also have been backed by the Pope, Mary's Guise family in France, and the Jesuits. This was the nightmare foreshadowed in Ridolfi's schemes and now almost come true at last – the grand, united Catholic conspiracy. Once again, to her councillors' despair, Elizabeth baulked at bringing Mary to trial, despite the damning evidence of several cipher letters, but the Scots queen's frustration at the foiling of her plans found vent in the famous 'scandal letter' – a missive supposedly from Mary herself discovered among Cecil's papers and presumed never to have been delivered by him in its full enormity.

Mary was writing to Elizabeth nominally to clear herself of the charge that she had become involved with her gaoler, the Earl of Shrewsbury – but she also vented a stream of spiteful gossip that, she said, had been passed on to her by the earl's wife, Bess of Hardwick, the Countess of Shrewsbury. Bess (wrote Mary) had said that one to whom Elizabeth

> had made a promise of marriage before a lady of your chamber, had made love to you an infinite number of times with all the license and intimacy which can be used between man and wife. But that undoubtedly you were not like other women ... and you would never lose your liberty to make love and always have your pleasure with new lovers.

(She also accused Elizabeth of sleeping with Simier as well as Alençon, and of pursuing Hatton with her attentions until he was forced to leave court to protect his modesty.) Mary must have been almost the only highly placed personage still to see Elizabeth and Robert as lovers in the physical sense. But their relationship was still a target for scandal that was meant to be spread wider afield, and aimed at an audience less discriminating. As 1584 wore on, that would be proved in the most horrible way.

It was indeed an *annus horribilis*. On 10 June Alençon died, and Elizabeth wrote to Catherine de Medici that his mother's grief 'cannot be greater than my own . . . I find no consolation except death, which I hope will soon reunite us. Madame, if you were able to see the image of my heart, you would see the portrait of a body without a soul.' Next came the assassination (by handgun; a new menace) of William of Orange by a Catholic fanatic presumed to be in Spain's pay. One result – as of any Catholic activity – could only be tighter security around the Queen of Scots. But the threat to Elizabeth was very real, as witness the assassination attempt made by a Welsh MP named Parry. One of the expenses in Leicester's disbursement book was for a 'standing' at Parry's execution.

Leicester was (Camden says) a prime mover behind the Bond of Association by which the loyal gentlemen of Elizabeth's realm vowed to band together and avenge her death, if necessary. It was in many ways a dubious document – essentially a charter for vigilante action, since the document's first form, before the Queen's own amendments, swore vengeance not only against Elizabeth's putative assassin but against the person they had hoped to put on the throne (and a document, moreover, which tied its signatories for eternity, since its terms spelt out that to renege on it was to make oneself the enemy). But in the climate of the times it must have seemed the only defence against a situation where anyone who wanted the throne could be placed there by a casual assassin, not officially connected to them in any way.

But these things were as nothing compared to the body blow that struck Leicester in July: the dangerous sickness of the 'noble Impe', the adored young Denbigh. Leicester was with the court at Nonsuch when the news of Denbigh's condition came; he rushed straight to Wanstead and Lettice's side, without stopping to take formal leave of the Queen.

We do not know why the child died, nor whether there was any warning illness: the only hint is the unreliable *Leicester's Commonwealth* comment that he suffered from 'the falling-sickness [epilepsy], in his infancy'. It has been suggested that the tiny suit of armour rumoured to have been made for him seems to have one leg slightly shorter than the other: key to some underlying malady? But in an age of such high infant mortality no-one felt it necessary to spell out the details.

Robert and his wife had both suffered a great personal loss. Leicester seems to have been fond of children in general (William of Orange's wife, when he escorted Alençon to the Netherlands, wrote of how kind he had been to her little daughter), and this longed-for son had been cosseted with all the magnificence of crimson velvet cradles, a portrait to display his naked form and a little chair decked out in green and carnation tinsel cloth. The inscription on his tomb wrote that he was a child 'of great parentage but far greater hope and towardness'. But now, since Lettice was in her mid-forties, and he himself in poor health, Leicester must have known he had probably lost the last chance of a dynasty. He wrote to Shrewsbury that the loss of his young son was indeed great, 'for that I have no more and more unlike to have, my growing now old'. The surviving pages of the disbursement book do not cover the period of Denbigh's death itself. But, with aching frequency, they record Leicester's gifts to the nurses and midwives of other people's babies.

Hatton wrote to Leicester:

What God hath given you, that hath He chosen and taken to Himself, whereat I hope you will not grudge . . . if the love of a child be dear, which is now taken from you, the love of God is ten thousand times more dear, which you can never lack or lose. Of men's hearts you enjoy more than millions, which, on my soul, do love you no less than children or brethren. Leave sorrow, therefore, my good Lord, and be glad with us, which much rejoice in you.

He had told Elizabeth the reason for Leicester's sudden departure, 'whereof I assure your Lordship I find her very sorry, and wisheth your comfort, even from the bottom of her heart'. She would write herself, 'and therefore she held no longer speech with me of the matter'. That letter has not survived, sadly.* But from the letters she wrote under other similar circumstances, we might guess that she would have taken the same tone of religious forbearance. Three years later, on the death of his adult son, she wrote to Shrewsbury:

> remember that God, who hath been the worker thereof and doth all things for the best, is not to be controlled. Besides, if we do duly look into the matter in true course of Christianity, we shall then see that the loss hath wrought so greater gain to the gentleman whom we now lack, as we have rather cause to rejoice than lament.

Leicester's letter to Hatton, thanking him for 'your careful and most godly advice', has on the surface of it the requisite resigned and religious tone. But underneath there is a more stormy story. 'I must confess I have received many afflictions within these few years, but not a greater,' he wrote, adding carefully, 'next [after] her Majesty's displeasure.' Disconcertingly, he seems to be striking almost a bargain with fate (though not, he says punctiliously, with God). He hopes that 'the sacrifice of this poor innocent might satisfy' those who are offended, who have taken 'long hard conceits' of him; 'if not, yet I know there is a blessing for such as suffer; and so is there for those that be merciful'. In what sounds like an implied rebuke to Elizabeth, he says that princes are never the best for mercy, 'therefore men fly to the mighty God in times of distress for comfort', even though they may have neglected Him when younger in order to 'run the race of the world'. He had, after all, good reason to feel that everyone's hand was against him at this time.

For the summer and autumn of 1584 also saw the publication in Antwerp of the laboriously entitled work more snappily known as *Leicester's Commonwealth*,† that scurrilous publication that

---

* Almost everything Elizabeth wrote to Robert until the very last years of his life is presumed to have been destroyed in the Civil War sack of Kenilworth.
† The full title was *The Copy of a Letter Written by a Master of Arts at Cambridge*.

took every action in his life and imputed to it the worst possible motives – 'the most malicious-written thing', as Walsingham wrote to Leicester, 'that ever was penned since the beginning of the world'. It would take far too long to detail its two hundred pages' worth of accusations (and the chief of them have been dealt with already), but, in sum, he stood accused of treachery, lechery, murders in plenty. The murders of Amy Dudley and of Douglass's and Lettice's husbands, certainly: 'His Lordship hath a special fortune, that when he desireth any woman's favour, then what person so ever standeth in his way hath the luck to die quickly for the finishing of his desire'; but also the murders of Throckmorton (who had died at his house 'after eating salads'), of the Earl of Sussex, and of several foreign dignitaries.

Then there was 'the intolerable license of Leicester's carnality', as evidenced in 'the keeping of the mother with two or three of her daughters at once or successively'. There was the accusation that none of the Queen's gentlewomen was safe from his lustful eye; and another that, conversely, he was now so worn out by his efforts that he had to buy pint bottles of an 'Italian ointment' in order 'to move his flesh' (and that he had 'a broke belly on both sides of his bowels').

Of course, the real accusation, to which these were only the salacious trimmings, was that he ruled the Queen completely, that he had on all occasions prevented her marriage, that his ambition knew no bounds; that 'his reign is so absolute . . . as nothing can pass but by his admission'. It was the old 'evil counsellors' argument, as Francis Bacon noted of a similar pamphlet directed at Cecil; a way 'to cover undutiful invectives' that might not so safely be aimed against the Queen herself.

The Queen and council moved to suppress the book's circulation in England; Philip Sidney wrote a spirited defence. But of course some copies were still passed around secretly. And it is possible that Elizabeth – for all her proclamation that 'none but an incarnate devil himself' could dream of believing such malicious slurs – also half resented the man who had been the unwitting instrument of involving her name in such ignominy.

The publication has to be seen in context: Elizabeth herself, and

Leicester on other occasions, had been and would be the victim of other such calumnies. They were a fact of political life. But this one was particularly extensive, and particularly damaging. Its slurs have haunted Leicester's reputation through the centuries.* Some of the mud stuck even with contemporaries. (Camden, writing within thirty years of Leicester's death and from a broadly anti-Leicester stance, spoke of 'defamatory libels' launched against him, 'which contained some slight untruths', and mentions the suspicions held against him in the deaths of Throckmorton and Essex, even while he describes the evidence to the contrary; however, by his sheer lack of comment he tacitly acquits him of the murders of Lord Sheffield and of Amy Dudley.)

The author of *Leicester's Commonwealth* was of course anonymous, and various theories have been put forward as to his identity. It may have been to some degree a group effort, with English Catholics in France such as Lord Paget and Charles Arundel (a member of the Howard clan whom Leicester had persecuted for his Catholic sympathies) among the moving spirits. Both Cecil and Edward Stafford have also been mooted as contributors; but for a long time the most popular contender was the exiled Jesuit Robert Persons, and Jesuit missionaries were certainly instrumental in getting the book into the country. There were personal animosities involved, and the publication's modern editor, D. C. Peck, has also drawn attention to its specific political goals, like the promotion of the Scottish claim to the throne. But surely you could also see this broadside as a perverse, backhanded tribute to Leicester's importance as acknowledged leader of the aggressive puritan party. That was certainly the opinion of the Italian Protestant (and legal expert) Alberico Gentili, who wrote that Leicester's praise lies not only in those who took his part, but in the very hostility of his Catholic enemies, with their 'infamous howling against a good man and true'.

Later that year, Leicester would call a two-day conference in

* The caption to a picture in *Harmsworth Magazine*, from July 1902, describes him as 'England's most celebrated poisoner'.

which he attempted to mediate between Elizabeth's bishops and the puritan ministers. But he cannot be said to have succeeded to any great degree. Indeed the conservative Whitgift, Elizabeth's new Archbishop of Canterbury, blocked his moves in every way. Elizabeth's difficult 'second reign' has been dated from this point in the middle 1580s; certainly a new generation of servants and favourites was waiting in the wings.

The ever-changing parade of personalities at court no longer affected Leicester quite as it had done. He did take the warmest interest in the career of his golden nephew Philip Sidney – 'my boy' – including his perennial quarrels with the Earl of Oxford and his growing reputation as a writer. (Even when Philip, as a twelve-year-old, had been taken to see the Queen, it had been Leicester who, with the boy's father away, had sent his own tailor scurrying around to make the child doublets of green taffeta and crimson velvet, bright trunk hose with their matching stockings, and six pairs of double-soled shoes.) But the appearance of the new star Walter Ralegh, with his own dark good looks and his Devon accent, his rough brand of charm and his big dreams, could not really affect his position. Ralegh, after all, was knighted only in 1584 and would not become Captain of the Guard for three years after that; and though he would by then be one of the chief 'backbiters' against Leicester, it was not the attack of an equal. (Indeed, when Ralegh first came to court at the start of the decade, he was one of the many who clung to Leicester for patronage.) Whatever Leicester's present relationship with Elizabeth, they had done the damage themselves; and though Ralegh made himself felt as a thorn in the flesh of all the established courtiers, it pricked Leicester less deeply. It was Hatton who had to be warned by Heneage that 'water' ('Walter' Ralegh) had been 'more welcome than were fit for so cold a season'; and then reassured by the Queen's message that water and the creatures who belong to it were not so appealing to her as some thought, 'her food having been ever more of flesh than of fish', and that (Heneage reassured Hatton) the Queen swore she 'would rather see [Ralegh] hanged than equal him with you'. But Hatton's own letters to Elizabeth were becoming less lover-like than they had been; more practical, more prone to quarrel and apology.

All the same, it was 1584 when Robert Cecil, William Cecil's son, took his Westminster seat; the first step in what would be a towering career. Perhaps it was to counter these new influences that Leicester, also in 1584, first brought his stepson Robert Devereux, the young Earl of Essex, to court. Eighteen years old, with auburn hair like his mother's and eyes dark like Leicester's own, he was ardent and athletic, his egotism and ambition hardly apparent, yet, under the veil of his undoubted brilliance and his youthful charm. 'Your son,' he signed himself in his letters to Leicester, 'most ready to do you service'; though nothing more fundamental than step-parenthood can be read into his words, by the language of the sixteenth century.*

It was only a short space of time before (with Leicester himself occupied elsewhere) Essex became such a favourite with Elizabeth that he often sat up with the Queen in her rooms over music or cards 'until the birds sing in the morning'; and it is worth stepping out of time and sequence again to look at Essex's future attitudes, because of what the comparison – the contrast – says about Robert Dudley.

Yes, both Roberts made themselves champions of the Protestant cause. Yes, they both believed that England's cause should be aggressively promoted abroad. Yes, they both (for Essex entered into negotiations with James of Scotland, far more autonomously than Leicester had done) wanted a hand in shaping the future of their country. But if you make a direct comparison between their letters, between their very different comportments under rebuke, the difference shows up clearly.

Perhaps Leicester might in the end have been brought to write, as Essex did: 'What, cannot princes err? Cannot subjects receive wrong? Is an earthly power or authority infinite? Pardon me, pardon me, my good lord, I can never subscribe to these principles.' But the quarrel that had provoked this letter had seen Elizabeth box Essex's ears at the privy council table – and seen

---

* Indeed, one thinks of the successors who called Potemkin 'Papa'.

Essex, momentarily, reach for his sword. It is impossible to imagine Leicester committing such *lèse-majesté*. Essex said once, in anger, that 'The Queen's conditions are as crooked as her carcass.' Leicester could never have said that, and not only because of his ability to 'put his passions in his pocket'. His affection would have forbidden it.

It was estimated that Elizabeth had four favourites of the first rank: Leicester and Hatton, Ralegh and Essex. (The Cecils, father and son, were in a different category.) Perhaps it was the loss of Leicester's undivided allegiance that prompted Elizabeth to turn to other men. On the other hand, there was something almost vampiric in the way Elizabeth moved on to younger 'lovers'.

Another picture hanging at Penshurst, dated just four years later than the supposed date of the 'Volta' tableau, shows Leicester portly and plump of face, a man whose square beard, now, is nearly white and bushy. Only the lambent, wary eyes could even begin to be recognizable as belonging to the dashing earl of earlier days. (Ambrose, whose portrait hangs alongside Robert's, seems with his trim, grizzled crop and quirking eyebrows to have aged more gracefully.) A foreigner who saw Leicester, and Hatton, and all the Queen's old circle at this time described them as 'charming old gentlemen'; and, as one of their contemporaries noted, forty heralded 'the first part of the old man's age'. No, certainly Leicester was no longer the figure he once had been: the dancer, the jouster, the darling of the Queen's eye; no longer the slim, youthful (and blond!) figure who, in the 'Volta' tableau, twirls 'Elizabeth' aloft so confidently. Perhaps that is why she had let him get away.

17

'Her Majesty will make trial of me'
1585–1588

IN THE DARK TIME AFTER LITTLE DENBIGH'S DEATH, ROBERT DUDLEY
had talked of retiring – told Cecil he did 'more desire my liberty,
with her Majesty's favour, than any office in England'. But his
public career was not yet over. It was both ironic and significant
that his moment of greatest official responsibility – and what
should have been the fulfilment of his dream – should come so
close to the end of his life, at a time when he was perhaps beginning to feel himself unfit for heavy duties. For years he had been
pressing for closer involvement in the Netherlands. Almost a
decade ago, he had already been holding himself in readiness to
lead an English army to the aid of his co-religionists. When in
autumn 1585 Elizabeth was finally persuaded she had to send a
force to help the Dutch Protestants, Leicester was the obvious,
the only, choice to command the expedition. But he was in the
position of the understudy in a long-running play finally called in
front of the footlights; just when hope deferred, after making the
heart sick, has worked its own cure and bred a kind of
resignation.

There is no reason to doubt he seized the chance. When
Elizabeth's summons back to court reached him he was at
Stoneleigh in Warwickshire, and wrote at once that he wished he
had a hundred thousand lives to spend in her service (although

that service might be delayed a little: he could not yet pull his boot on after a bad fall from his horse). Camden later wrote that he went 'out of an itching desire of rule and glory', but the cause, to one of his belief, was a holy war. Spain used the seventeen Netherlands provinces as a milch cow for the whole Spanish empire; but Spanish rule was about more than cold politics and economic calculation. In this police state, where each man was required to inform on his neighbours, stories spread of religious persecution on an appalling scale. Fifty thousand Netherlanders died (in the Prince of Orange's admittedly partial estimate) during the first seven years alone of Philip's rule. The numbers Mary Tudor had had killed were tiny by comparison – but this must have looked like a chance to reverse the Marian story. Moreover, Leicester must have hoped at long last to follow in his father's military footsteps, and set an unequivocally glorious seal on what was hitherto a rather amorphous and unpopular career.

But the fact was that he had not seen active service since his twenties (when, ironically, he had been fighting for the Spanish). Ever since, it was Ambrose who had been the warrior in the Dudley family; now it was possibly Ambrose's health – that old leg injury, which had never completely healed – that prevented him taking part in the new campaign. Island England had not bred commanders for a land army in quite the way it had for its navy; and there could be no thought that an army might be commanded by anyone but a senior member of the nobility, which reduced a poor field considerably. It was Leicester's bad luck that he would be facing the Duke of Parma; not another gentleman amateur but a general of wide experience, who combined noble blood with the abilities that might have made him a military genius in any century.

An inexorable pressure of events had brought Elizabeth's government to this point; had made war seem inevitable even to a moderate like Cecil. The appearance of Spanish troops in Ireland at the turn of the decade had been followed by Spain's annexation of Portugal, with Portugal's foreign territories, and its sea-going fleet; the voluntary return of the southern provinces of the Low Countries to Spain's rule, further isolating the rebellious north; and the assassination of William of Orange. Key, perhaps, had been Spain's alliance with France, raising the unacceptable spectre of a Europe dominated by the Habsburgs as far as the Channel coast.

Though the privy council's discussions were long and hard, Cecil reluctantly concluded that it was better to act now, to prevent Philip reaching the 'full height of his designs and conquests', rather than wait to suffer the full brunt of his 'insatiable malice'. Now he too was 'greatly discouraged' by the Queen's 'lack of resolutions', as he wrote to Leicester. But when Spain seized English vessels lying in Spanish harbours (while Antwerp, besieged and starving, finally fell that August), the Queen was left with no choice but to act. The treaty between England and the rebellious Netherlands, the States General, was concluded at Nonsuch, that lovely fantasy palace of stucco, in August 1585 – albeit not without further debate and acrimony.

This is no place to try to analyse the Netherlands campaign, or Leicester's performance in it. His failure – for so it has always been called – was perhaps inevitable. His personal skills and Parma's apart, he was up against the staggering Spanish war machine, equipped himself with only a ludicrously underfunded army, and under the authority of a queen never really committed to the war. Historians have regretted that the war was not better fought; that it was fought at all; or that it had not been fought a good decade earlier, when William of Orange was himself in the field against a less well-prepared Spain. But England, too, was in one way better equipped in the second half of the 1580s than it had been in the early 1570s. Its naval defences were far better. If England's open intervention in the Netherlands can be seen as one of the triggers for the launch of the Spanish Armada, then in the end the English team, Leicester among them, did not do so badly. Their worst fears, after all, never came to pass: England never became a Spanish-speaking, Catholic colony.

Leicester's commitment (like his personal courage, when it came to it) cannot be doubted. It was, he said, 'God's cause and her Majesty's'. His qualms (as he wrote to Walsingham at the beginning of September) were that the Queen had not 'a full persuasion indeed that the cause was as it was'. How well he knew her. By contrast, Leicester himself raised £25,000 (more than £4 million today) by sale and mortgage of his own land to fit himself out for the expedition. Mortgaging the lordship of Denbigh raised £15,000 from a group of London merchants; and he borrowed £13,000 from the Queen to pay for another troop of horse. He sent out some two hundred letters to the gentry of his affinity – 'gentlemen of good likings and callings in their countries, though my servants' – to rally a thousand heavy cavalry. This should be remembered when he is blamed for raising his own salary as Lieutenant-General from £6 to £10 13s a day. (He also raised the salaries of his men, to the level of campaigners in the Irish wars.)* He was doing no more than might be expected of a man of his rank, since to raise their own troops in time of war was a moral obligation of the nobility. And, of course, much of what he mortgaged would originally have been given to him by Elizabeth. But still, it shows that he cannot be viewed entirely as a parasite.

He had the devil's own work to make Elizabeth let him go. A dozen times she bade him farewell, and then summoned him back again, saying she could not do without him. One Tuesday in September he was writing to Walsingham of how desirous she was to stay his journey; of how she was doubtful of herself 'by reason of her oft-disease taking her of late, and this night worst of all'; of how 'she used very pitiful words', her 'fear that she shall not live, and would not have me from her'; of how he 'did comfort her as well as I could' . . . and of how Walsingham should send word to Lettice that there was no way her husband could get away from the court immediately. He was – he wrote to Walsingham again, as the delays continued – 'weary of life and all'.

'Her Majesty I see will make trial of me how I love her and what will discourage me from her service, but resolved I am that

---

* Nor was this money he could well afford: in 1587 he was in danger of forfeiting property worth £13,000, and more besides, if his creditors foreclosed on just a percentage – £4,300 worth – of his debts.

no worldly respect shall draw me back from my faithful discharge of my duty towards her, though she shall show to hate me, as it goeth very near, for I find no love or favour at all.' Elizabeth, for her part, when her claims of illness did not move him, accused Leicester of seeking more his 'own glory than her true service'. Finally, he got away. But on the very eve of sailing, he knew that he and his men were being sent without the backing they needed. As he wrote to Walsingham:

> I am sorry her Majesty doth deal in this sort, content to overthrow so willingly her own cause. Look to it, for by the Lord I will bear no more so miserable burdens; for if I have no money to pay the soldiers, let them come away, or what else. I will not starve them or stay them. There was never gentleman or general so sent out as I am. My cause is the Lord's and the Queen's. If the Queen fail I trust in the Lord, and on him I see I am wholly to depend.

In the Netherlands they took it very kindly that the Queen was sending someone so close to her: a personage, as she herself wrote to them, 'whom she did make more accompt of than any of her subjects'. Philip Sidney told Leicester that his coming was awaited like that of 'the Messiah'. In Middleburg he was given the lodgings which had been deemed worthy of Alençon, and a firework display with the like of which the Valois prince had been honoured. Everyone – so Leicester wrote home ecstatically – was crying Elizabeth's name 'as if she had been in Cheapside'. Delft staged for him 'the greatest shows that ever I saw'. He made his torchlit entrance into The Hague, where he was to keep 'his standing court', under arches made like the Dudleys' ragged staff, and past galleries staffed with maidens who made obeisance as he passed. Town gates were hung with his arms, as well as those of the Queen and of Prince William's son, Maurice, and banners twinned him with Elizabeth as saviour of the people:

> Blessed be the Virgin Queen, that sent this Good,
> And blessed be he that comes to save our blood.

Poems were hung up in streets decked with Tudor roses. 'Never was there people I think in that jollity that these be.' Elizabeth, he wrote, in a rare moment of blindness as to her character, 'would think a whole subsidy well spent' if she could only see a few of these towns as he had, and know they held for England.

The States had repeatedly offered Elizabeth sovereignty, after the assassination of their own prince, William the Silent. Now, in the spring of 1586, they offered a proxy version to Leicester. It was the very official recognition Elizabeth in England had always denied him. Perhaps he was simply tempted – and fell: 'tickled', Camden said, 'with such flatteries, as if he had been seated in the highest and amplest degree of honour; he began to assume royal and Kingly thoughts of Majesty'. (Alençon, as a jealous Leicester would have been well aware, had gone further in accepting an elected sovereignty before abdicating in 1583. But then, Elizabeth had not taken that kindly, reacting almost hysterically to the idea that the putative marriage between them might have meant involvement in the Netherlands war for her country: 'shall it ever be found true that Queen Elizabeth hath solemnized the perpetual harm of England under the glorious title of marriage with Francis, heir of France? No, no, it shall never be.')

If Leicester did simply fall, he did so (he said) only after a week of negotiations in which he himself was careful to take no part, spending the time in fasting, prayer and even, it was said, psalm-singing. He presented himself, even in his letter to Cecil, as being 'far unprovided' to answer the States' request. But in fact it is at least possible that some of the council in England, himself among them, had long decided that this would be the only way to establish 'some well settled government' in the fractious States – and that the only way to handle Elizabeth would be to present her with a *fait accompli*. By contrast, Mary, Queen of Scots took a different view: that it was Leicester who, by over-reaching him-self, had fallen into a trap: 'and there be instruments that help to push forward this subject to his ruin'.

He had every reason to claim he needed a fairly free hand, if he were to stand any chance of doing the job successfully. From the start, he said that if his hands were to be tied, he 'had as lief be dead'. As the States seemed happy to give him, in their own words, 'absolute power and authority', so he seemed eager to do his part in opening England's purse-strings, writing in strong terms to Cecil, after his arrival, that any slackening of English support would be 'a sin and a shame'. But for Leicester, in many ways, this was also the enactment of a fantasy.

An allegorical entertainment played out before him embodied the city of Leiden as a female figure assaulted by Spanish soldiers, before leaping off stage to take refuge under Leicester's cloak. He led her off to his lodgings, delightedly; at last, a woman who wanted to be rescued by the protective male! One of the first spectacles that greeted him represented a symbolic marriage between himself and Elizabeth: their personal emblems joined along with the inscription *Quod Deus coniunxit homo non separet*. Received as a prince – named as a prince in legal documents – he made no bones about accepting the title of governor general, rather than merely captain general. When Leicester told Cecil about his access of honours, he wrote optimistically: 'It is done for the best, and if so her Majesty accepts of it, all will be to the best.'

But Davison, the royal secretary Leicester sent, rather belatedly, to inform Elizabeth he had accepted the 'absolute governorship', was delayed by bad weather and arrived only after she heard of it from another source. She railed at Davison 'in most bitter and hard terms'; and the letter she sent to Leicester himself was coruscating in its fury.

How contemptuously we conceive ourselves to be used by you . . . We could never have imagined (had we not seen it fall out in experience) that a man raised up by ourself and extraordinarily favoured by us, above any other subject of this land, would have in so contemptible a sort broken our commandment in a cause that so greatly toucheth us in honor . . . And therefore our express pleasure and commandment is that, all delays and excuses laid apart, you do presently of your allegiance obey and fulfill whatever the bearer hereof shall direct you to do. Whereof fail you not, as you will answer the contrary at your uttermost peril.

The words 'of your allegiance' signal that this was regarded as possibly a treasonable offence, and what Leicester was commanded to do was to relinquish his new honour, publicly. 'At the least I think she would never have so condemned any other man before she heard him,' wrote Leicester painfully. 'For my faithful, true and loving heart to her and my country, I have undone myself.'

To the States General Elizabeth wrote that she found it 'very strange' they would offer such a position to her subject without consulting her, 'as though she wanted judgement to accept or refuse what was competent'. Besides the personal affront, of course, she feared the fact of an English governor general would make it appear that England had accepted sovereignty.

It was not Leicester who was at odds with public opinion here. He was backed up by most of the privy council, including even Cecil. At the very time Leicester was sailing off to fight, Elizabeth had secretly been opening negotiations for peace with Parma, and Cecil's sympathies in this lay Elizabeth's way. But all her ministers, even the least hawk-like, accepted that at least an initial show of strength was necessary in order to establish a good negotiating position. Cecil knew (and, later, wrote to Walsingham) that only disaster could come from this blatantly half-hearted attempt to prosecute a war. As he left England, Leicester had begged Cecil ('seeing that mine and other men's poor lives are adventured for her [Majesty's] sake') to 'have me thus far only in your care that . . . I be not made a metamorphosis, that I shall not know what to do'. Now Cecil told Leicester that 'I, for my own part, judge this action both honourable and profitable,' reassuring the distant earl he had told the Queen that if she continued her hostility, he himself would wish to be 'discharged of the place I held'. But Elizabeth 'would not endure to hear speech in defence' of her old favourite. Cecil found her attitude, as he said several times, to be 'both perilous and absurd'.

Elizabeth had probably been unrealistic in expecting that a commander in a foreign country, given the slowness of communications, could do anything other than act autonomously. But to her, surely, it was just as if the consort she had feared to take were indeed sidelining her and sweeping England towards a war of his own making . . . that old, bad, bogey.

Thomas Heneage – once Leicester's rival – was designated the Queen's emissary, to tell Leicester he had to relinquish his office, on the spot where he had accepted it in a formal ceremony. Heneage protested, which brought him his own slashing rebuke from the Queen. 'Jesu! What availeth wit when it fails the owner at greatest need? Do that you are bidden and leave your considerations to your own affairs . . . I am assured of your dutiful thought but I am utterly at squares with this childish dealing.' The States General too protested, and Elizabeth was finally persuaded that thus to reveal the divisions in her ranks could only be of comfort to the enemy. So Leicester was allowed to keep an emasculated title; but his prestige had been seriously damaged (as had that of the Queen, shown up as having been kept in the dark for weeks about a matter of such sensitivity). What had annoyed her most may have been that Leicester was preparing to act politically, rather than as merely her obedient military arm – though his instructions had ordered him to 'use all good means to redress the confused government' of the Low Countries.

But worst of all may have been the rumour that Lettice had been planning to join her husband, 'with such a train of ladies and gentlewomen, and such rich coaches, litters and side-saddles as her Majesty had none such, and that there should be a court of ladies as should far pass her Majesty's court here'. She 'would have no more courts under her obeisance than her own', Elizabeth declared furiously; and in early March Ambrose was warning his brother that the Queen's anger seemed to grow rather than diminish; that she seemed set on a course to make England the slave of Spain – 'and that which passeth all the rest, the true religion of Jesus Christ to be taken from us. She giveth out great threatening words against you,' Ambrose said.

Make the best assurance you can for yourself. Trust not her oath, for that her malice is great and unquenchable . . . Have great care for yourself, I mean for your safety, and if she will needs revoke you, to the overthrowing of the cause, if I were you, if I could not be assured there, I would go to the furthest part of Christendom rather than ever come into England again.

Incredible though such a thought might be, it sounds as if Ambrose Dudley at least was remembering the Tudors' record of abruptly turning on their ministers: Wolsey and Cromwell; Empson and Dudley . . .

Leicester was curiously slow to write to Elizabeth himself. Whether he was simply 'extremely overtoiled with business', as he complained, or whether there was some deeper resentment at work, it was a failure with which his adherents reproached him anxiously. Davison urged him to use 'more diligence entertaining her with your wise letters and messages, your slackness wherein hitherto appears to have bred a great part of this unkindness'. Finally he wrote, and the old charm worked: at the end of March, Ralegh (to whom Leicester had written asking for the services of some foot-soldiers) was reassuring the earl that 'the queen is in very good terms with you, and, thanks be to God, well pacified, and you are again her "sweet Robin" '. In April the Queen's next letter to Leicester was haughty, but conciliatory.

> Right trusty and well-beloved cousin and councillor, we greet you well. It is always thought in the opinion of the world a hard bargain when both parties are leasoned [slandered], and so doth fall out the case between us two . . .
>
> We are persuaded that you that have so long known us cannot think that ever we could have been drawn to have taken so hard a course herein, had we not been provoked by an extraordinary cause. But for that your grieved and wounded mind hath more need of comfort than reproof . . . whosoever professeth to love you best* taketh not more comfort of your welldoing or discomfort of your evildoing than ourself.

Elizabeth herself was feeling battered by the pressure of events. (That May, Walsingham wrote to Leicester that he found her

---

* One of her frequent digs at Lettice, here!

'daily more and more unapt to embrace any matter of weight'.) Perhaps she could face a permanent estrangement no more than could he. At the St George's Day banquet, Leicester – protesting that he was 'not ceremonious for reputation' – was careful to have an empty chair of state laid for the absent queen, while he himself took a stool.

Leicester continued to be widely addressed as 'Excellency'; to be allegorized, in the entertainments that marked his progresses, as 'a second Arthur'. But a great price had been paid; not only in terms of his relationship with the Queen, but, more seriously, in terms of the fate of the English soldiery. The task of the Netherlands was one to which Leicester had always been ill-suited. Maybe it was an impossible task. But it was certainly no job for this ill, ageing and irascible Leicester, smarting from the wound Elizabeth had dealt his dignity. His letters to his fellow councillors were full of reproaches for what he saw as their lack of support: Elizabeth's men tended to scatter like scolded school-boys, faced by the full display of her authority. But Cecil for one wrote to him with a personal sympathy. Leicester would find the Queen's latest letters to contain 'as much comfort from her as you have recent discomfort' – but that earlier anger 'I know hath deeply wounded your heart and these [letters] cannot suddenly sink so low as the wound is but your lordship must add to this your own fortitude of mind'.

Many of the troops he had were disaffected ones; he would have needed the tact he was lacking to deal not only with his allies, but with his own army. A lot of his puritan friends had joined up – as well as a lot of the far from puritanical Thames watermen! – but too many of the men were ragged conscripts who started the active campaign already owed a backlog of pay. 'There is much due to them,' he wrote in March 1586. 'They cannot get a penny; their credit is spent; they perish for want of victuals and clothing in great numbers.' He would write of them, with feeling, that he had 'no soldier yet able to buy himself pair of hose, and it is too too great shame to see how they go, and it kills their hearts to show themselves among men'. This was a problem to which he often returned: 'I assure you it will fret me to death ere long to see my soldiers in this case and cannot help them.' Elizabeth might grumble (so Leicester himself had heard, with pain) that there 'lacked a Northumberland in his place' – that he could not do the job his father did – but amid all the stories of his huffiness and hauteur, his quarrels with the experienced deputy whose advice should have saved him, one's heart warms to Leicester as he writes again: 'pity to see them'. When the 'poor starved wretches' deserted, he could not bring himself to execute too many of those recaptured: he understood too well why they had run away.

There were problems with corruption: money handed out to captains who were supposed to pay their men, but instead hung on to the loot and left the soldiers in penury. Leicester himself has been accused of peculation, but it looks more like a lack of financial competence all round, in which he was far from the only offender. The treasurer sent out to assist him was summoned back to account for his mistakes, but could never be charged, since no-one could understand his paperwork. There were endless disputes with the States General over who was to pay what; and over far more besides. 'I never did deal with such heady people as these States are,' he would complain. There was dissent among his own commanders: 'I will be master whilst I remain here, will they nill they.' While he protested that he would not be overbearded by 'churls and tinkers', the Queen was lamenting that she had ever let herself in for this war, calling it 'a sieve, that spends as it receives to little purpose'.

As early as that same March, Leicester was writing pathetically to Walsingham of how he longed to be at his own 'poor cottage' again. In May he wrote from Arnhem: 'I am weary, indeed I am weary, Mr. Secretary, but neither of pains nor travel [travail?]; my ill hap that can please her majesty no better hath quite discouraged me.' By August, writing to Walsingham again, he was thoroughly demoralized: 'if I have wanted wit, the fault is hers and yours among you for the choice, and that would not better assist me'. 'Would to God I were rid of this place!', he said bitterly.

And yet, when the summer campaign got finally under way, the army under Leicester's command did not at first do so badly; well enough, indeed, if you consider he was fighting on behalf of a queen who actually expected him to avoid too punishing a conflict with the enemy. Parma certainly wrote of the toughness of those ragged English troops. For much of 1586, the Spanish general had to battle for every small victory, while the long descriptions Leicester wrote of his first battles show the sense of vindication he felt in acting like a soldier at last.

But the underlying problems – the uncertainty of the mission, the inexperience of the command, the inadequacy of the army's supplies – did not go away. In an army plagued by 'danger, want and disgrace', Philip Sidney complained that 'if her Majesty were the fountain, I would fear . . . that we should wax dry'. He put his faith in God's support, in what seemed a holy war to him and to many of his contemporaries.

That summer Leicester wrote to Elizabeth in unusually straight terms.

> As the cause is now followed it is not worth the cost or the danger. Your Majesty was invited to be sovereign, protector, or aiding friend. You chose the third, and . . . if your Majesty had taken their cause indeed to heart, no practices could have drawn them from you. But they now perceive how weary you are of them, and how willing that any other had them so that your Majesty were rid of them.

It had, he said, 'almost broken their hearts' – and it is hard to doubt he meant his own, too. ('I pray God I may live to see you employ some of [his critics], to see whether they will spend £20,000 of their own for you in seven months . . .') To do the best he could for England still, he would try to get into his hands three or four most significant places in the northern states, and then she would 'make war or peace as you will'. 'But your Majesty must deal graciously with them at present, and if you mean to leave them keep it to yourself. Whatever you mean really to do, you must persuade them now that you mean sincerely and well by them. They have desperate conceit of your Majesty.'

His raising again that old question of Elizabeth's taking the crown herself, instead of reassuring her that he had at least had no thought of usurping her, provoked another hysterical outburst. But this time at least she followed it up with a letter of explanation to Leicester himself, and what was in effect an apology. 'Rob, I am afraid you will suppose by my wandering writings that a midsummer moon hath taken large possession of my brains this month . . .' She signed off:

> Now will I end, that do I imagine I talk still with you, and therefore loathly say farewell, [eyes symbol], though ever I pray God bless you from all harm, and save you from all foes with my million and legion of thanks for all your pains and care. As you know, ever the same, E.R.

Perhaps Elizabeth, too, had felt the distress of their real, their shattering, quarrel. That autumn, addressing a deputation from a Parliament she had felt unable formally to open, she spoke of how she had 'found treason in trust, seen great benefits little regarded, and instead of gratefulness, courses of purpose to cross'. She saw, she said, no great reason to live.

In September 1586 came the battle of Zutphen and, famously, the death of Philip Sidney, the young man seen as the flower of England's chivalry. His friend Fulke Greville described the scene much later: how, 'the weather being very misty', the English came suddenly upon the enemy – almost literally fell over them – and found themselves caught in the range not only of the great guns from the town ramparts but of musket fire from the trenches; how Sidney's thigh bone was broken by a musket shot (he having lent his leg armour to a friend), and his panicked horse swept him from the field.

> In this sad progress, passing along by the rest of the army, where his uncle the General [Leicester] was, and being thirsty with excess of bleeding he called for drink, which was presently brought him; but as he was putting the bottle to his mouth, he saw a poor soldier carried along, who had eaten his last at the same feast, ghastly casting up his eyes at the bottle; which Sir Philip perceiving, took it from his head

before he drank, and delivered it to the poor man with these words: 'Thy necessity is yet greater than mine!'

'Your son and mine', as Leicester wrote of him to Walsingham, whose daughter Sidney had married, died of gangrene, almost an agonizing month later.*

Leicester had now lost 'the comfort of my life'. If 'I could buy his life with all I have to my shirt I would give it', he wrote to Heneage bitterly. He continued to write of Philip's pregnant widow as his daughter, and enquired often and urgently after the fate of her child. Both Philip Sidney's parents – Sir Henry, and Robert's sister Mary – had died that summer. But there was no shortage of mourners. Though the young man who dared to criticize her planned marriage with Alençon had never been a personal favourite of Elizabeth's, she was sufficiently in tune with the public mood to order a state funeral for him, and crowds followed the body to its tomb in St Paul's.

But Zutphen (where Parma won only by a thread; where Leicester's stepson Essex fought valiantly, and was knighted by Leicester upon the field) proved a high point for the English force. Things went from bad to worse after that, until Leicester could only write: 'My trust is that the Lord hath not quite cast me out of your favour.' But it was probably as much because the Queen was missing him as for the poverty of his performance that, at the end of the year, she acceded to his request to come back home.

There was, after all, a crisis in England, and Elizabeth needed his support to sustain her through it. Holding Elizabeth's hand was always the best, the real, way that he could help his country.†
The question of Mary, Queen of Scots was coming to a head. Early that summer Walsingham's spies had got wind of yet another plan to set Mary on the throne of England, with the help

---

* He was thirty-one. A brilliant career, and then a moment of great danger in his thirty-second year, had been Dr Dee's prediction for him.
† As Potemkin told an Englishman two centuries later, towards the end of his relationship with Catherine, 'When things go smoothly, my influence is small but when she meets with rubs, she always wants me and then my influence is as great as ever.'

of a foreign Catholic army; the plan that would be known as the Babington conspiracy. This time, instead of stifling the plot in its infancy, it was decided to let it run – even to foster it a little – effectively, to give the Scots queen enough rope to hang herself. The opportunity never needed to be proffered twice; not with Mary. Besides Walsingham and his assistants, Leicester and the Queen herself were probably among the very few to know about what amounted to a set-up. By the end of the summer, Walsingham had what he needed: direct documentary proof of Mary's treasonable complicity.

In September, Babington and his fellow plotters died the horrible traitor's death. In October a commission was called (Warwick among the commissioners) to try Mary under the terms of the Act of Association, which had decreed that one on whose behalf the throne was attempted was herself guilty. There could be only one verdict. Both Houses of Parliament called for her death. From the Netherlands, Leicester too had urged that due process of law should go ahead. 'It is most certain if you would have Her Majesty safe,' he wrote to Walsingham in October, 'it must be done, for justice doth crave it besides policy.' When the verdict was published, it caused a bell-ringing, bonfire-lighting explosion of savage relief throughout the country.

But councillors, and even country, had called for Mary's death before. The problem was bringing the Queen to agree. So, from the viewpoint of his colleagues, Leicester's return on 23 November was timely. 'Never did I receive a more gracious welcome,' he wrote. It was a welcome from Elizabeth – and from everybody. That evening Leicester had supper with the Queen. That night, she sent word that she would proclaim the sentence against Mary. His was still the only voice (as the rest of the council were now happy to acknowledge) that could persuade her to proceed against the Scots queen. Archibald Douglas, one of the Scots commissioners, wrote in the first week of December that Leicester 'doth govern the Court at this time at his pleasure'.

But a warrant drawn up was not a warrant signed. As the Queen dithered still, Leicester's brief was communication with

Mary's son James, who to everyone's relief proved more interested in preserving his place in the English succession than in preserving his mother – although when it came to public pronouncements, as he warned Leicester, 'Honour constrains me to insist for her life.' A paper dedicated to Leicester (which suggests the writer was under his patronage) called for Mary's death, but also described Elizabeth's merciful reluctance: now as ever Leicester was safeguarding his queen's image, was giving Elizabeth an 'out'.

In December the council were forced reluctantly to deliver to Elizabeth a letter from Mary herself which, in its requests about the fate of her servants and the disposal of her body, was calculated to bring home the full enormity of the prospective death. Leicester wrote to Walsingham: 'There is a letter from the Scottish Queen, that hath wrought tears, but I trust shall do no further herein: albeit, the delay is too dangerous.' Elizabeth kept herself very private as the new year came in, but Camden reported that as she sat alone she could be heard murmuring: 'Strike, or be stricken, strike, or be stricken.' In the end it was her kinsman Lord Howard of Effingham (Douglass Sheffield's brother) who on 1 February persuaded her that this excruciating delay was shredding the nerve of the whole country. This is the day she sent for Davison and signed the warrant for Mary's execution, famously handing it back to him with just enough vagueness (on second thoughts, she said, perhaps Mary's gaoler should be sounded out about having her quietly put out of the way . . .) as to allow her later to claim she had never meant for it to be sealed and delivered immediately.

Leicester – with Walsingham, and Howard, and Knollys – was among the ten councillors who, under Cecil's leadership, agreed to take upon themselves the responsibility for the warrant's being put into effect. On 8 February the great hall at Fotheringhay saw a famous scene. A report sent to Cecil described how the executioners helped Mary's women strip her of her ornaments and outer clothes, and how she herself helped them make speed, 'as if she longed to be gone'.

All this time they were pulling off her apparel, she never changed her countenance, but with smiling cheer she uttered these words: 'that she never had such grooms to make her unready, and that she never put off her clothes before such a company' . . . groping for the block, she laid down her head, putting her chin over the block with both hands, which, holding there still, had been cut off had they not been espied . . . Then she, lying very still upon the block, one of the executioners holding her slightly with one of his hands, she endured two strokes of the other executioner with an axe, she making very small noise or none at all, and not stirring any part of her from the place where she lay: and so the executioner cut off her head, saving one little gristle, which being cut asunder, he lift[ed] up her head to the view of all the assembly and bade 'God save the Queen'.

Her lips, Cecil's correspondent wrote, 'stirred up and down a quarter of an hour' after she was dead.

Again, it had been the councillors – including Leicester – against the Queen, rather than Leicester against the rest of the councillors. Perhaps he had been in a particular position, as having persuaded her to the first move. But when the news was brought to Elizabeth at 9 a.m. the next day, all those responsible shared in her terrible anger (and none more so than the unhappy Davison, who found himself in the Tower). As Camden put it, she 'gave herself over to grief' – a hysterical and histrionic paroxysm, meant to convince a watching Europe of her innocence, but doubtless springing from a real and complex cocktail of emotions. Leicester, like Cecil, was told to stay away from the court (a fellow councillor, suffering the Queen's continued ill-humour, wrote to him that he was 'happy to be absent from these broils'). He betook himself that spring to the health-giving spa waters of the west, to Bath and Bristol. But, like Cecil, he was forgiven with revealing rapidity. At the end of March the ten councillors, with Cecil as their spokesman, were called upon to justify their actions before the Lord Chief Justice, the Lord Chancellor and the Archbishop of Canterbury. But by the beginning of April, an unidentified correspondent was writing to Leicester the universal gratitude owed to Ambrose Dudley, their intermediary to the

Queen, who had been 'the only means from God to qualify the Queen's bitter humour, and to stay the ruinous course provoked at home and abroad'. By June, good relations were restored; and debate turned once again to the foreign situation.

Philip of Spain had stepped up hostilities in the Netherlands, in preparation for using them as a springboard to launch his English invasion. The execution of the Queen of Scots gave him a pretext – and meant that he need no longer fear Elizabeth would be replaced by a Francophile Mary. In April, Drake's famous raid on the harbour of Cadiz had damaged enough of Spain's ships and property to force a delay in the invasion, but no-one doubted it was on the way. (And in January, two of the captains Leicester had left behind him in the Netherlands turned the defences at their command over to the Spanish enemy, choosing their Catholicism over their country. It must have been yet another blow to his confidence: Leicester had said he would stake his life on their loyalty.)

Again Leicester argued for more active armed intervention in the Netherlands; again the Netherlands begged for his return; again Elizabeth protested. He wrote to Walsingham: 'Seeing I find her Majesty's hardness continue still to me as it doth, I pray you lend me your earnest and true furtherance for my abode at home and discharge, for my heart is more than half broke.' Finally, at the end of June 1587, Leicester sailed back to the Netherlands, taking with him several thousand more men, but leaving behind him his stepson Essex who, by his stepfather's express permission, stayed in Leicester's apartments while he was away.

Leicester arrived just in time to preside, humiliatingly, over the loss of Sluys. The all-important port fell through what sounds horribly like an idiot blunder, and one that owes a lot to the poor communications between Leicester and his Dutch allies. 'Never were brave soldiers thus lost for want of easy succour,' wrote the commander of the English battalion inside the besieged town, bitterly. But the fact is that this second phase of Leicester's mission was from the start compromised even more gravely than the first had been. Even as he turned to war again, his queen (knowing that Philip of Spain did indeed have an 'Enterprise of

England' in preparation), began making overtures of peace to Parma – overtures Parma received with a tactical show of interest worthy of Elizabeth at her best. In November Leicester was recalled, having advised the Queen that he could be of no further use to her. He had failed – but it is hard to know exactly where success would have lain; nor, given the conflicting interests involved, was pleasing everyone a possibility.

Before he left he had a medal struck. It read: 'I reluctantly leave, not the flock, but the ungrateful ones.' Ungrateful, too, was what he found the Queen on his return; gracious enough in public, and prepared to defend him against the complaints of the States General, but ready to let him leave court to spend Christmas at his own house. He must have faced the year ahead, 1588, with small hope and less certainty.

18

'A thing whereof we can admit no comfort'
1588

EVERYONE KNEW THAT 1588 WOULD BE AN EXTRAORDINARY YEAR; and not only those who were aware that Philip's Armada was on the way. To students of the Bible the history of the world followed a discernible series of small cycles, each culminating in some great event; and the cycle of cycles would end in the grand climacteric of 1588. Even if land and seas did not collapse (in the words, translated, of the fifteenth-century mathematician Regiomontanus), then, at the very least, will 'the whole world suffer upheavals, empires / will dwindle and from everywhere will / be great lamentation'. The prophecies were discussed throughout Europe – everywhere, that is, government did not clamp down on them, as it did in England where, worst of all, the threatened second eclipse of the moon was forecast to come shortly before the Queen's birthday, and at the beginning of the season of Virgo, her ruling sign.

It hardly needed rumours of a Spanish fleet in the Channel in the December of 1587 to rattle the country (to rattle, particularly, anyone who, like Robert and Elizabeth, was old enough to remember 1539, and the child-scaring stories of the Catholic invasion force that had been awaited then). Even before Christmas, Howard of Effingham was appointed England's Lord Admiral, and the fleet put on standby. Harbours and ships were repaired, men and stores recruited. Next it was the turn of England's rusty land defences: seaport batteries and town walls unused for more than a century. A system of warning beacons was set up upon the hilltops, to spread the news of an invasion and summon the 'trained bands' of each locality.

At first it seemed as if Leicester's punishment was to be denied any part in this great national effort. In January he was reduced to begging the Queen ('after having so many months sustained her indignation') 'to behold with the eyes of your princely clemency my wretched and depressed state'. Had that situation continued, no doubt his enforced idleness would have hurt him bitterly – and Leicester must have known that the composition of the privy council had changed during the time he had spent in the Netherlands, had seen the addition of several of Cecil's conservative allies. 'The world was never so dangerous, nor never so full of treasons and treacheries, as at this day,' he had written to her from the Netherlands. 'God, for his mercy sake, preserve and keep you from them all! And it is one great part of my greatest comfort in coming home near your presence, that if these attempts fall out against your Majesty, that I shall be in place to do you a day's service.' As always when the pressure became too much for her, Elizabeth did send for him; and, as it became ever clearer that war was ahead, he was given a part to play in putting the country on a war footing, commissioned as Her Majesty's Lieutenant Against Foreign Invasion.

Just how important a part this was is perhaps up for dispute. It has been argued that Leicester, in being given titular command of the camp at Tilbury, was in fact being safely sidelined; that Parma's invasion force was far more likely to land either some distance away in Essex, or more probably on the south coast, in which case it would approach towards the other bank of the Thames. But it would have been risky, surely, knowingly to put up a straw man against a steel army, and Tilbury did command the route up the Thames to guard London. In any case, perhaps all such assessments founder on the sheer confusion of the preparations that summer. Elizabeth, again, was still negotiating frantically for peace: still negotiating as the Armada set sail; still negotiating as it neared English waters. It was only two days before the Armada was sighted off the Scilly Isles on 19 July – a fleet so great that they said the ocean groaned under it – that she brought negotiations to a close. For the past decade Leicester had been calling for a strengthening of England's coastal defences, a modernization of its methods of warfare. All this spring and summer, at the council table, Leicester's had been the leading voice urging Elizabeth that, in this latest crisis, to rely on words alone simply would not do; and his name headed the Spaniards' list of arrests to be made after their victory, first among 'the principal devils that rule the court'.

The trouble was that his Netherlands wars had cost a lot of money – too much of it frittered away – that England (especially with its once-lucrative cloth trade through the Netherlands in tatters) could ill afford. A cash-in-hand national balance of £270,000 just before Leicester first sailed had dwindled, by the eve of the Armada, to a mere £3,000. So now the ships put on war footing early in the spring were decommissioned again before the summer, and the sailors sent ashore to live at their own expense, not that of the government. (Some of the naval leaders would wind up feeding their starving sailors themselves, just as Leicester himself had done for his army in the Netherlands.)

Predictably, Leicester bickered with his experienced deputy, Sir John Norris. It was precisely the difficult relationship they had had in the Low Countries. As July ended (with the Armada and the English fleet engaging inconclusively off the Isle of Wight) there was still no camp at Tilbury. Leicester protested that even the men from Essex, ordered to report on Monday, had still not arrived by Thursday. 'If it be five days to gather the very country-men, what will it be, and must be to look for those who are forty, fifty and sixty miles off?' He had to provide for those who did turn up; when the four thousand men from Essex did arrive, 'there was neither a barrel of beer nor a loaf of bread for them'. The victuallers for whom he had been appealing by town criers in every market square had not yet appeared – nor, for that matter, had the official commission that would give him his authority. The boom that was to close the river broke; the bridge of boats to

allow the army to cross the river if necessary was not ready . . .
and yet, even hungry men 'said they would abide more hunger
than that to serve her Majesty and the country'.

Nevertheless, as flustered county officers were set dragging men
from the ungathered harvest to muster at armed camps through
England's southern counties, Leicester wound up with perhaps
something between 12,000 and 17,000 men at Tilbury, besides
the 6,000 at Sandwich who also fell under his command. By
August he could boast that his men appeared 'soldiers rather of a
year's experience than of a month's camping'. But then again, by
August – as we now know – the danger was past. As so often, his
real achievement was an oddly anomalous one, for which he himself has had little credit down the years, though it might cast him
as one of the spin doctors of history. It was, of course, the great,
the iconic publicity coup of Elizabeth's visit to Tilbury.

As the Armada drew close, towards the end of July, Elizabeth's
nerve storms had given way to calm. She spoke brave words to
Leicester, who 'spared not to blaze them abroad as a comfort
to all'. A lack of personal courage was never her problem, any
more than it was his. In that she was a woman, she had said in a
prayer once, she was inevitably 'weak, timid, and delicate' – but
in that she was queen, God had caused her to be 'vigorous, brave,
and strong'. Now, at Leicester's camp down on the Thames shore,
her councillors, so the story goes, had at least persuaded her to
wear a breastplate, though in Elizabeth's hands, the basic armour
had become a piece of graven burnished fantasy.

She had set out from London on 8 August accompanied by her
yeomen and gentlemen of the household. Careless of her personal
safety Elizabeth might seem to be, but she was not, at this
moment when she held the reins of history, so crazy as quite to
ignore security. But her guards had been impotent to help her
through the risky passage out of London, when unseasonable
rains had raised the tide rush through the arches of London
Bridge; and now, once her barge had successfully shot the rapids,
and borne her downriver to the Essex marshlands, she put them
away. Elizabeth disembarked at Tilbury fort (that bare gunpowder
store, set up by her father Henry). There she ordered the men of

her household to line up there on the shore and – in one of those gestures too risky to be altogether premeditated – advanced almost alone, with just four men and two boys, to meet her army.

In the famous image the Earl of Ormonde walked in front of her, carrying the sword of state. He was followed by two pages dressed in white velvet; one carrying her helmet on a cushion, the other leading her white horse. At the rear of the small procession walked Sir John Norris – but on either side of Elizabeth rode her Lieutenant General and her new Master of Horse: the Earls of Leicester and of Essex. Her old and her new favourites, you might say.

For almost thirty years Leicester had supported her, stood in for her, whenever she was required to display the masculine aspect of monarchy. And he was beside her now, as she rode towards the small hill where the army was encamped, above the stagnant pools of the waterside. How could he be anywhere else, at what both had every reason to believe was a moment of crisis in their country's history?

Elizabeth lay that night at a house in the vicinity, and returned the next day for a formal review of the army.

The speech Elizabeth gave that day to the troops that Leicester had, after all, so hastily assembled lives in posterity. It was always meant to have a resonance far beyond those muddy fields at Tilbury.

> My loving people, I have been persuaded by some that are careful of my safety to take heed how I committed myself to armed multitudes, for fear of treachery. But I tell you that I would not desire to live to distrust my faithful and loving people ... Wherefore I am come among you at this time but for my recreation and pleasure, being resolved in the midst and heat of the battle to live and die amongst you all, to lay down for my God and for my kingdom and for my people mine honor and my blood even in the dust.

Her words were written down by Lionel Sharp, a chaplain in the Earl of Leicester's service, who described Elizabeth riding through her squadrons like 'an armed Pallas', and who was, he says, commanded to read her 'excellent oration' to all the troops all over again on the next day. Reports of the scene, and of Elizabeth's stirring battle cry, were printed up and sent skimming through Europe within a week. Leicester had always intended that this scene should play widely.

> Now for your person, being the most sacred and dainty thing we have in this world to care for, a man must tremble when he thinks of it; specially finding your Majesty to have that princely courage, to transport yourself to the utmost confines of the realm to meet your enemies and defend your people. I cannot, most dear Queen, consent to that,

he had written, urging her, instead of taking up position on the south coast, to make the brief trip to see the troops at Tilbury. 'You shall comfort not only these thousands, but many more that shall hear of it. And thus far, and no further, can I consent to venture your person.'

It was (with the hindsight of some modern historians) an unreal and unnecessary heroism. 'God's wind' had already done its work and the Spanish fleet had been scattered. The pursuing English ships cleared Margate and Harwich as Elizabeth entered her barge in London. But the sneer is too easy. At the time, no-one yet knew that the Spanish fleet would be unable to regroup – and Spain had always planned a dual assault. While the Armada was to smash England's navy, transport vessels were to bring over from duty in the Netherlands the huge, waiting land army. As Elizabeth spoke at Tilbury, that army still waited, threateningly. The Duke of Parma had not yet finally decided that invasion without sea support was an impossibility. His first responsibility, after all, was to continue to hold the Netherlands for Spain, against that resistance the English had fostered so painfully.

The communications of the sixteenth century, moreover, guaranteed that word of England's salvation came only slowly. Indeed, as Elizabeth and her captains sat at dinner on 9 August, a false report had come to them that the Spanish army had embarked the day before, 'with 50 thousand men foot and 6000 horse'. The story was not disproved by the time one of Leicester's household officers put pen to paper on Sunday, adding that he himself was staying at the camp 'to see the end of so unhappy a matter'. An even more optimistic report reached Paris, where the Spanish diplomat Don Bernadino de Mendoza (expelled from England a few years before) took his sword in his hand and rushed into Notre Dame shouting 'Victory! Victory!' Others heard that England had been 'subdued, the Queen taken and sent prisoner and sent over the Alps to Rome, where, barefoot, she should make her humble reconciliation'. No wonder people in England itself needed a morale boost, a propaganda victory, after the years of painful uncertainty, years of waiting for the blow to fall.

The contemporary chroniclers on whose reports we depend recorded the gold-chased truncheon Elizabeth held in her right hand, and her stately 'King-like' pace.* One wrote of a coach decked with emeralds and rubies. To the balladeer Thomas Deloney she was 'attired like angel bright'. It is only later chroniclers who mention a white dress and a helmet with white plumes – but then Elizabeth usually wore black and white, the colours of perpetual virginity, and this time she would choose shining white; for impact and visibility, and to cast a flattering light on a 55-year-old's careworn face. (As for the armour, again, no-one at the time mentioned that piece of cross-dressing – but many years earlier, an ambassador had reported Elizabeth even as practising riding war horses to lead a charge against Spain; quite like a Boudicca of latter day.) No-one mentioned the clouds of stinging insects in which Tilbury abounds, either; or the absence of any money to pay Elizabeth's troops; or Leicester's complaint that he had had to be 'cook, caterer and huntsman' to the whole company.

It seemed like just another triumph of publicity – great, but of the kind Elizabeth and Leicester together had so often pulled off

---

* Camden, two decades later, described her as carrying 'the truncheon of an ordinary Captain', and walking up and down 'sometimes like a Woman, and anon, with the countenance and pace of a Soldier'.

before. No-one, except the Queen herself, understood her image better than he.

'I know I have the body but of a weak and feeble woman,' she had continued, as Leicester looked on approvingly,

> but I have the heart and stomach of a king and of a king of England too – and take foul scorn that Parma or any prince of Europe should dare to invade the borders of my realm. To the which rather than any dishonor shall grow by me, I myself will venter my royal blood; I myself will be your general, judge, and rewarder of your virtue in the field . . . In the meantime, my lieutenant general shall be my stead, than whom never prince commanded a more noble or worthy subject.

There is no reason to suppose either of them troubled with fore-knowledge that their long association was drawing to a close; that it was Leicester's body which would prove all too 'weak and feeble', and that very shortly.

It took weeks, after Tilbury, for sure news to filter through that the Spanish had lost two-thirds of their men and forty-four ships, to the English one ship and a hundred men. In the middle of August Leicester was writing optimistically to Shrewsbury that he trusted the Spaniards 'be too much daunted to follow their pretended enterprise'; that God – he said, foreshadowing the words Shakespeare gave to Henry V – 'hath also fought mightily for her Majesty'; and that, should invasion still come, Elizabeth's visit 'hath so inflamed the hearts of her good subjects, as I think the weakest person amongst them is able to match the proudest Spaniard that dares land in England'. It was 17 August before Leicester had word that the camp at Tilbury was to be disbanded (and in September, Mendoza in France was still writing optimistic despatches, believing the Armada could re-form). But then at least Leicester had the pleasure of returning to London like – as spectators remarked – a king.

His is not one of the names associated with England's triumph in popular history. That credit (rather forgetting the part played by wind and weather) has gone to sailors like Francis Drake –

himself once Leicester's protégé. But the Queen, at least, felt he had played a major part in the events of that summer – unless, again, she was simply feeling guilty. In the weeks following the Armada's defeat, as she wrote to James about the failure of 'this tyrannical, proud and brainsick attempt', as she triumphed that '[the Spanish king] hath procured my greatest glory that meant my sorest wrack', Camden says she was also having papers drawn up to make Leicester 'Lieutenant Governor' of the country. She was, he says, dissuaded only by Hatton and Cecil from placing so much power in one man's hands, and setting up what was in effect a vice-regency. (They clearly saw it as a danger. But one wonders whether, alternatively, Elizabeth were not specifically trying to set up a safe 'second person' in the realm, now that she was finally rid of the woman who had shown what a threat the position could be.)

But even without that extraordinary title, Leicester was still riding high. When the Earl of Essex led the first victory celebrations, Leicester watched from a window with the Queen. He dined every night with her, and a Spanish agent reported to Mendoza in Paris that he had seen the earl driving through London in a coach alone, accompanied by his household and a troop of light horse, as though at this late date he had indeed become the royal consort he had so long aspired to be.

His health was poor, but then so was Elizabeth's own; and when Leicester set off towards his beloved Kenilworth and the medicinal springs at Buxton late that summer, as he had so often done before, exhaustion must have warred with satisfaction. From Rycote in Oxfordshire on 29 August he wrote Elizabeth a note, the note of a man who expects to write many more.

> I most humbly beseech your Majesty to pardon your poor old servant to be thus bold in sending to know how my gracious lady doth, and what ease of her late pain she finds, being the chiefest thing in the world I do pray for, for her to have good health and long life. For my own poor case, I continue still your medicine . . . hoping to find perfect cure at the bath . . .

It was not to be. Only a few miles later, he grew sicker, and was forced to take refuge at the manor of Cornbury near Oxford (and also, ironically, near Cumnor). It is usually described as his own house, and indeed he had for several years exercised control over the deer and timber of the ancient, evocatively named, Wychwood Forest that lowers over the site. But there is nothing to suggest that this was a home to him – that, had he been able to choose a place and a moment, this was where he would choose to die.

But his ague turned into 'a continual burning fever' – perhaps a bout of malaria, made worse by his experience on the Tilbury marshes. That, at least, was the official conclusion, when his fellow councillors were called on to consider the results of the post-mortem. He died early in the morning on 4 September; and when the rumours gathered steam this time, he featured as victim, rather than villain. In the next century it was whispered that he 'hath ratsbane put in his porridge at Cornbury'; that a gentleman of his chamber, one William Haynes, said 'that he had seen the Lady Lettice give the fatal cup to the Earl'. Camden reported gossip that Leicester had suspected Lettice's lust for the younger man she married shortly thereafter – that Leicester, from the Netherlands, had attempted the assassination of his rival; and the scandal story ran that this was her pre-emptive strike. But in reality, it is hard to be sure Lettice was even there at Cornbury (and harder still truly to suspect the two men investigated by the privy council on the charge that they had procured his death by sorcery). It is just another one of the sticky smears that have dogged Leicester's memory. He had been unwell a long time – had complained of 'the stone', that catch-all name for an intestinal malady. It has been speculated that he had stomach cancer, and if this were the underlying cause of his death, then it would have accounted for any gastric symptoms that suggested poison to the suspicious minds of his contemporaries.

We have no record as to how Lettice mourned him. But Elizabeth was condemned to an extraordinary conjunction of public rejoicing and private agony. This was her own personal sorrow – it would be folly to try to damp the mood of the country – and against a background of the national victory celebrations she shut herself into her own chamber to grieve. According to the report from a Spanish agent, indeed, she shut herself in 'for some days', until her councillors had the doors broken forcibly; and though that may be an exaggeration, Walsingham too wrote that she would not tackle affairs 'by reason that she will not suffer anybody to have access to her'. Nothing in her early life – the fraught deaths of her mother, brother, Thomas Seymour and more – could have taught her to see grief as anything other than a dangerous emotion, best indulged solitary. A Genoese resident in London, one Marco Antonio Micea, noted, when she was seen about again, that she looked 'much aged and spent'.

Elizabeth kept that final note from Cornbury in a box in her closet until the end of her life. Labelled in her own hand as 'His last letter', it is held in the National Archives today. But no-one else seems to have mourned him, said the ubiquitous ambassadors, smugly. Though the Queen was 'much grieved' at Leicester's death, yet the joy of the country as a whole 'was never a whit abated', wrote Camden wryly. Worse than that: 'All men, so far as they durst, rejoiced no less outwardly at his death than for the victory lately obtained against the Spaniard,' lamented the writer and antiquarian John Stow, who said he owed his career to Leicester's encouragement. As another of his protégés, the poet Spenser, wrote a year later, with a certain amount of sharp sympathy:

> He now is dead, and all his glories gone.
> And all his greatness vapoured to nought.
> His name is worn already out of thought,
> (Nor) any poet seeks him to revive,
> Yet many poets honoured him alive.

But that was for the future. So, too, was Camden's not wholly unsympathetic epitaph:

He was reputed a complete Courtier, magnificent, liberal, a protector and benefactor of Soldiers and Scholars . . . very officious, and cunning towards his ill-willers; for a time much given to Women, and finally, a good husband in excess . . . to say the truth, he was openly held to be in the rank of those which were worthy of praise, but the things which he secretly plotted displeased many.*

For the moment, when Shrewsbury (in nervous association with his guest the Earl of Derby) wrote to Elizabeth the difficult letter that combined congratulations on her victory with commiserations on 'so great a loss', she replied to him as if writing of a green wound that cannot bear the touch: 'Although we accept and acknowledge your careful mind and good will, yet we desire rather to forbear the remembrance thereof as a thing whereof we can admit no comfort, otherwise [than] by submitting our will to God's inevitable appointment.' There is no letter that really reveals Elizabeth's feelings – no equivalent, even, to that she wrote to Catherine de Medici after Alençon's death. But then there was really no-one to write to: the death of Robert certainly would not bring her closer to Lettice in any way.

Court cynics might whisper that Elizabeth always got over her grief. (When Cecil died a decade later, Lettice's brother Sir William Knollys would sneer that the Queen 'seemeth to take [it] very grievously, shedding tears and separating herself from all company. Yet I doubt not but she in her wisdom will cast this behind her, as she hath done many other before time of like nature.') Elizabeth had, indeed, to develop a measure of hardihood, when her own life was so much longer than that enjoyed by most of her contemporaries. Nor would she place private feelings above public responsibilities. But for the moment at least – perhaps for ever – the loss of 'a personage so dear unto us', as she described Robert to Shrewsbury, was without remedy.

But while Elizabeth, shutting herself away, was capable of the sudden, savagely dramatic gesture, she also expressed herself less directly. As in life, so in death she and Leicester often spoke to

---

* Later, too, came the epitaph of one Thomas Digges, who in 1601 wrote that 'when the Earl of Leicester lived, it went for current, that all Papists were Traitors, in action, of affection. He was no sooner dead, But . . . Puritans were trounced, and traduced as troublers of the state.'

each other obliquely. Perhaps it is to the years ahead that we should look for Elizabeth's last (and almost disastrous) great loving gesture towards her lost companion – to her relationship with Leicester's stepson and surrogate, Essex. Leicester had brought Essex to court as he himself began to tire and age, willing still to perform necessary duties, but unable any longer to flatter Elizabeth with the conviction he had once had; unable to provide the energetic, exciting pageant of eager masculinity. Elizabeth obediently would follow his programme almost to her destruction; would try to believe Essex was another Leicester. The Queen's long, her extraordinary, indulgence towards Robert Devereux was her long lament for Robert Dudley.

The so-called 'Armada Portrait' of Elizabeth painted in 1588 must be one of the glummest ever celebrations of victory. Her right hand resting possessively on the globe, the crown at her side and pictures of the sea defeat behind her, she is clad with an almost unimaginable magnificence of embroidery and jewellery. But her pouched and hooded eyes gaze into the distance, past the viewer, with an effect almost of melancholy. Against the black velvet of her dress, her pearls – perhaps those Leicester bequeathed to her – stand out clearly. Nothing can be read, in the Armada portrait, into Elizabeth's choice of black and white clothes. They had become, as the years wore on, her favourite colours. But she might well have been in mourning, and not for one man merely. The end of the glory years of her reign was upon her, even as it reached its apogee.

While the Spanish war wore on – while Elizabeth at last, too late for Leicester, was forced to commit to it wholeheartedly – over the next few years all the greatest aides and adorers of her heyday would slip away. Ambrose died in 1590 – of gangrene, ten days after the amputation of the leg that had been wounded in France almost thirty years earlier. Walsingham too died in 1590; and Hatton in 1591, also without a son to inherit his dignities. Cecil lived until 1598, but as the decade passed even he began to take less part in affairs. There remained Cecil's son Robert and Leicester's stepson Essex (as well as the maverick Walter Ralegh). With these young men Elizabeth would try to recreate the pattern of earlier years; but those days, when bickering would in the end be subsumed into co-operation, were never again to be. The 1590s – a difficult decade of famine and uncertainty, with the succession still unsettled and Elizabeth's death ever more likely – did at last see the outbreak of the factionalism once attributed to Leicester's day. Arguments concerning the nature of monarchy became more explicit. Courtiers split into camps, with Essex positioning himself in opposition to the Cecils, and the Queen's efforts to balance opposites leading to stasis, rather than to a fruitful collegiality.

Essex's career is too well known to need more than the briefest description here. It was speculated early in his heyday, in 1591, that he was 'like enough, if he had a few more years, to carry Leicester's credit and sway'. That was before it became clear that Essex's ambition went much further that his stepfather's (fired, perhaps, by the smidgin of royal blood running through his veins; the thought that if only the line of succession had run differently . . .). Then came his bid for political as well as personal power; his increasing dissatisfaction with the limitations on a favourite; his disastrous campaign in Ireland; and his famous intrusion into Elizabeth's bedroom to explain it away. Think of Leicester's very different reaction when Elizabeth criticized his conduct in the Netherlands. Think, too, of Elizabeth's horrified reaction, all those years ago, when men had burst into the chamber of the Scots Queen Mary.

Time and again Elizabeth forgave Essex; punished him, at most, but leniently. It was probably the withdrawal of his income that pushed him into armed rebellion; maybe Elizabeth's refusal to renew his 'farm' of sweet wines, which Leicester had held before him, was a symbolic rejection. Leicester's stepson died on the headsman's block as Leicester's father and grandfather had done. But even before Essex's downfall, the Queen was turning away from him. She knew the difference between the presence, and the absence, of loyalty. Elizabeth's first and last favourites were in essence very different men.

19

'*To end this life for her service*'

ROBERT DUDLEY, EARL OF LEICESTER, WAS BURIED IN HIS FAMILY stronghold of Warwick; in the Beauchamp Chapel of St Mary's church, built more than a century before.

Five days before the October ceremony, the procession had set out from Kenilworth: a hundred poor; a hundred gentlemen servants to the attending lords 'in cloaks' (the mourning garment given to those of this class; anyone who ranked esquire or above was given a whole gown); a hundred of Leicester's own gentlemen similarly attired; chaplains, doctors and secretaries; the Mayor of Coventry; attendants bearing Leicester's guidon, and leading his horse. Mourners of rank being customarily of the same sex as the one mourned, the names of the women present come at the end of the long list of attendees preserved in the records of the College of Arms. They include such humble personages as the dairy woman at Wanstead, and 'Mary the poor scullery'. The body itself was followed by the Earl of Essex, the chief mourner, with Sir Robert Sidney (Philip Sidney's brother) as his assistant, and a trainbearer behind them, presumably to deal with the yards of black. (From an earlier list of preparations it looks as though Ambrose had planned to attend, but was in the end prevented, perhaps by his health.) Several of Lettice's male relatives were there, as well as Leicester's brother-in-law the Earl of

Huntingdon; but there is no mention of the 'base son', the younger Robert Dudley.

On Leicester's tomb, in Latin, the inscription lists his titles under Queen Elizabeth ('who distinguished him by particular favour'), and describes him as 'the best and dearest of husbands' to Lettice, who erected it and who shares the vault under the gaudy effigies. Ambrose Dudley lies nearby, as does the 'noble Impe', his effigy still dressed in a young child's gown, rather than the breeches which, had he lived to seven, would have marked his entrance into maturity.

Leicester's funeral seems to have been unremarkable, for a major nobleman of the sixteenth century – but then, he had planned it that way. In the will he had written a year before his death, in 1587 on his return to the Netherlands, he had required that his friends should bury 'the wretched Body of mine' (when it pleased God to separate it from the soul) 'with as little Pomp or vain Expenses of the World, as may be'; he was 'persuaded that there is no more vain Expenses' than a lavish tomb. Unless the Queen's majesty appointed otherwise, or unless it proved too inconvenient, he had always wished to be buried at Warwick, 'where sundry of my Ancestors do lie'.

His will, he wrote, was of necessity an amateur effort, since he found himself in the Netherlands, and was 'no Lawyer, nor have any Counsel now with me'. The result is a document more moving than any lawyer could achieve – and, before anything else, a statement of his religious conviction, and the almost Calvinist trend thereof. 'First I take it to be the Part of any true Christian, to make a true Testimony of his Faith at all Times . . .' His continues for a long paragraph, stating his anticipation of the forgiveness of his sins ('be they never so great or infinite'); his trust in an Almighty whose 'Graces Goodness and Mercy I most faithfully take hold on, being so promised by himself, who is the only Truth itself, that I am the Child of Salvation', one of the 'faithfull Children, and Saints of God'.

Lettice figures in his will as his 'dear and poor disconsolate wife'. He has, he writes, 'always found her a faithfull, loving, and a very obedient, carefull Wife'; it was in this perception that he made her his executor. Before a year was out, Lettice was married again – to the 32-year-old Christopher Blount, a friend of her son Essex; a Catholic member of the minor gentry who had served as Leicester's Master of Horse in the Netherlands. And although remarriage was to be expected, and rapid remarriage common, this might seem almost like *Hamlet* speed.* On the other hand, the Blounts were connections and clients of the Dudleys – Christopher (to whom Leicester wrote as 'Kytt') was a younger son of that 'Cousin Blount' to whom Leicester had written on the death of Amy Dudley – and might be said to be 'in the family'. Blount never publicly claimed Lettice as his wife, referring to her rather as a 'friend', and she continued to be known as the Countess of Leicester. When Essex's outrages and obsessions finally brought him and some of his supporters to rebellion and the headsman's block, his stepfather Blount was among the fellow victims. Lettice was thus doubly bereft. She spent the rest of her life in comparative retirement, dying only in 1634, in her nineties.

To his 'most dear, and most gracious Sovereign, whose creature under God I have been, and who hath been a most beautiful, and a most princely Mistress unto me', Leicester left a 'Rope of fair white Pearls, to number six hundred'. Elizabeth had exalted him

as well in advancing me to many Honours, as in maintaining me many Ways by her Goodness and Liberality. And as my best Recompense to her most excellent Majesty can be from so mean a Man, chiefly in Prayer to God, for whilst there was any Breath in this Body, I never failed it, even as for mine own Soul. And as it was my greatest Joy, in my Life Time, to serve her to her Contentation, so it

* It is a reasonable speculation that Shakespeare (who worked with several former 'Leicester's Men') based the character of Hamlet in part on Lettice's son Essex – whether or not we take Shakespeare (as do the authors of a new book) actually to have been the diplomat Neville, with whose family the Dudleys were at enmity. The said authors point out that this leaves Leicester as Claudius: the second husband who killed the first. His advocates might resent that characterization of Robert Dudley – but Lettice as Gertrude, with her 'fever in the blood', would work out nicely!

is not unwelcome to me, being the Will of God to die, and end this Life for her Service.

He was thinking of death on a Dutch battlefield – but in fact, since his whole life had been spent in her service, his death could hardly be seen differently whenever it occurred.

If you exclude the sole involuntary betrayal of Leicester's dying and leaving her, then, for Elizabeth, you might say their relationship had worked. Whether she regretted not marrying him, in the first shock of grief – or whether her wary sense of self-preservation kicked in, to keep the pain at bay – in the course of their thirty-year alliance she had achieved a relationship that gave play both to her power, and to her vulnerability.

And of course, he had not done so badly. The tale of the prince who adventured and won a kingdom and a princess was not new even in the sixteenth century; and if he did not quite win the kingdom, then he went a good way of the journey. As Robert bolstered Elizabeth's majesty, he had shared the benefits of her sovereignty. But dynastically, he gambled and lost. He was robbed of his posterity. Leicester's earldom eventually (after being in abeyance for thirty years) was recreated by James I for Leicester's nephew, Sir Robert Sidney. The great Sidney house of Penshurst in Kent remains one of the chief shrines to the dissipated Dudley legacy.* But effectively the direct line of Dudley dignities dwindled and died out (since Ambrose too died without child), and it is safe to say that Robert would have seen his great failure as this: the failure of his dynasty.

It seems ironic but apposite that, in the same generation, the Tudors died out in much the same way.

Appendix I:

The second Robert Dudley

THE YOUNGER ROBERT DUDLEY – LEICESTER'S ACKNOWLEDGED BUT illegitimate son – was brought up under his father's auspices, his mother having (she said) been frightened into relinquishing him before her own marriage to Edward Stafford at the end of 1579, when the boy was around five years old. The young Robin went to live with his father's kinsman John Dudley, in Stoke Newington, and it seems Leicester (like Douglass) visited him there, since a servant later remembered that Leicester did 'very often times discover his love and care he had of his son, and the desire he had to have him receive good usage and education'. By 1583 (with Douglass and her new husband in Paris, and the elder but illegitimate boy's prospects having fallen on the birth of Leicester's legitimate heir), Leicester had sent the child to be tutored at Offington near the Sussex coast, Ambrose having property nearby.

He was only fourteen when Leicester entered him at Christ Church, Oxford, in 1587, with the rank of 'an earl's son' and a notable tutor in the shape of Thomas Chaloner, who would go on to tutor James's son Prince Henry. The following year he begged to be allowed to volunteer for Elizabeth's army at Tilbury, where (or so he boasted) his father commissioned him as a colonel of foot, under the guidance of an older officer. Leicester's sudden death put an end to a relationship that seems to have been unmarred by any resentment, and two years after that the death of Ambrose (to whom Leicester had left a life interest in his disposable lands, his son being still 'young and casual') left young Robert in possession of a great inheritance.

Leicester had died with huge cash debts: little short of £60,000, of which his wife would be required to repay the crown more than £20,000. 'Touching my Bequests, they cannot be great, by Reason my Ability and Power is little, for I have not dissembled with the World my Estate, but have lived always above any Living I had (for which I am heartily sorry) lest that, through my many Debts, from Time to Time, some Men have taken Loss by me.' (There were those moneys to the London merchants, from whom he had raised cash for the Netherlands ... he desired his executors to satisfy everybody.) Elizabeth moved instantly to recover those moneys owed to her, even those that had been spent in her cause. (Fondness, as Camden noted, never lessened her sense of what was owed to her treasury.) But she concentrated her attentions on those properties that had been left to Lettice rather than those destined for the young Robert Dudley.

By the time the young Robert successfully took full possession of Kenilworth at last, another avenue of opportunity had opened up when his mother returned from Paris and was appointed lady of the bedchamber. He joined the fringes of the court – a young man 'of exquisite stature, with a fair beard and noble appearance', as he was later described – before being briefly banished for marrying (and kissing, in Elizabeth's presence!) Margaret Cavendish, cousin to the famous explorer Thomas and sister-in-law to the travel writer Richard Hakluyt. The sea had, from his childhood, drawn young Robert's 'natural sympathy'; and now began his own long involvement with affairs maritime when he fitted out three ships to go venturing in the south seas – the Queen having firmly vetoed his desire to sail with them.

The failure of this expedition left him undaunted, and in 1594 he did indeed set sail himself, to test his carefully acquired skills in navigation on a voyage to the West Indies. The records of the journey show him to advantage, not only taking possession of the island of Trinidad in the Queen's name, but winning the admiration of his sailors and establishing friendly relations with the Arawak people – 'a finely shaped and gentle people, all naked and painted red'.

The ore he found proved to be not gold but marquisite; though he was given word of a town called El Dorado, only a few of his men were able to penetrate up the Orinoco; and back home, he found his voyage eclipsed by the almost simultaneous venture of Ralegh. But he had put into personal action his father's dream of empire and interest in the sea. Shortly afterwards he sailed on the Cadiz expedition against the Spanish led by his half-brother Essex, who knighted him at the end of the voyage. The young Dudley had some part in Essex's rebellion; but his involvement was not such as to incur any major penalty.

His first wife Margaret Cavendish having died of plague while he was in the West Indies, he married the daughter of a Kenilworth neighbour, Alice Leigh, and it may have been his new wife's family who encouraged him to press the cause of his legitimacy. He first approached an ecclesiastical court, where less stringent inquiries would be made into the supposed marriage, and where his reluctant mother would not be asked to testify. This attempt, however, came to an end when, in October 1603, Robert Sidney arrived with a mandate from the privy council, moving the case to the jurisdiction of the Star Chamber.

Dudley's timing had been appalling. Elizabeth, had he launched his claim some months earlier, might well have been sympathetic. But the new King James was determined to reward those who had been helpful to him, which included the martyred Essex (as represented by his mother Lettice) and Robert Sidney; while Leicester had been high on the list of those James felt necessary to blame for his mother's execution. The identification of the crown with the opponents to young Dudley's case was shown when it was announced they would be represented by the Attorney General Sir Edward Coke, on whose advice Lettice charged

Dudley and all his associates with defamation of character.*
The trial opened in June 1604, and by this time Douglass had been persuaded by her son's urgency to rally to the cause. Douglass's description of her wedding ceremony was supported by five witnesses who had already given written testimony, but these Coke dismissed as being 'all not worth a frieze jerkin'. The most material among them were, after all, servants or people of lower rank – 'a base and poor carpenter', 'a common drunkard', 'a lying tailor' – the aristocratic witnesses to the wedding being dead. Even the single most important witness, Douglass's gentlewoman Magdalen Salisbury, was dismissed as being 'an infamous instrument', procured for pay.†

The papers kept in Robert Sidney's family include reports about one Mr Christmas, a companion of Leicester's who (said someone who had known Christmas's servant thirty years before) had tried to dissuade the earl from the match, and claimed until his last hour that 'had it not been for him' then Leicester and Douglass would have been married; but, as it was . . . One Owen Jones had been examined. He had been a servant hired by Leicester to wait on the young Robert, and claimed that Leicester once said to him, 'Owen, thou knowest that Robin, my boy, is my lawful son; and as I do charge thee to keep it secret, so I charge thee be careful of him.' It was an important part of Robert Dudley's case; but Owen had taken money from him, and was now described, in the report to Robert Sidney, as 'a lewd fellow', who could easily be 'laid out

---

* Leicester had been barely cold when James had been writing south to Elizabeth his hopes that Robert Sidney, then on a mission to Scotland, should not suffer from having been absent when the 'unfortunate and displeasant' event of his uncle's death occurred – that 'in anything concerning this gentleman fallen out by the death of his uncle, ye will have a favorable consideration of him for my sake'.

† A cryptic letter from Robert Dudley to his father's one-time secretary Arthur Atye, quoted by Adlard from Lansdowne MSS, 89, refers to 'an instrument my father made, of this last reputed marriage, under the hands and seals and oathes of them that were at it' – and yet, this putative document itself seems to have a dubious history, to have been the subject of some controversy. No wonder Atye, whatever he was able to reply to the younger Robert Dudley, 'refused my father to be any actor in this matter'.

in his [true] colours'. (And indeed, Sidney's agent pointed out with some reason 'how unlikely it was to be true that [Owen] should be of my lord's secrets and know these matters'.

There were lists of questions to be put to family friends:

Do you know or believe in your conscience that the said Earl was ever lawfully married to Douglasse Lady Sheffield?

Did the Earl ever say to you that he was married to her?

Hath not the Lady Sheffield many times since the birth of Sir Robert Dudley said unto you that she was never married to the said Earl of Leicester?

Did not the said Earl in all conferences betwixt you and him always accompte Sir Robert Dudley to be his base son?

A 'statement of case for Counsel: together with Counsel's opinion thereon' declared that:

A marriage is pretended [claimed] to be secretly celebrated in a chamber in *anno* 15 Eliz. [the fifteenth year of Elizabeth's reign] between A [the Earl of Leicester] and B [the Lady Sheffield]. This marriage is never published: the parties do never cohabit as man and wife . . . A and B both subsequently marry. A married C and B marries E. The marriage of A and C is never contradicted by B by suit on the Ecclesiastical Court nor does B ever claim any marriage with A but always . . . protesteth she was never married to A but only promised marriage by A.

But in fact, it was not the events of 1573, but those of 1603, upon which Robert Sidney and Lettice made their case.

Robert Dudley's witnesses in the hearing at Lichfield, so his opponents claimed, were 'all suborned and long time before and after maintained with meat, drink, lodging and apparel by the plaintiff in this suit'. Three of the witnesses said the marriage had been in '*anno* 15 Eliz.', but two others said it had been in *anno* 14. Two out of that first three said it had been at Assher (Esher) House in Surrey in that year, where they had been in Douglass's service; but other witnesses could be found who claimed

Douglass was never at Esher then, and that indeed it was *anno* 17 before the pair became Douglass's servants. Counsel's opinion was that witnesses being once 'disabled, shall be of no credit'. (And as for Douglass's own testimony, when counsel was asked, 'Of what force in law will be the affirmation of B to prove the marriage, being party &c.', the answer came: 'We take it the affirmation of the said B not to be anything available in law to prove the said marriage.')

Coke's demand that Dudley's witnesses 'should be damned' formed the basis of the decision of Star Chamber, who took until 10 May 1605 to deliver their judgment, having examined more than 150 witnesses. Dudley's three chief witnesses were fined and declared for ever suspect, and the Star Chamber further ordained that all the depositions should be 'sealed up and suppressed until the King should order the enclosures to be broken', thereby impeding further enquiry. A later lawyer called the judgment 'infamous', and even in its day it received some comment. 'The matter of marriage was not handled at all,' wrote Rowland White to Gilbert Talbot, now the new Earl of Shrewsbury, 'only the practice was proved [Dudley's legal methods were queried] in the proceedings'. Through the centuries since, it has been riveting to trace the labyrinthine path of the legal manoeuvres, but impossible to reach any hard conclusions about the original story.

The seventeenth-century antiquary Sir William Dugdale (author of *Antiquities of Warwickshire*, and of *Baronage*) did manage to see copies of the witness depositions in the library of Sir Robert Cotton; and his conclusion was that on the whole, whatever ceremony had taken place at Esher (and no-one seemed to deny there had been something, in an age when a betrothal was attended by as much ceremonial as a wedding day) would have constituted a valid marriage. (And, he added, in a belt and braces kind of way, the couple's cohabitation and their child together would be enough, combined with any kind of contract, to constitute a marriage anyway.) Dugdale's decision was influenced by the claim that Leicester had told a servant (Owen Jones?) that Robert was his true son, and 'likewise by what Ambrose, Earl of Warwick, had uttered, which for brevity's sake I omit'. One

wishes he had been less brief: in 1731 many of the Cotton manuscripts were destroyed by fire, and later researchers were unable
to find Ambrose's statement, or to echo Dugdale's certainty.

In 1824 Sir John Shelley-Sidney of Penshurst tried to establish his
claim to the barony of Lisle and Dudley, by then in abeyance, but
the Committee of Privileges of the House of Lords rejected his
request, which could have been granted only if the descendants of
Robert Dudley could be declared illegitimate with certainty. But in
1899 Sir George Warner, writing an introduction to *The Voyage of
Robert Dudley to the West Indies* (Hakluyt Society, second series 3)
examined all the documents he could lay his hands on and decided
the marriage was not valid ... Perhaps the most one can say with
certainty is that the very manner of proceeding of Robert Dudley's
opponents suggests that he did have some sort of a case that could
not have been dismissed by more straightforward means.

Within weeks of the final failure of his claim, Robert Dudley
left England in disgust. Though he and Alice had been married
almost ten years, and had a bevy of young daughters, he took with
him on his travels a page who proved, once safely in France, to be
the young beauty of the court (and his own distant kinswoman)
Elizabeth Southwell. They were married with the aid of a papal dis-
pensation that forgave them their consanguinity, but made no
mention of the fact that Robert was married already, presumably
because it had been an Anglican ceremony. He was long a loving
husband to Elizabeth, and father to their children, but never again
showed any interest in Alice or in their daughters; displaying at last,
it was said, almost a resentful pleasure in doing 'what his father, as
he contended, had been allowed to do with impunity'. He abandoned his lands, which were sequestered by the crown; Kenilworth
(purchased for a knock-down price) eventually became part of
Queen Henrietta Maria's marriage portion, before falling victim to
parliamentary forces when the outer, defensible, portions were
'slighted' – destroyed – during the Civil War.*

---

* Over the subsequent centuries, only Leicester's gatehouse, converted into a
private dwelling, stood aloof from the decay; today English Heritage, which runs
the property, has completed a considerable restoration project.

Robert and Elizabeth having converted to Catholicism, they made their way to Florence, where Ferdinand de Medici was waging a naval war against the Turks and could use the services of a young man who already had theoretical and practical experience of fitting vessels for the sea. Dudley's interests were enormously wide, with his mathematics and astronomy, his experiments in medicine and civil engineering, his invention for use in the silk industry (like his father's concern for the cloth trade!) – and the pamphlet he once wrote, in the hope of regaining King James's favour, suggesting money-making mechanisms for the monarchy, and control by standing army. 'In policy there is a greater tie of the people by force and necessity than merely by love and affection . . .' He would be responsible not only for some important new designs in shipbuilding, but for the draining of the Tuscan marshes and the creation of the port of Livorno (and, since many of the thirteen children he had with Elizabeth survived and married well, for a fair proportion of the Italian nobility).*

Dudley's career in Tuscany lasted until his death in 1649. Though James sequestered his English estates, Europe acknowledged the titles he claimed – even his grandfather's title of Duke of Northumberland – and he retained the favour both of the Medici and of the papacy, which gave him the singular honour of allowing him the right of mapping out his own order of chivalry. When he gave up his practical responsibilities he kept high ceremonial rank (though never political power) as Grand Chamberlain at the Florentine court, thanks to the favour of three successive grand duchesses. In his last years, as Charles I finally issued a letter of redress accepting his legitimacy, he published his great work of charts and navigations, *Dell'arcano de mare*, and plans for the future exploration of the sea. Leicester would have been pleased. Elizabeth too, maybe.

* Sadly, one of his surviving sons, Carlo, instead took to brigandry. A granddaughter of Carlo's would marry the Duke of Shrewsbury – descendant of Leicester's friend – but her brother, accompanying her to London, was hanged at Tyburn for stabbing his manservant to death; he asked to be hung separately from the other convicts in his cart, lest they should touch him in their plebeian death throes.

Appendix II:

The Arthur Dudley mystery

AMONG THE MANY LEGENDS ABOUT ELIZABETH, ONE OLD CHESTNUT of a story has come back into favour very recently. It has, after all, the useful attribute of seeming to offer the most certain proof of all that Elizabeth was no virgin (though it leaves open the question of whether it was from purely political or also psychological motives that she was forced to deny, even as she indulged, her sexuality). The story is worth examining in some detail because it shows just how long-lived any tale about a high-profile woman's sexuality can be – shows, too, how the same set of facts can also fit a political reading that reinterprets the whole story.

In the summer of 1587, the year before the Armada, a young man was brought to the Spanish court, claiming to be the son of Elizabeth Tudor and Robert Dudley. The bald statement opens up – if one chooses to follow it – a path of dizzying possibility. The name 'Arthur Dudley' has not rated so much as a mention in the index of most biographies of either of his putative parents. Historians almost universally dismiss his claim – and I should say at once that I share the general scepticism. None the less, the past few years have seen a renewed bout of interest – equivalent, in a minor key, to the nineteenth century's interest in the Amy Dudley mystery. Mystery births and secret bloodlines clearly catch the mood of our moment, as witness The Da Vinci Code.

The story 'Arthur Dudley' told comes to us from four letters sent by Sir Francis Englefield, a Catholic renegade living at the Spanish court, to King Philip. Once a councillor of Mary Tudor (and a correspondent of Leicester), Englefield was now old and blind, but still considered fit to be entrusted with the investigation of this English prisoner, apparently shipwrecked on the Spanish coast and brought to Madrid as a possible spy. The first of these letters is a very lengthy verbatim report of what 'Arthur Dudley' had told him. Stripped down to its essentials, the story was this.

'Dudley' claimed to have been raised by a man called Robert Southern (a former servant of Elizabeth's confidante Kat Ashley) who, many years before, had been summoned to Hampton Court and there handed a baby, born in secret to one of the Queen's ladies, which he was told to name Arthur, and raise as his own. This he accordingly did, giving the boy, indeed, a better education than he could give his own offspring. When Arthur was eight years old, Robert Southern was given a post at one of the Queen's houses, in Enfield. Arthur grew up spending summers there, and winters in London, until he was fourteen or fifteen years old when, in a fit of adolescent rebellion, he stole a handful of silver from his foster-father's purse and set out to run away to sea. He was stopped, bizarrely, by a letter from seven of Elizabeth's privy councillors, ordering that he instead be brought to London immediately. The letter, Arthur said, showed him to be 'a person of more importance than the son of Robert Southern', but when he was met by John Ashley, Kat's husband, little more was told to him. Not enough, at any rate, to quench his desire to see those lands beyond the sea. Finally he obtained permission, and, travelling in the care of a servant of the Earl of Leicester's, was sent abroad into the care of a Monsieur de la Noue, a Frenchman fighting in the Flanders wars. When La Noue was taken prisoner he ran away and adventured around France, until urgent letters recalled him to England, at the end of 1583.

Robert Southern was dying, and told Arthur he was not his real father. He refused, however, to say who the real parents might be. Arthur left the house in anger, but Southern sent a schoolmaster named Smyth to bring him back, and, on Arthur's return, admitted the young man was in fact the son of the Queen and Robert Dudley. Arthur begged him to put it in writing, but Southern was paralysed and unable to do this.

When John Ashley learnt that the secret was out, he was so horrified that Arthur was panicked back into flight. He racketed around France, approaching several Jesuit colleges and Edward Stafford, the English ambassador in Paris, but always found himself unable through nerves to tell his story, or them unwilling to listen to it. (It is, is it not, beginning to sound like a paranoid fantasy?)

Returning to England, Arthur was brought before Leicester by two of the earl's officers named Blount and Fludd. (Blount, of course, is a name familiar from Leicester's service; the name of the man who sent him the reports on Amy's death. Fludd was indeed really the name of one of Leicester's Netherlands secretaries. But to some degree these – like, of course, the more senior officials mentioned – were public personages.) In an extraordinary interview, Leicester 'by tears, words, and other demonstrations' showed his great affection . . . 'You are like a ship under full sail at sea, pretty to look upon but dangerous to deal with,' he told the younger man. Leicester sent Arthur to Walsingham to expedite his safe passage back out of the country, but Walsingham's manner and his curious questions so put the wind up Arthur that he fled once again, and at Gravesend signed up with a party of English soldiers heading to service in Flanders.

From there, the narrative becomes yet more confused. (Indeed, Englefield himself said as much, and sent only an abridged version to his master.) It seems that Arthur schemed to hand a Flanders town over to the Spanish, and actually sent his story to the Pope and to the Duke of Parma. He was on pilgrimage in Spain when he learnt of Mary Stuart's death. The news made him set sail again for France; and it was at this point that shipwreck in the Bay of Biscay landed him on the Spanish shore, where he was seized on suspicion of espionage. (Back in the middle of April, the Venetian envoy in Madrid had heard it slightly differently: that a Catholic Englishman had been arrested at Fontarrabia on the French frontier and that King Philip was 'in great doubt' whether to keep him prisoner or let him go.)

Englefield's own statement was accompanied by a private letter from Arthur Dudley:

> If God grants that his Majesty [King Philip] should take me under his protection, I think it will be necessary to spread a rumour that I have escaped, as everybody now knows that I am here, and my residence in future can be kept secret. I could then write simply and sincerely to the Earl of Leicester all that has happened to me, in order to keep in his good graces; and I could also publish a book to any effect that might be considered desirable, in which I should show myself to be everybody's friend and nobody's enemy . . .

If real, it was an extraordinary naïveté.

This account was sent to Philip on 17 June. On the eighteenth, the twentieth and the twenty-second, Englefield sent further, brief letters giving his limited conclusions (of which more later) after successive waves of further questioning. At the end of the first letter he suggested installing Arthur in 'San Geronimo, the Atocha, or some other monastery'. At the end of the fourth Englefield says clearly: 'I am of the opinion that he should not be allowed to get away, but should be kept very secure to prevent his escape.' The letter is endorsed with a note in Philip's own hand, to the effect that it would indeed be 'safest to make sure of his person until we know more about it'. A few days later the Venetian ambassador in Madrid reported that Arthur had been sent to the castle of Lameda. By now, so the Venetian understands it, Arthur is definitely believed to be a spy.

In May 1588 an English agent 'BC' was writing to Cecil that Dudley was still in Spanish hands, 'very solemnly warded and served', at a cost to the King of six crowns a day, and 'taketh upon him' [behaves] 'like the man he pretendeth to be'. 'BC' has been identified by Robert Hutchinson, in *Elizabeth's Spy Master*, as Anthony Standen alias Pompeo Pellegrini, one of Walsingham's chief collectors of news in Spain.*

---

* Standen was a member of Lord Darnley's household in 1565; soon after that (it has been suggested), Darnley was murdered by the English.

In September the same year, another letter mentions in passing that 'The varlet that called himself Her Majesty's son is in Madrid, and is allowed two crowns a day for his table, but cannot go anywhere without his keepers, and has a house for a prison.' From six crowns to two crowns . . . Perhaps his value had dropped, once the Armada was well away. Two years later again, a report sent to England on the state of Spain mentions Alcantara, 'where an Englishman of good quality and comely personage was imprisoned who avowed himself Leicester's son by no small personage'. From then on, Arthur Dudley disappears from history. His claim seems never, in his own day, to have been debated more widely.

Was he just an adventurer, spinning a yarn for his own advantage? That has been the most popular assumption, but it is one with which the historian and novelist Paul Doherty would not agree. His credence for Arthur's claim has been recently expressed in a 'factional' book, *The Secret Life of Elizabeth I*, and a television documentary. (A few years earlier, Robin Maxwell's novel *The Queen's Bastard* supported much the same theory.) Doherty can cite a certain amount of circumstantial evidence for his claim. When 'BC' wrote in 1588, he described Arthur as being about twenty-seven years of age. That would probably date his birth to 1561, and the records for Elizabeth's movements that summer are scanty. It was always her progresses that were considered to have given her the best opportunity for closet action. One contemporary scandal-monger said that she never went on progress but to be delivered of an illegitimate infant . . . Though when you think just how many courtiers went on progress with her, it becomes a little harder to envisage her as out of the public eye.

In the summer of 1561, one woman said she looked like one come from childbed, and the Spanish ambassador reported her as dropsical and 'swelling extraordinarily' – though she had been reported as dropsical and swelling on other occasions in her medical history (from February right through to July, in 1554), and though the ambassador also said she was 'extremely thin and the colour of a corpse'. Still, it all seems to fit together: the probable date of conception (in winter 1560/61, right after the Amy Dudley scandal, when marriage would have been impossible); the name Arthur, which figures in both the Tudor and the Dudley family tree. And of course, it would explain why the next year, when she thought she was dying, Elizabeth wanted Robert made Lord Protector of the country.

But the convenience of the timing starts to crumble when one looks at it more closely. In mid-June 1561, when Elizabeth was sharing a barge with that same Spanish ambassador, and joking that he might then and there perform a marriage ceremony, de Quadra clearly noticed nothing unusual about her shape. A cleverly cut disguising costume? Well – maybe. But it was high summer when the gentlewoman in Ipswich said that Elizabeth looked pale (not big!), as one come from childbed, and not until September that de Quadra wrote she had begun to swell; October when the full record of her movements resumes again. (It was that summer, too, when Elizabeth's kinswoman and putative heir Katherine Grey gave up the attempt to conceal her pregnancy, and was put in the Tower for her pains.)

All the nitpicking over dates, of course, is only to dodge the central great improbability. Do we really believe that someone as closely watched, as incessantly accompanied, as Elizabeth could have carried a pregnancy to term and given birth with no-one knowing? Do we really believe that her ladies and councillors, her chambermaids and doctors, were in on the act? And that no-one, ever, would have breathed a word about the most saleable secret of the century?

Doherty and Maxwell cite the case of the maid of honour Anne Vavasour, who in the early 1580s did conceal her condition until she gave birth in the maidens' chamber. But Anne would not have been watched as Elizabeth was watched – even assuming she were at court throughout her pregnancy. It's easy to hide when no-one is looking for you. Anne might, moreover, had had some help from fashions: a surviving portrait shows her in the long stomacher and huge wheel-shaped French farthingale that first appeared around 1570, though it did not become common wear for more than another decade.

The Tudor century had seen impostors as plausible and as widely accepted as Perkin Warbeck and Lambert Simnel. It had seen, too, such madwomen as Anne Burnell, who in this same year of 1587 announced in England that she was the daughter of Philip of Spain and that 'it might be Queen Mary was her mother', since she had a birthmark like the coat of arms of England 'upon the reynes of her back'. There had been other reports that Robert had children by Elizabeth: twice in 1560; in 1563, 1570 and 1575 – this last, by a Spanish ambassador, asserting that the two had a daughter. The putative daughter recurs in other reports – along, by the next century, with 'a Son bred in the State of Venice'. The daughter (said to be thirteen years old, by the end of 1575) was to be married, so Spanish agents reported, to Katherine Grey's son; and even the papacy briefly took this one seriously, suggesting war between England and Spain might thus be averted, spurred on thereto by the fact that Elizabeth's own ambassador was said himself to be leaking the story . . . Needless to say, no daughter ever appeared, but it is interesting to see just what games Elizabeth was prepared to play with her own reputation in the sacred causes of peace and policy.

The conjecture that Arthur Dudley may have been born during Elizabeth's dropsical episode of 1561 is not a new one. The Catholic historian Lingard hinted at it in the early nineteenth century. (Others have suggested 1562, when Elizabeth was ill of smallpox; but to deny that diagnosis is to forget the scars she – and Mary Sidney – afterwards bore.) The collection of documents described above is not new either; Englefield's letters, with Philip's endorsement and the report of 'BC', are all reprinted, for example, in Chamberlin's book of 1920, *The Private Character of Queen Elizabeth*. Paul Doherty has, however, unearthed one fascinating new piece of evidence: a Robert Southern living in Enfield, as Arthur described, whose will was indeed witnessed by a John Smyth. Of course, it hardly proves the rest of Arthur's story about his relation to Southern – especially as Southern's will lists bequests under the name of his children, and there is no Arthur among them. But the real existence of this obscure individual does at least suggest that the story was not one hundred per cent fabrication. It suggests, you might say, either that his story contained some elements of truth, or that he had been well briefed by somebody.

What it does not do is make me think that Elizabeth and Robert really did have a baby. In the end, I feel like the White Queen in *Alice*, asked to believe too many impossible things before breakfast. But you could follow all the facts that Doherty adduces, and yet find yourself on a different pathway.

Francis Englefield says not once, but twice, that he believes Elizabeth herself is aware of Arthur's claims. At the end of his first letter, Englefield writes:

> I think it very probable that the revelations that this lad is making everywhere may originate in the queen of England and her Council, and possibly with an object that Arthur himself does not yet understand. Perhaps, if they have determined to do away with the Scottish throne, they may encourage the lad to profess catholicism, and claim to be the queen's son, in order to discover the minds of other princes as to his pretensions, and the queen may thereupon acknowledge him, or give him such other position as to neighbouring princes may appear favourable. Of perhaps in some other way they may be making use of him for their iniquitous ends.

That is, he effectively suggests that Arthur, wittingly or not, is on an English mission.

In his last letter, Englefield adds:

> it is also manifest that he [Arthur] has had much conference with the Earl of Leicester, upon whom he mainly depends for the fulfillment of his hopes. This and other things convince me that the queen of England is not ignorant of his pretensions; although, perhaps, she would be unwilling that they should be thus published to the world.

Does it sound almost as though Englefield is being convinced by Arthur's story? If it does, then it is only briefly. He seems to have regarded Arthur ('this lad') with a certain sympathy – but not, surely, with the excitement that would greet what he believed to be a real Tudor heir, and living proof of Elizabeth's immorality. He continues: 'It is true his claims at present amount to nothing, but . . . it cannot be doubted that France and the English heretics, or some other party, might turn it to their advantage . . .' Spain above all feared an Anglo-French alliance, and it is for this reason that Arthur cannot be allowed to get away.

Englefield seems to be suggesting that 'Arthur Dudley' is a stooge: not of the Catholics, but of Elizabeth I – and, presumably, a government that included Robert Dudley. But it is equally possible (and again, this is not a new theory, having been mooted by Hume at the very beginning of the twentieth century) that he was not a stooge, but – as the usually shrewd Venetians always believed – nothing more nor less than a spy. Hume saw him as an operative caught out, presumably on a mission to report on Spain's preparations for warfare, and forced for self-preservation to disgorge a pre-planned cover story. But it is surely also possible that he had been sent on purpose to deliver this very tale.

If Englefield were right and 'Arthur Dudley' were in any sense an English agent or an English tool it would explain, heaven knows, why the Spanish decided to keep him close. It would explain (even better than his being a complete adventurer) why they never made any publicity capital out of his claim, even at a time when nothing would have been more useful than a universal condemnation of the Protestant Elizabeth's immorality. It would spare us the problem of trying to swallow the spectacle of an Elizabeth surrounded by 'Argos eyes' but yet managing to conceal a pregnancy and a delivery. It would also explain another improbability: the chance that supposedly just threw this man of all men – at this moment of all moments – into the hands of those who might receive his claim most favourably. That chance looks a little less implausible if Arthur were not a half-blood prince shipwrecked on the Spanish shore but a professional looking for an opportunity that could be seized – or staged. (We have, after all, no details of this so-convenient shipwreck.) And it would explain why 'Arthur Dudley' (who, if he didn't make his escape and resume his own identity, would surely have been executed by the Spanish) then fades out of the story.

The question that might be asked is this: what motive could the English have, in sending a fake heir to the Spanish court? The answer may be: plenty.* In 1587, Elizabeth and her government were trying everything in order, first, to learn what the Spanish plans were, and second, if possible, to trick, force or tempt Spain into postponing them at least for a year, until England could be ready.

The spring of 1587 saw Drake's famous raid on Cadiz, which did indeed set Spanish preparations back a year. In these months Walsingham also wrote a lengthy plan of action for gathering information on the Queen's foreign enemies. Agents were sent into Spain to pose as disaffected Englishmen. (One of Walsingham's memos to himself was to get a spy into the very Spanish court.) He was, moreover, at the same time conducting against the Spanish a war of propaganda and morale, feeding them disinformation wherever possible. Mendoza (the former Spanish ambassador now expelled from England) wrote to Philip of reports which, although they 'have some appearance of probability, they are really hatched by Walsingham's knavery'. From the Spanish side, Englefield himself had written of a war 'we must fight with paper and pens', as he laid out suggestions for an extended edition of *Leicester's Commonwealth*.

Neither King Philip nor the daughter to whom he planned to pass his claim showed any sign of wanting to occupy the English throne themselves. Philip's time in England as Mary's husband had shown him the difficulty; and one clause in the treaty of July 1587 whereby the papacy gave financial backing to the Armada

---

* I am assuming that if 'Arthur Dudley' was an agent, he was not Elizabeth's real son. It is, I suppose, theoretically possible that a baby born with Elizabeth's bloodline just happened to have also the qualities that make a successful agent – but there might surely be better uses for a real Arthur Dudley, and Elizabeth never squandered her resources. In an age before genetic testing, the most general resemblance – height, dark or red hair – would qualify an experienced, and expendable, professional for the role.

specifically allowed Philip to bestow the crown on whomsoever he wished. He wanted the restoration of the Catholic faith and an England under Spanish, rather than French, influence. A puppet pretender might have done him nicely, especially one as compliant as 'Arthur Dudley'. In the summer of 1587, at exactly this time, Elizabeth invited her young kinswoman and putative heir Arbella Stuart to court, suggesting that she might be married to a Spanish prince, and Anglo-Spanish relations secured that way. Or – so Arthur in his statement declared – 'they' might instead choose to marry her to Arthur Dudley.

One of Walsingham's chief tools in his disinformation campaign was Sir Edward Stafford. Whether he were really a traitor, or playing his own deep game, the English ambassador had long been passing information to the Spanish, taking money also from the Duke of Guise to show him England's diplomatic correspondence. It may well be he who features as 'the new friend' in Philip and Mendoza's letters. But Walsingham was well aware of whatever Stafford was doing, and used it as a conduit to feed the Spanish erroneous intelligence. (One of the letters of the Armada years shows Mendoza catching Stafford out in inaccuracy, and suggesting his news should be treated with some caution.) It was of course Stafford to whom 'Arthur Dudley' had made his initial abortive approach in France.

It had long been a tactic of Walsingham's to insert *agents provocateurs* into the prisons where Catholics were being held, or into the Catholic seminary at Douai. A pretender could trick the Spanish into showing him their hand (remember that offer of writing a book to 'whatever end' they considered desirable?). If they were persuaded even to accept him as real, then the English government could expose him at any convenient moment (which never came, since the Spanish didn't take the fly), dealing a devastating blow to their credibility. It sounds convoluted, but no more than other schemes Walsingham carried out in these years, and not just against the Scots queen Mary. That same year, 1587, it was probably he – desperate to jolt Elizabeth into action against the Catholic powers – who sent William Stafford (Edward's brother) on a fake attempt to assassinate the Queen, simply in order to convince her of her danger.*

Is 'BC''s letter a problem here? A slight one, maybe. It is a puzzling document. 'BC' starts out on this subject by telling Cecil the old news of Arthur's arrival and claim, adding that if only he himself had his 'alphabet' or cypher with him he would say more touching Arthur's 'lewd speeches'. None the less he assures Cecil that 'if I may I will do [Arthur] pleasure'. Gain his confidence – or help preserve his cover? 'BC' believes he may soon be called on by the Spanish to help establish or disprove Arthur's identity. His purposes are unclear; but unless he is just taking caution to extremes, it does sound as if he is unaware that Dudley may also be in Walsingham's pay. But again, this is far from conclusive evidence: the tangled chronicles of these espionage years show countless examples of agents operating in tandem, with a firewall between them; of agents set to spy on (double) agents. (Walsingham had one of his agents spying on Sir Edward Stafford in Paris, and another reporting back to him on Leicester's activities in the Netherlands.)

To bring the Arthur Dudley mystery back to the most basic terms: we do not know that Elizabeth slept with any man, still less that she ever had a baby. We do know that she and those around her used *agents provocateurs*; that the English were using black propaganda against the Spanish at this time. But this remains only the most speculative theory – one I raise, indeed, only as counterweight to that other claim, that Arthur really was the child of Elizabeth and Robert Dudley.

In the Afterword, I suggested that perhaps the simple fact of sex itself would not have changed everything about their relationship. The knowledge of so potentially explosive a secret as an unacknowledged son might, however, be a different story. It was, after all, a secret Robert could have held over Elizabeth's head,

* Doherty hints that Englefield, who was still allowed to collect his English revenues while in Spain, may himself have been a double agent; and of course there is a chance that Edward Stafford – who similarly never suffered any penalties for his treachery – was actually playing a triple, rather than a double, game. But perhaps this is taking paranoia a step too far.

since she was more vulnerable here than he. I tried to fit such knowledge into the dynamics of this relationship, as our explorations have revealed them, but this time the exercise failed. I no longer saw the relationship ring true.

That's the final reason why, at the end of the day, I don't believe the claims of 'Arthur Dudley'. In the world of fact, not fiction, I still believe that the 'Virgin Queen' was more than just mythology.

Afterword:

Some fictional treatments

WE ALL MAKE ELIZABETHS AFTER THE IMAGE OF OUR OWN AGE, AND find evidence for them, too. In the long history of writings on the Elizabethan era, our sense of the importance of the relationship between Elizabeth and Robert Dudley has ebbed and flowed, depending on how successive generations have chosen to see the Queen herself.

Leicester's near-contemporaries were on the whole hostile to his memory. No-one loves a lost favourite. By the later seventeenth century, however, Elizabeth's whole era was already beginning to look like a golden age, by contrast with the foibles of the Stuart monarchy. Indeed, Leicester and his queen alike could even be seen as epitomes of lost virtue. In the so-called 'Armada pack' of playing cards (a protest against the threat of James II's Catholicism), Leicester's portrait, clearly labelled, appeared as the King of Hearts. Besides being Elizabeth's lost love he had, after all, been a Protestant hero. It was, you might say, one of the first fictional versions of their story.

The latter half of the eighteenth century found a certain peripheral use for the relationship. The cult of female sensibility could accommodate Elizabeth in the character of victim, forced by a cruel fate to throw her chance of love away. The age found it harder to deal with her exercise of power – witness the juvenile

History of Jane Austen, who infinitely preferred the romantic Queen of Scots. Schiller's 1800 play *Mary Stuart* (recently revived in the West End) had Leicester, a weak if well-meaning man tormented by his own inadequacies, in thrall to a dominant Elizabeth, but yearning for an emotionally powerful Mary.

The Victorians – while relishing the brave and beruffed ruler as an icon of empire – were troubled by the whole question of Elizabeth's sexuality (so different from the home life of their own dear queen!). In so far as she had chosen to present herself as an eternal virgin, she was unwomanly; if on the other hand she were in any way sexual without the marriage tie ... 'when the character of a lady is at issue, to doubt is to condemn', as *Fraser's Magazine* put it memorably. (Elizabeth, wrote Jacob Abbott in 1849, in what he clearly considered the ultimate put-down, 'would not have been a desirable wife for any of us'.) The influence of Sir Walter Scott's *Kenilworth* in 1821 was slow to die away – *Kenilworth*, which conflates the stories of Amy Dudley's death, of the 1575 visit and of Leicester's subsequent secret marriage. The novel casts him as a murderer who repents too late; though Elizabeth, more forgivingly, is seen as the ruler who had already decided to choose her sovereignty over her suitor when the assassin crept up on Amy. Scott had himself disclaimed any historical veracity – but as the Reverend Canon J. E. Jackson pointed out more than half a century later in his influential article for *The Wiltshire Archeological and Natural History Magazine*, for every person who read the scholarly refutations, there were many more who knew only the novel, and more again who had seen the subsequent melodrama, complete with hissing villains, at the Covent Garden Theatre. Scott's book had even (so the canon reported with incredulity) got an early version of a film adaptation – been 'repeated at the Polytechnic, in Dissolving views!'

Thomas Hardy wrote that 'No historian's Queen Elizabeth was ever so perfectly a woman as the fictitious Elizabeth of *Kenilworth*.' And in the beginning of the twentieth century, the real Elizabeth's 'unwomanly' qualities were again used against her when Kipling, in his eerie fantasia of 1910, *Puck of Pook's Hill*, saw the rejected Leicester as a ghost levelling reproaches at Elizabeth:

> The Queen was in her chamber, a-weeping very sore,
> There came Lord Leicester's spirit and it scratched upon the door,
> Singing, 'Backwards and forwards and sideways may you pass
> But I will walk beside you till you face the looking-glass
> The cruel looking-glass that will never show a lass,
> As hard and unforgiving or as wicked as you was!'
>
> The Queen was in her chamber; her sins were on her head;
> She looked the spirits up and down and statelily she said: –
> 'Backwards and forwards and sideways though I've been,
> Yet I am Harry's daughter and I am England's Queen!'

Just eighteen years later, the story took a new twist. Lytton Strachey in his psychobiography *Elizabeth and Essex* (not, obviously, a fictional presentation; but well within the sphere of creative writing) reinvents Elizabeth yet again as 'a post-Freudian hysteric . . . not quite fully heterosexual'. The words are those of the authors of *England's Elizabeth: An Afterlife in Fame and Fantasy*, and it is hard to disagree. As Strachey wrote of Essex's downfall (and Essex was Leicester's stepson, successor and surrogate): 'Manhood – the fascinating, detestable entity, which had first come upon her concealed in yellow magnificence in her father's lap – manhood was overthrown at last, and in the person of the traitor it should be rooted out.'

This interpretation has never (to date!) quite gone away. Certainly it stuck around long enough to influence the Bette Davis/Errol Flynn movie, *The Private Lives of Elizabeth and Essex*. But by the middle of the twentieth century the tale of Elizabeth and Essex, that intrinsically abortive relationship, was once again out of fashion, and Leicester came back to the foreground for the first time in more than a century. The purview of 'the woman's film and the woman's novel' (as *England's Elizabeth* puts it) relied on Leicester to exhibit an Elizabeth who 'despite her public chastity . . . had been quiveringly alive with bona-fide reproductive heterosexuality'.

You can see this reliance in many of the pictures of Elizabeth still around us; on the screen, on the bookshelves, or in our memory. In the middle of the last century there were (among many other lesser luminaries) the novels of Margaret Irwin and Jean Plaidy. In Irwin's trilogy – *Young Bess, Elizabeth, Captive Princess* and *Elizabeth and the Prince of Spain* – Robin is the romantic lead to whom Elizabeth is several times on the point of yielding until abruptly prevented; as much by the demons in her psyche as by any outside agency. Irwin's edgy, haunted, intelligent Elizabeth, treading the knife-edge between heroism and hysteria, long remained a staple of the public libraries, and indeed might still convince today. (It seems an anomaly that her works are long out of print, while those of Jean Plaidy – like the far less considerable *Gay Lord Robert* – are back in the shops.) Certainly nothing in them seemed to jar when I read them as a young teenager, as late as the 1970s. This was an Elizabeth who gave first place to her own powers, her own priorities.

In the same decade, the BBC's great *Elizabeth R* copped out, a little, from this particular dilemma. Glenda Jackson's Elizabeth was in love with Robert; was prepared, even (in the second play of the series, written by Rosemary Anne Sisson), to promise a secret marriage ceremony. But she arrived too late for the date; he had not waited long enough . . . It was a fictional reprise of the London Bridge story told on page 196).

In the last decades of the twentieth century, an alternative portrayal of Elizabeth as a career woman's role model tended to downplay her personal relationships, to see them as just one weapon in the armoury of a woman who had it all, and at a price many of us might be prepared to pay. Books on the management secrets of Elizabeth I, and 'Elizabeth CEO', compete with feminist academic study.* But of course the more romantic portrayal has never gone away; indeed, it has had some important outings

---

* In the mid-1980s, copies of Neale's 1930s biography of Elizabeth circulated among Tory MPs. Among the marked passages were some felt particularly appropriate to the favour Margaret Thatcher showed towards, for example, Cecil Parkinson and Jeffrey Archer. Which presumably means that *Blackadder II*, first screened in 1985, should rank as political satire . . .

recently. In print, the most familiar example is probably Philippa Gregory's *The Virgin's Lover* (with *The Queen's Fool*), which follows the relationship through the death of Amy Dudley. Gregory's Elizabeth – while manipulative enough to take a tacit part in Amy's murder, as a way to make sure she could enjoy Robert without ever having to marry him – is essentially the foolishly passionate creature, guided by a wiser Cecil, painted by the great historian Froude in the nineteenth century. No question here but that she and Robert go all the way . . . but to assume that all fictional interpretations now choose to believe Elizabeth no virgin is still a jump too far.

It's true that Shekhar Kapur's feature film *Elizabeth*, starring Cate Blanchett and Joseph Fiennes, at the very least suggested plenty of bona fide sexuality. The sequel *Elizabeth: The Golden Age*, though set in the run-up to the Armada, will not feature a Robert or indeed a Cecil. But the personal drama of the Elizabeth/Ralegh/Bess Throckmorton story acted out here surely borrows from the emotional dynamic of the Elizabeth/Robert/Lettice story. In the first film, Elizabeth moved away from Robert, assuming the white mask of an iconic virginity at the end of the movie. Perhaps this second film, by contrast, portrays a lover figure who (as Leicester did) ultimately moves away from Elizabeth to choose a less challenging model of humanity.

Of the two recent British television dramas, the Channel Four version starring Helen Mirren and Jeremy Irons was set towards the end of Robert's life, when not even their worst enemy seriously believed that these two were still the last of the red-hot lovers. (A doctor who had just given Elizabeth the near-obligatory gynaecological examination did mutter 'virgo intacta' to Cecil at the very start of the programme.) The BBC's longer but in some ways less considerable *The Virgin Queen* [*sic*] did indeed have to tackle the question of the relationship more directly – but cheated, you might say. Twice, we saw a red-headed woman writhing in Robert Dudley's arms. Once it was indeed Elizabeth – but only in a dream, from which she abruptly awoke. Once, it proved to be another woman in her dress: the Queen's cousin Lettice Knollys, the one Robert married, eventually. The substitute lover in the

Queen's dress had of course already been seen in *Elizabeth*; and indeed a number of dramas, filmed and written, have chosen to play the sex life of one of Elizabeth's ladies as a kind of surrogate for her own . . . Striking how the same devices do come round with regularity. Quite a number of fictional stories bring Lettice into the tale rather earlier than is justified by history. The surrogate theme is a neat way for the reader or viewer to experience what they want without compromising the notion of Elizabeth's virginity . . . It is interesting to see that all the actors interviewed for either of the two recent dramas declared their belief in that virginity, incidentally – rather like the ambassadors of the sixteenth century! There are sometimes surprising similarities to be found between modern attitudes and those of Elizabeth's own day.

But as we discuss the precise nature of Elizabeth's relationship with Robert Dudley – as we edge around the precise limits, in fact or fiction, to their physical intimacy – perhaps we are missing the real, the final point. Just assume, for a moment, that uncontrovertible evidence were to be discovered, showing that Elizabeth had full sex with Robert. How much difference would it make, really? We are, after all, the first generation of historians to be able to ask the question – *not* to feel that if Elizabeth were guilty of 'immorality', she would be less worthy to rule her country.

Knowledge that Robert and Elizabeth had full (rather than partial) physical relations would, it is true, offer a new prism through which to consider every aspect of their dealings. But try to do it, just as an exercise, and you still, in even sharper focus, see an Elizabeth notable for her refusal to commit. You still see a Robert who (long keeping a secret he could have used to become the power behind the throne) was notable for his loyalty.

When Martin Hume, in 1896, wrote the first version of his classic *Courtships of Queen Elizabeth*, he was (he said, introducing the extended version eight years later) staggered by the number of letters he received, most of them making a particular plea. Correspondents from around the world lamented that 'the actual relations that existed between the Queen and various favourites' had not been dealt with more thoroughly. 'As a political historian,' Hume wrote, 'I must confess that this phase of the subject did not appear to me to be one of any great importance.' His job was to tackle 'the national results' of Elizabeth's various courtships, while 'a study of the non-political philanderings' seemed to him a very minor matter. At the safe distance of a century, perhaps one might venture to disagree.

Starting from a different standpoint, I too none the less set out with a curious reluctance to write on the subject of Elizabeth and Robert Dudley. It's not a question of the historical high ground, to which I can hardly stake a claim – but there is surely a kind of shame in seeming to reduce Elizabeth I to a romantic story. To approach a great stateswoman primarily through her love life seems at first distinctly retrograde.

Writing this book showed me I was wrong. The Arthur Dudley story described in Appendix II is just one of many episodes capable of either a personal or a political interpretation, neither to be assessed without some awareness of the other. Elizabeth's statecraft and her sexuality were inextricably intertwined. (Perhaps it is that very unusual fact that makes her so interesting to us today.) That 'the personal is political' was a slogan of modern feminism. But one thing I've learnt is this – it was just as applicable in the court of England in the late sixteenth century.

Notes on sources

General

The last quarter-century alone has seen an impressive list of biographies of Elizabeth, notably those by (in alphabetical order) Carolly Erickson (*The First Elizabeth*, Macmillan, 1983), Christopher Hibbert (*The Virgin Queen: The Personal History of Elizabeth I*, Viking, 1990; Wallace MacCaffrey (*Elizabeth I*, Edward Arnold, 1993), Maria Perry (*The Word of a Prince: A Life from Contemporary Documents*, The Folio Society, 1990), Jasper Ridley (*Elizabeth I*, Constable, 1987), Anne Somerset (*Elizabeth I*, Weidenfeld & Nicolson, 1991) and Alison Weir (*Elizabeth the Queen*, Jonathan Cape, 1998; following on from *Children of England: The Heirs of King Henry VIII*, 1996, and *The Six Wives of Henry VIII*, 1991).

Of the recent more academic studies, I was especially interested by the work of Susan Doran (*Monarchy and Matrimony*, Routledge, 1996), Carole Levin (*The Heart and Stomach of a King*, University of Pennsylvania Press, 1994), and Julie M. Walker, ed. (*Dissing Elizabeth: Negative Representations of Gloriana*, Duke University Press, 1998).

Among the older biographers of Elizabeth, first place now and always must go to Agnes Strickland, whose *Lives of the Queens of England* (vols 7 and 8, London, 1844) is an invaluable guide back to original sources (even though she does occasionally cite the late-seventeenth-century chronicler Gregorio Leti, some of whose most succulent 'finds' appear to have begun and ended in his own imagination). The works of Frank Arthur Mumby are useful in that his 'lives in letters' reprint much original correspondence in full. See *The Girlhood of Queen Elizabeth* (1909); *Elizabeth and Mary Stuart* (1914); *The Fall of Mary Stuart* (1922), all published by Constable. *Queen Elizabeth and Her Times,* edited by Thomas Wright in 1838, is likewise a collection of contemporary correspondence.

No-one can ignore the biography by J. E. Neale (*Queen Elizabeth*, Jonathan Cape, 1934); or that of Elizabeth Jenkins (*Elizabeth the Great*, Victor Gollancz, 1958) – who, of course, is also the author of *Elizabeth and Leicester* (Victor Gollancz, 1961). Earlier books on the pair include those of Milton Waldman (*Elizabeth and Leicester*, Collins, 1944) and Frederick Chamberlin (*Elizabeth and Leycester*, Dodd, Mead & Co., 1939), whose *The Private Character of Queen Elizabeth* (John Lane, 1920) includes such invaluable oddities as the collection together of all Elizabeth's medical records, and of all the ambassadorial statements concerning the existence or otherwise of her sexual relations; while his *The Sayings of Queen Elizabeth* (John Lane, 1923) groups together her most famous and/or revealing remarks. Perhaps it is here, too, that one should mention Martin Hume's classic *The Courtships of Queen Elizabeth* (extended edition, Eveleigh Nash, 1904), and Josephine Ross's *Suitors to the Queen* (Weidenfeld & Nicolson, 1975).

Three biographies of Robert Dudley appeared in less than a decade: Alan Kendall's *Robert Dudley, Earl of Leicester* (Cassell, 1980); Alan Haynes's *The White Bear: Robert Dudley, the Elizabethan Earl of Leicester* (Peter Owen, 1987); and Derek Wilson's important *Sweet Robin: A Biography of Robert Dudley Earl of Leicester 1553–1558* (Allison & Busby, 1988). Anyone writing on Leicester now must acknowledge a particular debt to Wilson's work, not only in *Sweet Robin* but in *The Uncrowned Kings of England: The Black Legend of the Dudleys* (Constable, 2005). The study of Robert – unlike that of Elizabeth herself, but with obvious ramifications for their relationship – is still one where new material may be explored; the other immense debt one must acknowledge here is to Simon Adams, whose *Leicester and the Court: Essays on Elizabethan Politics* was published by Manchester University Press in 2002; his edition of the *Household Accounts and Disbursement Books of Robert Dudley, Earl of Leicester, 1558–1561, 1584–1586* was published by Cambridge University Press (for the Royal Historical Society) in 1995. See also Adams's articles: 'The Papers of Robert Dudley, Earl of Leicester', in *Archives*, xx (1992), 63–85; xx (1993), 131–44; xxii (1996), 1–26.

A selection of Elizabeth's own letters, and a collection of her speeches, prayers and poems were recently gathered together into an authoritative and comprehensively annotated volume (superseding the older collection edited by G. B. Harrison in 1935): *Elizabeth I: Collected*

Works, ed. Leah S. Marcus, Janel Mueller and Mary Beth Rose (University of Chicago Press, 2000). The poem quoted by way of epigraph can be found on pp. 303–5, with a discussion of the attribution to Elizabeth. The letters selected include those Elizabeth wrote to Alençon; her teasing letters to the Shrewsburys about Leicester's diet; and of course her letters to Leicester and others concerning his acceptance of the governorship of the Netherlands. In this volume can also be found some other relevant documents from the collections of state papers – for example, Parliament's pleas to Elizabeth to marry (as well as her responses to those pleas) and Cecil's letter urging her to the Alençon match; also the most important correspondence on the Thomas Seymour affair.

State and official papers

As always, the HMSO *Calendars* are an essential source; we today are all indebted to those tireless Victorians (and neo-Victorians) who docketed and in some cases transcribed the collections of manuscripts that are the building blocks for any attempt at Tudor history.

Several volumes of the *Calendar of State Papers, Domestic Series*, ed. Robert Lemon and M. A. E. Green, 1856–72, hereafter abbreviated to *CSP Dom.*, contain letters to, from and about Elizabeth and Leicester. (See also *Miscellaneous State Papers from 1500 to 1726*, ed. the Earl of Hardwicke, London, 1778, which has, for example, in vol. I interesting correspondence from Mary to Norfolk, and Walsingham to Stafford.)

CSP Dom. 1547–1580: This and the following volume are often frustrating, in giving abstracts of or extracts from letters, rather than the whole thing. Among the multitude of more political documents, however, are several letters from Robert either to or about Elizabeth (see e.g. pp. 448, 503).

CSP Dom. 1581–1590: This volume includes on p. 116 a memo of a letter from Robert to the Queen suggesting that he was indeed behind the Bond of Association; on p. 265 his letter to Walsingham about the 'very pitiful words' she used to keep him back from the Netherlands; on p. 276 his plea (after returning from there) that she should pity his 'wretched and depressed estate'; on p. 514 his letter inviting her to Tilbury; and on p. 538 his last letter.

The two volumes labelled 'Addenda' are more satisfying, as usually containing complete letters. *CSP Dom. Addenda 1566–79* includes Leicester's despairing letter to Throckmorton (pp. 28–9) and the letters from Kenilworth in the winter of 1569–70 (pp. 575, 198–9); for others of his letters to the Queen in this period, see pp. 231–2, 339–40, 360, 361. There is also a good deal of material about the Norfolk affair. In *CSP Dom. Addenda 1580–1625*, see pp. 95–6 for Leicester's 'goodness of God' letter to Elizabeth; also pp. 99, 141.

Letters to and from English emissaries abroad are to be found in the *Calendar of State Papers, Foreign Series*, ed. Joseph Stevenson et al., 1863–1950. For example, the volume that covers 1558–59 includes, on the first page, Cecil's memorandum about sending out the news of Elizabeth's accession; the next (1560–61, from p. 347 on) contains the letters Throckmorton in Paris wrote after Amy Dudley's death.

Letters exchanged with Ireland, however, get their own series of volumes – as (more importantly in this particular context) do those with Scotland. The *Calendar of State Papers Relating to Scotland and Mary Queen of Scots, 1547–1603*, ed. Joseph Bain et al., Edinburgh, 1898–1952 (CSP Scottish), contains in the second volume (1563–69) much correspondence concerning Elizabeth's attempt to marry Robert to Mary, and in the fourth (pp. 32–40) Norfolk's confession.

The reports home of the Spanish ambassadors are an invaluable source on this relationship – especially the letters of Feria and de Quadra on Elizabeth's early relationship with Robert and the Amy Dudley affair. See the *Calendar of Letters and State Papers relating to English Affairs, preserved principally in the Archives of Simancas*, ed. M. A. S. Hume et al., 1892–99 (*CPS Spanish*). The all-important letter about Amy's death is on pp. 174–6 of vol. I (*but* see the proviso under Chapter 6 below); that on Elizabeth's near-fatal smallpox attack on pp. 262–4 of the same volume. The scene in which Elizabeth promised to marry the Duke of Alençon is pp. 226–8 of vol. III; Englefield's correspondence on the Arthur Dudley affair is in vol. IV, pp. 101–12.

The other ambassadorial calendar of especial relevance is perhaps that of the Venetians (*Calendar of Letters and State Papers relating to English Affairs, preserved in the Archives of Venice and in the other Libraries of Northern Italy*, ed. Rawdon Brown et al., 1864–98) – though Venice did not keep an envoy at Elizabeth's court for much of her reign. Other vital ambassadorial sources are the *Correspondance Diplomatique de Bertrand de Salignac de la Mothe Fénelon* (London and Paris, 1838); particularly the first volume, pp. 233–7, for his account of the famous scene where Leicester and Norfolk challenged Cecil; also vol. II, p. 112, on the aftermath of the St Bartholomew's Day Massacre.

The important letters of the envoy of the Holy Roman Emperor in the first years of Elizabeth's reign are reproduced in *Queen Elizabeth and Some Foreigners*, ed. Victor von Klarwill, trans. Prof. T. H. Nash (John Lane, 1927).

Private papers

The following are some of the most relevant for Elizabeth and Leicester of the 'calendars' of private collections of papers commissioned by the Historic Manuscripts Commission.

Calendar of the Manuscripts of the Most Honourable the Marquess of Bath Preserved at Longleat, Wiltshire, vol. V, *Talbot, Dudley and Devereux Papers 1533–1659*, ed. G. Dyfnallt Owen, HMSO, 1990. The Talbot Papers contain some relevant material (running in tandem, you might say, with that which appears in Lodge; see notes for Chapter 13 below); as do the Devereux Papers. But the real point, here, is some ninety pages of transcripts of Robert Dudley's own papers: inventories of the contents of his properties; letters of business addressed to him about everything from the manipulation of the patronage networks to the mulcting of estates; from the total of his debts at his death to the excellence of his dogs. Tyndall's statement as to Leicester's marriage with Lettice is on pp. 205–6; Hatton's letters about the Queen's dream of a marriage on p. 197.

Calendar of Manuscripts of the Most Honourable the Marquess of Salisbury, Preserved at Hatfield House (published in the 1880s). This huge collection of the papers in William Cecil's possession – the cogs that made the wheels that ran the Elizabethan state – includes, for example: in vol. I, a good deal about the Norfolk affair; in vol. II, letters written by Simier and Anjou/Alençon to Elizabeth; in vol. III, materials on the execution of Mary and on Netherlands affairs. However, perhaps its real point, in this particular context, is that it serves to show just how large a part Robert Dudley played in greasing those wheels – just how many, and how varied, bits of business involved him.

For some particularly interesting documents, readers of this *Calendar* will sometimes find themselves referred back to 'Murdin', i.e. to *A collection of State Papers relating to affairs from the years 1542–1570 left by William Cecil Lord Burghley*, ed. William Murdin, 1759. Other sources refer one back to 'Haynes', i.e. to the collection under the same title edited by Samuel Haynes in 1740, which includes, for example, on pp. 361–2 Robert's letter to Cecil after Amy's death, on p. 444 one version of Cecil's memo about Robert's unsuitability as a husband as compared to the archduke, and (pp. 52ff.) a great deal of self-exculpatory correspondence from the accused Norfolk.

Report on the Manuscripts of Lord de L'Isle and Dudley preserved at Penshurst Place, ed. C. L. Kingsford and William A. Shaw, 1925–36. Vol. II includes the inventory of the contents of Kenilworth. These Sidney papers, however, are chiefly notable for what light they can throw on Lettice, her later relations with Robert Sidney, and (vol. III, pp. 142–7) her efforts to overthrow the claims of the younger Robert Dudley.

Report on the Pepys Manuscripts preserved at Magdalene College, Cambridge (1911). The first 175 pages of the volume are very largely concerned with Leicester and his affairs: letters to Leicester from Throckmorton and from Mary, Queen of Scots; a letter (pp. 178–9) concerning that plan to use cats and dogs in the Kenilworth fireworks; and (p. 180) one to Christopher Blount ('Mr Kytt'). Only a note (p. 3) is made of the Blount letters of 1560, since these are reproduced elsewhere (see notes for Chapter 6, below); however, Blount's evidence in the Appleyard inquiry is given on pp. 111–13.

Some contemporary chroniclers

Camden, William (1551–1623): antiquary and headmaster of Westminster School, whose *Annales rerum Anglicarum et Hibernicarum regnante Elizabetha*, the first part of which was published in 1615, provides one of the chief sources for contemporary opinion on Elizabeth's reign (albeit always in the knowledge that, since Camden wrote in Latin, the English quotes with which we are familiar were penned by other hands).

Clapham, John (1566–1619): author of *Elizabeth of England*; a historian and poet who (like Camden and Naunton – like so many of those who formed our image of the age!) was at one time a protégé of the Cecil family.

Foxe, John (1516–87): Protestant martyrologist whose *Actes and Monuments*, more popularly known as the *Book of Martyrs*, was first printed in English in 1563. Appended to it was a tract from which come many of the old tales about Elizabeth's time in the Tower: *The Miraculous Preservation of the Lady Elizabeth, now Queen of England*.

Harington, Sir John (1560–1612): Elizabeth's 'witty godson', whose letters and personal writings (as distinct from his satires and treatises) were collected together as *Nugae Antiquae* in the late eighteenth century.

Hayward, Sir John (?1564–1627): author of *Annals of the First Four Years of the Reign of Queen Elizabeth*; also *The Life and Raign of King Edward VI*. Hayward was later imprisoned by Elizabeth for his support for Essex's rebellion.

Holinshed, Raphael (d. 1580?): historian famous for his *Chronicles*, a collection of pieces – some by other hands – which in some editions include, for example, Richard Mulcaster's description of Elizabeth's passage through the City on the day before her coronation, and which continued to be revised by others after his death.

Naunton, Sir Robert (1553–1635): staunchly Protestant professional courtier who eventually rose to high office under James. *Fragmenta Regalia, or Observations on Queen Elizabeth her Times and Favorites*, published posthumously in 1641, was probably intended to provide an example to the Stuart monarchy.

Speed, John (1552?–1629): most widely remembered now as a cartographer, Speed was also a member of the Society of Antiquaries and author (with help from Camden et al.) of *The History of Great Britain . . . with the Successions, Lives, Acts and Issues of the English Monarchs from Julius Caesar to . . . King James*, published in 1611.

Stow, John (1525–1605): London chronicler and antiquary patronized by Leicester. His *Chronicles* [in later editions, *Annales*] *of England* were published in 1580.

Other works particularly relevant for individual chapters

Chapter 1

The comparison of Tudors and Dudley to a tree and the ivy that twines around it comes from David Starkey's *Elizabeth: Apprenticeship* (Chatto & Windus, 2000). Of course, anyone writing today on Elizabeth's youth – a subject he revitalized – is indebted to Starkey for a great deal more than that. Apart from anything else, it was he who pricked the balloon of myth concerning the different sources on Elizabeth's accession day. To the classic popular studies on the reign of Henry VIII (Alison Weir's and Antonia Fraser's; and of course Starkey's own *Six Wives*, Chatto & Windus, 2003) one should add two biographies of Anne Boleyn: Eric Ives's *The Life and Death of Anne Boleyn* (Blackwell, 2004) and Retha M. Warnicke's revisionist work *The Rise and Fall of Anne Boleyn* (Cambridge University Press, 1989).

Besides the works of Derek Wilson, noted above, further information on the background of Robert's family can be found in the recent *The Sidneys of Penshurst and the Monarchy, 1500–1700* by Michael G. Brennan (Ashgate, 2006). I am grateful to Robin Harcourt Williams of Hatfield House for his help on 'the oak story'.

Chapter 2

For the theory that Henry had Cushing's Syndrome, see *The Last Days of Henry VIII: Conspiracies, Treason and Heresy at the Court of the Dying Tyrant* by Robert Hutchinson (Weidenfeld & Nicolson, 2005).

For the Dudley connection with Prince Edward, see the 'biographical memoirs' in the *Literary Remains of Edward VI*, vol. I, ed. J. G. Nichols, Roxburghe Club, 1823.

The Queen's Conjuror: The Life and Magic of Dr Dee is by Benjamin Woolley (HarperCollins, 2001).

Chapter 3

For the new trends in thinking about Edward's reign I found particularly helpful Stephen Alford's *Kingship and Polity in the Reign of Edward VI* (Cambridge University Press, 2002), and *Intrigue and Treason: The Tudor Court, 1547–1558* by David Loades (Longman, 2004). For John Dudley's role in particular, see Loades, *John Dudley, Duke of*

Northumberland, 1504–1553 (Oxford University Press, 1996), especially pp. vii–viii for the growth of the 'bad duke' bogey; also B. L. Beer, *Northumberland: The Political Career of John Dudley* (Kent State University Press, 1973).

Starkey's interpretation of the Seymour affair quoted is found on pp. 76–7 of *Elizabeth*; see also Sheila Cavanagh's article in Walker's *Dissing Elizabeth*.

Chapter 4

Robert's poem (from the Arundel Harington MS) is reprinted as an appendix in Haynes's *The White Bear*.

Simon Adams's work on Robert's early adulthood has corrected some important errors, notably the assumption that he was living wholly retired in the country – and thus presumably out of touch with affairs – for the last years of Mary's reign: see *Leicester and the Court*, p. 160. By the same token David Starkey has done much to redraw the picture of an Elizabeth living simply retired. An analysis of Dee's role under the Marian regime is to be found in Benjamin Woolley's *The Queen's Conjuror*.

Chapter 5

The *Collected Works* (pp. 53–5 and notes) not only gives accounts of but discusses the sources for different accounts of Elizabeth's coronation. Susan Frye's *The Competition for Representation* (Oxford University Press, 1993) is particularly interesting on the coding of the festivities. On the likelihood of dissolving a marriage, see Lawrence Stone's *The Road to Divorce* (Oxford University Press, 1990), pp. 301–5.

Chapter 6

The most recent analyses of Amy's own letters, and her whereabouts, are to be found in Adams, *Leicester and the Court*, p. 150n, and Appendix I to the *Disbursement Books*.

I am indebted to Faith Marshall-Harris for her opinion, as a coroner, on the evidence as to Amy's death. On the theory that breast cancer could have caused it, see I. Aird, 'The Death of Amy Robsart', *English Historical Review*, lxxi (1956), pp. 69–79.

The Victorian period was the great age of writing on Amy Dudley.

George Adlard, whose *Amye Robsart and the Earl of Leicester* was printed in London in 1870, gives the Blount correspondence in full; the originals are in the Pepys Library in Magdalene College, Cambridge. Walter Rye's *The Murder of Amy Robsart: A Brief for the Prosecution* (Norfolk, 1885) reprints, by way of appendices, the documents on Appleyard's accusation. Among the substantial body of other writings, I found particularly helpful the article by Canon J. E. Jackson, 'Amye Robsart', *Wilts. Archeological Magazine*, xvii, 1898.

I do have, however, in sourcing this chapter to add a big 'NB'. The conventional – the invaluable! – source for the quotations from foreign ambassadors is the relevant *Calendar*. The version of the all-important letter from de Quadra I have used comes not from the *CSP Spanish*, however, but from the twelve-volume *History of England from the Fall of Wolsey to the Defeat of the Armada* published by James Anthony Froude between 1856 and 1870.

No-one with the faintest sympathy or respect for Robert Dudley can take very much from Froude's commentary. However, Froude did his own research in the archives at Simancas (writing evocatively of how he often found grains of sand still glittering on the pages – sand scattered when the letters were written, and untouched until that day), and his translation sometimes varies significantly from Hume's in the *Calendar*. One phrase in particular (*'se ha hecho senor de los negocias y de la persona de la Reyna'* – 'had made himself master of the business of the state, and of the person of the Queen') is hardly recognizable in the *Calendar* version.

To replace all quotations from the *Calendar* with the equivalents from Froude is not an option: he himself quotes only as and when he chooses. I am aware, moreover, that errors have been detected in his work: he made his own transcriptions, and worked at great speed. (Mind you, no less a person than J. E. Neale, in the article on Stafford cited under Chapter 14 below, pointed out that Hume in the *Calendar* could also be challenged; at least that his footnotes frequently make identifications 'with a certainty that others cannot share'.) None the less, in this and the following two chapters (Chapters 6–8, after which the Spanish reports become less crucial for a time), the quotations I use are taken from his book: see esp. pp. 277–81. I prefer Froude's version on aesthetic grounds if no other: they read far more naturally, to me.

Wherever possible I have also referred back to the *Colección de Documentos Inéditos para la historia de España*, better known as *Codoín*, vols 87 and 89; however, these too are often frustrating, with some of the most relevant letters absent. De Quadra's letter of 11 September 1560, for example, appears not in *Codoín*, but in *Relations Politiques des Pays-Bas et de l'Angleterre sous la règne de Philippe II*, ed. M. Kervyn de Lettenhove (Brussels, 1883), vol. 2, pp. 529–33. I am indebted to Daniel Hahn for his help in reading it.

Chapter 7

On favourites in general, see Ronald G. Asch and Adolf M. Birke, eds, *Princes, Patronage and the Nobility: the Court at the Beginning of the Modern Age* c.*1450–1600* (Oxford University Press, 1991); Simon Adams, 'Favourites and Factions', in John Guy, ed., *The Tudor Monarchy* (Arnold, 1997); also J. H. Elliott and Laurence Brockliss, eds, *The World of the Favourite*, c.*1550–1675* (Yale University Press, 1999). My picture of the relationship between other rulers and their favourites is drawn particularly from *Prince of Princes: The Life of Potemkin* by Simon Sebag Montefiore (Weidenfeld & Nicolson, 2000); also Virginia Rounding's *Catherine the Great: Love, Sex and Power* (Hutchinson, 2006); Ophelia Field's *The Favourite: Sarah Duchess of Marlborough* (Hodder & Stoughton, 2002); and Maureen Waller's *Ungrateful Daughters: The Stuart Princesses Who Stole their Father's Crown* (Hodder & Stoughton, 2002). See also Stella Tillyard, *A Royal Affair: George III and his Troublesome Siblings* (Chatto & Windus, 2006), for Caroline Mathilde's relationship with Johann Struensee.

On ideas of monarchy, see John Guy's essay on Tudor monarchy and its critiques in the anthology he edited, cited above. See also several other essays in the same volume: David Starkey, 'Representation through Intimacy'; Patrick Collinson, 'The Monarchical Republic of Elizabeth I'; Stephen Alford, 'Reassessing William Cecil in the 1560s'.

On Elizabeth's relationships, see Susan Doran's article, 'Why Did Elizabeth Not Marry?', in Walker, ed., *Dissing Elizabeth*; her own *Monarchy and Matrimony* is a fuller exploration of the practical difficulties that beset any choice of husband Elizabeth might make, and of Doran's belief that, had her advisers all united to promote any one suitor, Elizabeth might have ceased to resist. See also Alan Haynes, *Sex in Elizabethan England* (Sutton, 1997), and Anne Laurence, *Women in England 1500–1760* (Weidenfeld & Nicolson, 1994). For contemporary opinions as to the nature of Elizabeth's sexual relationships with Robert and others, see Chamberlin, *Private Character*, pp. 276–81.

For courtly love, see C. S. Lewis, *The Allegory of Love: A Study in*

Medieval Tradition (Oxford University Press, 1936) and Friedrich Heer, *The Medieval World* (Weidenfeld & Nicolson, 1962); also the more recent works by Roger Boase, *The Origin and Meaning of Courtly Love* (Manchester University Press, 1977), and Bernard O'Donoughue, *The Courtly Love Tradition* (Manchester University Press, 1982).

For references on the Arthur Dudley story, see the section below on Chapter 19, Afterword and Appendices.

Chapter 8

There has obviously accrued an enormous literature on Mary Queen of Scots. Notable recent additions, however, are: Jane Dunn's *Elizabeth and Mary: Cousins, Rivals, Queens* (HarperCollins, 2003); John Guy's *My Heart is My Own: The Life of Mary Queen of Scots* (Fourth Estate, 2004); Alison Weir's *Mary Queen of Scots and the Murder of Lord Darnley* (Jonathan Cape, 2003).

The *Memoirs* of Sir James Melville of Halhill were reprinted by the Folio Society in 1969.

Chapter 9

For sources for this chapter, see the *Calendars* noted under 'General' above, especially *CSP Scottish*. For Norfolk himself, see Neville Williams's *Thomas Howard, Fourth Duke of Norfolk* (Barrie & Rockliff, 1964); also the sections on the Howards in David Starkey, ed., *Rivals in Power: Lives and Letters of the Great Tudor Dynasties* (Macmillan, 1990).

Chapter 10

Neville Williams's *All the Queen's Men* (Weidenfeld & Nicolson, 1972) has a lucid and readable reprise of the conventional story as to the events of 1569. For more recent thinking see G. Parker's article, 'The Place of Tudor England in the Messianic Vision of Philip II of Spain', *Transactions of the Royal Historical Society*, 6th series, xii (2002) – to which my attention was first drawn by John Guy's picture of the Ridolfi plot in his biography of Mary. To this I would add *CSP Dom. 1547–1580*, p. 345, for evidence of Leicester and Cecil acting in concert.

For current thinking on Cecil see Stephen Alford, *The Early Elizabethan Polity: William Cecil and the British Succession Crisis, 1558–1569* (Cambridge University Press, 2002), and M. A. R. Graves, *Burghley: William Cecil, Lord Burghley* (Longman, 1998).

Chapter 11

Most of the biographies of Leicester have extensive chapters on his financial affairs and enterprises. Rye, *The Murder of Amy Robsart*, prints as appendix XV a list of Elizabeth's gifts and grants to him. For the tale of the missed meeting, see *Old London Bridge* by Patricia Pierce (Headline, 2001).

For Leicester's discussion of his religious position, see the *Letters of Thomas Wood, Puritan*, ed. Patrick Collinson (Athlone, 1960); the introduction offers an extensive and authoritative discussion of his attitudes. See also the religious implications of his patronage in Eleanor Rosenberg's *Leicester, Patron of Letters* (Columbia University Press, 1962).

Chapter 12

It is possible to trace the progress of the Valois marriage negotiations from, so to speak, both angles. Walsingham's correspondence with Leicester (and Cecil) is transcribed as *The Compleat Ambassador*, ed. Dudley Digges (1655), while the French ambassador's version can be seen in *Correspondance Diplomatique de la Mothe Fénelon*.

The letter Leicester wrote to Norfolk is reprinted in Starkey, ed., *Rivals in Power*.

Dyer's letter is in *Memoirs of the Life and Times of Sir Christopher Hatton, K.G.*, by Sir Harris Nicolas (London, 1847), which also quotes Hatton's letters to Elizabeth; the bulk of the book is an important source for court correspondence of the period, including that between Hatton and Leicester himself, the supposed rivals.

Chapter 13

Gilbert Talbot's letter about the sisters in love with Leicester is to be found in Edmund Lodge, *Illustrations of British History* (1791; edition used 1838), which indeed contains the bulk of the Talbot (Shrewsbury) family correspondence quoted, a good deal of it with Leicester himself.

Information on Douglass's background is to be found in the first chapter of Arthur Gould Lee's biography of her offspring, *The Son of Leicester: The Story of Sir Robert Dudley* (Victor Gollancz, 1964); chapters IX and X give an account of the trials, with an appendix on the validity or otherwise of the supposed marriage. While the surviving Cotton manuscripts wound up in the British Library, other manuscripts are in the Dudley Papers at Longleat, boxes 6–8, and the Sidney Papers from Penshurst, now held in the Centre for Kentish Studies at Maidstone, vols 698, 699, 755; the *Report on the Manuscripts of Lord de L'Isle* transcribes three of them. For the identification of Douglass Sheffield as the recipient of Leicester's letter see Conyers Read, 'A Letter from Robert, Earl of Leicester, to a Lady', *Huntingdon Library Quarterly*, April 1936.

The main first sources on Elizabeth's progresses in general, and her visit to Kenilworth in particular, are respectively *The Progresses and Public Processions of Queen Elizabeth*, ed. J. G. Nichols (Roxburghe Club, 1823), and Robert Laneham's *A letter; wherein the Entertainment and Killingworth Castle is signified* (1575), which is reproduced therein. An important modern source, however, is Zillah Dovey's *An Elizabethan Progress: The Queen's Journey to East Anglia, 1578* (Farleigh Dickinson Press, 1996). For Susan Frye's analysis of the entertainments Leicester provided, see *The Competition for Representation*, esp. p. 61.

Chapter 14

For Wood's letters, see notes for Chapter 11.

For the Irish situation, see Susan Brigden, *New Worlds, Lost Worlds: The Rule of the Tudors 1465–1603* (Allen Lane, 2000); also Walter Bourchier Devereux, *Lives and Letters of the Devereux Earls of Essex* (1853).

For the marriage day, see Dovey, *An Elizabethan Progress*, p. 74. For Lettice's subsequent life, see Sylvia Freedman's *Poor Penelope: Lady Penelope Rich, an Elizabethan Woman* (Kensal Press, 1983); also E. W. Dormer, 'Lettice Knollys, Countess of Leicester', *Berkshire Archaeological Journal*, xxxix, 1935.

Information on Stafford's dubious activities can be found in Robert Hutchinson, *Elizabeth's Spy Master: Francis Walsingham and the Secret War that Saved England* (Weidenfeld & Nicolson, 2006), which is also fascinating on the machinations of the years ahead: see esp. pp. 224–5. A belief in Stafford's guilt was shared by Conyers Read, who expressed it in his classic biographies of Walsingham and also of Cecil: the opposite view, however (that Stafford was himself trying to deceive Spain in England's best interests) was expressed by J. E. Neale in 'The Fame of Sir Edward Stafford', *English Historical Review*, xliv (1929).

Chapter 15

It is the delicate mating game with Alençon (or, properly, 'Anjou') that sees Hume's *Courtships* really come into its own; out of all Elizabeth's 'philanderings', this was the single episode that most interested Hume in the entire chronicle of what he called 'the longest and most eventful comedy in the history of Europe'. See especially chs 9 and 10. See also C. F. H. de la Ferrière, *Les Projets de mariage de la Reine Elisabeth* (1882).

Once again, Simon Adams (*Leicester and the Court*, p. 232) has corrected an important error in redating the birth of Leicester's son.

Chapter 16

The *Disbursement Books* as edited by Adams is the invaluable source on Leicester's daily life.

See Nicolas, *Memoirs of Sir Christopher Hatton*, for Aylmer's letter (p. 348), for changes in Leicester (p. 351), for his letter about Lord and Lady Norris (p. 269), and for letters about Denbigh's death.

A modern edition of *Leicester's Commonwealth* (ed. D. C. Peck, Ohio University Press, 1985) has a valuable introduction; for authorship of the book, see also Alice Hogge, *God's Secret Agents* (HarperCollins, 2005), p. 172n.

Chapter 17

The first and most significant of Leicester's two sojourns in the Netherlands, and his quarrels with the Queen, are chronicled in *The Correspondence of Robert Dudley, Earl of Leicester, during his Government of the Low Countries in the Years 1585 and 1586*, ed. J. Bruce (Camden Society, 1844). Wright's *Queen Elizabeth and Her Times*, vol. ii, gives what you might call the behind-the-scenes view. For an analysis of the ceremonials, see Roy Strong and J. A. Van Dorsten, *Leicester's Triumph* (Oxford University Press, 1964); Strong's many books on the significance of Elizabeth's own portraits are obviously also essential reading for anyone working on her today.

Chapter 18

Garrett Mattingly's *The Defeat of the Spanish Armada* (Jonathan Cape, 1959) was the book that converted many of us to history. More recently, see James McDermott, *England and the Spanish Armada: The Necessary Quarrel* (Yale University Press, 2005); Neil Hanson, *The Confident Hope of a Miracle: The True History of the Spanish Armada* (Bantam, 2003); and Bertrand T. Whitehead, *Brags and Boasts: Propaganda of the Year of the Armada* (Sutton, 1994).

The *Collected Works,* pp. 325–6n, has a discussion of the sources for Elizabeth's Tilbury speech: two contemporary poetical accounts of the visit are James Aske's *Elizabetha Triumphans, with a Declaration of the Manner how her Excellency was entertained by her Souldyers into her Campe Royall at Tilbery, in Essex,* and Thomas Deloney's *The Queen . . . at Tilsburie* (in Edward Arber's *An English Garland,* 1877–96, vol. VII). See also Miller Christy's important article, 'Queen Elizabeth's Visit to Tilbury in 1588', *English Historical Review,* xxxiv, 1919, and A. J. Collins's 'The Progress of Queen Elizabeth to the Camp at Tilbury', *British Museum Quarterly,* x (1936).

Chapter 19, *Appendices and Afterword*

For Leicester's will, see appendix in Wilson, *Sweet Robin;* and see the details of his funeral in the *Disbursement Books.*

For the theory that Shakespeare was Neville, see Brenda James and William D. Rubinstein, *The Truth Will Out: Unmasking the Real Shakespeare* (Longman, 2005).

On Essex, see Robert Lacey, *Robert, Earl of Essex: An Elizabethan Icarus* (Weidenfeld & Nicolson, 1970); G. B. Harrison, *The Life and Death of Robert Devereux, Earl of Essex* (Cassell, 1937); John Guy, ed., *The Reign of Elizabeth I: Court and Culture in the Last Decade* (Cambridge University Press, 1995); Paul Hammer, *The Polarisation of Elizabethan Politics: The Political Career of Robert Devereux, 2nd Earl of Essex, 1585–1597* (Cambridge University Press, 1999).

On Sir Robert Dudley, see Gould Lee, *The Son of Leicester;* G. K. Warner, *The Voyage of Robert Dudley to the West Indies,* Hakluyt Society, 2nd series, iii (1899); J. Temple Leader, *Sir R. Dudley* (1895); Vaughan Thomas, *Italian Biography of Sir R. Dudley* (1881).

On 'Arthur Dudley', see Paul Doherty, *The Secret Life of Elizabeth I* (Greenwich Exchange, 2006); letters reprinted in Chamberlin, *Private Character,* pp. 309–18; also the additional chapter of Hume's *Courtships.* Englefield's letter about the propaganda war is quoted in Peck's introduction to *Leicester's Commonwealth,* p. 12. For espionage practices in general, see Hutchinson, *Walsingham;* also Alan Haynes,

Invisible Power: The Elizabethan Secret Service 1570–1603 (Sutton, 1992).

For the fascinating saga of Elizabeth's posthumous reputation, see Michael Dobson and Nicola J. Watson, *England's Elizabeth: An Afterlife in Fame and Fantasy* (Oxford University Press, 2002). For that of Robert, the best source is Chamberlin, *Elizabeth and Leycester*. In the first fifty pages of his book, and in a series of appendices, Chamberlin analyses the picture of Leicester presented in some eighty books from the sixteenth century to the early twentieth.

Acknowledgements

One often says, 'It's all thanks to you . . .', but in this case, it happens to be true. I want to thank first and foremost Alison Weir, who gave me this idea for a book. And Alison, thanks again, for correcting some of the errors in the text: I can only hope that not too many escaped your eagle eye! By the same token, I should like to thank Mary Lovell and Margaret Gaskin, both of whom suggested some very important changes to the presentation of the material; Carole Myer and Leonie Flynn, who were also kind enough to read and comment upon earlier versions of this story; and also Leanda de Lisle, who sent me information on some unpublished letters of Leicester's. I am, as always, very grateful to Selina Walker, my commissioning editor, and to Sheila Lee at Transworld; to my agent Araminta Whitley at LAW; and especially to Gillian Somerscales for her endlessly patient copy-editing. Family and friends, I hope, can by now take my gratitude for granted! So let me give the last thanks to the many anonymous friends not mentioned in the source notes – to helpful ladies at Hever and Penshurst, at the Kent county archive and at Kenilworth; not to mention the ever-resourceful staff of the London Library.

Picture acknowledgements

First colour section

Portrait of Elizabeth as a young girl by William Scrotts, *c.*1546–7: the Royal Collection © 2006 Her Majesty Queen Elizabeth II

Anonymous portrait of Anne Boleyn, 1533–6: National Portrait Gallery, London; *The Family of Henry VIII* by an unknown artist, *c.*1545: the Royal Collection © 2006 Her Majesty Queen Elizabeth II; view of the Knot Garden and the Old Palace, Hatfield House, Hertfordshire/The Bridgeman Art Library; anonymous portrait of Thomas Seymour, second half of the 16th century: National Portrait Gallery, London

Portrait of Robert Dudley by Nicholas Hilliard, 1576: National Portrait Gallery, London; map of London, from *Civitates Orbis Terrarum*, by Georg Braun and Frans Hogenburg, *c.*1572: © Guildhall Library, City of London/The Bridgeman Art Library; Dudley coat of arms carved by Ambrose and Robert Dudley, 1553–5, Beauchamp Tower, Tower of London: photo © Historic Royal Palaces; drawing of the coronation procession of Elizabeth I, 14 January 1559, detail, London College of Arms MS M6 f.41v: The Art Archive/Eileen Tweedy

Drawing of Elizabeth and drawing of Robert Dudley, both by Federico Zuccaro, 1575: British Museum, London; *Elizabeth I's Procession arriving at Nonesuch Palace* by Joris Hoefnagel, *c.*1568: British Museum, London/The Bridgeman Art Library; *Figures Dancing la Volta* by an unknown artist, late 16th century: by kind permission of Viscount De L'Isle from his private collection at Penshurst Place

Execution of Mary, Queen of Scots in the Great Hall at Fotheringay, 8 February 1587, Scottish school: © Private Collection/The Bridgeman Art Library; anonymous portrait miniature of Mary, Queen of Scots, c.1560–65: National Portrait Gallery, London; detail of a portrait of Queen Elizabeth by Federico Zuccaro, late 16th century: Pinacoteca Nazionale, Siena/Alinari/The Bridgeman Art Library

Second colour section

Portrait of Robert Dudley, 1st Earl of Leicester, 1560s, by Steven van der Meulen: © Yale Center for British Art, Paul Mellon Collection/The Bridgeman Art Library

Anonymous portrait of Christopher Hatton: National Portrait Gallery, London; anonymous portrait of François de Valois, Duke of Alençon, 1560s, Hermitage, St Petersburg/The Bridgeman Art Library; portrait miniature of Sir Walter Ralegh by Nicholas Hilliard, c.1585: National Portrait Gallery, London; portrait of Robert Devereux, Earl of Essex, by William Segar: National Gallery of Ireland, Dublin; portrait of William Cecil, 1st Baron Burghley, by Arnold von Brounckhorst, 1560–70: © National Portrait Gallery, London/The Bridgeman Art Library; portrait of Robert Cecil, 1st Earl of Salisbury, by John de Critz: © Courtesy of the Warden and Scholars of New College, Oxford/The Bridgeman Art Library

View of Kenilworth Castle c.1620, 18th-century copy of a 17th-century wallpainting: photo English Heritage; east elevation of Leicester's Building, Kenilworth Castle: photo English Heritage; portrait of Lettice Knollys, Countess of Leicester, by George Gower, c.1585: Longleat House, Wiltshire/The Bridgeman Art Library

Queen Elizabeth Receiving the Dutch Ambassadors, c.1585: Staatliche Museen, Kassel; anonymous portrait of Robert Dudley, Earl of Leicester, 1575, Parham Park, Nr Pulborough, West Sussex: Mark Fiennes/The Bridgeman Art Library; portrait of Philip II (mounted on a cow), the Duke of Alençon, the Duke of Alba, William of Orange and Queen Elizabeth I by Philip Moro: Private Collection/The Bridgeman Art Library; portrait of Elizabeth, known as the 'Armada Portrait', c.1588, attributed to George Gower: Woburn Abbey, Bedfordshire/The Bridgeman Art Library

Portrait of Robert Dudley by Nicholas Hilliard: photo The National Museum of Fine Arts, Stockholm; tomb of Robert Dudley, Earl of Leicester, and Lettice Knollys, Beauchamp Chapel, Collegiate Church of St Mary, Warwick: © Trevor Haywood/fotoLibra

Index

Abbott, Jacob, 344
Accession Day, 207
Adlard, George, 115–16, 122
Aird, Ian, 117
Alane, Alexander (Alesius), 20
Albert, Prince Consort, 136
Alençon, François, Duke of: appearance, 214, 273; religion, 214, 266–7, 281; titles, 208n; first question of suit to QE, 214; Netherlands involvement, 267, 283, 287, 310; suit to QE resumed, 265, 267–9; Simier's mission, 269–71; arrival in England, 273; relationship with QE, 274–7, 282–3, 284–5, 296; QE's virginity, 132, 284–5; English view of, 277–9, 282, 319; marriage articles, 279, 282, 284; opinion of QE, 283; return to England, 285–6; QE's promise and refusal, 286–7; money for Netherlands campaign, 287; departure for Netherlands, 287, 288, 298; Netherlands sovereignty, 310; death, 297, 336
Allen, William, 266
Alva, Duchess of, 67
Alva, Duke of, 189, 211, 266
ambassadors: French, 71, 72, 145, 195, 196, 200, 206, 273, 292, see also Castelnau, Fénelon; Imperial (Habsburg), 38, 48, 96, 100, 206, see also Chapuys; Scottish, 144, 155, 161, see also Maitland; Spanish, 16, 35, 63, 89, 95, 128, 129, 146, 155, 184, 189, 192, 199, 210, 216, 237, 269, 278, 286, see also de Quadra, de Silva, de Spes, Feria, Mendoza (Bernardino de); Venetian (in England), 60, 72, 73, 92, 132, 174; Venetian (in Madrid), 353, 354, 359; Venetian (in Paris), 283, 286
Anatomy of Melancholy (Burton), 244
Andreas Capellanus, 131
Anjou, Duke of, *see* Henri III
Anne, Queen of Great Britain, 136, 141–2
Anne of Cleves, Queen, 23, 27, 93
Antwerp, fall of, 307
Appleyard, John, 105, 114–15, 177n
Archer, Jeffrey, 367n
Arden, Edward, 251n
Aristotle, 45
Armada, Spanish, 307, 325–33
Arran, James Hamilton, second Earl of, 94, 147, 159
Arthur, King, 88
Arundel, Charles, 301
Arundel, Henry FitzAlan, nineteenth Earl of, 58, 93, 126
Arundel House, 290
Ascham, Roger, 29, 35, 42, 45–6
Ashley, John, 45, 352, 353
Ashley, Kat (Champernowne): family background, 26; education of Elizabeth, 26, 35; Seymour's conspiracy, 43; evidence on Seymour's behaviour, 40–2, 44; First Lady of the Bedchamber, 95; concern for QE's reputation, 95–6; death, 173, 352
Ashridge House, 25, 32
Association, Act of, 320
Atye, Arthur, 346n
Austen, Jane, 365
Aylmer, John, 90n, 135, 199, 294

Babington, Anthony, 320
Bacon, Francis, 13, 300

Baddesley Clinton, 239, 250, 252
Bayly, Dr, 121
Baynard's Castle, 152
Bedford, Francis Russell, second Earl of, 75, 80, 199, 229, 238
Belvoir Castle, 226
Blanchett, Cate, 368
Blois, Treaty of (1572), 214
Blount, Christopher, 341
Blount, Thomas: background, 103, 341; correspondence with RD, 103–7, 114, 116, 122, 341, 353; investigation of Amy's death, 105–7, 121, 122, 353
Boleyn, Anne, Queen: family background, 12–13, 226, 259; education, 26; Henry's courtship, 15; status at court, 16; marriage, 16, 31; coronation, 64; birth of daughter Elizabeth, 16–18; relationship with Mary, 18–19; miscarriage, 19; relationship with daughter, 19–21; blamed for Henry's decisions, 141; accusations against, 21, 22, 29; in Tower, 22, 64; marriage annulled, 23; execution, 12, 21–2, 23, 24, 25, 32, 45, 64; grave, 80
Boleyn, George, 21, 32, 64, 80n
Boleyn, Mary, 16, 172
Boleyn family, 12–13
Bond of Association, 297
Borgarucci (or Borgherini), Dr Giulio, 230, 232
Bothwell, James Hepburn, fourth Earl of, 178–9, 182–3, 195, 257n
Boulogne, recapture of, 33
Brockett, Sir John, 9
Brown, John, 142n
Bryan, Margaret, Lady, 18, 20, 24
Bullinger, Henry, 199
Burbage, James, 123
Burcot, Dr, 153, 154
Burnell, Anne, 357
Burton, Robert, 244
Buxton, spa waters, 254–5, 261, 333

Cabot, Sebastian, 28
Cadiz: Drake's raid, 323, 360; Essex's expedition, 345
Calais, 73, 160, 209
Calendars of State Papers, 147, 159
Calvin, John, 293
Cambridge, 244
Camden, William: on relationship of QE

and RD, 9; on QE's character, 11; on RD's character, 11–12, 289; on Amy's death, 119n; on QE and marriage, 144, 286; on RD's influence on QE, 171n; on Norfolk, 186, 187; on Walsingham, 208; on Hatton, 219–20; on death of Essex, 253n; on Simier, 269, 270; on RD's marriage, 271–2, 289; on Bond of Association, 297; on Leicester's Commonwealth, 301; on RD in Netherlands, 306, 310; on QE and Mary's execution, 321, 322; on Tilbury speech, 331n; on alleged plan to make RD Lieutenant Governor, 333; on RD's death, 335–6; on QE's attitude to money, 344
Carew, Lady, 235
Carlos, Don (son of Philip II), 71
Castelnau, Michel de, Sieur de Mauvissière, 276, 295
Castiglione, Baldassare, 30, 193
Catherine de Medici, Queen Regent of France: regency for sons, 96; on slander, 130; Huguenot rebellion, 159; sons' marriage proposals, 165, 209, 214, 273; jewellery, 180; St Bartholomew's Day massacre, 215; Alençon's death, 297, 336
Catherine the Great, Empress of Russia, 142–4, 247n, 319n
Cavendish, Elizabeth, 256
Cavendish, Margaret, 344
Cavendish, Richard, 213
Cavendish, Thomas, 344
Cecil, Robert, 151, 252, 303, 304, 337
Cecil, William, Lord Burghley: family background, 77; character, 77; education, 91; religion, 77; secretary to John Dudley, 49; opinion of RD's marriage, 49; list of RD's associates, 70; RD's letters, 12, 110, 189, 217–18, 223–4, 254–5, 272, 280–1, 305, 310, 311, 312; relationship with RD, 74, 77, 95, 98, 99, 108–9, 110, 119, 150–1, 183–4, 188–90, 210, 217–18, 223, 315; relationship with Elizabeth, 74, 77, 90, 110, 119, 189, 205, 223, 254, 304, 322; Elizabeth's accession, 7, 75, 76; state secretary, 77; QE's marriage question, 82; Scottish mission, 97–8, 155; Amy Dudley's death, 99, 100, 108–12, 116, 118–20, 123;

Throckmorton correspondence,
111–12, 119, 134, 148, 166; on QE's
childbearing potential, 133; RD's
Scottish marriage plan, 157, 161; on
Howards, 169; support for Habsburg
marriage, 170, 171–2; memoranda
comparing archduke and RD, 171–2;
relationship with Norfolk, 172, 185,
186–7, 210–11; on QE and RD,
172–3; policy towards Mary, Queen of
Scots, 181–2, 183, 185, 217, 254, 296;
casket letters, 182n; plot against,
183–4; Ridolfi plot, 189; privy council
meetings, 192; influence in government,
192, 326; Burghley title, 210; Knight
of the Garter, 210; Ridolfi plot,
211–12; response to St Bartholomew's
Day massacre, 216; daughter's
marriage, 221; view of Hatton, 223;
on royal progresses, 237, 238, 242,
244; Irish policy, 252; guardianship of
Devereux children, 260; view of
Alençon suit, 267–8, 276, 279, 282;
relationship with Lettice, 272;
accusations against, 300; *Leicester's
Commonwealth*, 301; Netherlands
policy, 306, 307, 312; Mary's
execution, 321–2; banished from
court, 322; response to Lieutenant
Governor proposal, 333; Arthur
Dudley story, 353; death, 337; fictional
treatment of, 368
Chaloner, Thomas, 343
Chamberlain, Sir Thomas, 112n
Champernowne, Kat, *see* Ashley
Chapuys, Eustace, 16, 18–19
Charles, Archduke of Austria, 93, 94, 95,
137, 160–1, 165, 169–70, 177
Charles I, king of England and Scotland,
232, 350
Charles V, Emperor: rule, 16n; aunt's
divorce, 17; question of Elizabeth's
marriage, 27; son Philip's marriage, 60,
81; abdication, 16n, 73n, 93; death,
73n
Charles IX, King of France, 165, 208,
209, 267
Charlotte, Princess of Orange, 298
Charterhouse, 78
Chartley, 251
Chastelard, Pierre de, 167
Chatsworth, 255

Cheke, John, 28, 32, 35, 46, 77
Chelsea, 39
Christina, Queen of Sweden, 142n
Christmas, Mr, 346
Churchill, Sarah, Duchess of
Marlborough, 141–2
Churchyard, Thomas, 237
Cicero, 29, 45
Clapham, John, 10n, 140, 193, 255
Clinton, Geoffrey de, 239
Clinton, Gervase, 259
Coke, Sir Edward, 365–6, 348
Coleshill, 251
Coligny, Admiral, 215–16
Company of Kathai, 198
Cornbury, RD's death, 334
Cotton, Sir Robert, 348–9
Cox, Richard, 35
Cranmer, Thomas, 37
Cromwell, Thomas, 14, 21, 24, 183, 314
Cumnor Place, 102–5, 114, 121, 178

Dacre, Lady Margaret, 233
Darnley, Henry Stewart, Earl of: family
background, 165–6; appearance and
character, 165–6, 174; religion, 166;
marriage to Mary, 137, 173–4, 177–8;
murder of Rizzio, 175–6; death, 178,
179, 182, 353n; brother's marriage,
256
Davis, Bette, 366
Davison, William, 271, 311, 314, 321,
322
Dee, John, 28–9, 74–5, 89, 319n
Dekker, Thomas, 68
Denbigh, 151, 198, 308
Denbigh, Robert Dudley, Lord (RD's son),
see Dudley
Denny, Sir Anthony, 42
Denny, Joan, Lady, 42
de Quadra, Alvaro: on relationship
between QE and RD, 97, 112, 127,
148–52; on Amy's death, 99–100,
108–10, 120; on QE's childbearing,
132, 356; on QE's illness, 154; death,
157
de Silva, Diego Guzman, 164–5, 169,
170–1, 176
de Spes, Guerau, 187
Deloney, Thomas, 331
Derby, Henry Stanley, fourth Earl of, 336
Despenser, Hugh le, 139

Devereux, Dorothy, *see* Perrot
Devereux, Penelope, 253n
Devereux, Robert, *see* Essex
Devereux, Walter, *see* Essex
Diana, Princess of Wales, 4
Digby, Sir George, 251
Digges, Thomas, 336n
Douglas, Archibald, 320
Douglas, Lady Margaret, *see* Lennox
Dowe, Anne, 98
Drake, Sir Francis, 198, 283–4, 292, 323, 332–3, 360
Drayton, Michael, 206
Dublin, Archbishop of, 252
Dudley, Ambrose (RD's brother), Earl of Warwick: appearance and character, 158, 304; Kett rebellion, 46–7; titles, 50, 152; imprisonment in Tower, 56, 57–9, 66–7; trial and sentence, 62; release from Tower, 67; revenues, 72; French campaign, 72–3; Master of the Ordnance, 78; marriages, 80, 89, 229; QE's coronation, 80; earldom of Warwick, 152; Scottish marriage proposal, 157–8; French campaign, 160; Scots inquiry, 182; campaign against northern earls, 188, 190–1; interest in exploration, 198; QE's Warwick visit, 215; godfather to RD's son, 233; rumours about RD, 249; health, 254–5, 306, 337; RD's wedding to Lettice Knollys, 261; portrait, 304; RD's son, 343, 348–9; Netherlands campaign, 306, 313–14; trial of Mary, 320; intermediary role after Mary's execution, 322–3; RD's funeral, 339; death, 337, 344; tomb, 340
Dudley, Amy (Robsart, RD's wife): family background, 49, 101; appearance and character, 100, 229; marriage, 49, 128; visiting RD in Tower, 64, 100; relationship with husband, 100–2; childless, 171; lands, 74, 101; lifestyle, 101; at court, 101; rumours concerning, 91–2, 97, 99, 116–17; death, 3, 4, 6, 99–100, 133–4, 145–6, 178, 179, 254, 300, 301, 355–6; inquiry into her death, 103–7; inquest, 104, 107, 113, 114–15, 122; funeral, 109–10; suicide theory, 115, 118, 120–3; murder theory, 116, 118–20; illness theory, 116–18, 119, 120; fictional treatments

of, 100, 118, 365, 368
Dudley, Anne (Russell), Countess of Warwick, 229
Dudley, Arthur: story of birth, 4, 129, 350–2; story of childhood, 352; story of travels, 352, 353; story of interview with RD, 353; arrival in Spain, 129, 351, 353–4; taken to be a spy or stooge, 354, 358–61; life in Spain, 354–5; likelihood of story, 55–8, 362–3, 370
Dudley, Carlo (RD's grandson), 35n
Dudley, Edmund (RD's grandfather), 13–14, 27, 31, 62, 138, 314
Dudley, Elizabeth (Grey, RD's grandmother), 14, 91
Dudley, Guildford (RD's brother), 50, 52, 56, 62, 80n, 91
Dudley, Henry (RD's brother), 56, 57–9, 62, 66–7, 72
Dudley, Sir Henry, 70, 74
Dudley, Jane (Guildford, RD's mother), 14, 15, 27–8, 32, 66–7, 70
Dudley, John, Earl of Warwick, Duke of Northumberland (RD's father): childhood, 14; marriage, 14; career, 14, 27, 32, 33, 34, 40, 47–9; relationship with King Henry, 14, 27, 32, 38, 78; children, 14, 15, 27, 33, 49; lands, 14–15, 151, 240; relationship with Seymour brothers, 27, 38, 43, 44, 47–8, 49; London home, 30–1; titles, 32, 33, 37, 47, 50; relationship with King Edward, 38, 47–9, 51, 52–3, 152; Kett rebellion, 46–7; rise to power, 47–9, 138; children's marriages, 49, 52, 67; illness, 49, 54; King Edward's last illness and death, 52–3, 152; expedition in favour of Lady Jane Grey, 54; proclamation of Mary as Queen, 54; arrest, 55; in Tower, 55, 56; trial, 57, 169n; recantation, 57–8, 201; last letter, 58, 114n; execution, 58, 59; grave, 80; attainder, 50, 72; reputation, 47–8, 51–2, 58, 138
Dudley, John (RD's brother), Earl of Warwick: marriage, 49; title, 13, 50; career, 50, 78; expedition to secure Mary, 53–4; in Tower, 56–9; trial, 57; release from Tower, 66–7; death, 67
Dudley, John (RD's kinsman), 34

Dudley, John Sutton, first Baron (RD's
great-grandfather), 13, 14
Dudley, Katherine (RD's sister), *see*
Hastings
Dudley, Lettice (RD's wife), *see* Knollys
Dudley, Mary (RD's sister), *see* Sidney
Dudley, Robert, Earl of Leicester: birth,
12, 14; childhood, 15, 25n; education,
12, 27–30, 34, 35, 39, 87; first
meeting with Elizabeth, 31–2; at court,
39, 194–5; Kett rebellion, 46–7;
military career, 47, 72; marriage to
Amy Robsart, 49, 91–2, 171; court
career, 50–1; sent to secure Mary,
53–4; proclamation of Lady Jane Grey
as Queen, 54; arrest, 55; imprisonment
in Tower, 12, 55, 56–9, 64–5; father's
execution, 58; trial and sentence, 61–2;
release from Tower, 66–7; mother's
death, 67; life after release, 67–8;
access to revenues, 72; French
campaign, 72–3, 102; QE's accession,
8–9; Master of Horse to QE, 11, 78–9,
85–6, 239; QE's coronation, 74, 80;
Knight of the Garter, 88; talk of
marriage to QE, 91–2, 95–8, 112–13,
133–5, 145–6, 149–53, 164–5; wife's
death, 99–100, 103–23, 133–4, 145–6,
179, 254; peerage question, 112, 113,
151, 157, 159; Spanish sponsorship,
149–51; QE's illness, 153–5; Lord
Protector proposal, 154; 356 privy
councillor, 155, 192–3; Scottish
marriage plan, 156–63, 166; Earl of
Leicester, 159, 162–3; quarrel with
Norfolk, 168–70; flirtation with
Lettice Knollys, 172, 250; Scots
inquiry, 182; plot against Cecil, 183–4;
support for Norfolk's marriage to
Mary, 184–7; rebellion of northern
earls, 188, 190; Ridolfi plot, 189;
influence, 192–5; Norfolk's release,
210–11; policy towards Mary, Queen
of Scots, 217, 320–1; view of Hatton,
223–4; affair with Douglass, 225–34,
256–8; wish for children, 229, 257,
298; story of secret wedding, 230–1,
256, 345–9; birth of son by Douglass,
230, 257; entertainment of QE at
Kenilworth (1575), 239–48, 251;
rumours about, 249–50; Irish policy,
252; taking the waters at Buxton,

254–5, 261, 333; marriage to Lettice
Knollys, 231, 256–62, 281; wedding
ceremonies, 261, 264; Netherlands
policy, 266, 268, 305–6; view of
Alençon suit, 267–71, 273, 274,
278–9, 281–2, 283, 285–6; birth of
son by Lettice, 285; married life,
289–95; dynastic scheming, 294–5;
son's death, 297–9, 305; *Leicester's
Commonwealth*, 299–301; religious
conference, 301–2; thoughts of
retirement, 305; Netherlands
campaign, 306–19, 323–4, 327;
governor general of Netherlands,
310–12; execution of Mary, 320–2,
345; Tilbury command, 326–9;
Lieutenant Governor proposal, 333;
death, 1–2, 30, 334–6; funeral,
339–40; tomb, 259, 339–40; will, 230,
259, 337, 340–2, 344; fictional
treatments of, 365–9
FINANCES: access to revenues, 72;
accounts, 101, 289–94, 297; business
ventures, 198; debts, 308n, 344;
dress costs, 84; export licence, 151;
'farm' of sweet wines, 338; funds for
Netherlands expedition, 308; gifts
from Elizabeth, 88, 151, 194, 204;
household, 194–5, 290–1; living
beyond means, 198; Netherlands
campaign, 316, 327; pension, 151;
rights over customs duties, 151; will,
344
HEALTH: broken bones, 294; corns,
294; diet, 255; eyesight, 294; fever,
294, 334; ill health, 261, 264; last
illness, 333–4; mentioned in letters,
53, 218; 'the stone', 334; taking the
waters at Buxton, 254–5, 261, 333
INTERESTS: exploration, 197–8;
gardens, 290; horsemanship, 85–6;
science, 87; theatre, 87
LANDS: building projects, 198; gifts
from Elizabeth, 88, 151–2; Norfolk
rental plans, 100–1; sale to raise
funds for Elizabeth, 74; volunteered
sale under Mary, 72
LETTERS: to Blount, 103–5, 107; to
Cecil, 12, 110, 189, 217–18, 223–4,
242–3, 254–5, 272, 280–1, 305, 310,
311, 312; to court official in
Netherlands, 267; to Douglass,

Dudley, Robert, Earl of Leicester (*cont.*)
227–9; to Elizabeth, 160, 190–1,
196–7, 203, 218–19, 295–6, 314,
317–18, 319, 326, 330, 333, 335; to
Forster, 197; to Hatton, 272–3, 293,
299; to Heneage, 293, 319; to
Morton, 217; to Shrewsbury, 197–8,
298, 332; to Sussex, 189; to
Throckmorton, 202, 203; to
Walsingham, 194, 208–9, 212–13,
214, 216, 236–7, 268, 269, 307–9,
316, 319, 320, 321, 323; to Warwick
burghers, 198; to Wood, 200–1
PERSON: appearance, 10, 49, 84, 192,
304; character, 11, 87–8, 294; diet,
255; dress, 84, 192, 199, 271, 291;
family, 12–14; motto, 162;
nicknames, 10, 29, 84, 139, 205,
224; portraits, 192, 234, 250, 288–9,
304; symbols, 10, 86, 89–90, 241
RELATIONSHIP WITH ELIZABETH:
before her accession, 74–5; flowering
of, 83–8; Amy's death, 123–4; love
and sex, 125–30; courtly love,
130–1, 205–6; question of marriage,
148–53, 174–5, 204–5, 224;
earldom, 162–3; flirtations, 172–3;
favourite courtier, 193–4; religious
differences, 202; estrangements,
202–4; closeness, 218–19, 223–4,
255–6; twin portraits, 234;
Kenilworth entertainment, 247–8;
her response to his marriage, 272–3,
281–2, 294–5; Netherlands
campaign, 308–9, 311–15; her
response to his death, 334–6, 342;
fictional treatments, 364–70
RELIGION: books dedicated to, 199;
conversion suggestion, 149–51;
Denbigh church, 198; different from
Elizabeth's, 91, 202; at Mary's
accession, 54; Netherlands policy,
266; prayer, 65; Protestant hero, 343;
puritanism, 35, 199–202; reading,
293; will, 340
Dudley, Robert (RD's 'base' son by
Douglass Sheffield): birth, 230, 233;
godparents, 260; childhood, 230,
291–2, 363–4; father's death, 340,
344; inheritance, 230, 364, 369;
appearance as a young man, 364;
marriages, 213, 344, 345, 349;

banished from court, 344; voyages,
344–5, 349; knighted, 345; claim to
legitimacy, 231–2, 345–9, 350;
conversion to Catholicism, 260, 350;
career in Tuscany, 350; known as
Duke of Northumberland, 231, 350;
writings, 350; descendants, 350n
Dudley, Robert, Lord Denbigh (RD's son
by Lettice), 256, 285, 294, 297–8,
305, 340, 343
Dudley Castle, 15, 233n
Dudley family: background, 12–15;
motto, 9; relationship with Tudors, 9,
39, 47–8; power, 88–9; emblem, 191,
241; end of dynasty, 342
Dugdale, Sir William, 251n, 368–9
Durham House, 48
Dyer, Edward, 114n, 221–3

Earl of Leicester's Men, 87, 123, 341n
Edinburgh: peace treaty (1560), 98, 155;
Mary and Bothwell, 178–9
Edward II, King of England, 139
Edward IV, King of England, 14, 52
Edward VI, King of England: christening,
24; babyhood, 18, 24; education, 26,
33–4, 48–9, 141; household, 32, 33–4,
78; religion, 15, 35, 38, 46, 48, 51; in
family portrait, 36; father's death, 37;
coronation, 37; reign, 38, 46, 88, 154;
court, 39, 48, 195; Thomas Seymour's
plot, 43; fall of Somerset, 47; at RD's
wedding, 49; health, 51; rumours of
poisoning, 51; last illness, 52–3; will,
52, 136, 144; death, 7, 53; succession,
33, 51–2, 53
Eleanor of Aquitaine, 130, 131
Elizabeth I, Queen of England: birth, 12,
16–18; babyhood, 15, 18–21; childhood,
23–4, 25, 32; brother's christening, 24;
education, 12, 26–7, 34–6, 45–6, 70;
mother's death, 21–2, 25; bastardy, 23,
53; marriage prospects, 27, 40, 43–4, 48,
70–1; first meeting with Robert, 31–2;
at father's court, 32, 36; place in father's
will, 36; father's death, 37; at Chelsea,
39–42; relationship with Seymour,
39–45; life with Dennys, 42; illness,
42–3; at brother's court, 48, 195; London
visits, 49–50, 59; status at court, 49–50,
51; succession question, 51–2, 53;
sister Mary's accession, 59; at sister's

court, 59–60, 67–8; Wyatt rebellion, 62–3, 69; imprisonment in Tower, 12, 62; house arrest in Woodstock, 65, 66, 68; return to Hatfield, 69; Philip of Spain's policy towards her, 69–72, 75, 81–2, 147, 149–50; Dudley plot, 70; Duke of Savoy marriage question, 71; King of Sweden marriage question, 71–2, 93; plans for future government, 73–4; accession, 7–11, 75, 76, 162, 207; advisers, 75, 76; privy council, 76–7, 88, 236–7, 244, 270–1, 326; appointments, 78; entry into London, 78; coronation, 74, 79–81, 168; marriage question, 81–3, 91–8; court, 39, 193–4, 234–5; government, 90, 138, 192, 236–7; talk of marriage to RD, 91–2, 95–8, 112–13, 133–5, 145–6, 149–53, 164–5; Philip of Spain's suit, 92–3, 273; suitors, 93–5; Amy Dudley's death, 99–100, 105, 107–8, 117, 122, 123–4, 133–4, 145–6, 179; RD's peerage question, 112, 113; smallpox, 153–5, 356, 357; succession question, 154, 155, 157; marriage plans for Mary, Queen of Scots, 157–63; French wars, 159–60; flirtation with Heneage, 172–3, 174; response to Rizzio's murder, 175–6; response to Mary's flight, 180–2; response to plot against Cecil, 183–4; rebellion of northern earls, 187–8, 190; Valois suitors, 207–10, 212–13, 214–15, 216; papal bulls against, 207, 282; Accession Day, 207; Norfolk's execution, 213–14; Warwick visit, 215; Kenilworth visits, 215, 216, 239–48, 251; response to St Bartholomew's Day massacre, 216–17; policy towards Mary, Queen of Scots, 217; relationship with Hatton, 219–24; RD's marriage to Lettice Knollys, 261–4, 295; Alençon suit, 265–71, 273–9, 281–7, 319; Netherlands policy, 266, 268, 305–6, 310; news of RD's marriage, 271–2; Throckmorton plot, 295–6; assassination attempt, 297; new favourites, 302–3; Netherlands campaign, 305–13, 327; execution of Mary, 320–2; Spanish Armada, 325–38; Tilbury speech, 328–32; plan to make RD Lieutenant Governor, 333; response to RD's death, 2–3, 334–5; RD's will, 337, 341–2; fictional treatments of, 364–70
FINANCES: debts, 73; household, 234–6; land holdings, 48; progresses, 237–9
HEALTH: energy, 85; ill-health, 333; illness in cold weather, 164; illness over execution of Norfolk, 213–14; mentioned in letters, 53, 218; nerve storms, 42, 46, 84; pregnancy question, 355–6; pregnancy risks, 128; smallpox, 153–5, 356, 357; swelling of face and body, 63, 355; toothache, 264
LETTERS: to Alençon, 275–6, 279, 284–5, 289; to Ambrose Dudley, 160; to father, 138; to Mary Queen of Scots, 138; to Queen Katherine, 35, 42; to RD, 202, 311–12, 314, 318; to Shrewsbury, 299, 336; to Simier, 270; to Somerset, 44; to Walsingham, 216
PERSON: appearance, 10, 20, 40, 84, 213; beds, 125; character, 11, 87–8, 123, 148, 203, 213, 282, 328; diet, 246, 255; dress, 21, 24, 46, 79, 164, 331, 337; equestrian skill, 85–6; falcon badge, 22; motto, 22, 213; phoenix emblem, 11; poems, 275; portraits, 36, 40, 234, 264, 284n, 288–9, 337; progresses, 234–9, 262–3, 293, 355; rumours of secret pregnancies, 42–3, 63, 98, 129, 222, 355, 357; virginity, 3–4, 81, 83, 125, 129, 132–3, 145
RELATIONSHIP WITH DUDLEY, see under Dudley (relationship with Elizabeth)
RELATIONSHIPS: with father, 22–3, 25, 32; with favourites, 137–8, 140, 172–3, 193–4, 219–22, 223–4, 302–4; with Mary, Queen of Scots, 138, 161–2, 164, 179, 180–2, 296, 320–2; with mother, 19–21, 22; with sister, 8, 10, 22, 23, 60, 63
RELIGION: conversion possibility, 150; different from RD's, 91, 202; instruction in Catholicism, 60; Netherlands policy, 266–7; 'new religion', 50; prayers, 65, 77, 128, 201; religious views, 199–202; response to St Bartholomew's Day massacre, 216–17

Elizabeth II, Queen of Great Britain, 136
Elizabeth R (BBC TV drama), 1, 367
Ely Place, Holborn, 30–1
Elyot, Thomas, 30, 139
Empson, Sir Richard, 13–14, 314
Englefield, Sir Francis, 352, 353–4, 358–9, 362n
Eric XIV, king of Sweden, 71–2, 93, 94
Erisa, Mrs, 231n, 233
Esher, 230, 233, 347–8
Essex, Robert Devereux, second Earl of: parentage, 250; character, 338, 341; relationship with QE, 45, 303–4, 337–8; mother's letters, 258; mother's relationship with QE, 272; relationship with RD, 323; at Tilbury, 329; Armada victory celebrations, 333; Cadiz expedition, 345; execution, 45, 140, 338, 341; tomb, 80n; fictional treatments of, 341n, 366
Essex, Walter Devereux, first Earl of, 250–4, 260, 300, 301
Etheldreda, St, 25, 31n
Euclid, 29

Family of Henry VIII, The (painting), 36
Fénelon, Bertrand Salignac de la Mothe, 184, 189, 209, 216
Ferdinand I, Emperor, 93, 170
Ferdinand de Medici, Grand Duke of Tuscany, 350
Feria, Gomez Suarez de Figueroa, Duke of, 75, 81–2, 84, 91, 137
Fiennes, Joseph, 368
Fitzwilliam, George, 212
Flynn, Errol, 366
Forster, Anthony, 102–3, 105, 107, 197
Foxe, John, 64, 67
Francis II, King of France, 94, 147, 159, 165, 167
Fraser's Magazine, 365
Frobisher, Martin, 29, 198
Froude, James Anthony, 193–4, 254, 368

Garter, Bernard, 238
Garter knights, 88, 210
Gascoigne, George, 243, 246–7
Gaveston, Piers, 139
Gentili, Alberico, 301
Gentleman Pensioners, 220, 236

George, Prince (husband of Queen Anne), 136n
Gheeraerts, Marcus, 264
Gillions, Roger, 289
Golden Hind, 283
Goldingham, Harry, 245n
Gomez de Silva, Ruy, 139
Gorboduc, 152
Grafton, 219
Greenwich, 18, 19, 32, 94, 196, 272n, 273, 291
Gregory, Philippa, 1, 118n, 368
Greville, Fulke, 140, 318
Grey, Lady Frances, Marchioness of Dorset, Duchess of Suffolk (Lady Jane's mother), 52
Grey, Henry, Marquess of Dorset, Duke of Suffolk (Lady Jane's father), 63
Grey, Lady Jane, Queen of England: at Sudeley, 42, 43; marriage, 52, 91, 145; pregnancy, 52; proclaimed Queen, 53, 54; in Tower, 54; execution, 62, 63, 65; grave, 80n
Grey, Lady Katherine, see Hertford
Grindal, William, 35, 42
Guildford, Sir Edward, 14
Guise family, 215, 361

Hakluyt, Richard, 344
Hamlet, see Shakespeare
Hampton Court, 33, 34, 36, 68–9, 136, 352
Hardy, Thomas, 365
Harington, Sir John, 145
Harvey, Gabriel, 39
Hastings, see Huntingdon
Hatfield House: Elizabeth's childhood, 18, 25, 59; Mary at, 18, 25; Elizabeth's residence during Mary's reign, 69, 75, 145; Elizabeth's accession, 7, 9–10, 76, 78, 86n
Hatton, Christopher: family background, 219; appearance, 219–20; arrival at court, 219–20; relationship with QE, 219–24, 263, 296, 302–3, 304; at Ely Place, 31n; relationship with RD, 223–4, 272, 293, 298–9; on QE's progresses, 235; view of Alençon suit, 278, 286, 287; Mary's view of, 296; attitude to RD as Lieutenant Governor, 333; death, 337
Hawkins, John, 198, 212

Haynes, William, 334
Hayward, Sir John, 10, 51, 79, 80
Heneage, Thomas, 172–3, 174, 293, 302, 313
Henri II, King of France, 83, 94
Henri III, King of France (earlier Duke of Anjou), 208–10, 213, 214, 267, 269, 286
Henri IV, King of France, 125
Henrietta Maria, Queen, 349
Henry I, King of England, 239
Henry III, King of England, 240
Henry IV, King of England, 162
Henry V, King of England, 240, 332
Henry VII, King of England, 13
Henry VIII, King of England: character, 102; accession, 13; court, 9, 50, 78; Kenilworth lodgings, 240; sports, 14; divorce, 15, 60; marriage to Anne Boleyn, 16, 31; birth of Elizabeth, 16–18; Katherine's death, 19, 20; relationship with daughters, 19, 25, 32; courtship of Jane Seymour, 19; execution of Anne Boleyn, 21; marriages, 23, 32, 258; birth of son, 23; French wars, 33, 34; portraits, 36; will, 36, 52, 156, 165n; health, 36–7; death, 37, 39; succession, 23, 33, 36, 46, 51–2
Henry, Prince of Wales, 363
Hertford, Sir Edward Seymour, Earl of, 233
Hertford, Lady Katherine (Grey), Countess of, 154, 233, 356
Hertford Castle, 25
Hever Castle, 73
Holles, Gervase, 226
Holy Maid of Kent, 31
Horace, 29
Horsey, Sir Edward, 230
Horsey, Jerome, 198
Howard, Charles, second Baron Howard of Effingham, 260, 321, 325
Howard, Frances, 225
Howard, Katherine, Queen, 23, 32, 80n
Howard, Lord William, first Baron Howard of Effingham, 225
Huicke, Robert, 144
Hume, Martin, 348–9, 359
Hunnis, William, 290
Hunsdon, Henry Carey, first Lord, 187, 203

Hunsdon House, 25, 53–4
Huntingdon, Francis Hastings, second Earl of, 80, 89, 109, 154
Huntingdon, Henry Hastings, third Earl of: family background, 52, 109; marriage, 52, 73; Lord President of the Council in the north, 89, 187; claim to throne, 109; on Amy's death, 117–18; father's death, 154; Mary's imprisonment, 188; guardianship of Devereux children, 260; RD's funeral, 339–40
Huntingdon, Katherine (Dudley, RD's sister), Countess of: marriage, 52, 73; relationship with QE, 78n, 89; father-in-law, 80; husband's title, 154; illness, 175; at Kenilworth, 191; household, 260

Inner Temple, 152, 219
Ireland, 251–2, 268, 306
Irons, Jeremy, 347
Irwin, Margaret, 1, 367
Isabella, Queen of England, 139, 140
Isabella of Castile, Queen, 26

Jackson, Glenda, 1, 367
Jackson, J. E., 365
James I (VI), King of England and Scotland: birth, 176, 181; mother's abdication, 178; Scottish rule, 282; English gifts to, 292; marriage question, 294; mother's execution, 321; relationship with Essex, 303; Spanish Armada, 333; accession, 231; Leicester inheritance case, 231, 342, 365, 346n; Dudley estates, 350; favourites, 139, 140
James II, King of England and Scotland, 364
John, Duke (brother of Eric of Sweden), 94
John of Gaunt, Duke of Lancaster, 162, 240
Jones, Owen, 346–7, 348
Jones, Robert, 112–13
Jonson, Ben, 132
Journal of matters of state (anon. tract), 116
Julio, Dr, *see* Borgarucci

Kapur, Shekhar, 368

Katherine of Aragon, Queen: education,
26; marriage, 18, 60; daughter, 18, 20;
connection with Jane Dudley, 28;
divorce, 15, 17; death, 19; marriage
declared valid, 60
Kenilworth (Scott), 100, 118, 365
Kenilworth Castle: John Dudley's
ownership, 151; QE's gift to RD,
151–2; RD at, 190; RD's plans, 191;
QE's visits, 100, 215, 216, 239–48,
251; RD's marriage to Lettice, 256;
RD's last illness, 333; RD's funeral,
339; RD's will, 259; sequestered by
crown, 349
Kett, Robert, 46, 47
Kett rebellion, 46–7
Kew, 104, 110, 185
Keyle, Robert, 153
Killigrew, Henry, 112n
Kingston, Lady, 22
Kipling, Rudyard, 365–6
Knole Park, 88
Knollys, Sir Francis, 192n, 259–60, 321
Knollys, Katherine (Carey), 172, 259
Knollys, Lettice, Viscountess Hereford,
Countess of Essex, Countess of
Leicester (RD's wife): family
background, 259–60; appearance, 172,
258; character, 258–9; first marriage,
172, 250–1, 260; flirtation with RD,
172, 173, 250; children, 251, 258–9,
294; relationship with RD, 257–8;
marriage to RD, 260–2; QE's response
to marriage, 262–3, 271–2, 280, 294;
birth of RD's son, 285; finances, 291;
married life, 291, 295; son's death,
297–8; RD's death, 334, 336; RD's
funeral, 339; RD's tomb, 340; RD's
will, 340–1, 344; third marriage, 259,
260, 334, 341; young Dudley's case,
345–6; death, 341; tomb, 259, 340;
fictional treatments of, 368–9
Knollys, Richard, 261
Knollys, Sir William, 336
Knollys family, 259, 284
Knox, John, 90n, 135, 199

La Noue, M. de, 351
Laneham, Robert, 240–5, 247
Laws and Statutes of Geneva, 199
Le Havre, 159–60
Lee, Sir Henry, 233, 239, 260

Leicester, Earl of, *see* Dudley (Robert),
Montfort (Simon de), Sidney (Sir
Robert)
Leicester House, 197, 233, 261, 290–1, 292
Leicester's Commonwealth (pamphlet):
publication, 141, 299–301; authorship,
301; allegations against RD, 116, 117,
140, 300–1; on Amy's death, 116, 117,
121, 122; on RD's son, 298; editions,
360; reprinted, 141
Leigh, Alice, 345, 349
Lennox, Lady Margaret Douglas,
Countess of, 33, 165
Lennox, Matthew Stewart, fourth Earl of,
33, 161, 165
Leslie, John, *see* Ross, Bishop of
Lichfield, 238
Lincoln, Henry Clinton, second Earl of,
239, 279
Lingard, John, 357
Lok, William, 20
London, 30–1, 80–1, 196–7
London Bridge, 31, 196, 367
Loseley, 186
Luther, Martin, 15

Maitland of Lethington, William, 157, 185
Margaret, Regent of the Netherlands, 26
Margaret (Tudor, sister of Henry VIII),
Queen of Scotland, 165
Marguerite of Navarre, 96
Marlborough, John Churchill, Duke of,
141, 142
Marsham, 129
Martyr, Peter, 199
Mary I, Queen of England: childhood,
18–19, 20; education, 26; bastardy, 17,
18, 23, 53; mother's death, 19;
relationship with sister, 8, 10, 22, 23,
60, 63; at father's court, 25, 28, 32;
marriage prospects, 27, 40; brother's
christening, 24; in family portrait, 36;
father's death, 37; at brother's court,
48, 51; religion, 50, 96, 145; brother's
illness, 51; succession question, 51–2,
53; proclaimed Queen, 54; reign, 8,
11, 145; marriage to Philip of Spain,
60–1, 66, 81, 136–7, 144–5; Wyatt
rebellion, 61–3, 69, 136; imprisonment
of sister, 63–5; supposed pregnancies,
8, 66, 68–9, 73; burnings of
Protestants, 8, 67–8; childlessness, 7–8,

69; Philip's departure, 8, 69; sister's marriage question, 71–2; succession, 33, 69–70, 75; last illness, 75; will, 8, 75; death, 8, 75, 81; funeral, 78

Mary II, Queen of Great Britain, 136

Mary, Queen of Scots: claim to English throne, 70, 83, 154, 155, 156; heir, 94; appearance, 162; marriage to Francis, 160, 162, 167; view of Elizabeth, 112, 113, 129, 179; death of husband Francis, 147; remarriage question, 147–8, 150, 155; peace treaty issue, 155–6; scandals concerning, 167; question of marriage to RD, 156–63; Darnley's visit, 165–6; infatuation with Darnley, 166, 167; marriage to Darnley, 137, 173–4, 177–8; pregnancy, 174; relationship with Elizabeth, 138, 164, 179, 180–2; Rizzio's murder, 175–6, 338; birth of son, 176, 181; Darnley's death, 178, 179, 182; marriage to Bothwell, 178–9, 182–3, 195; abdication, 178–9; jewellery, 180; flight to England, 180–2; Cecil propaganda against, 109; imprisonment, 129, 181–2, 254; casket letters, 182; talk of marriage to Norfolk, 182–6, 211; plotting, 185, 211, 296, 320; rebellion of northern earls, 187–8; Anjou marriage question, 209–10; Ridolfi plot, 211–12; response to St Bartholomew's Day massacre, 216; taking the waters at Buxton, 254; new of QE's suitors, 265; Throckmorton conspiracy, 296; cipher letters, 296; on RD in Netherlands, 310; Walsingham's schemes, 361; Babington conspiracy, 319–20; execution, 120, 321–2, 353; fictional treatment of, 365

Mary of Guise, Dowager Queen of Scotland, 50, 96

Mary of Hungary, 96

Mary (Tudor, sister of Henry VIII), Duchess of Suffolk, 52, 165n

Matilda, Empress, 52n

Maurice of Nassau, Prince of Orange, 309

Mauvissière, see Castelnau

Maximilian II, Emperor, 170

Melville, Sir James, 161–3, 164, 181

Mendoza, Bernardino de: on QE's response to RD's marriage, 261–2; on

QE's Alençon marriage plans, 273, 274, 279, 282, 284, 285, 287; expulsion from England, 331, 360; in Paris, 331, 332, 333

Mendoza, Don Diego de, 67

Merchant Adventurers, 198

Micea, Marco Antonio, 335

Mildmay, Sir Walter, 203

Mirren, Helen, 2, 368

Montfort, Simon de, Earl of Leicester, 13, 239–40, 248n

Moray, Lord James Stewart, Earl of, 178

More, Sir William, 186

Mortimer, Roger, 139, 140

Morton, James Douglas, fourth Earl of, 217

Mulcaster, Richard, 80

Muscovy Company, 29, 198

Nashe, Thomas, 132

Naunton, Sir Robert: on QE's accession, 9; on RD, 10, 11; on QE's favourites, 139, 140; on relationship between QE and RD, 173; on Hatton, 219

Neale, J. E., 367n

Netherlands: Spanish wars, 177, 266, 268, 278; QE's policy, 266–7, 305–7; Alençon's involvement, 267, 283, 287, 298, 310; RD's command, 305–9; RD's arrival, 309–10; RD's governorship, 310–15; RD's campaign, 315–19, 323–4, 327; RD's departure, 324; Spanish forces, 330

Neville, Sir Henry, 189

Nonsuch, 290, 297, 307

Norfolk, Thomas Howard, third Duke of, 13, 38, 167–8, 169

Norfolk, Thomas Howard, fourth Duke of: family background, 167–8; Knight of the Garter, 88; relationship with RD, 95, 115n, 126, 168–9, 210–11; relationship with QE, 168–9, 177, 211; support for Habsburg marriage, 170, 176; relationship with Cecil, 172; wives, 144n; Scots inquiry, 182; question of marriage to Mary, 182–7, 211; plot against Cecil, 183–4; rebellion of northern earls, 187; in Tower, 259–60; release from Tower, 210–11; Ridolfi plot, 211–13; in Tower, 212; trial, 213; execution, 213–14, 260

Norfolk, Thomas Howard, fifth Earl of, 230

Norris, Sir Henry, Baron Norris of Rycote, 293

Norris, Sir John, 327, 329

Norris, Marjorie, Lady, 293

North, Roger, second Baron North, 229, 261

Northampton, Elizabeth, Marchioness of, 145

Northampton, William Parr, Marquess of, 88, 177, 184

Northumberland, Duke of, see Dudley (John)

Northumberland, Henry Percy, ninth Earl of, 253n

Norwich: Kett rebellion, 46–7; QE's visits, 237, 264

Odingsells, Mrs, 106

Ormonde, Thomas Butler, tenth Earl of, 329

Ovid, 166

Owen, George, Dr, 102

Owen, Mrs, 106

Oxford, Edward de Vere, seventeenth Earl of, 28, 196, 221, 233, 302

Oxford University, 89, 226

Paget, Lord, 301

Palavicino, Sir Horatio, 292

Parker, Matthew, 21

Parkinson, Cecil, 346n

Parliament: reassembled (1548), 43; declaration on marriage of Henry VIII, 60; on QE's marriage, 82, 144, 156, 176; RD's seat, 87; role in government, 90; question of Mary's marriage, 150, 161; called by QE, 176; national security acts, 211; conspiracy fears, 214; execution of Mary, Queen of Scots, 320

Parma, Duke of: Netherlands campaign, 268, 278, 312; RD's campaign against, 306, 307, 312, 317, 324; invasion force, 326; Arthur Dudley story, 353

Parr, Katherine, Queen: relationship with Dudleys, 27, 28, 32; marriage to Henry, 32, 34; court, 34, 36; religion, 35; relationship with Elizabeth, 35–6, 39, 41–2; marriage to Thomas Seymour, 39–41, 144; death, 42, 43, 144

Parry, Thomas, 41, 43, 44, 66, 75, 77, 173

Parry, William, 297

Pembroke, Henry Herbert, second Earl of, 197, 261

Pembroke, Mary (Sidney), Countess of, 230, 261

Pembroke, Sir William Herbert, first Earl of, 152, 177, 180, 230

Penshurst Place, 288, 304, 342

Perrot, Dorothy (Devereux), 253n, 294–5

Perrot, Thomas, 294

Persons, Robert, 301

Philip II, King of Spain: marriage to Mary, 60–1, 66, 136–7, 144–5; consort status, 66; dress, 84; Mary's supposed pregnancy, 66, 69; godfather to Philip Sidney, 67; policy towards Elizabeth, 69–72, 75, 81–2, 109, 127, 147, 149–50; leaves England, 69; returns to England, 71; French wars, 72–3, 102; father's abdication, 16n, 93; final departure, 8, 73; suitor to Elizabeth, 92–3, 133; favourite, 139; Netherlands wars, 177, 267, 268, 307, 330; response to St Bartholomew's Day massacre, 216; Irish policy, 268; annexation of Portugal, 283, 306; Throckmorton plot, 296; religious policies, 306; Enterprise of England, 296, 323–4; response to execution of Mary, Queen of Scots, 323; Armada, 325, 330; Arthur Dudley story, 352, 354, 360–1

Pickering, Sir William, 93

Pirto (maid), 106, 121

Pius V, Pope, 207

Plaidy, Jean, 1, 367

Plantagenet, Arthur, 14, 50, 91

Pliny, 29

Potemkin, Grigory, 142–4, 247n, 303, 319n

Private Lives of Elizabeth and Essex, The (film), 366

Progresses of Queen Elizabeth (Nichols), 226

Ptolemy, 29

Ralegh, Walter: appearance, 302; arrival at court, 302; relationship with QE, 302, 304, 337, 368; relationship with RD, 314; marriage, 271; writings, 197

Randolph, Thomas: Cecil's correspondence, 98, 110; ambassador to Scotland, 110, 159, 160, 161; RD marriage proposal, 160, 161; on Darnley marriage, 166, 175; on Rizzio, 167, 174; on RD's quarrel with Norfolk, 168–9

Reformation, 15–16

Regiomontanus (Johannes Müller), 325

Regnans in Excelsis (papal bull), 207

Rich, Penelope, Lady, 253n

Richard II, King of England, 139

Richelieu, Cardinal, 139

Richmond Palace, 66, 125, 185

Ridolfi, Roberto, 184, 188–9, 211–13, 296

Rizzio, David, 167, 174, 175–6, 179

Robsart, Amy, *see* Dudley

Rochford, Jane, Lady, 32

Rogers, John, 67–8

Ross, Bishop of (John Leslie), 217

Russell, John, Baron, 43

Rutland, Henry Manners, second Earl of, 88

Rye, Walter, 115–16

Saffron Walden, 238

St Bartholomew's Day Massacre, 215–17, 239

St Quentin, siege, 72

Salisbury, Magdalen, 231n, 346

Sandwich, 235

Savoy, Emmanuel Philibert, Duke of, 71

Sawston Hall, 54

Saxony, Duke of (John Frederick II), 74, 153

Schiller, Friedrich, 1, 365

Scott, Sir Walter, 100, 118, 365

Seymour, Edward, Earl of Hertford, Duke of Somerset: character, 38–9; relationship with John Dudley, 27, 38, 43, 44, 47–8, 49; career, 33, 37; titles, 33, 37; religion, 35, 39; Lord Protector, 37, 43, 46, 154; relationship with King Edward, 37, 38, 43, 47–8; brother's plot, 43–4; relationship with Elizabeth, 44; Kett rebellion, 46; in Tower, 47; restoration, 49; execution, 50, 53; widow in Tower, 59

Seymour, Edward (son of Katherine Grey), Lord Beauchamp of Hache, 357

Seymour, Jane, Queen, 19, 23, 27, 36

Seymour, Thomas: appearance and character, 40; marriage to Katherine Parr, 39–42; relationship with Elizabeth, 39–45, 111, 126; Katherine's death, 42; plot against King Edward, 43–4; execution, 44–5; grave, 80n

Shakespeare, William: birth, 123; on Ely Place, 31; theatrical career, 123, 126, 341n; will, 125; works: *As You Like It*, 86; *Hamlet*, 106, 122–3, 152, 341; *Henry V*, 332; *Midsummer Night's Dream*, 245

Sharp, Lionel, 329

Sheffield, Douglass (Howard), Lady: family background, 225–6; character, 233–4; Sheffield marriage, 226; relationship with RD, 225–30, 256–8, 260, 262; Sheffield's death, 226–7; secret marriage with RD, 225, 230–3, 343, 346–8; birth of son, 230, 233, 260; son's claim to legitimacy, 231–2, 345–8; remarriage, 279–80, 343

Sheffield, John, second Baron, 226–7, 254, 300, 301

Sheffield, Robert, 230

Shelley-Sidney, Sir John, 349

Shrewsbury, Bess of Hardwick, Countess of, 256, 294, 296, 298

Shrewsbury, Charles Talbot, Duke of, 350n

Shrewsbury, George Talbot, sixth Earl of: RD's letters, 197–8, 298, 332; son's letters, 225, 255, 269, 287; Buxton spa, 254; Mary's imprisonment, 254, 296; RD's visit, 254–5; QE's letters, 255–6, 299, 336; RD's gifts to, 291; letter to QE on RD's death, 336

Shrewsbury, Gilbert Talbot, seventh Earl of: letters, 225, 226, 227, 230, 255, 269, 287; Rowland White's letter, 348

Sidney, Frances (Walsingham), 319

Sidney, Sir Henry: Edward's death, 53; marriage, 67, 73; Spanish mission, 67; career, 89; on relationship between QE and RD, 127, 149; wife's smallpox, 155; question of marriage between Mary and RD, 161; Ridolfi plot, 212; Irish policy, 89, 252; death of Essex, 253; death, 319

Sidney, Lady Mary (Dudley, RD's sister): marriage, 67, 73; QE's lady of the bedchamber, 78, 89; Habsburg marriage mission, 94; smallpox, 155, 356; at Kenilworth, 191; family, 197, 229; view of Alençon suit, 274; death, 319

Sidney, Sir Philip: Philip II's godson, 67; relationship with RD, 12, 197, 262, 300, 302; relationship with QE, 262, 278n, 319; writings, 39, 253n, 262; Irish policy, 252; in masque, 284; marriage, 319; Netherlands campaign, 309, 317, 318; death, 318–19; funeral, 319

Sidney, Sir Robert, Earl of Leicester, 339, 342, 345–7

Simier, Jean de, 269–71, 273, 279, 296

Simnel, Lambert, 357

Sisson, Rosemary Anne, 365

Sluys, fall, 323

Smeaton, Mark, 21

Smith, Sir Thomas, 73, 190, 213, 214

Smyth, John, 352, 357

Somerset House, 48, 78

Southern, Robert, 352–3, 357–8

Southwell, Elizabeth, 349–50

Speed, John, 64

Spenser, Edmund, 88, 205, 238, 335

Stafford, Dorothy, Lady, 292

Stafford, Sir Edward: religion, 260; marriage, 260, 279, 343; French mission, 279–80; *Leicester's Commonwealth*, 301; Arthur Dudley story, 353, 361; passing information to Spain and France, 361; Walsingham's use of, 361, 362; Robert Dudley's legitimacy claim, 346

Stafford, Sir William, 279–80, 361, 346

Standen, Anthony, 354

Star Chamber, 231, 232, 233, 292, 345, 348

Stephen, King of England, 52n

Stoneleigh, 305

Stow, John, 335

Strachey, Lytton, 366

Stuart, Arbella, 256, 294, 361

Stubbs, John, 277–8, 282

Succession, Acts of: (1536), 23; (1544), 33, 156

Sudeley Castle, 42

Suffolk, Lady, *see* Grey (Lady Frances)

Surrey, Henry Howard, Earl of, 168

Sussex, Anne, Countess of, 145

Sussex, Henry Radcliffe, second Earl of, 169n

Sussex, Thomas Radcliffe, third Earl of: QE's views on marriage, 145; attitude to QE's marriage, 169, 170, 279; Norfolk plot, 184, 187; relationship with RD, 189, 271, 294, 300; on RD's marriage, 271; death, 300

Talbot, Francis, Lord Talbot, 299

Talbot, Gilbert, *see* Shrewsbury

Tamworth, John, 155n

Thatcher, Margaret, 367n

Throckmorton, Bess, 271, 368

Throckmorton, Francis, 295–6

Throckmorton, Sir Nicholas: on Thomas Seymour, 40; relationship with QE, 75, 111, 203; correspondence, 111–13, 116, 119; on Amy's death, 111, 119; on question of RD's marriage, 112, 134; on question of Mary's remarriage, 147–8, 158, 166; relationship with RD, 172, 184, 202–3; Scottish policy, 181; Norfolk marriage question, 184; in Tower, 188; death, 210, 300, 301; nephew's conspiracy, 295

Tilbury, camp, 326, 327–30, 343

Titchfield Abbey, 186

Topcliffe, Richard, 191

Tower of London: Elizabeth's servants in, 44; Somerset in, 47; King Edward's death, 53; Lady Jane Grey in, 54; Dudley family in, 55, 56–9; RD in, 12, 56, 64, 100; Wyatt in, 61; Elizabeth's imprisonment, 12, 63–5; Elizabeth's coronation, 79–80; Katherine Grey in, 154, 356; Throckmorton questioning, 188; Norfolk in, 210, 212; Ralegh and Bess Throckmorton in, 271

Tree of Commonwealth, The (Dudley), 138n

Trent, Council of, 150

Turbeville, George, 243

Tyndall, Humphrey, 260–1

Tyrwhit, Lady, 44

Tyrwhit, Sir Robert, 44

Valois, royal house, 207

Vavasour, Anne, 233, 356

Vere, Robert de, 139

Very brief and profitable Treatise, A, 139
Victoria, Queen of Great Britain, 136, 142n
Villiers, George, Duke of Buckingham, 139, 140
Virgil, 29
Virgin Queen, The (BBC TV drama), 118n, 368
Virgin's Lover, The (novel), 118n

Walsingham, Francis: relationship with RD, 188, 266; Ridolfi plot, 188; influence, 192, 266; RD's letters, 194, 208–9, 212–13, 214, 216, 236–7, 268, 269, 307, 308–9, 316, 319, 320, 321, 323; French marriage question, 208–9, 210, 212–13, 214–15, 269, 277, 282, 285–6; St Bartholomew's Day massacre, 216; Netherlands policy, 237, 264, 268, 312; secretary of state, 266; religion, 266; *Leicester's Commonwealth*, 300; spies, 319, 360, 363; *agents provocateurs*, 361; Babington plot, 319–20; execution of Mary, 321; on QE's response to RD's death, 335; Arthur Dudley story, 353, 360–1; death, 337
Wanstead: RD's purchase, 197; RD's wedding, 261; QE at, 262, 264; RD's retirement to, 272, 273; life at, 290;

Denbigh's death, 297
Warbeck, Perkin, 357
Warner, Sir George, 349
Warwick, 198, 215, 339
Warwick, Richard Neville (the Kingmaker), sixteenth Earl of, 13
Warwick Castle, 152, 298
Westminster, Palace of, 31, 81, 278
Westminster Abbey, 31
Westmorland, Charles Neville, sixth Earl of, 187
White, Rowland, 348
Whitehall, 31, 50, 63, 79, 125, 214, 283, 285
Whitgift, John, 302
William III, King of Great Britain, 136
William I (the Silent), Prince of Orange, 266, 287, 297, 306, 307, 310
Wilson, Thomas, 264, 268, 269
Windsor, 47, 172–3, 187, 190
Wolsey, Thomas, 14, 15, 139, 314
Wood, Thomas, 200, 249–50
Woodstock, 65, 66, 68, 216
Wotton, Sir Henry, 250
Wyatt, Sir Thomas, 61, 63, 65, 136
Wyatt rebellion, 61–3, 69, 70
Wychwood Forest, 334

Zuccaro, Federico, 234
Zutphen, battle (1586), 318–19

Few relationships fire the imagination like that of Elizabeth I and the Earl of Leicester, Robert Dudley. Scandalizing the royal court with her passionate fondness for the married courtier, the Queen took Leicester on as a counselor, unofficial consort, army commander, and emissary. But she also fought with him, made him act as go-between with her other suitors, and even tried to have him imprisoned. Reigniting this four-hundred-year-old love story in lush detail, Sarah Gristwood reveals a complex, strikingly modern relationship fueled by scandal and intrigue—and a uniquely detailed portrait of two outsized personalities that transformed their age.

VISIT WWW.VPBOOKCLUB.COM
WWW.PENGUIN.COM

COVER IMAGES: *The Ermine Portrait of Queen Elizabeth I* BY NICHOLAS HILLIARD, HATFIELD HOUSE, LONDON, ENGLAND © SUPERSTOCK.COM; *Robert Dudley (1532–88) 1st Earl of Leicester* BY STEVEN VAN DER MEULEN © YALE CENTER FOR BRITISH ART, PAUL MELLON COLLECTION, USA / THE BRIDGEMAN ART LIBRARY; *Pink and Rose Wallpaper* BY WILLIAM MORRIS © GETTY IMAGES.
COVER DESIGN: NATALIE SLOCUM